Reading the Past, Writing the Future

Task Force on Council History and 2011

Leila Christenbury, Chair, Virginia Commonwealth University, Richmond

Andy Anderson, Johnson County Community College, Kansas

Akua Duku Anokye, Arizona State University West, Phoenix

Janet Emig, Naples, Florida

Jeanne Gerlach, University of Texas at Arlington

Julie Jensen, Hutchinson, Minnesota

Ken Lindblom, Stony Brook University, New York

Erika Lindemann, University of North Carolina at Chapel Hill

James Marshall, University of Georgia, Athens

Jesse Perry, Hayward, California

R. Joseph Rodríguez, The University of Texas at Austin

Renita Schmidt, Furman University, Greenville, South Carolina

Patricia Lambert Stock, Michigan State University, East Lansing

Paul Thomas, Furman University, Greenville, South Carolina

Kathleen Blake Yancey, Florida State University, Tallahassee

Bill Younglove, Lakewood, California

Reading the Past, Writing the Future

A Century of American Literacy Education and the National Council of Teachers of English

Edited by

ERIKA LINDEMANN
University of North Carolina at Chapel Hill

NCTE 100 YEARS READING THE PAST. WRITING THE FUTURE.

National Council of Teachers of English
1111 W. Kenyon Road, Urbana, Illinois 61801-1096

Staff Editor: Bonny Graham
Interior Design: Jenny Jensen Greenleaf
Cover and Divider Page Design: Pat Mayer
Images supplied by NCTE staff and archives.

NCTE Stock Number: 38762

It is the policy of NCTE in its journals and other publications to provide a forum for the open discussion of ideas concerning the content and the teaching of English and the language arts. Publicity accorded to any particular point of view does not imply endorsement by the Executive Committee, the Board of Directors, or the membership at large, except in announcements of policy, where such endorsement is clearly specified.

Every effort has been made to provide current URLs and email addresses, but because of the rapidly changing nature of the Web, some sites and addresses may no longer be accessible.

Library of Congress Cataloging-in-Publication Data

Reading the past, writing the future : a century of American literacy education and the National Council of Teachers of English / edited by Erika Lindemann.

p. cm.

Includes bibliographical references and index.

ISBN 978-0-8141-3876-2 ((pbk))

1. National Council of Teachers of English—History. 2. English teachers—United States—Societies, etc.—History. 3. English language—Study and teaching—United States—History. I. Lindemann, Erika.

PE11.N33.R43 2010

428.0071—dc22

2010008701

To those who came before
and those who will come after

CONTENTS

Foreword

Deborah Brandt
University of Wisconsin at Madison

If you ask everyday people to talk about reading and writing in their lives, their accounts teem with the consequences of teaching and learning, the politics of language and literacy, and the systems of access and reward—fragile, contradictory, and ruthless—by which educational opportunity is given and denied. So a son recalls how his romantic father, caught up in the reading of western novels, moved his family to California and into financial ruin. An ailing farm woman discusses typewritten letters received from her daughter who writes during downtime at her bank job in a distant city. A milliner's daughter recalls studying Latin and Greek at the Norwich Free Academy in Connecticut in the 1920s before going off to secretarial school in Boston. A Mississippi sharecropper's son remembers in the 1930s riding with his classmates to his school, located in a church two towns away, on the back of a pickup truck driven by his teacher. A utility worker and story writer from Chicago remembers writing as a four-year-old with a fountain pen lent to her by her grandmother, a teacher who lost her career when schools for African Americans in the South were closed after official desegregation. A Vietnam War refugee recalls teaching himself English as a child under headphones in a language lab for the blind, where he was placed because his school district lacked an ESL program. A former editor of a high school newspaper describes how her staff defied their principal's censorship edict by finding refuge in the shop of a sympathetic local printer, where the newspaper continued to publish.

When we listen to the stories of language learners over time, we appreciate the enormous responsibilities that fall to English teachers—the potential for what we teach and how we teach it to reverberate in relations between parents and children; to affect decisions at the levels of individual conscience and institutional power; to condition identity; or to cultivate the resources, individual and collective, to sustain tradition and adapt to change. We also can appreciate that we do our work in larger arenas of social struggle, where other interests can color and even upend our efforts, giving them negative outcomes we cannot anticipate, even as our own egregious failures can be redeemed by resilient spirits. While there is an overwhelming immediacy to what teachers teach and learners learn, this work leaves residues, unintended legacies that can make things easier or harder later on, easier or harder on future teachers and future learners. In short, we operate in fraught circumstances.

The essays in this volume document how one professional organization, the National Council of Teachers of English, understood those fraught circumstances over the first one hundred years of its history. This is an instructive story of how efforts at mass professionalization emerge in support of mass education. Certainly we can see that NCTE has taken its responsibilities seriously. Since its founding in 1911, the organization has chosen to stand in the same baffling gaps between desire and possibility that shape individual pursuits of literacy and education—and then has figured out how to proceed. This sense of responsibility no doubt accounts for the breadth of the NCTE agenda: its complex set of collaborations, initiatives, resolutions, publications, committees, and caucuses, its ever widening sphere of concerns and contacts. It also explains why NCTE has construed its constituency so broadly, understanding that the quality of teachers' professional lives can only rise with the desire of a mass citizenry to want something better for itself. This approach has shaped NCTE into a multiliterate multitasker: publisher, critic, advocate, conciliator, ally, convener, lobbyist, researcher and research analyst, and global communicator, among other roles. NCTE has published books for parents, broadcast radio shows, bestowed media awards, sponsored workshops on how to organize anticensorship protests, hosted film festivals, and initiated such national happenings as the African American Read-In and the National Day on Writing. Its members have moved publishers, industrial leaders, judges and juries, and Congress to action. Along the way, NCTE has advocated for inclusive and dynamic definitions of literacy, as pluralistic skills of give-and-take that befit a diverse, globally involved, multimediated democracy. Like the efforts of literacy learners, though, these organizational undertakings leave mixed results, shifting, tentative residues that are sometimes hard to discern and gauge—except that, as with so many literacy memories, they express what our members have yearned for.

In this volume, a dream team of scholars revisits key moments from the one-hundred-year history of NCTE. Each chapter offers a different emphasis, in a cumulative and kaleidoscopic manner that invites multiple perspectives and deepening understanding of those events. For instance, we visit NCTE's reformist beginnings: *An Experience Curriculum in English*, Project English, *Students' Right to Their Own Language*, *Standards for the English Language Arts*. Sometimes the perspective is from within the organization; in other chapters, we see NCTE from the intellectual and social milieu around it. The chapters use a fascinating archive of organizational documents, photographs, and other artifacts, supplemented at times by the testimony of key participants in the history. Throughout we are invited to reflect on how a consistent core of commitments—developing sound practices, advancing scholarship, professionalizing teachers, and educating the public—persists amid escalating pressures and relentless change.

How NCTE has chosen its campaigns and its alliances, where it has fallen silent, where it has succeeded, and where it has failed can provide guidance for teachers and learners in the new century. That is the value of this volume. As you read these astute chapters, here are a few themes worth noticing:

> *What we take for granted in our professional background is there as a result of somebody's insight and effort.* In retrospect we appreciate how the activism of forebears built the house in which we do our work today: Reading as constructive. Writing as process. Language as a heritage right. Assessment as formative. Teachers as leaders. Scholarship and pedagogy as one. We assume these truths to be self-evident—but only because NCTE members studied, taught, argued, and pressed

them into existence, making them programmatically real to the wider field. And so this begs the question: Whose forebears are we? What do they need from us now?

Low expectations are never reliable. Again and again in the story of literacy and education in the twentieth century, various commentators have assumed incapability on the part of some learners or groups—invariably those with the least political and economic padding around them. Often, tests are involved in these processes of limitation. And again and again, when opportunity knocks, the stigmatized resist and shatter those limits: Leaders who are told they can't, lead. Parents who are told they can't, parent. Students who are told they can't, learn. Teachers who are told they can't, teach. Again and again the myths of low expectations are proven wrong, and the circle of talent is expanded—but only at a great cost to the oppressed and a great drag on the wider society. Today we continue this pattern of low expectations, using testing to stigmatize, underestimate, and malnourish human potential, repeating these same miserable myths. How do we stop the loss?

The need to articulate a relationship between language learning and civic life is ongoing and urgent. Every success that NCTE can claim has involved articulating the dependency of a healthy democratic society on the broad and equitable development of people's language and literacy. Each generation has had to rethink and remake the link. Over the last twenty years, economic, technological, and social change has only intensified the relationship between a person's language arts and their viability in the world. What Manuel Castells calls *communication power*—the capacity to change minds through words—is becoming the dominant political, cultural, and economic resource in a connected and conversing world. Controlling communication or breaking through such control is the political struggle of these times. As a professional organization, NCTE has always focused its attention on the power of communication—in speaking, listening, reading, writing, and the interpretation of literature. How do we leverage this tradition in these times? How do we make our voices better heard and our knowledge more respected?

In 1911, NCTE stood in the breach between a constricting regime of education and an American populace that was reaching for something better. In 2010, we stand there again—different regime, different populace, different conditions, but the same magnitude of yearning for something better. Thanks to the editor and all of the authors in this volume for reminding us what time it is.

Work Cited

Castells, Manuel. *Communication Power*. New York: Oxford UP, 2009. Print.

CHAPTER ONE

NCTE and the Shaping of American Literacy Education

LEILA CHRISTENBURY
Virginia Commonwealth University

> The fact remains, nevertheless, that there are numerous unsolved problems of English teaching; witness the discontent.
>
> JAMES FLEMING HOSIC, *English Journal* inaugural editorial, 1912

To assess the National Council of Teachers of English (NCTE) and its influence on literacy education in the United States, it may be useful to linger over the above sentence, written by one of NCTE's founders. James Fleming Hosic was NCTE's first secretary (an office that is today known as the executive director), eventual president (1920), and editor of its major and, for many years, its only journal. In his inaugural *English Journal* editorial, published in 1912 at the very onset of NCTE's formation, Hosic asserts the existence of "unsolved problems" of English teaching. That may be hardly startling, but, more significantly, in the same sentence Hosic bluntly sounds an almost ominous reality: the times are marked by nothing less than "discontent."

James Fleming Hosic, a professor at Chicago Teachers College, was a highly energetic, charismatic individual but also, by contemporary accounts, not one inclined to drama. We can take his characterization as accurate: NCTE was born in discontent, specifically in resistance and opposition to powerful East Coast educational forces that, in an effort to make consistent the course of study in high school English, had established the Uniform Entrance Requirements. First seen as progress, the requirements included specific books all students should read in their high school English classes and on which they would be examined in order to enroll in college. The arrangement, however, in effect dictated the shape of the curriculum of English classes in American high schools as well as the testing. This dominance, particularly in localities near and west of the Mississippi River, was viewed as onerous, if not without historical precedent (see Trachsel for further discussion). It was also incompatible with what the English Round Table, a smaller group allied with the National Education Association (NEA), called in 1911 "the kind of training in English best fitted to develop [students] and to prepare them for life" (National Education Association 597) and seen as a "confused" approach to the aims of American secondary education (Mason 42). As former NCTE Executive Director Miles Myers observes, "The Uniform Book List put the control of the high school curriculum in the hands of colleges and universities, named the canonical works of English literature . . . and . . . mandated once again that secondary schools should focus their primary attention on college preparatory students" (83). Fifty years later, Dora V. Smith, 1936 NCTE president, would articulate the aversion to this kind of uniformity:

> [We must] educate each pupil in terms of *his own uniqueness within the context of the group*. All this has special import for the curriculum. It cannot be done adequately if the aim is the reading of specific books by every member of the class, mastery of a set number of rules by all pupils, or attainment by everybody of specific standards in speech or writing during any given year of the school system, regardless of the point from which each pupil starts and his own individual rate of learning. (Smith 7, emphasis in original)

But what could any individual teacher or school do? English teachers of the time had "little unity and no effective means of working together" (Radner v). After discussion and debate, the NEA's answer was to form a committee to make recommendations, a committee that ultimately would lead to the creation of a new and more specifically English-focused organization. Although he did not work alone, the undeniable center of that effort was James Fleming Hosic. Appointed by the NEA to survey college entrance requirements and to report back, Hosic was charged by his peers in the summer of 1911 to organize "an independent national society of English teachers" (Hook 14).

Thus organized, motivated, and cheered on by Hosic, some sixty educators—mostly from the American Midwest and East Coast, representing eleven states (Hook 7), men and women, college and high school teachers and administrators—met in Chicago in December 1911. There, guided by the preparatory work of Hosic and the NEA, they agreed to create an organization that could give voice and power to oppose the status quo. They decided to name it the National Council of Teachers of English, and, today, some one hundred years later, NCTE still works to influence and shape literacy education in the United States. Within this volume are a number of accounts of the founding of NCTE, but the contributors offer particular perspectives on this history, depending on the focus of their essays. What follows is an overview.

NCTE and Issues in American Literacy Education

As one of the oldest active educational organizations in this country (an NCTE affiliate, the New England Association of Teachers of English, was founded in 1901, and the Illinois Association of Teachers of English, in 1908), the history of NCTE is, in many ways, the history of American literacy education. Initially focused on the relatively narrow concern of high school English teaching and teachers and on the literature curriculum in the high school, the organization has since expanded to embrace the entire range of English language arts from prekindergarten students and their teachers to those studying and teaching in postdoctoral settings. Unlike the Modern Language Association and its major journal *PMLA*, which early in the twentieth century turned from pedagogy to research, NCTE has embraced both. Virtually every area of English, English studies, and English teaching has found its niche in NCTE publications (including books, monographs, newsletters, and academic journals), websites, research studies, workshops, conventions, institutes, and constituent groups and subgroups. The organization embraces language, linguistics, literature of all kinds and genres, speaking, writing, listening, media, technology, professional teaching concerns, standards, accountability, testing, English language acquisition, and, not least, issues of social justice in education and society. Over the decades, the sponsor of and participant in numerous international ventures and organizations, NCTE has reached beyond the boundaries of the United States and cosponsored conferences and research studies in Canada, the United Kingdom, Germany, France, Australia, South Africa, and numerous other countries (in 1965, NCTE sponsored the first International Conference on the Teaching of English). With headquarters first in its founding city of Chicago (the organization was, in its early days, housed in a desk drawer in Hosic's Chicago Teachers College office), NCTE in 1954 moved to Champaign, Illinois. In 1971 the organization relocated to neighboring Urbana, and today NCTE has additional offices and staff in Berkeley, California (established in 2003), and Washington, DC (established in 2005), and a membership that grew from its initial group of under 100 to as many as 120,000 in the late 1960s.

What is characteristic of NCTE and its work is the close connection the organization and its members have had to the challenges of the times. NCTE took and continues to take stands on pertinent social and political issues. Through resolutions and position papers, the organization asserts the need for inclusive materials that represent all students and inclusive language that embraces both genders. It maintains the principle that in its meetings there be open access to all and freedom from menace, regardless of color or sexual orientation. It challenges the use of language to further political ends, to obscure or intimidate, and recognizes and highlights the honest use of words. As a professional and academic organization, NCTE reminds the country of the centrality and utility of language even when it is at war and even when the national focus, as in the recent past, was overwhelmingly on science and foreign language study. NCTE has also continued to address powerful changes in literacy. As media—first newspapers, then radio, motion pictures, television, and now computers and assorted forms of wireless and digital communication—have surged in influence in the culture, NCTE has crafted and disseminated guides to selecting, watching, using, and creating media in and outside the classroom. Finally and possibly most important, the organization has also fostered the scholarship of English teaching, conducting research studies and disseminating the results.

Because NCTE has been a factor in shaping the teaching and learning of English in this country, a voice to be reckoned with—if not always to be followed in specific—this introduction looks at the past one hundred years through a discussion of five general areas and numerous selected documents. NCTE's broad and inclusive agenda has especially encompassed the following activities:

- Shaping classroom materials for literacy study
- Fostering the professional development of literacy teachers
- Guiding the literacy profession
- Taking a stand on social justice issues impacting literacy education
- Advancing the scholarship of English and literacy

In the following pages, these areas are addressed in turn, tracing in broad and general outline NCTE's influence on and efforts to shape American literacy education.

Shaping Classroom Materials for Literacy Study

It is no surprise that an organization formed largely in response to a restrictive reading list for English classes should take an avid interest in providing teachers with materials that can be incorporated into the literacy classroom and used with students. While the following section provides a general overview of this issue, Chapter 5 by Arthur N. Applebee, Judith A. Langer, and Marc A. Nachowitz details NCTE's persistent, "important role in helping the profession assimilate new ideas about curriculum and instruction in literature as they emerge from the larger educational and social context" (p. 204).

The Recommending and Selection of Books

As early as 1913, just two years after its founding, NCTE published its first booklist, the pamphlet *Books for Home Reading*. Decades later and frequently revised and updated, *Books for Home Reading* remained a bestseller; 150,000 copies were distributed in 1931 alone (NCTE Annual Business Meeting Minutes, 27 Nov. 1931), and over its lifetime, hundreds of thousands of copies were produced (Hook 24, 25). NCTE's fostering of booklists continued into midcentury with the publication of the senior high school series *Books for You*, the middle level *Your Reading*, and the elementary series *Adventuring with Books* (as well as other series such as *Kaleidoscope* and *Reading Ladders for Human Relations*). These resources provided teachers with up-to-date, annotated lists of hundreds of books, grouped by topic and theme, that could be used in the classroom to broaden student literacy and appeal to student interests. From 1960 to 1967, 350,000 copies of these NCTE booklists were sold (Hook 203). In addition, to foster the reading of other literary genres, NCTE established the Excellence in Poetry for Children Award in 1977, and the Orbis Pictus Award, begun in 1989, gives recognition to outstanding nonfiction materials for the English classroom (Zarnowski, Kerper, and Jensen). Some members of NCTE also took special interest in promoting young adult literature; NCTE President Dora V. Smith (1936) was a pioneer in advocating for the reading of what were then called "junior" or "juvenile" books, and NCTE President G. Robert Carlsen (1962) was similarly engaged. In 1973 the Assembly on Literature for Adolescents of NCTE (ALAN) was established, and *The ALAN Review* a year later became its journal, providing book reviews and pedagogical articles for teachers (Kelly and Small 323–33) as well as sponsoring a highly popular two-day workshop on young adult literature.

For the teachers of younger readers, NCTE published materials on children's literature and, through numerous subgroups, among them the Whole Language Umbrella (which became an NCTE conference in 2000), fought to keep unexpurgated, full-text literature in the hands of children. These teachers opposed basal readers peppered with excerpted texts, controlled and restricted vocabulary, and directed responses for students. In addition, NCTE sponsored annotated book lists for striving readers (at one time termed *hi/lo* books, for "high interest/easy reading") as well as information in NCTE journals and books about using such materials. The goal was to ensure that young people left school not just with diplomas but also as lifelong readers.

NCTE also provided lists for university students. *The College and Adult Reading List of Books in Literature and the Arts* was an NCTE publication in the 1960s that recommended books of canonical poetry, prose, drama, biography, and literary criticism, as well as books on art, music, and drawing. In more recent publications, NCTE has attempted to expand teacher and student awareness of mature and adult literature suitable for use in the college classroom.

Other Media: Newspapers, Radio, Recordings, Comic Books, Film, Computers

As the chapter by Mary Christel and Sandy Hayes in this volume further details, established and even conventional print materials were not NCTE's only focus. The first president of NCTE, Fred Newton Scott (1912, 1913), was highly interested in the influence of newspapers and called them, in a presidential speech of 1913, "the most pervasive influence of our day and nation" (Scott 3). Scott urged English teachers to use critical approaches to newspaper reading in the classroom (Radner 9–10). This acknowledgment of the power of the press (termed the *cheap press*) was reiterated by subsequent NCTE presidents, who encouraged attention to this compelling and, at the time, widespread and popular form of reading.

Radio, an innovation in its day, drew attention to the importance of listening, a special concern of NCTE President Stella S. Center (1932), who worked to teach students to be "critical listeners, alert and challenging" (Radner 10). In 1945, NCTE gave its first Radio Award to the CBS program "On a Note of Triumph," further highlighting the significance of the medium.

Also in the early 1930s, NCTE began to produce literary recordings of writers reading their works and of professional readers rendering versions of poems. The program continued to be successful; the January 1950 catalog of NCTE publications offered *Poets' Recordings of Their Own Poems*, *Masterpieces of Literature,* and linguistic recordings such as *General American Vowels: Explanation and Performance by J. S. Kenyon . . . Authoritative and Clear.*

While graphic novels are increasingly making their way into today's libraries and classrooms and onto recommended lists from such literacy organizations as the American Library Association, in an earlier time the precursors of graphic novels, comic books, were not so kindly greeted. Nevertheless, as early as the mid-1940s, *English Journal* featured an article contending that "comic books are here to stay" and that English teachers could use them to encourage student reading (Dias 145). Today, NCTE provides numerous resources for teachers using graphic novels, including lesson plans on the NCTE-cosponsored website readwritethink.org, articles in NCTE journals and newsletters, and books such as James Bucky Carter's *Building Literacy Connections with Graphic Novels: Page by Page, Panel by Panel.*

From the 1930s through the early 1960s, film emerged as a powerful medium in the country and in the classroom. Again, NCTE President Stella S. Center was active, creating an NCTE committee to provide "standards of photoplay [film] appreciation" (Radner 11). Later, two NCTE publications, *Photoplay Studies* and *Studies in the Mass Media,* featured writing by NCTE members and provided classroom study guides for current famous movies. *Photoplay Studies*, first published in 1935, was a journal in which NCTE President Max J. Herzberg (1943) had a direct interest. Volume I, number 1 of *Studies in the Mass Media,* the direct successor to *Photoplay Studies*, appeared in October 1960. Edited by NCTE President Joseph Mersand (1959), the inaugural, sixteen-page publication was directed toward students and their teachers and featured material written by NCTE Second Vice President Hardy R. Finch (1960) on the recently released Warner Brothers film *Sunrise at Campobello.* The journal had NCTE-member advisors, including Robert E. Shafer and Walter J. Ong, soon-to-be NCTE Executive Secretary Robert F. Hogan (1968), and NCTE President Marion C. Sheridan (1949). Mersand's opening editorial, "By Way of Introduction," noted

> We hope that [the journal] will meet the needs of our students and teachers for a greater understanding of the tremendous resources of the mass media of communication and for developing criteria of judgment in these times of false and superficial values. The National Council of Teachers of English has long been interested in developing such standards . . . [and has] endeavored to assist its members in understanding the educational significance of the medium and the most effective ways to teach its appreciation. (3)

Studies in the Mass Media, however, did not last beyond 1964, although editor Mersand noted in "Vale," his farewell, that

> the termination of *Studies in the Mass Media* with this issue does not mean that the National Council of Teachers of English will discontinue its interest in the better utilization of the mass media. This interest has been traditional with the Council almost since its inception, and will, I am sure, continue in the other Council journals, in the Council committees, in the annual meetings. (20)

In a similar vein, NCTE advocated the incorporation of television in the schools. As early as the late 1930s, NCTE President Holland D. Roberts (1937) noted that English teachers who did not use this new medium in their teaching "will be swept into the dust bin of the past" (Radner 11). By the mid-1940s, NCTE was noting that mass media were "one of the three basic functions of English teaching" (Radner 11). The organization featured many convention sessions on media, and as late as 1984, the NCTE Committee on Television Literacy prepared a pamphlet, "Helping Children Use Television Wisely: A Guide for Parents," which advocated a "positive relationship with television" and offered eleven guidelines for television watching, some of which are remarkably similar to contemporary advice about young people's use of the computer, such as "do not put a television in your child's bedroom" and "watch *with* your child as often as possible" (NCTE Committee on Television Literacy 1, 2).

Computers and digital literacy have expanded in influence and have become a significant focus of the organization in the past twenty-five years. Among more recent developments, NCTE, the International Reading Association (IRA), and the Verizon

Foundation inaugurated in 2002 the website readwritethink.org, which offers free Internet-based teaching resources crafted by English teachers. At this writing, approximately 400 lesson plans appear on the site, which receives, on average, approximately 1.7 million "hits" per month (Gallivan, 4 Mar. 2009), an indication of the power of this digital teaching resource. In addition, NCTE continues to create and update guidelines for media study and use, both inside and outside of the classroom.

Fostering the Professional Development of Literacy Teachers

While Patricia Lambert Stock's chapter in this volume traces in detail NCTE's efforts to foster the professional development of literacy teachers, this section offers an overview. From its inception, NCTE has stressed the importance of teachers' being prepared for their work and, even after years in the classroom, continuing to learn and to refine their skills. The 1917 *Reorganization of English in Secondary Schools* (also known as the "Hosic Report" after its compiler, James Fleming Hosic) asserted the need for English teachers to have both "knowledge, but also skill" (148) and affirmed Massachusetts Board of Education official Clarence D. Kingsley's call for "the continued training of teachers after they have entered upon their work" (150). Today, professional development through NCTE takes many forms: books, journals, conventions and meetings, workshops, institutes, and numerous digital communities. Students entering teaching have also been extended membership at a reduced rate, a practice that began in 1944, when NCTE began its "junior membership" program, and that still applies today. In addition, NCTE has sponsored multiyear projects such as the 1997 Reading Initiative and, in digital format, CoLEARN (begun in 2003), Pathways (inaugurated in 2007), and Web seminars to help teachers access research, learn about classroom best practice, and build professional learning communities. Human resources are also available to NCTE members through the Consulting Network, which offers trained experts in many areas of literacy teaching to groups seeking continued professional development.

Professional Meetings and Conferences

NCTE has held an annual convention almost every year since 1911. The deadly influenza epidemic postponed the 1918 Annual Convention to February 1919, and World War II cancelled the 1942 sessions and abbreviated the 1943 gathering, but apart from these exceptions, the Annual Convention traditionally has been held every November, right before Thanksgiving (earlier conventions extended into Thanksgiving Day). Attendance was, at first, without charge; in 1916 a cost of twenty-five cents was assessed. By contrast, the registration fee in 1971 was $10, and in 2008, $210. The conventions were held in Chicago, New York, and Boston until 1922, when Chattanooga became the first southern city to host NCTE. In 1929, NCTE went west of the Mississippi and met in Kansas City, Missouri. The organization continued to expand its geographical horizons after that date, meeting in 1947 in San Francisco and, in 1967, even farther west, in Honolulu. From the outset, attendees have been able to access high-quality, often famous speakers; examine displays of professional materials; convene in smaller committees and interest groups; and, in the convention presentations and workshops, hear other teachers and scholars discuss a range of literacy practices and current research findings. While many of these convention presentations found their way into print, in the early 1970s NCTE recorded convention presentations and offered them for sale as cassette tapes, a program that ended as recently as 1998 (Gallivan, 4 Mar. 2009). These recorded presentations were not exactly new, since CBS and NBC had broadcast NCTE convention speakers on the radio as early as 1934.

NCTE convention attendance figures have ranged from a hundred or so in early meetings to several thousand. The 2007 Annual Convention in New York set a record of 8,040 attendees (Wagner). Over the decades, in gatherings extending from one to eight days, writers, poets, playwrights, filmmakers, teachers, and scholars have shared their expertise, learned from one another, and developed ways to support the work of their students. While the professional and social importance of these conventions cannot be overestimated, these annual gatherings represent a dedicated time and space for learning about new developments in the profession, building community, working on policy and scholarly statements, and sharing concerns about the education of America's young. The Annual Convention also provides an opportunity to recognize outstanding professionals through extensive awards programs that honor exemplary scholarship, service to the profession, and other meritorious achievements. In recent decades, the Annual Convention has extended over a week, with events beginning as early as 7:00 a.m. and other functions, such as poetry readings, going on until close to midnight.

In addition to the Annual Convention, NCTE has sponsored numerous smaller, regional and spring conventions as well as hundreds of institutes and workshops on reading, composition, literature, and new technologies. NCTE affiliates also have held yearly or twice yearly meetings to serve the teachers in a particular city, state, or region. In many ways, these meetings have been the lifeblood of the organization because they have given rise to grassroots movements, enabled teachers to adapt pedagogical research to local settings, created important special interest groups and task forces, sponsored NCTE resolutions, originated policy statements, and supported affiliate publications, an important venue for young teachers as well as veterans.

Professional Books

The first NCTE books were published reports of committee work, and the 1913 *Books for Home Reading* was one of the first, if not the first, NCTE publication (Austin). Decades later, in 1930, NCTE established the Committee on Publications with Holland D. Roberts (later NCTE president) as chair; this committee became the NCTE Editorial Board in 1973 (Austin). The Editorial Board serves as the "chief advisory group" for the NCTE Books Program, and while it does not make policy, it provides "strategic oversight" (Austin).

In the recent past, bestselling NCTE books include a true range of topics embracing writing, grammar, poetry, film, and vocabulary. Some of the bestsellers from the past thirty years include Gene Stanford's edited collection, *How to Handle the Paper*

Load (1979); Stephen Dunning and William Stafford's *Getting the Knack: Twenty Poetry Writing Exercises* (1992); Katie Wood Ray's *Wondrous Words: Writers and Writing in the Elementary Classroom* (1999); John Golden's *Reading in the Dark: Using Film as a Tool in the English Classroom* (2001); Victor Villanueva's edited collection *Cross-Talk in Comp Theory: A Reader* (2nd ed., 2003); Brock Haussamen, Amy Benjamin, Martha Kolln, and Rebecca S. Wheeler's *Grammar Alive! A Guide for Teachers* (2003); and Chris Jennings Dixon's *Lesson Plans for Teaching Writing* (2007) (Austin).

Almost all of the books published by NCTE are intended for teachers, not students, and over time, these works have made a significant contribution to literacy education. Among the most influential are two important research studies, Janet Emig's *The Composing Processes of Twelfth Graders* (1971) and Arthur N. Applebee's *Literature in the Secondary School: Studies of Curriculum and Instruction in the United States* (1993). The 1996 *Standards for the English Language Arts,* copublished by NCTE and the International Reading Association, has also been an influential and bestselling work. Currently, NCTE releases about a dozen new titles a year.

Professional Journals

In its one-hundred-year history, NCTE has sponsored a variety of monthly, bimonthly, and quarterly periodicals, all focusing on issues of English, language, and media teaching and materials. As previously noted, NCTE's inaugural publication, *English Journal,* was published just one month after the organization's December 1911 founding and continues to serve members through articles, columns, and reports. To provide information for college members, NCTE inaugurated a "College Edition" of *English Journal* in 1928; eleven years later, *College English* became a separate publication. In time, NCTE expanded its journal offerings to meet the increasingly varied needs of members. For elementary teachers, NCTE launched *Elementary English Review* in 1924, renamed it *Elementary English* in 1947, and then titled the journal *Language Arts* in 1975. *College Composition and Com-*

munication, intended for teachers of rhetoric, composition, and communication, began publication in 1950; *English Education*, meant for teacher educators, was initiated in 1969; and *English Leadership Quarterly*, of interest to those in positions of leadership in college and school English departments, first appeared in 1971. *Teaching English in the Two-Year College* (*TETYC*) began in 1974; *Classroom Notes Plus*, in 1983; *Talking Points*, in 1989 for elementary language arts teachers; *Voices from the Middle*, in 1994 for middle level English teachers; *School Talk*, in 1995 for elementary teachers; *Research in the Teaching of English*, begun in 1967, filled a vital niche by disseminating pedagogical and literacy research. The number of subscriptions to these journals has often exceeded membership figures and has been as high as 200,000 (Gallivan, 19 Mar. 2009).

In addition, NCTE's affiliate organizations have published their own journals in almost every state. Affiliate journals such as the New England Association of Teachers of English's *The Leaflet*, the Virginia Association of Teachers of English's *Virginia English Bulletin*, and the California Association of Teachers of English's *California English* have all served useful functions, providing forums for discussing professional issues and sharing pedagogical strategies. Traditionally, the affiliate journals have served as important venues for publishing the writing of classroom teachers rather than that of university and college instructors.

For scholars in the field, analyzing the content of these NCTE journals provides a unique window into the issues that, over time, have concerned those who teach English. Contemporary dissertations have used the tables of contents and journal articles extensively as a basis for gauging the temper of the times and the nature of discussions surrounding educational and literacy issues. A recent example is Mark Faust and Mark Dressman's analysis of populist perspectives on teaching poetry, based on *English Journal* articles printed from 1912 to 2005. NCTE journals also have been vehicles for discussing research and exploring outside forces that impact the teaching of literacy. The journals often have been a forum for dissent and argument as well; the discontent that runs through much of the profession has found expression in lead articles, letters to the editor, and often pointed exchanges between writers and readers. Although NCTE publishes these journals, field editors and contributors are free to print articles and take stances critical of some of the organization's platforms (see Christenbury's "Entering the Whirlwind").

Guiding the Literacy Profession

NCTE has consistently been involved in debates regarding issues affecting literacy teaching and teachers in America. Though all of the organization's recommendations and policy statements have not been enacted on the national stage, NCTE and its members have attempted to be an influence, a force, and a source of information and timely research. In the early years of NCTE, NCTE and the NEA sponsored the *Reorganization of English in Secondary Schools* (1917) to provide guidance for shaping the high school English curriculum. This report is an early example of the kind of collaboration with other professional organizations that continues to this day. NCTE also has served as the launching place for several new organizations that are still active in their own right. The Association for Supervision and Curriculum Development (ASCD), the National Communication Association (NCA), Teachers of English to Speakers of Other Languages (TESOL), and the International Reading Association (IRA) all emerged from NCTE (Hook 6, 50, 61,151).

Early Initiatives

Early initiatives by NCTE to guide the profession, especially in response to the exigencies of the times, are the 1919 appointment of the first NCTE Commission on the English Curriculum and the 1935 publication of *An Experience Curriculum in English*. In *An Experience Curriculum*, as former NCTE Executive Director and literacy researcher Miles Myers points out, "NCTE leaders . . . pushed for [John] Dewey's [progressive] ideas, recommending in 1935 that the nation adopt" a progressive, Dewey-centric curricular form (86). Beginning in 1945 through *English Journal*, NCTE promoted the use of the term *language arts* to characterize the education of younger students, an inclusive term intended to convey a more complex understanding of reading, writing, listening, and speaking than "English" as a traditional school subject had come to mean. In 1949, acknowledging the central importance of teaching writing (often neglected in relation to reading), NCTE established within the organization the Conference on College Composition and Communication (CCCC), a specialized, large group that by the 1980s had developed an entire discipline within English: composition studies. The history of this conference and the relationship between national and local developments in the teaching of writing is treated in Anne Ruggles Gere's chapter in this volume.

Establishing Organizational Groups

As developments and concerns in the larger world have affected literacy education, NCTE has attempted to cover the waterfront, establishing a myriad of study, research, and organizational groups to address both curricular and workplace issues. The list includes the formation of several commissions: the Commission on the Profession (1958); the Commission on the English Language (1961); the Commission on Literature (1964); the Commission on Composition (1967); the Commission on Reading (1969); the Commission on Media (1979); and most recently, the Commission on Assessment (2009). The commissions have served the Council by studying trends and research and providing recommendations for policy decisions.

In addition to establishing CCCC, NCTE periodically has sponsored other groups to address the specialized interests of its members. The Conference on English Education (CEE) was established in 1964 for those who prepare English language arts teachers. For those who teach at two-year colleges, NCTE sponsored regional conferences in 1966 in Chicago, San Bernardino, San Antonio, Charlotte, Cazenovia, Vancouver, and St. Louis. These meetings led to the formation of the National Two-Year College Council, today known as the Two-Year College English Association, or TYCA. TYCA has been particularly active not only in addressing pedagogical issues but also in bringing public attention to a daunting list of concerns about the professional treatment of two-year college teachers and the conditions in which they work, among them

> increased teaching loads (larger class sizes or a requirement to teach more sections), colleges replacing full-time instructors with adjunct instructors, unjustified firings, threats to academic freedom, salaries that don't keep pace with the cost of living, loss of tenure, reduction or loss of shared governance, reduction of professional development opportunities, and micromanagement by suspicious administrators. (Bateman 241)

In 1970 the Conference of Secondary School English Department Chairmen (CSSEDC) was established. Renamed the Conference on English Leadership (CEL) in 1991, CEL responded to changes in the organization of American schools as high schools compressed and established new configurations for younger students (known alternately as junior high schools, intermediate schools, and middle schools). In 2000, NCTE acknowledged the special needs and contributions of middle school teachers by establishing the Middle Level Section, a division of the Council equal in rank and power with the members who align themselves with the interests of the traditional, historic Secondary, Elementary, and College Sections.

A Consideration of Three Documents

Let us pause here to examine how NCTE's meetings, commissions, and publications have guided the literacy profession in the face of forces shaping American public education. Throughout much of NCTE's history, discontent has characterized members' concerns about their profession and the times, just as conflicting views of the role of public education have persisted in the larger society. While discontent can be expected in an organization as large and diverse as NCTE, what matters most is the tone of the discussion and how inevitable tensions are resolved. It may be instructive to take a closer look at one such moment to appreciate the scope of NCTE's interest in literacy education. The report resulting from the Basic Issues conferences of 1958 and two parallel NCTE documents produced virtually at the same time, "What Are the Responsibilities of Teachers of English?" and "Selective Annotated List of Recent Readings on the Profession of English Teaching," represent pertinent examples of how, at one point in the history of the organization, the 1950s, both conservative and progressive streams of thought coexisted and, in different ways, competed to shape the literacy profession and attempted to resolve a moment of dissent and discontent. I begin with a quotation from *The Basic Issues in the Teaching of English* (1959):

> There is . . . much reason to believe that English teaching can be radically improved, given the right approaches to the problems and an effort of sufficient magnitude and strength. . . . [A] broad attack upon the whole problem of the teaching of English from the kindergarten through the graduate school is essential. (NCTE 5, 14)

The urgency expressed in this excerpt (cobbled together from the preface and the conclusion of the document) is clear, as is the belief that "attack" is the solution to the "problem." The devil, however, is in the details, requiring the "right approaches" and an "effort of sufficient magnitude and strength." *The Basic Issues in the Teaching of English* defines thirty-five areas of discussion, most presented in the form of questions, and was the product of several meetings throughout 1958 of almost thirty individuals representing the American Studies Association, the College English Association, the Modern Language Association, and NCTE. One impetus for the post-*Sputnik* meetings was a national concern that the country was inferior—the document refers to the "scientific and political crises which have aroused the interest and concern of the public" (NCTE, *Basic Issues* 15)—and that its schools were not living up to any sort of promise or potential. This was an era of impassioned calls for new rigor as well as for new approaches and new beliefs.

Of the thirty-five "basic issues" the document addresses, none is more important than the underlying theme that English has both practical and intrinsic value but that it also carries "*civilizing value*" (4, emphasis in the original): "ignorance of it would leave one a barbarian" (4). *The Basic Issues in the Teaching of English* acknowledges the "communications revolution" (5) but asserts that a major goal of the English program is to acquaint students with "the best thought and expression of their own time and the cultural heritage which is rightfully theirs" (6). Younger students should come to high school with an understanding of "narrative point of view, blank verse, irony, and poetic justice"

(7). In addition, the document posits that a "truly sequential and cumulative program in English" is essential to shape "the teaching of English from the kindergarten through the graduate school" (14).

By contrast, the newly constituted NCTE Commission on the Profession saw the situation very differently in its 24 May 1958 document, "What Are the Responsibilities of Teachers of English?" The commission certainly identified "problems"—twelve of them. Some were related to issues in teaching English; others addressed professional challenges and needs; many overlapped with concerns taken up in *The Basic Issues in the Teaching of English.* The tone of the commission's document, though, is significantly different. "What Are the Responsibilities of Teachers of English?" expects readers to accept, for example, that the "vast complex which the teaching of English undeniably is . . . [is] the normal development of our culture" (NCTE Commission on the Profession 1). In the current age, the document observes, we should "raise questions about old assumptions" (1). In addition to acknowledging a "revolution in communication" (2), the document asserts that in teaching English, "*learning to learn* has become an important goal" (4, emphasis in the original), as has "responsibility for the growth of each individual" (7). Reading "What Are the Responsibilities of Teachers of English?" gives the sense that the old is not to be conserved but is to yield to the new. In response to the question "What has happened in the world beyond the classroom to suggest the need to re-interpret our [English teachers'] responsibilities?" the answer is that "Aspects of our culture may call for new approaches to old problems and may create new problems which cannot be solved by old methods" (1). The document also calls for a "modified concept of 'literary experience' on the part of teachers" (2).

Underscoring these progressive ideas is a third document from the Commission on the Profession, "Selective Annotated List of Recent Readings on the Profession of English Teaching." The thirty-eight articles listed appeared in academic and popular journals published, with few exceptions, in 1958 and 1959. The list reflects a different philosophy of English teaching at all levels. Mass media and television are the topics of at least five articles, and the state of Russian education is the focus of two. The list includes conservative pieces as well as those written by NCTE leaders: former presidents Helen K. Mackintosh (1957), Robert C. Pooley (1941), Alfred H. Grommon (1968), Luella B. Cook (1956), Dora V. Smith (1936), and Lou L. LaBrant (1954). The contrast, however, between the conservative nature of *The Basic Issues in the Teaching of English* and the more forward-looking documents from the Commission on the Profession demonstrates that larger social forces were prompting a reassessment of literacy education and raising questions that had contradictory answers. As one annotation in the reading list notes, "the essential task of English is to help students look at everyday relationship [sic] in 'their self-searching, in their motivations, in their reactions to the culture patterns that surround them'" (NCTE Commission on the Profession, "Selective Annotated List" 2), a far different aim from the desire to "civilize" students through the study of English expressed in *The Basic Issues in the Teaching of English*.

Policy Meetings, Policy Statements, Standards, and Digital Literacy

In addition to guiding the literacy profession by providing opportunities for specialized subgroups of teachers to meet and by responding to shifting understandings of the role of English in public education, NCTE has sponsored meetings and developed policy statements that helped shape the profession by redefining the curriculum to meet the changing needs of students. Early efforts included the *Reorganization of English in Secondary Schools*, *An Experience Curriculum in English*, and the Basic Issues conferences. The Dartmouth Conference of the mid-1960s, the Impact conferences of the early 1980s (discussed in Donna Alvermann's chapter in this volume), and the English Coalition Conference of the late 1980s represent sustained efforts to review research and align it with current thinking about appropriate courses of study and teaching methods. While few of these meetings transformed the profession overnight, they remain landmark efforts to redefine "English" and offered a foundation upon which subsequent teachers and scholars could build new understandings of their work.

Policy statements also have helped to redefine "English." One salient example is the publication in 1996 of the jointly produced IRA and NCTE *Standards for the English Language Arts*, an effort to meet a national call to articulate agreed-upon principles for the content area and to provide "national consensus on the nature of English and the needs of teachers and students in the field" (Nelms 49). As John Mayher, the architect of one of many draft documents in the standards project, observed in 1999,

> A consistent theme in the school reform efforts of the past decade has been the mantra that "Our schools are failing because our standards are too low." . . . One of the significant limitations of the involvement of educators . . . in the standards movement is that we failed to insist on a sufficiently complex conception of standards to make them worth achieving. This allowed the term to become a kind of Rorschach blot in which everyone saw what they wanted to see, and in which the things we were to have higher—always higher!—standards about could vary widely. (106, 107–08)

Despite the challenges, NCTE joined with IRA and received federal support to craft standards for the English language arts. When the draft standards did not suit federal representatives, financial support for the project was withdrawn, but NCTE and IRA proceeded with the work nevertheless, funding it themselves. Mayher adroitly details the complex history of the drafts and the different conceptions of English as a subject that shaped the final document. *Standards for the English Language Arts* was the product of years of consensus-sharing within the membership and in alliance with IRA. The final document, though, was not met with applause or approval. Virtually no one within or outside the literacy profession was pleased with the result, and after *Standards for the English Language Arts* was published, it became clear that the document would never have the impact of the highly successful and, at least at the time, well-received 1989 standards from another important professional organization, the National Council of Teachers of Mathematics. Nevertheless, the *Standards for the English Language Arts* asserted principles collaboratively developed in a field in which consensus is often elusive, and the many individuals who worked on the project struggled through discontent to produce a document that met a national demand for articulating important principles of literacy teaching and learning. Both Donna E. Alvermann and John Mayher return to the IRA–NCTE standards project in their chapters for this volume, taking up subsequent calls for standards that characterize the political context in which today's literacy educators work.

As digital literacy issues have become broader in the twenty-first century, NCTE has also attempted to lead the profession and is, to date, the only professional organization to define *twenty-first-century literacies* (2008) so that literacy instruction and assessment, as well as acknowledgment of the power of social networking in most students' lives, is intelligently conducted. NCTE in 2008 sponsored an important Summer Institute on 21st Century Literacies and continues to develop resources, lesson plans, guidelines, and resolutions regarding the use of digital media in the classroom—all part of the information and advocacy of NCTE regarding digital literacy. These efforts are elaborated throughout this volume but especially in Chapter 6 by Mary Christel and Sandy Hayes.

Taking a Stand on Social Justice Issues Impacting Literacy Education

In advocating for social justice, NCTE has had considerable company among academic organizations and other sectors of American society. Even so, while progress has sometimes seemed too slow, over the decades many NCTE members have contributed their time and talents toward ensuring that fairness, equal opportunity, and democratic principles are the standard, both within and outside the profession, in schools, in communities, and in the nation.

Addressing Issues of Gender and Race

Women were part of the founding and very first meeting of NCTE. A photo of the December 1911 gathering features thirteen identifiable women in a room of thirty-four individuals, albeit all of them white. A year later, the first slate of NCTE officers included Emma J. Breck as first vice president, a fact made more impressive when we remember that women in the United States did not have the right to vote until the passage of the Nineteenth Amendment in 1920. Nine years later, in 1929, Rewey Belle Inglis was the first woman to be elected president of NCTE. (WILLA, the Women in Literature and Life Assembly of NCTE, established in 1991, annually presents the Rewey Belle Inglis Award for Outstanding Woman in English Education.) NCTE struggled, however, with equal gender representation, especially in leadership roles, and for half a century the language in Council publications consistently used the traditional *man/men* and *he/him* for all references to human beings. In the 1970s, the NCTE Women's Committee actively advocated for the use of nonsexist language in all NCTE communications and attempted to highlight the dearth of women in leadership roles. (More information on this topic and the role of NCTE's women presidents can be found in Jeanne Gerlach and Virginia Monseau's edited collection *Missing Chapters: Ten Pioneering Women in NCTE and English Education.*) By 1975, when guidelines for nonsexist language were adopted, having been affirmed in a 1974 NCTE resolution (Reed 1), inclusive, nonsexist language became the norm in virtually all NCTE print material. Women also entered leadership roles in increasing numbers, consistent with the expansion of women's presence in the teaching profession at all levels. Today, women leaders are the rule, not the exception.

Though NCTE has not always been in the forefront of social change, it has had leaders who strongly objected to racial inequality. NCTE conventions located in segregated cities posed significant challenges for members early in NCTE's history. At the 1932 NCTE Annual Convention in Memphis, for instance, meetings for white and black members were held in separate hotels across the street from each other. Major speakers gave their presentations twice, once in each of the two segregated locales. Jacqueline Jones Royster's chapter in this volume provides a fuller account of this meeting. In 1945, NCTE adopted the policy to meet only in cities providing hotels and dining facilities "regardless of race or religion" ("The Buffalo Convention" 108). It was not until 1962 that NCTE conventions returned to the South (Hook 129). By 1964 the NCTE Board of Directors also had prohibited racial restrictions on membership in NCTE affiliates. Later, NCTE also would not meet in states that had failed to ratify the Equal Rights Amendment and, in subsequent decades, where laws put gay and lesbian members at risk of arrest.

In addition to asserting freedom of assembly for all NCTE members, the organization sponsored efforts to educate teachers, parents, and the public about a more inclusive curriculum. In 1941, Charlemae Hill Rollins published through NCTE *We Build Together*, an annotated volume "which described books by and about blacks" for young readers (Hook 107); the book was revised and reissued in 1948 and 1967. Inclusive instructional materials were also the concern of the Task Force on Racism and Bias, established in 1969 under the leadership of Ernece B. Kelly, who served until 1980 (Brown). This important task force issued in 1970 a statement setting forth "Criteria for Teaching Materials in Reading and Literature." The task force found "crucial deficiencies" in instructional materials used in English language arts classrooms and enumerated some of them in a 1971 *College English* article:

> Specifically, educational materials now suffer from the following crucial deficiencies: the inadequate representation of literary works by members of non-white minorities in general anthologies which serve as basic texts and in basal readers and other Language Arts kits inclusive of audio-visual materials, in most elementary, secondary, and college English courses; representation of minority groups which is demeaning, insensitive, or unflattering to the culture; the inclusion of only popular and proven works by a limited number of "acceptable" writers, resulting in a misrepresentation of the actual range of the group's contribution to literature; biased commentaries which gloss over or flatly ignore the oppression suffered by non-white minority persons; and still other commentaries in anthologies which depict inaccurately the influence of non-white minority persons on literary, cultural, and historical developments in America. (713–14)

The document calls for "balance," and asserts that "non-white minorities must be represented in basic texts in a fashion which respects their dignity as human beings and mirrors their contributions to American culture, history, and letters" (714). To help educate students and teachers about the range of excellent literature by authors of color, NCTE and the NCTE Black Caucus hosted in 1990 the first African American Read-In, a day in which teachers, students, and the general public read African American literature.

The work of the Task Force on Racism and Bias was considered influential regarding the selection of teaching materials, but the movement was much broader. Two actions emerged from an NCTE study group, meeting before the 1970 NCTE Annual Convention in Atlanta (Prichard; NCTE Annual Business Meeting Minutes, 28 Nov. 1970). First, NCTE members passed a resolution, "On Items Testing Competence in Black Literature on Qualifying and Certifying Examinations," calling for the inclusion of test items "designed to test and examine competence in Black Literature" for "all teacher certification and recertification examinations, all English achievement tests, and the Graduate Record Examination." A second, less binding but still significant sense-of-the-house motion urged similar attention to Chicano literature, noting that "the cultural contribution of the Chicano Community . . . be recognized" through examination and test items (NCTE Annual Business Meeting Minutes, 28 Nov. 1970, 25).

At NCTE meetings, the Task Force on Racism and Bias also provided leadership and focus:

> At both the 4C's and NCTE Conventions, the Task Force maintained a booth exhibiting publications of every genre penned by minority authors. Recordings were also on display. The materials spanned elementary to college level reading abilities, and occasionally, an author of color was featured at the booth. This person would talk about the publishing process and answer questions.
>
> Because the TF booth was competing for the attention of conference-goers with the more expensive-looking booths of publishers, ethnic music was played there. The booth acted also as a means for enhanced cooperation between the caucuses because TF relied on non-members to help maintain a presence there. (The now-deceased, African American poet Sarah Webster Fabio scrawled her thanks to the Task Force on one of her spoken word LP's for helping increase her visibility in the English teacher/publisher communities.) (Brown)

To further the work of scholars of color and to reinforce a commitment to diversity, in the spring of 2000 the NCTE

Research Foundation established the Cultivating New Voices Among Scholars of Color (CNV) program, sponsoring scholars of color and fostering their research. Forty-three individuals were selected for the program between 2000 and 2007, each developing a proposal for research and participating in a mentored cohort of young scholars:

> The mentors, many long-standing members of NCTE, are asked to work across two years with fellows to develop research theory, methods, and implementation in support of the fellows' dissertations or related research projects. The mentors and fellows meet annually during the NCTE Fall Convention and in the Spring for a research retreat. Since 2004, CNV fellows and mentors have met in conjunction with the Research Foundation Spring meeting so that Trustees may also attend and support the work of CNV. (NCTE Research Foundation 1)

Providing such mentoring for new leaders of color represents an ongoing effort to diversify NCTE membership. NCTE's first African American president (as well as the first African American editor of an NCTE journal, *Language Arts*) was William A. Jenkins, who served in 1969. Since then, other members of color have held leadership positions in the Council, including the presidency. Beginning in the late 1960s, NCTE also saw the formation of several caucuses: the Chicano Caucus (1968; now known as the Latina/o Caucus), the Black Caucus (1970), and the Jewish Caucus (2002). Within CCCC, the Asian/Asian American Caucus was organized in 1995; the Caucus for American Indian Scholars and Scholarship, in 1997. These groups had their genesis in the membership and deliberations of the Task Force on Racism and Bias, which worked to correct "crucial deficiencies" in instructional materials used in English classrooms. While the Gay Caucus began meeting at NCTE annual conventions in 1976, by 1994 the Gay Straight Educators' Alliance (GSEA) was established as the NCTE Assembly for Gay Lesbian Academic Issues Awareness (AGLAIA). These groups not only provide an important intellectual and social space within the organization but also help mentor future leaders and urge NCTE toward greater inclusiveness. Some of the contributions of these caucuses to the

Council's policy work are discussed in chapters by Jacqueline Jones Royster and by Carol D. Lee and Anika Spratley.

These authors, together with Stephen Tchudi in his chapter, "Teaching Language," detail NCTE's efforts to address misconceptions about the English language, specifically the place of a student's "home" language in the classroom and the role of Standard English. The influential—and, for some, still controversial—*Students' Right to Their Own Language* resolution was approved in 1972 by CCCC and later adopted, slightly revised, by NCTE and reaffirmed in 2003. Reflecting decades of linguistic research and a belief in the importance of respecting all language varieties, the statement asserts, in the language of the 1972 resolution,

> the students' right to their own patterns and varieties of language—the dialects of their nurture or whatever dialects in which they find their own identity and style. Language scholars long ago denied that the myth of a standard American dialect has any validity. The claim that any one dialect is unacceptable amounts to an attempt of one social group to exert its dominance over another. Such a claim leads to false advice for speakers and writers, and immoral advice for humans. A nation proud of its diverse heritage and its cultural and racial variety will preserve its heritage of dialects. (NCTE, *Students' Right* 2–3)

The significance of the *Students' Right to Their Own Language* statement is attested by virtually every contributing author in this volume. While it grew out of "the Council's evolving consciousness of issues of race, class, and dialect" (p. 152), as Tchudi puts it, it also helped to educate teachers, parents, and others about linguistic research and language variation. (For additional information, see Scott, Straker, and Katz.)

Confronting War and Advocating for Peace

Insularity was not an issue for NCTE during the world wars, nor were members indifferent to the need for harmony between nations. After the First World War and fearing a second, NCTE's International Relations Committee was alarmed enough about the state of the world to present, at the 29 November 1935 annual business meeting, a number of resolutions. The resolutions noted concerns for "a thoroughgoing peace policy for the United States and for the world"; opposition to "a war and to the supplying of munitions and all materials that might be used toward the breaking of world peace"; and, with regard to education, opposition to the "prevailing tendency to militarize the schools and colleges of the nation" by means of ROTC programs and war propaganda in classroom instructional materials (Minutes 19).

At subsequent pre–World War II annual business meetings, members understood that the United States faced "troubled times" (NCTE Annual Business Meeting Minutes, 22 Nov. 1940, 29) and adopted a resolution calling for "specific training in the use of . . . contemporary materials" such as magazines and radio scripts, and for the "spiritual defense of our democracy" (28–29). Two years later, during the November 1942 Board of Directors meeting, NCTE members present observed that "[a]s English teachers we are mobilized for war" (Minutes 270) and noted how literacy could be effective in the conflict.

What possible relevance could English and the teaching of English have in a time of war? For NCTE the answer lay in what literacy education could do for victory, and the organization asserted the importance of language and communication early on. During World War II, NCTE went all out with war-related articles, pamphlets, and, in an apparent contradiction, advice to teachers on how to help students interpret propaganda. A 28 December 1941 "English in Wartime" resolution from the NCTE College Section, approved by one hundred members in attendance at the Indianapolis College Section luncheon, noted that "[t]eachers, as citizens, are obligated to support civilian morale. In time of war as in time of peace the defense of our country involves the preservation and extension of democracy, its institutions, its hopes, and its ideals" ("English in Wartime" 578).

Because the war restricted travel, no NCTE Annual Convention was held in 1942, though smaller, local conferences served "to increase intelligent and effective support of the war effort on the part of the schools and teachers" ("News and Notes" 564). In 1943 a business meeting only was offered. Yet despite the suspension of large meetings, NCTE contributed to the war effort in other ways. As an example, in 1943 "Pre-Induction Needs in Language Communication and Reading" was published in *Education for Victory*, a newsletter cosponsored by the U.S. Office of Education and the War Department. Written by NCTE members and then-NCTE President Max J. Herzberg, the article offered numerous strategies to strengthen communication skills for soldiers. After World War II, *College English* in 1945 conducted and published a survey of "English for Ex-Service Personnel," addressing the needs of soldiers adjusting to peacetime and to their work in college English classes.

During the Cold War, the federally sponsored National Defense Education Act (NDEA) was established in 1958 to support subjects that were considered vital to national defense—science, mathematics, and foreign language. To assert the centrality of literacy education to national defense, a 1960 NCTE resolution called for the NDEA to include English in the program; in 1961 the argument was reinforced by NCTE's publication of *The National Interest and the Teaching of English*. NDEA did not immediately include English as a subject vital to national defense, but a second publication, *The National Interest and the Continuing Education of Teachers of English* (1964), proved effectively compelling, and in 1964, NDEA was expanded to include English. Scholar Robert P. Yagelski marks the event:

> [*The National Interest and the Continuing Education of Teachers of English* convinced] Congress to include English as a vital subject of study in schools. . . . It seems a watershed, if short-lived, movement in the history of English as an academic discipline, bringing together conservative, rationalist, moderate, liberal, and progressive educators in a rare moment of relative agreement about the importance of the study of English in American society. (7–8)

The support for war efforts and defense-related teaching shifted around the time that the Vietnam War entered the national consciousness. In that era, one of the consistent tensions within NCTE was what position the organization should take on the Vietnam War. Like many organizations of the time, NCTE fought its own battles over the issue. In 1969, NCTE President William

A. Jenkins noted that individuals who opposed the war could be more effective "as private citizens than as members of NCTE" (Hook 237). But just weeks later, NCTE members disagreed and passed a resolution demanding an end to the Vietnam War and calling it "not only a threat to [NCTE's] educational objective but a threat to the very culture it is expected to educate young people for" (Hook 238). At almost every subsequent NCTE meeting until the conflict ended, issues regarding Vietnam emerged and were debated.

The response to war and the role of literacy has continued through NCTE publications and resolutions in recent decades. Over the years, war-related articles in *English Journal* have provided curricular responses to war, helped students develop patriotism and avoid xenophobia, and explored critical citizenship. Other war-related topics were addressed in NCTE books, such as Larry Johannessen's *Illumination Rounds,* and special issues of NCTE journals, among them the 2000 *English Journal* focus issue, *A Curriculum of Peace,* edited by Virginia Monseau, and the 2009 *Teaching English in the Two-Year College* special issue, *Teaching in a Time of War,* edited by Jeff Sommers. Just two months after the September 11 attacks on the Pentagon and the World Trade Center, members attending the 2001 NCTE Annual Convention passed a resolution "On Teaching in a Time of Crisis." The resolution urged NCTE to continue to support

> Literature and writing instruction as a means for understanding loss, anger, war, and difference;
>
> Language study as a vehicle for understanding conflict, propaganda, and democratic discourse; and
>
> Critical literacy as an instrument essential to an informed citizenship and global understanding. (NCTE Annual Business Meeting Minutes, 26 Nov. 2001, 4)

At the beginning of the twenty-first century, NCTE members continue to define how their teaching of the English language arts speaks to the larger forces that disrupt the peace between nations. Among the questions they attempt to address are those posed by *TETYC* editor Jeff Sommers:

> How are we now teaching students who are veterans of the wars in Iraq and Afghanistan, the first Gulf War, Panama, Somalia, Vietnam? Many students have parents, siblings, spouses, grandparents, even children who have served during wars in the past forty years. How is teaching English to these students influenced by our current war-time standing? What is the effect on classroom dynamics? teacher-student relationships? student-student relationships? pedagogical decisions about assigned reading and writing? (Sommers, "Editorial" 349)

Literacy, it would seem, does indeed have a place in times of conflict.

Intellectual Freedom for Students and Teachers

As a social issue, intellectual freedom and resistance to all forms of censorship have been central concerns for NCTE for decades. Censorship especially bears on the instructional freedom of teachers and their students because it often restricts or controls materials used in libraries and classrooms.

In the mid-twentieth century, many in the United States were concerned about the influence of communism, but for NCTE members, there were real limits to proving one's loyalty to the U.S. Constitution and one's love of democracy. At the annual business meeting on 23 November 1950, NCTE members passed several resolutions directly addressing the fear-mongering of the times: after some debate and a few changes in wording, the members "deplored[d] the unwarranted suspicions implied in hastily conceived and discriminatory teachers' oaths," which had a tendency to "divide and confuse by a questionable identification of the word with the thing, honest and conscientious teachers" (Minutes 63). At the annual business meeting on 26 November 1953, NCTE members expressed their concern regarding "restrictions upon the choice of classroom materials and the right of communists to teach in the public schools of the United States" (Minutes 77). The group went on to adopt a resolution, partially quoted here:

> The NCTE believes that freedom to teach includes freedom to examine and to dissent from, within the limits of loyalty and integrity, not only those beliefs which are safe and popular,

> but those which are held by the few and are unpopular with many. . . . [D]enying access to all relevant facts is as much a betrayal of responsibilities as is indoctrination with fanatic creeds and that both practices are indeed totalitarian. . . . It is the strong conviction of the NCTE that schools and colleges of the nation must be guarded not only against Communism, but also against those persons who use the fear of Communism as a pretext for their attacks upon the American educational system. (Minutes 77, 78)

Resolutions are important not only for solidarity but also because they frame responses that can promote further work. Opposition to censorship, "restriction upon the choice of classroom materials" in the words of the 1953 resolution just cited, prompted the publication in 1953 of the pamphlet "Censorship and Controversy," as well as "The Students' Right to Read" (1962), which affirmed the necessity of open materials for all students: "Censorship leaves students with an inadequate and distorted picture of the ideals, values, and problems of their culture. . . . [T]he real victims are the students, denied the freedom to explore ideas and pursue truth wherever and however they wish" (NCTE Committee on the Right to Read 7).

In one of the most important American judicial rulings regarding the censorship of classroom and library materials, NCTE affiliates contributed funds to permit filing a friend-of-the-court (*amicus curiae*) brief supporting a student's appeal of a decision in a book-banning case (*Pico v. Island Trees School District*) in 1979. The brief contended:

> At stake is the right of students and teachers to pursue their scholastic activities free from the intrusion of public officials who, because they are offended by certain passages, physically remove and ban books from public junior and senior high school libraries and forbid their use in the curriculum. . . . [S]uch conduct is abhorrent to the principles of a free society, and in direct contravention of the First Amendment.
>
> Government censorship in any form is suspect. It is especially unwelcome in the public school system, which must instill an understanding of, and respect for, democratic processes if our society is to remain viable. (*Brief* 3)

The Supreme Court's decision was split, but the justices ruled that library materials were protected and could not be removed from a school.

Today NCTE continues to assist teachers and other literacy leaders in resisting censorship by providing supporting letters, materials, and information and by joining with other organizations such as the American Library Association to make the public more aware of the continued pressure to censor or "ban" books.

NCTE also routinely calls attention to deceptive uses of language. In 1972 the first NCTE Committee on Public Doublespeak was appointed. The committee's title is a nod to George Orwell's novel *1984* and his influential essay on the deliberate misuse of language, "Politics and the English Language." Today, at the NCTE Annual Convention the Doublespeak Award highlights deceptive language, and the George Orwell Award recognizes individuals who support intellectual freedom. Donna E. Alvermann treats these and other issues of intellectual freedom in her chapter.

The involvement of NCTE in political activities and policy work is essentially inescapable. In 1972, when former NCTE President William A. Jenkins headed a subcommittee of the NCTE Commission on Reading, he wrote, in "Political Activities of the NCTE Commission on Reading," that an "activist" orientation to "keep our needs, intentions, and concerns before those who are in power should be carried out" (Jenkins 1). Jenkins offered a nineteen-point agenda with eight priorities, advocating that "the Commission [on Reading] re-establish contact and maintain contact with the 'gatekeepers' of the lands of political influence, financing, and other forms of support for the teaching of reading" (Jenkins 6). Shortly thereafter, in 1975, NCTE launched an "action wing," Support for the Learning and Teaching of English (SLATE), to provide members with information about political events and movements. As political pressures on education mounted, especially during discussions of federal No Child Left Behind legislation, NCTE hosted its first Advocacy Day on Capitol Hill in 2002 so that members could discuss literacy issues with congressional representatives. In 2006, NCTE leaders wrote their first legislative platform, which is updated annually to advance public policies supportive of effective literacy education.

Assessment

What historian Arthur N. Applebee calls "the movement for scientific management" (*Tradition* 81) in education was embodied early on by E. L. Thorndike, whose achievement tests in major school subjects were instituted in American classrooms around 1908. In the 1930s, NCTE Executive Director W. Wilbur Hatfield and eventual NCTE President John J. DeBoer (1942) were also involved in creating and advocating for objective tests for the English classroom. But as testing has expanded, largely through the influence of the College Entrance Examination Board (CEEB), NCTE has increasingly resisted large-scale, high-stakes assessments. In the past thirty-five years, the organization has adopted no fewer than twenty-four resolutions that address concerns about behavioral objectives, standardized tests, national testing programs, the National Assessment of Educational Progress (NAEP), alternative testing, mandated competency tests, and "excessive focus on subskills" testing. These concerns are not confined to younger students but also extend to those attending colleges and universities. Kathleen Blake Yancey's chapter in this volume charts "NCTE's role in *advocating for* and helping to create assessments in support of learners and learning, as well as *speaking against* measures that truncate learning or stigmatize students" (p. 284). A past president of NCTE, Yancey and others in 2005 helped address the widespread use of timed writing tests by virtually all school districts across the country in *The Impact of the SAT and ACT Timed Writing Tests* (NCTE). The report details the effects of this kind of testing on students' processes of composing and revising and raises four issues regarding the validity and reliability of such tests, the effect of the tests on curriculum and classroom instruction, the unintended consequences of the tests, and concerns about equity and diversity (2).

While assessment is central to responsible classroom instruction, the misuse and misinterpretation of tests remains a persistent concern of literacy teachers. The comments of John C. Sherwood, writing fifty years ago as the chair of the 1964 Committee on Testing, are salient today, especially as contemporary students are the most frequently assessed and tested individuals in American educational history:

> The field of objective testing is today a controversial one, and it is hardly surprising that controversies about testing in composition should be especially troublesome. . . . That many teachers hold violent opinions on these topics is hardly surprising. . . . We must recognize the dangers involved in objective testing . . . and [take] every care to avoid any undesirable influence on the teaching of English. (Sherwood 1, 6)

Advancing the Scholarship of English and Literacy

NCTE has long been a sponsor of research on the teaching and learning of English. The first article in the first issue of the organization's first periodical, *English Journal*, presents data on student–teacher ratios in a number of states and makes the case that composition teachers in particular are overburdened (Hopkins). This pattern of initiating and reporting on research and also asking for "teacher opinion on various professional problems" (Radner 13) has continued over a century. Research is central to the work of NCTE: it tells us that individuals put bias in language, and that language arts are processes (and how these processes develop). Research defines pedagogical practices and drives advocacy; it promotes teachers' studies of classroom practices, fosters ongoing professional development, and generates consulting networks. The research studies that NCTE has sponsored have been important and ultimately influential. They include, just to mention a few from recent years, the effect of grammar instruction on writing, the use of canonical works in secondary English classes, the writing behaviors of students, and the influence of digital communication on students' out-of-school literacy practices.

The Research Foundation and the James R. Squire Office

The NCTE Research Foundation, established in 1960 and supported by a portion of members' dues, has published influential research, helped draft and disseminate policy documents, and recognized exemplary studies and dissertations (through the Promising Researcher, Britton, Emig, Meade, and Russell Awards, just to mention five). The Research Foundation also fosters "research and scholarship related to diversity and equity in literacy education" (NCTE Research Foundation 1), and a 2007 report from the foundation notes a $700,000 investment in such research over a period of six years.

In 2004, NCTE also established the James R. Squire Office of Policy Research in the English Language Arts. Named in honor of former NCTE Executive Director James R. Squire, the office has researched and reported on timely topics impacting the work of literacy educators, among them writing, new media, twenty-first-century literacies, English language learners, traditional and alternative certification programs, and the working conditions of college composition teachers. Compilations of research through the Squire Office regarding assessment, writing across the curriculum, and teacher preparation not only strengthen NCTE's claims about effective teaching practices but also provide policymakers with current information about the work of literacy educators.

Scholarly Research Meetings and Seminars

Significant research meetings and seminars sponsored by NCTE have also contributed to the scholarship of the profession. As mentioned before, the 1966 Anglo-American Seminar on the Teaching and Learning of English, known as the Dartmouth Conference, still ranks as one of the most influential conferences in the latter part of the twentieth century. Also in the 1960s, NCTE administered and directed Project English, headed by NCTE Executive Director J. N. Hook and funded by the federal government. Project English supported curriculum study centers, conferences, and research. While the curriculum centers and other initiatives did not continue in influence much beyond the 1960s, Project English demonstrates that when literacy organizations conferred, they could create innovative approaches to teaching (Hook 196). The 1960s also saw NCTE and the University of Illinois at Urbana–Champaign collaborate on the National Study of High School English Programs (1963–1965). In addition to supporting and conducting research, NCTE, beginning in 1967 (Hook 267), became a major distributor of scholarship as the home of the English and then the reading divisions of the Education

Resources Information Center (ERIC) Clearinghouse, a vital center for collecting research materials, reports, conference presentations, and books that otherwise would not be accessible to educators.

Disseminating research was also one goal of a series of Impact Conferences on reading and literacy education, especially in the elementary schools (Goodman x). As part of the 1979 International Year of the Child, the presidents of NCTE and IRA formed a joint committee on the Impact of Child Language Development Research on Curriculum and Instruction. From 1979 to 1982, this group sponsored four national and three regional conferences on children's language and learning. What emerged from these conferences was the influential *Observing the Language Learner* (Jaggar and Smith-Burke), as well as the concept of "kidwatching" for observing young language learners. These conferences laid important groundwork for resisting an exclusive focus on phonics and basal readers and for promoting whole language approaches to reading instruction.

In 1986, NCTE joined with eight other organizations to cosponsor the English Coalition Conference. The focus of this gathering was, "[What] does it mean to be a teacher of English, from kindergarten through graduate school?" (Lloyd-Jones and Lunsford xvii), and the sixty participants discussed "English studies as a continuum from the earliest grades through undergraduate study" (xxi). Seen as a "follow-up to the Dartmouth Conference" (Elbow 3), attendees engaged in much "hope and idealism" (Nelms 58) and revisited many of the principles articulated at Dartmouth.

Scholarly Publications

As discussed earlier in this chapter, NCTE has a long history of publishing scholarly books and has vetted, printed, and distributed hundreds of titles over the years. NCTE books have furthered scholarship in the field, helped teachers with their own ongoing professional development, and offered materials for classroom study. Together with NCTE publications cited previously, the following books published or distributed by NCTE have been especially influential in changing literacy practice and research directions: Richard Braddock, Richard Lloyd-Jones, and Lowell Schoer's *Research in Written Composition* (1963); Kellogg W. Hunt's *Grammatical Structures Written at Three Grade Levels* (1965); George Hillocks Jr.'s *Research on Written Composition: New Directions for Teaching* (1986); Judith A. Langer and Arthur N. Applebee's *How Writing Shapes Thinking: A Study of Thinking and Learning* (1987); James Flood, Diane Lapp, James R. Squire, and Julie M. Jensen's *Handbook of Research on Teaching the English Language Arts* (2nd ed., 2003); books in the current Theory & Research Into Practice (TRIP) series, which translates research into instruction; and volumes in NCTE's Research Report series, which offered research findings based on various methods of research.

NCTE has also been active in chronicling its own history. Three major treatments are Arthur N. Applebee's *Tradition and Reform in the Teaching of English: A History* (1974); J. N. Hook's *A Long Way Together: A Personal View of NCTE's First Sixty-Seven Years* (1979); and Marjorie N. Farmer's *Consensus and Dissent: Teaching English Past, Present, and Future* (1986). In addition, two *English Journal* focus issues devoted to the history of literacy education were published by editors Judy and England in 1979 and one by *English Journal* editor Monseau in 2000. TYCA's history has been recently chronicled in four articles written by Jeffrey Andelora and published in *Teaching English in the Two-Year College. The ALAN Review* has been detailed in a collection of essays edited by Patricia P. Kelly and Robert C. Small, Jr., *Two Decades of* The ALAN Review (1999).

Connecting with International Scholars

According to *International Involvement, "Global English," and NCTE Focus Group White Paper,* an NCTE staff report that informs the following section, the organization has maintained an interest in the work of teachers outside the United States almost from the beginning. As early as 1925, NCTE member E. Estelle Downing of Michigan State Normal College, a pacifist and internationalist, made the case that the study and teaching of English could help ensure that the tragedy of World War I would never be repeated. At the 1925 NCTE Annual Convention, Downing asked,

> How can we teach composition so that assertion will not pass for argument, prejudice for reason, or passion for knowledge? How can we teach literature so as to lessen combative group loyalties, inhibiting prejudices, and dangerous hatreds? How through the teaching of English can we prevent standardization of opinions and beliefs and crystallization of a blind and deaf conservatism? How can we better foster faith in the ultimate force of friendship, honesty, and justice between classes, races, and creeds? (NCTE, *International Involvement* 1)

Downing was later appointed chair of NCTE's first International Relations Committee, a group that wrote extensively across the Council and sponsored International Good-Will Days. This concern for international relations continued, and by 1943, a motion was adopted to create an International Council of Teachers of English, formed by delegates from across the Americas. To support teachers who taught nonnative speakers of English, NCTE formed a committee on Teaching English as a Second Language in 1945. NCTE President Harold B. Allen (1961) created the English for Today series, distributed by McGraw-Hill, which became the primary set of English textbooks in many nations around the world in the 1960s and 1970s. Allen also published *A Survey of the Teaching of English to Non-English Speakers in the United States* (1966) and organized a series of national conferences in the mid-1960s that gave rise to the TOEFL exam and the organization TESOL. It was NCTE Executive Director Robert F. Hogan who drafted TESOL's constitution.

To encourage NCTE members to meet teachers in other countries, the Council organized study tours of England in the mid-1960s, and many American teachers came away impressed by the progressive teaching methods used in British schools. Drama, storytelling, and art were often interwoven with English study. Boris Ford, the president of NCTE's sister British professional association, the National Association for the Teaching of English (NATE), attended the NCTE Convention in 1964 and was so inspired by what he saw as similar challenges across the two organizations that, in the following year, he and James R. Squire organized the International Conference on the Teaching of English, held during the 1965 Annual Convention. The papers delivered during this gathering were published as *A Common Purpose: The*

Teaching of English in Great Britain, Canada, and the United States (1966). In 1967 the Canadian Council of Teachers of English was organized with NCTE's assistance, and the seeds were sown for the influential Dartmouth Conference that summer.

Despite the momentum from Dartmouth, international concerns faded in the fevered activism of the late 1960s. By 1972, however, NCTE sponsored its First International Conference on the Teaching of English in York, England, and that same year launched the International Exchange Assembly, one of the first four assemblies formed by NCTE. Although the assembly provided an institutional base for a few hundred members, no major structural steps were undertaken until selected NCTE leaders began participating in a loosely formed International Steering Committee in the late 1970s. This group would officially become the International Federation for the Teaching of English (IFTE) in 1982, and NCTE ratified its participation and the IFTE constitution in 1983.

As the 1990s began, international interest strengthened. NCTE President Miriam Chaplin (1995) went on a fact-finding trip to South Africa, and Presidents Jesse Perry (1993) and especially Shirley Haley-James (1991) pushed the Council to undertake new structures to support international scholarship and engagement. In the summer of 1995, under the American leadership of John Mayher and Gordon Pradl, the International Federation for the Teaching of English Tri-Annual Conference was held in New York City, bringing together teachers from Australia, the United Kingdom, and the United States. In the late 1990s, NCTE was involved in the International Conference for Global Conversations on Language and Literacy; a number of these meetings were organized and attended by NCTE officers and members in such locations as Heidelberg, Germany (1996); Bordeaux, France (1998); and Utrecht, Netherlands (2000).

Conclusion: Into the Twenty-First Century

> The ideological and material complexity that builds up around literacy . . . cannot be underestimated.
>
> DEBORAH BRANDT, *Literacy in American Lives* (193)

> Idealism remains a driving force in the profession of English teaching.
>
> ROBERT P. YAGELSKI, *The Relevance of English: Teaching That Matters in Students' Lives* (15)

One of the undeniable characteristics about English, the teaching of English, and the goals and ideals of any organization purporting to represent English teachers is the tremendous diversity of opinion about any topic. Put any three literacy professionals together, and they will offer you a dozen different opinions. But it has always been so. While most English teachers would agree on fundamental principles about students, the subjects they teach, and the balancing act that effective instruction requires, literacy educators also recognize that language and its uses are highly contextual, that their students are unique individuals, and that much about teaching depends on factors that can shift from day to day and year to year. Good teachers hold, on the one hand, conviction, and on the other, doubt and concern as they continually evaluate their work. This complexity coexists with the "idealism" described in the quotation above from Yagelski. Applied to an organization such as NCTE, holding conviction simultaneously with doubt and concern makes for a complicated, multifaceted, and often contradictory history.

In endeavoring to represent English teachers and provide a voice for important policy and research in the field, NCTE can count some undeniable victories. There are also defeats and stalemates and clear evidence that no single group of professional educators has been, at least in the last forty years, a significant influence on national policy and practice. At the same time, NCTE can claim a consistent effort to influence English classrooms and English teaching at all levels in this country, what John Mayher, later in this volume, calls a "progressive pattern that has informed the positions, beliefs, and practices of the Council" (p. 397). We can also acknowledge that the discontent that Hosic noted in 1912 is still with us. American public education is in constant foment, and depending on the exigencies of the time, change and conflict—and, yes, even discontent—appear and reappear, sometimes in new guises. As Deborah Brandt so eloquently illustrates in *Literacy in American Lives*,

> Throughout the past century, with nearly every new generation, learning to read and write has meant learning to read and write for new reasons and under new auspices. Literacy learning became part of a wider response to changes affecting individuals, their families, and their communities. (191)

What NCTE represents, then, is a focal point and a force, a movement if you will. Today, after almost a century, it remains a voice for English language arts teachers and an advocate for America's students.

An enduring value in the United States is the shaping of citizenry and the dissemination of democratic values within the classrooms of American public schools. Brandt calls "literacy's link to democracy" both "complicated" and "vital" (205). What happens in those classrooms affects our communities, our economy, our present, and our future. The consequences of both success and failure are immense. One of the compelling motivations behind the ongoing work of NCTE is the fact that power is rarely in the hands of those closest to students. The people who spend hours with students are the last to be consulted regarding policy. Often, curricular decisions, access to materials, funding, and institutional regulations are imposed from without and based on misplaced ideological allegiances, often without regard for sound pedagogical principles. As articulated by reading researcher and 1979 NCTE President Yetta M. Goodman, "the mission of NCTE [is] to respond to uninformed impositions by those outside of the classroom," and part of the organization's mandate is the need for "background knowledge, theory, and research" (Goodman viii) to resist those impositions. While the degree of teacher and student influence varies across teaching levels, access to power and voice in education is an ongoing concern for most literacy teachers. For one hundred years, marking some victories, some defeats, and some draws, NCTE has worked to be that voice, to be a professional home for those who teach language and literature and writing and speaking. The organization has also functioned, in a way, as a conscience: it has lent voice and prestige to those who work with young people in classrooms across the United States and who often have no one to speak for them. Through NCTE, the importance of literacy education and the principles whereby it is taught are asserted outside the schoolhouse.

On the fiftieth anniversary of NCTE, eight individuals were asked to predict what the world of teaching English would look like fifty years into the future, in 2010. Some of their predictions were more hopeful than realistic. Arno Jewett, for example, hoped that teachers at all levels would cooperate and not criticize one another; Paul Diedrich hypothesized an ideal teaching environment, with a reduced number of students and full days for individual meetings (17); and Lou LaBrant looked for an "improved" alphabet and "simplified" grammar (NCTE, *Golden Anniversary* 16–17). A number of observers, however, proved to be right on target:

> Lou LaBrant predicted that we would enjoy "daily television from around the globe" and that English would be a "world language";
>
> Robert Tuttle saw "automatic devices for learning" that would not only instruct but also correct errors;
>
> Patrick D. Hazard acknowledged the power of "the emergence of massive, extracurricular media of communication." (NCTE, *Golden Anniversary* 16–17)

As NCTE Executive Director James R. Squire looked into the future in 1967, he observed, "Every committee, every publication, every special conference . . . means Council members at work trying to improve the teaching of English in school and college. And to such involvement I am willing to trust the future of our profession" (22).

And what is the future? *Consensus and Dissent*, the 1986 publication celebrating the diamond jubilee of NCTE, affirmed the organization's role as "the continuing forum for the exploration of possible truths about the art and science of teaching English" (Farmer 144) but also cautioned that the organization could become "a kind of paper organization, continually passing rules, regulations, recommendations, and resolutions which have no impact on the teaching lives of its members or on the rest of the English teaching profession" (140), not to mention the country at large. Indeed, how any organization can effect systemic and permanent change is central to evaluating the role of NCTE in American literacy education.

What is clear, however, is the commitment of NCTE members, literacy teachers at all levels, to the cause and the work. In *The Relevance of English*, Robert P. Yagelski writes of the "hopeful vision that seems to run through the short history of the teaching of English" (16), the "building of a better world through the teaching of English . . . as we struggle to understand ourselves in a time of change and even as we battle among ourselves to define our mission while confronting uncertain prospects for the future" (15–16). Adherence to that "hopeful vision," which is amplified in the chapters that follow, marks the successes and explains the failures of NCTE, the literacy organization that, now after a hundred years, still works to create that better world.

Works Cited

Allen, Harold B. *A Survey of the Teaching of English to Non-English Speakers in the United States*. Champaign, IL: NCTE, 1966.

Andelora, Jeffrey. "Forging a National Identity: TYCA and the Two-Year College Teacher-Scholar." *Teaching English in the Two-Year College* 35.4 (2008): 350–62. Print.

———. "The Professionalization of Two-Year College English Faculty: 1950–1990." *Teaching English in the Two-Year College* 35.1 (2007): 6–19. Print.

———. "TYCA and the Struggle for a National Voice: 1991–1993." *Teaching English in the Two-Year College* 35.2 (2007): 133–48. Print.

———. "TYCA and the Struggle for a National Voice: 1994–1997." *Teaching English in the Two-Year College* 35.3 (2008): 252–65.

Applebee, Arthur N. *Literature in the Secondary School: Studies of Curriculum and Instruction in the United States*. Urbana, IL: NCTE, 1993. Print. NCTE Research Report No. 25.

———. *Tradition and Reform in the Teaching of English: A History*. Urbana, IL: NCTE, 1974. Print.

Austin, Kurt. "NCTE Staff Report." Message to the author. 8 Apr. 2009. E-mail.

Bateman, Eric. "Ideas for the Future of TYCA." *Teaching English in the Two-Year College* 36.3 (2009): 235–43. Print.

Braddock, Richard, Richard Lloyd-Jones, and Lowell Schoer. *Research in Written Composition*. Champaign, IL: NCTE, 1963. Print.

Brandt, Deborah. *Literacy in American Lives*. New York: Cambridge UP, 2001. Print.

Brief of National Council of Teachers of English, New York State English Council, National Council for the Social Studies, and Speech Communication Association, Amici Curiae. 20 Nov. 1979. Print. University of Illinois Archives (Record Series 15/73/009, Box 2, File 5), Urbana, IL.

Brown, Kelly. "The Black and Hispanic Caucus." Message to the author. 10 Oct. 2007. E-mail.

"The Buffalo Convention." *English Journal* 39.2 (1950): 106–10. Print.

Carter, James Bucky, ed. *Building Literacy Connections with Graphic Novels: Page by Page, Panel by Panel*. Urbana, IL: NCTE, 2007. Print.

Christenbury, Leila. "Entering the Whirlwind: Editing *English Journal* 1994–1998." *English Journal* 89.3 (2000): 60–67. Print.

Dias, Earl J. "Comic Books—A Challenge to the English Teacher." *English Journal* 35.3 (1946): 142–45. Print.

Diedrich, Paul. "The Change I Would Most Like to See in English Teaching during the Next Fifty Years." NCTE, *Golden Anniversary* 17. Print.

Dixon, Chris Jennings, ed. *Lesson Plans for Teaching Writing*. Urbana, IL: NCTE, 2007. Print.

Dunning, Stephen, and William Stafford. *Getting the Knack: Twenty Poetry Writing Exercises*. Urbana, IL: NCTE, 1992. Print.

Elbow, Peter. *What Is English?* New York: MLA; Urbana, IL: NCTE, 1990. Print.

Emig, Janet. *The Composing Processes of Twelfth Graders*. Urbana, IL: NCTE, 1971. Print. NCTE Research Report No. 13.

"English for Ex-Service Personnel: A Survey Conducted by *College English*." *College English* 6.4 (1945): 206–12. Print.

"English in Wartime: A Resolution from the College Section." *College English* 3.6 (1942): 578–84. Print.

Farmer, Marjorie N., ed. *Consensus and Dissent: Teaching English Past, Present, and Future*. Urbana, IL: NCTE, 1986. Print.

Faust, Mark, and Mark Dressman. "The Other Tradition: Populist Perspectives on Teaching Poetry, as Published in *English Journal*, 1912–2005." *English Education* 41.2 (2009): 114–34. Print.

Flood, James, Diane Lapp, James R. Squire, and Julie M. Jensen, eds. *Handbook of Research on Teaching the English Language Arts*. 2nd ed. Mahwah, NJ: Erlbaum, 2003. Print.

Gallivan, Sue. "NCTE Staff Report." Message to the author. 4 Mar. 2009. E-mail.

———. "NCTE Staff Report." Message to the author. 19 Mar. 2009. E-mail.

Gerlach, Jeanne Marcum, and Virginia R. Monseau, eds. *Missing Chapters: Ten Pioneering Women in NCTE and English Education*. Urbana, IL: NCTE, 1991. Print.

Golden, John. *Reading in the Dark: Using Film as a Tool in the English Classroom*. Urbana, IL: NCTE, 2001. Print.

Goodman, Yetta M. "Introduction: From the Beginning: Power for the Teacher." *What Research* Really *Says about Teaching and Learning to Read*. Ed. Stephen B. Kucer. Urbana, IL: NCTE, 2008. vii–xiii. Print.

Haussamen, Brock, with Amy Benjamin, Martha Kolln, and Rebecca S. Wheeler. *Grammar Alive! A Guide for Teachers*. Urbana, IL: NCTE, 2003. Print.

Hazard, Patrick D. "The Change I Would Most Like to See in English Teaching during the Next Fifty Years." NCTE, *Golden Anniversary* 17. Print.

Hillocks, George Jr. *Research on Written Composition: New Directions for Teaching*. Urbana, IL: ERIC/RCS and NCRE, 1986. Print.

Hook, J. N. *A Long Way Together: A Personal View of NCTE's First Sixty-Seven Years*. Urbana, IL: NCTE, 1979. Print.

Hopkins, Edwin M. "Can Good Composition Teaching Be Done under Present Conditions?" *English Journal* 1.1 (1912): 1–8. Print.

Hosic, James Fleming. "Editorial: The Significance of the Organization of the National Council." *English Journal* 1.1 (1912): 46–48. Print.

———, comp. *Reorganization of English in Secondary Schools: Report by the National Joint Committee on English Representing the Commission on the Reorganization of Secondary Education of the National Education Association and the National Council of Teachers of English*. Washington, DC: GPO, 1917. Print. Dept. of the Interior, US Bureau of Education, Bulletin 1917, No. 2.

Hunt, Kellogg W. *Grammatical Structures Written at Three Grade Levels*. Champaign, IL: NCTE, 1965. Print. NCTE Research Report No. 3.

International Reading Association, and National Council of Teachers of English. *Standards for the English Language Arts*. Newark, DE: IRA; Urbana, IL: NCTE, 1996. Print.

Jaggar, Angela, and M. Trika Smith-Burke, eds. *Observing the Language Learner*. Newark, DE: IRA; Urbana, IL: NCTE, 1985. Print.

Jenkins, William A. "Political Activities of the NCTE Commission on Reading." 21 Nov. 1972. TS. University of Illinois Archives (Record Series 15/73/007, Box 1, File 2), Urbana, IL.

Jewett, Arno. "The Change I Would Most Like to See in English Teaching during the Next Fifty Years." NCTE, *Golden Anniversary* 17. Print.

Johannessen, Larry R. *Illumination Rounds: Teaching the Literature of the Vietnam War*. Urbana, IL: NCTE, 1992. Print.

Judy, Stephen N., ed. *English since Sputnik*. Themed issue of *English Journal* 68.6 (1979): 1–112. Print.

Judy, Stephen N., and David A. England, eds. *An Historical Primer on the Teaching of English*. Themed issue of *English Journal* 68.4 (1979): 1–112. Print.

Kelly, Patricia P., and Robert C. Small, Jr., eds. *Two Decades of* The ALAN Review. Urbana, IL: NCTE, 1999. Print.

LaBrant, Lou. "The Change I Would Most Like to See in English Teaching during the Next Fifty Years." NCTE, *Golden Anniversary* 16. Print.

Langer, Judith A., and Arthur N. Applebee. *How Writing Shapes Thinking: A Study of Teaching and Learning*. Urbana, IL: NCTE, 1987. Print.

Lloyd-Jones, Richard, and Andrea A. Lunsford, eds. *The English Coalition Conference: Democracy through Language*. Urbana, IL: NCTE; New York: MLA, 1989. Print.

Mason, James Hocker. "The Educational Milieu 1874–1922: College Entrance Requirements and the Shaping of Secondary Education." *English Journal* 68.4 (1979): 40–45. Print.

Mayher, John S. "Reflections on Standards and Standard Setting: An Insider/Outsider Perspective on the NCTE/IRA Standards." *English Education* 31.2 (1999): 106–21. Print.

Mersand, Joseph. "By Way of Introduction." *Studies in the Mass Media* 1.1 (1960): 3. Print.

———. "Vale." *Studies in the Mass Media* 4.8 (1964): 19–20. Print.

Monseau, Virginia R., ed. *A Curriculum of Peace*. Themed issue of *English Journal* 89.5 (2000): 1–168. Print.

———, ed. *Our History, Ourselves*. Themed issue of *English Journal* 89.3 (2000): 1–140. Print.

Myers, Miles. *Changing Our Minds: Negotiating English and Literacy*. Urbana, IL: NCTE, 1996. Print.

National Council of Teachers of English. Annual Business Meeting Minutes. 27 Nov. 1931. TS. University of Illinois Archives (Record Series 15/71/001, Box 1, File 1), Urbana, IL.

———. Annual Business Meeting Minutes. 29 Nov. 1935. TS. University of Illinois Archives (Record Series 15/71/001, Box 1, File 1), Urbana, IL.

———. Annual Business Meeting Minutes. 22 Nov. 1940. TS. University of Illinois Archives (Record Series 15/71/001, Box 1, File 1), Urbana, IL.

———. Annual Business Meeting Minutes. 23 Nov. 1950. TS. University of Illinois Archives (Record Series 15/71/001, Box 1, File 2), Urbana, IL.

———. Annual Business Meeting Minutes. 26 Nov. 1953. TS. University of Illinois Archives (Record Series 15/71/001, Box 1, File 2), Urbana, IL.

———. Annual Business Meeting Minutes. 28 Nov. 1970. TS. University of Illinois Archives (Record Series 15/70/001, Box 1, File 3), Urbana, IL.

———. Annual Business Meeting Minutes. 26 Nov. 2001. Urbana, IL: NCTE, 2002. Electronic copy.

———. *The Basic Issues in the Teaching of English: Being Definitions and Clarifications Presented by Members of the American Studies Association, College English Association, Modern Language Association, and National Council of Teachers of English from a Series of Conferences Held throughout 1958*. Champaign, IL: NCTE, 1959. Print.

———. Board of Directors Meeting Minutes. 27 Nov. 1942. TS. University of Illinois Archives (Record Series 15/71/001, Box 1, File 6), Urbana, IL.

———. *Golden Anniversary*. NCTE Convention Program. Urbana, IL: NCTE, 1960. Print.

———. *The Impact of the SAT and ACT Timed Writing Tests: A Report from the NCTE Task Force on SAT and ACT Writing Tests*. Urbana, IL: NCTE, 2005. Print.

———. *International Involvement, "Global English," and NCTE Focus Group White Paper*. Unpublished staff report for the NCTE Executive Committee, April 2009.

———. "Resolution on Teaching in a Time of Crisis." Annual Business Meeting for the Board of Directors and Other Members of the Council, Baltimore, MD. *National Council of Teachers of English*. NCTE, 2001. Web. 8 Aug. 2009.

———. *Students' Right to Their Own Language*. Spec. issue of *College Composition and Communication* 25.3 (1974): 1–32. Print.

National Council of Teachers of English Commission on the Profession. "Selective Annotated List of Recent Readings on the Profession of English Teaching." Champaign, IL: NCTE, 1958. TS. University of Illinois Archives (Record Series 15/73/006, Box 1, File 1), Urbana, IL.

———. "What Are the Responsibilities of Teachers of English? A Preliminary Inquiry." Champaign, IL: NCTE, 1958. TS. University of Illinois Archives (Record Series 15/73/006, Box 1, File 1), Urbana, IL.

National Council of Teachers of English Committee on Censorship of Teaching Materials for Classroom and Library. *Censorship and Controversy: Report of the Committee on Censorship of Teaching Materials for Classroom and Library*. Chicago: NCTE, 1953. Print.

National Council of Teachers of English Committee on National Interest. *The National Interest and the Continuing Education of Teachers of English*. Champaign, IL: NCTE, 1964. Print.

———. *The National Interest and the Teaching of English: A Report on the Status of the Profession*. Champaign, IL: NCTE, 1961. Print.

National Council of Teachers of English Committee on Television Literacy. "Helping Children Use Television Wisely: A Guide for Parents." Urbana, IL: NCTE, 1984. TS. University of Illinois Archives (Record Series 15/71/010, Box 21, File 12), Urbana, IL.

National Council of Teachers of English Committee on the Right to Read. *The Students' Right to Read.* Rev. ed. Champaign, IL: NCTE, 1962. Print.

National Council of Teachers of English Curriculum Commission. *An Experience Curriculum in English: A Report of the Curriculum Commission of the National Council of Teachers of English.* New York: Appleton, 1935. Print.

National Council of Teachers of English Research Foundation. *NCTE Executive Committee Reports: Report on a Sustained Investment in Diversity and Equity.* Urbana, IL: NCTE, February 2007. Print.

National Council of Teachers of English Task Force on Racism and Bias in the Teaching of English. "Criteria for Teaching Materials." *College English* 32.6 (1971): 713–15. Print.

———. "Criteria for Teaching Materials in Reading and Literature." 26 Nov. 1970. TS. University of Illinois Archives (Record Series 15/73/008, Box 1, File 4), Urbana, IL.

National Education Association. "Round Table Conferences." *Journal of Proceedings and Addresses of the Forty-Ninth Annual Meeting Held at San Francisco, California, July 8–14, 1911.* Winona, MN: National Education Association, 1911. 592–98. Print.

Nelms, Ben F. "Reconstructing English: From the 1890s to the 1990s and Beyond." *English Journal* 89.3 (2000): 49–59. Print.

"News and Notes." *English Journal* 31.7 (1942): 564–69. Print.

Orwell, George. *1984.* 1949. New York: Penguin, 2003. Print.

———. "Politics and the English Language." *Eight Modern Essayists.* 3rd ed. Ed. William Smart. New York: St. Martin's, 1980. Print.

"Pre-Induction Needs in Language Communication and Reading." *Education for Victory* 2.11 (1943): 1, 16–24. Print. University of Illinois Archives (Record Series 15/71/806, Box 1, File 4), Urbana, IL.

Prichard, Nancy. Memo to Ernece B. Kelly. [1971]. TS. University of Illinois Archives (Record Series 15/73/008, Box 1, File 1), Urbana, IL.

Radner, Sanford. *Fifty Years of English Teaching: A Historical Analysis of the Presidential Addresses of NCTE*. Champaign, IL: NCTE, 1960. Print.

Ray, Katie Wood. *Wondrous Words: Writers and Writing in the Elementary Classroom*. Urbana, IL: NCTE, 1999. Print.

Reed, Linda. "Statement in Favor of the Continued Use of Nonsexist Language in Publications of the National Council of Teachers of English." NCTE Board of Directors Meeting Minutes, 1979. TS. University of Illinois Archives (Record Series 15/71/010, Box 21, File 14), Urbana, IL. Print.

Rollins, Charlemae Hill. *We Build Together: A Reader's Guide to Negro Life and Literature for Elementary and High School Use*. Chicago: NCTE, 1941. Print.

Scott, Fred Newton. "The Undefended Gate." *English Journal* 3.1 (1914): 1–14. *JSTOR*. Web. 5 Aug. 2009.

Scott, Jerrie Cobb, Dolores Y. Straker, and Laurie Katz, eds. *Affirming Students' Right to Their Own Language: Bridging Language Policies and Pedagogical Practices*. New York: Routledge; Urbana, IL: NCTE, 2009. Print.

Sherwood, John C. "Committee on Testing: Terminal Report." [1964.] TS. University of Illinois Archives (Record Series 15/71/010, Box 14, File 17), Urbana, IL.

Smith, Dora V. "Curriculum during the Next Fifty Years: The American Way." NCTE, *Golden Anniversary* 7. Print.

Sommers, Jeff. "Editorial: Teaching English in a Time of War." *Teaching English in the Two-Year College* 35.4 (2008): 349. Print.

———, ed. *Teaching English in a Time of War*. Spec. issue of *Teaching English in the Two-Year College* 36.4 (2009): 336–437. Print.

Squire, James R., ed. *A Common Purpose: The Teaching of English in Canada, Great Britain, and the United States*. Champaign, IL: NCTE, 1966.

———. "The Future of the Council." Memo to the 1966 and 1967 NCTE Executive Committees. 6 Dec. 1967. TS. University of Illinois Archives (Record Series 15/71/200, Box 2, File 5), Urbana, IL.

Stanford, Gene, ed. *How to Handle the Paper Load: Classroom Practices in Teaching English 1979–1980*. Urbana, IL: NCTE, 1979. Print.

Trachsel, Mary. *Institutionalizing Literacy: The Historical Role of College Entrance Examinations in English.* Carbondale: Southern Illinois UP, 1992. Print.

Tuttle, Robert. "The Change I Would Most Like to See in English Teaching during the Next Fifty Years." NCTE, *Golden Anniversary* 16. Print.

Villanueva, Victor, ed. *Cross-Talk in Comp Theory: A Reader.* 2nd ed. Urbana, IL: NCTE, 2003. Print.

Wagner, Carol. Message to the author. February 2009. E-mail.

Yagelski, Robert P. "The (Ir)relevance of English at the Turn of the Millennium." *The Relevance of English: Teaching That Matters in Students' Lives.* Ed. Robert P. Yagelski and Scott A. Leonard. Urbana, IL: NCTE, 2002. 1–19. Print. Refiguring English Studies series.

Zarnowski, Myra, Richard M. Kerper, and Julie M. Jensen, eds. *The Best in Children's Nonfiction: Reading, Writing, and Teaching Orbis Pictus Award Books.* Urbana, IL: NCTE, 2001. Print.

NCTE READING THE PAST. WRITING THE FUTURE.
100 YEARS

A Blast from the Past

Did you know that James Fleming Hosic, NCTE's founder and first executive director, later founded a second significant professional organization? It is known today as ASCD, the Association for Supervision and Curriculum Development, founded in 1943.

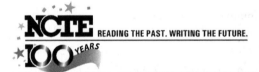

...mes, Addresses, and Positions of the

Charter Members

of the

...lly S. Maury Louisville Girls High Sch...
Louisville, Ky...

...e M. Wingate, Head of Eng.
Oak Park, Illinois

H. F. Kling
Prin Spencer School Chic...

...R. Rounds, Head of Dept. of
English, West Division H...
Milwaukee, ...

...rnon P. Squires, Professor of English,
University of North Dakota
Grand Fork, N. D...

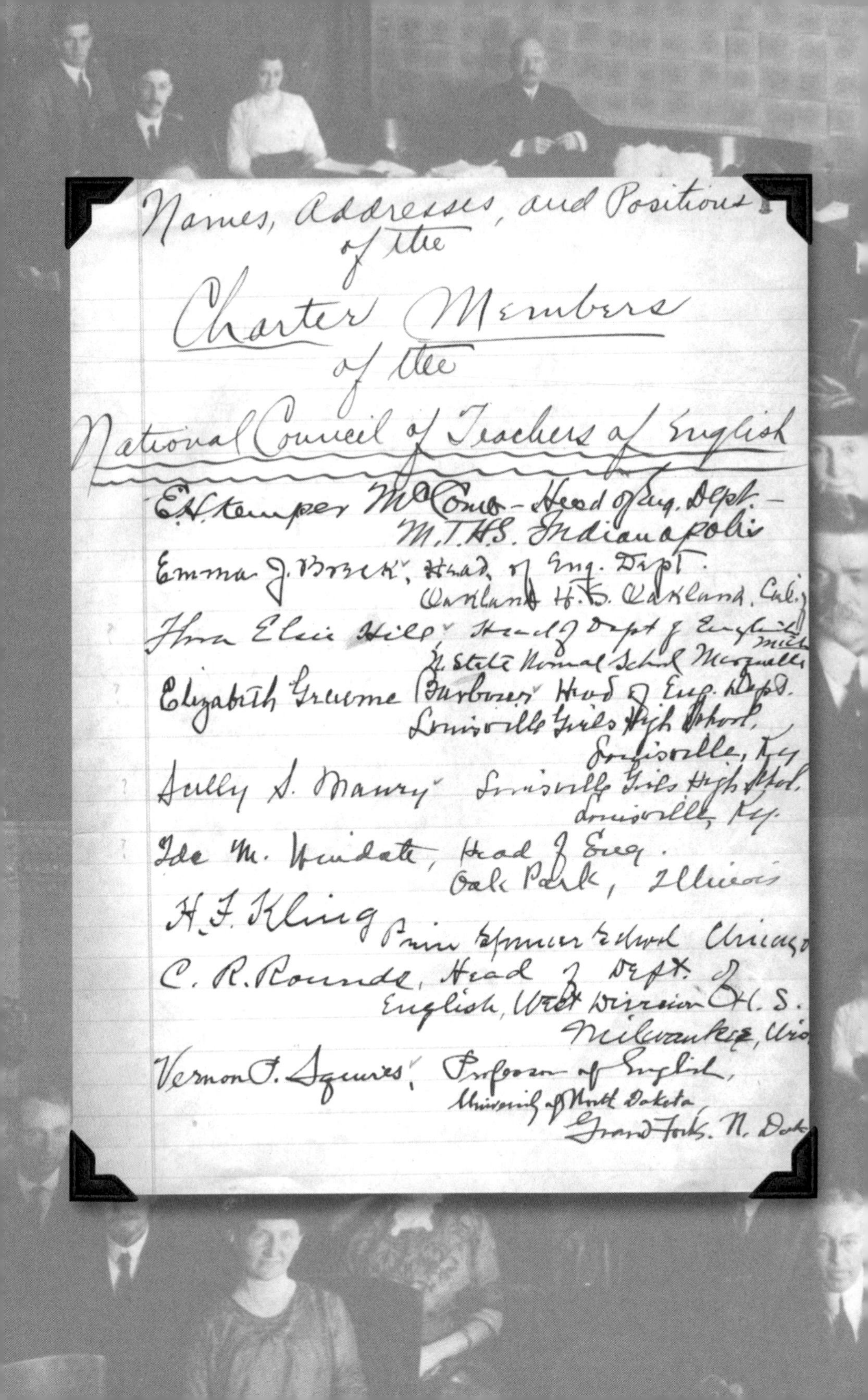
Names, Addresses, and Positions
of the
Charter Members
of the
National Council of Teachers of English

E. H. Kemper McComb – Head of Eng. Dept. – M.T.H.S. Indianapolis

Emma J. Breck, Head of Eng. Dept. Oakland H.S. Oakland, Cal.

Flora Elsie Hill, Head of Dept of English N. State Normal School Marquette Mich

Elizabeth Graeme Barbour, Head of Eng. Dept. Louisville Girls High School, Louisville, Ky

Sally S. Maury, Louisville Girls High Schl. Louisville, Ky.

Ida M. Windate, Head of Eng. Oak Park, Illinois

H. F. Kling Prin Spencer School Chicago

C. R. Rounds, Head of Dept. of English, West Division H.S. Milwaukee, Wis

Vernon P. Squires, Professor of English, University of North Dakota Grand Forks, N. Dak

Chapter Two

The Teaching of Reading

Donna E. Alvermann
University of Georgia

Entangled beginnings are sometimes the most telling of an organization's sense of purpose and contribution to the field over time. This opening statement previews in no small way NCTE's response to the social, cultural, and political forces that have historically shaped the teaching of reading since the early twentieth century and that continue to define it today. Founded forty-five years before the International Reading Association (IRA), the National Council of Teachers of English (NCTE) was for nearly half a century the sole authority on what constituted appropriate ways for motivating students to read and reflect on various kinds of texts.

Joined by other voices in the latter half of its hundred-year history, NCTE continues to exert due influence on the teaching of reading as part of the English language arts through its political activism, research on reading instruction, and professional development. In this chapter, I focus on NCTE's contributions to each of these three areas after first examining how the mixed origins of reading instruction in the early 1900s laid the groundwork for all that followed.

Entangled Beginnings

The year 1910 marked for Nila Banton Smith, the grande dame of American reading instruction, a notable juncture. It signaled the start of a fifteen-year period in which "an emphasis on scientific investigation in reading" (Smith 148) led to what she viewed as major innovations in the field. Most notable was the transition from oral reading instruction and rote drills (e.g., the McGuffey

Readers) to silent reading instruction. Smith attributed this change largely to Edmund Burke Huey's influential research on reading for meaning, or what Huey described in 1908 as "thought getting and thought manipulating" (359) while reading silently. Another innovation, according to Smith, was the development of remedial reading techniques that were necessary once standardized reading tests had made the sorting of readers possible.

Although both would have ripple effects on what should count as reading, and hence on how reading should be taught, in the first three decades of NCTE's existence it is difficult to pinpoint to what degree, if any, these two so-called innovations influenced the content of Franklin T. Baker's presidential address at the fourth annual meeting of NCTE in Chicago on 27 November 1914. Speculation aside, we do know that President Baker opened his address by quoting from an editorial in a leading New York newspaper, *The Tribune*. The editorial, "Teaching Light Reading," critiqued English educators for "making work of play"—for turning reading that might be done for pure enjoyment into a pedantic task, for the sake of self-improvement. Baker used the editorial to make a countercase for what he perceived as a weakness among those in the teaching ranks who were, in his words, "making play of work" (Baker 2). He claimed that high school English teachers coddled students in their gravitation toward contemporary works, thereby losing sight of the need for rigor in helping youth "grow into the power of enjoying good books" (2). For such growth to occur, he reasoned, teachers would need to hold high school students accountable by teaching them to "read in a serious and earnest manner" (5). Baker proceeded in his speech to outline the following approach to reading literature at the high school level: "We shall study the best approach to each classic: what needs to be known before reading, what needs to be looked for while reading, and what reflected upon afterward" (6). Interestingly, with the possible exception of his emphasis on the classics, Baker's before–during–after reading approach is still touted as effective pedagogy in the major content area reading methods texts of the twenty-first century (Alvermann, "Exemplary").

When newspapers rather than the canon constituted what counted as reading, a slightly different approach to teaching students to read surfaced—this time in the second presidential address of Fred Newton Scott, in 1913. According to Sanford Radner, who compiled a history of the first fifty years of English teaching by analyzing the first fifty NCTE presidential addresses, Scott had taught journalism at the University of Michigan before assuming the NCTE presidency and thus knew both the pervasiveness of the newspaper in people's lives and the medium's potential for "corrupting American youth by its sensationalism and distortion" (qtd. in Radner 9). Rather predictably, then, President Scott called on the English teachers in his audience to instruct students in their junior and senior years to read newspapers critically.

Yet another way of defining what counted as reading (and hence a different approach to reading instruction) was the notion that students should be allowed to bring their everyday life experiences to comprehending literary texts. Teachers, however, were to monitor students' uses of such experiences in an effort to ensure that they did not interfere with the intellectual and aesthetic values associated with a good literary education. Advocates of this practical approach to teaching reading included Charles Swain Thomas, who, in his presidential address in 1935, alluded to a vastly different and growing population of students in schools. Thomas referred to this population as students "with reading and writing retardation" (Radner 26) who needed assistance in reading good literature if they were to be promoted and eventually graduate from high school. To underscore the urgency of the situation, Thomas told the assembled group, "I stand firmly upon the principle that the larger portion of our expended energies in English teaching must rest upon the broadly extended base of the practical, for it is there that we meet the workaday needs of every individual pupil" (qtd. in Radner 26). In his call to English teachers to build on their students' background knowledge for comprehending text, NCTE's twenty-third president foreshadowed by at least four decades the recommendations that would come from reading research conducted in the late 1970s and early 1980s.

School Librarians Vie for Footing in Reading Instruction

Despite what might seem the case from the preceding presidential addresses, reading instruction in the early twentieth century did not lie solely within the domain of English teachers; other educators entered into the mix as well. For example, a book titled *The High-School Library* (1913) lists the guidance of students' reading as second in importance in a series of responsibilities allocated to school librarians, although such guidance referred to helping students select appropriate reading materials rather than teaching them to read per se. Nevertheless, an opportunity to influence young people's reading habits was deemed "the greatest privilege and pleasure which comes to the high-school librarian" (Ward 11). Less desirable aspects of such guidance included a librarian's responsibility for "questioning cases of suspiciously irrelevant reading, and making suggestions as necessary" (Ward 12).

School librarians were also responsible for developing home reading lists, a fact that deserves brief commentary in light of NCTE's early history. Because the Council was founded partially in response to complaints that the reading lists of eastern colleges were overly prescriptive in their content for high school students seeking college admission, it is somewhat ironic that one of the first items of business for the newly formed organization was to consider a request by the delegation from the Illinois Association of Teachers of English for a home reading list (Hatfield). Unlike the college lists, NCTE's home reading lists consisted of relatively current selections for high school students' enjoyment, such as modern fiction, poetry, essays, and travel and adventure (Ward).

Home reading lists were considered the sine qua non of a well-functioning school library. In a paper read at the 1915 NCTE Annual Convention in Chicago, Emma J. Breck, a librarian at University High School in Oakland, California, enumerated the principles that should guide a librarian's choices in establishing a collection. Among them was a set of criteria for the home reading list, which consisted not only of the usual high-quality books but also of books that had what Breck later described as the strongest "modern appeal" (15). In this category, she included books on science and invention for boys and specifically noted that the girls' "desire for a love-story may be granted, if with discretion" (16). At the close of the reading, a resolution to accept the principles offered by Breck was passed, with the added recommendation that they be published in *English Journal* and distributed by the NCTE Publicity Committee. In later years, the summer reading lists for junior and senior high school students appeared regularly in *English Journal.*

More than the preparation of summer reading lists was entrusted to school librarians, however. After disentangling the origins of the school library media center, Latrobe found that librarians had always been committed to sharing responsibility for teaching students to read. Moreover, she noted, "The school library lies at the very root of the new pedagogy of individual differences. . . . [and] is at the heart of any program of socialized effort and individual responsibility" (xi). Reports of public librarians stepping up to the plate as reading instructors also abound. For example, Sabra Vought, who was secretary of the Chicago Library Club in 1923 and later head librarian in the U.S. Office of Education, is alleged to have said that she believed a library should be "a working laboratory [whose] principal aim . . . is to teach the child how to read" (qtd. in Drury and Masters 25). Clearly, as Latrobe and others have shown, NCTE's support of libraries in the early years pretty much ensured that the responsibility for the advancement of reading, at least at the secondary level, would not rest solely with English teachers.

World War II Ushers in High School Reading Skills Instruction

As the twentieth century neared its midpoint, what counted as reading—for example, reading for meaning, for evaluating newspaper accounts, and for practical purposes, such as understanding technical manuals—coalesced in an agenda aimed at the development of reading skills deemed necessary for supporting the wartime effort. Once again, NCTE was ready. On 1 December 1943, NCTE, in cooperation with the U.S. Office of Education and the War Department, issued a report that appeared in *Education for Victory*. The first part of that report, "Pre-Induction Needs in Language Communication and Reading," made explicit the necessity of specific skills in reading for high school students who were within one or two years of being inducted into the armed forces. Preinduction training, according to the War Department, was not a policy handed down to the schools; rather, it was an invitation to schools to prepare potential inductees in a manner that would instill a sense of national unity and at the same time ensure that essential skills, such as reading, were being taught in the context of existing English courses.

A year later, an article authored by Robert C. Pooley, a professor of English at the University of Wisconsin and past president of NCTE, appeared in *English Journal.* Essentially, it exhorted high school English teachers to take stock, among other things, of their adherence to instruction focused on specific skills itemized in the "Check List of English Pre-Induction Skills." For reading, these items included answering the following questions:

- Are pupils encouraged to *read newspapers* and keep informed on current events?
- Are students given instruction and practice in *comprehending* the *main points* of paragraphs, articles, and chapters?
- Are *samples of technical literature* available, such as soldiers are called upon to read in the Army? (Pooley 356, emphasis in original)

In an attempt to assure teachers that "the reading goals [were] not new, but [called] for changes of emphasis and the provision of materials to meet needs made critical by war" (356), Pooley went on to list six experiences with books and magazines that teachers needed to attend to on the "Check List of English Pre-Induction Skills":

- Is opportunity given for studying materials which describe the *nature of military life*?
- Are students encouraged to read books and magazines bearing on *the background of the war*, the character of our allies and enemies, and the like?
- Is opportunity given for reading books and magazines proclaiming and interpreting the *principles of American democracy*?
- Is opportunity provided through reading and discussion to understand the *rights of the individual* which a democracy guarantees?
- Do students read books and articles creating an *understanding of different races and cultures*?

- Are students encouraged through reading and discussion *to form a plan of life* which extends beyond the period of the war? (Pooley 357, emphasis in original)

While reading skills instruction entered the secondary English classroom largely through wartime needs, and entered the college curriculum through remedial reading classes that served students needing assistance (Clifford), it grew more pervasive throughout the curriculum as a result of increased attention to standardized tests and what they might (or might not) have to say to teachers. Regardless of the impetus, teaching students how to read in the elementary grades took on added significance with the push from NCTE to promote language arts as a separate school subject.

Elementary Teachers Find a Niche in Reading Instruction

NCTE's Elementary Section, a part of the Council from the start and traditionally the domain of early reading instruction, experienced a significant growth in membership as a result of the Council's decision in 1945 to promote the use of the term *language arts* to signify its place in the curriculum, separate from subject English (Hook, *Long Way Together* 147). This pedagogical and political move by NCTE to delineate differences in curricular areas led to reopening a conversation begun some thirty years earlier by Charles Swain Thomas in a book chapter he titled "Articulation of Elementary-School English with Secondary-School English." In advocating for a curriculum that would span kindergarten through college, Thomas found common ground in a goal to which he believed all English teachers, regardless of grade level, aspired: namely, teaching students to interpret and express themselves in relation to what they read.

NCTE President Ruth Strickland picked up on earlier calls for an articulated English language arts curriculum in her keynote at the organization's Golden Anniversary Annual Convention in Chicago in 1960. Strickland called for approaches to reading instruction that would foster meaning-making and lifelong reading habits. Noting that the field had passed a time in which students were given "books that ooze boredom—silly books or empty or pedantic books" (304), Strickland stressed the importance of viewing reading as an integral part of the language arts, not as a separate subject for teaching word-level skills in isolation. This view, supported by Huey's influential research at the turn of the twentieth century on reading as meaning-making, would become a touchstone argument for the whole language movement and other integrated language arts approaches to teaching reading. It would also thrust NCTE into the national spotlight by the late 1980s, shortly after the publication of *Becoming a Nation of Readers* (Anderson, Hiebert, Scott, and Wilkinson)—a book that was roundly critiqued by some members of NCTE (e.g., Goodman, Shannon, Freeman, and Murphy) for supplanting elementary teachers' instructional authority with scripted basal reading programs that underestimated what children knew about reading as a meaning-making process.

In looking back, NCTE's entangled beginnings were predictable in many ways, especially in relation to how they played out against a backdrop defined by the social, cultural, and political currents of the time. Yet they were not merely coincidences; nor would they disappear with time. Changes in what counts as reading (and hence how reading is taught), along with broadened constituencies and pressures for reform from external sources, are still visible today. Glimpses of these lingering entanglements take center stage in the next section.

Political Activism

Founded at a time when high school teachers' authority over curricular and pedagogical matters had been seriously challenged from the outside (Applebee; Hook, *Long Way Together*), NCTE was neither naïve nor passive when similar attempts were made to regulate both the type of reading materials at teachers' disposal and the approaches they could take to reading instruction. The organization's response in these instances was to assume a political stance from which it could lend support through resolutions and policies democratically adopted by the membership. While reading-related issues were numerous during NCTE's first one hundred years, three in particular stand out: (1) the National

Reading Panel's endeavor to influence how reading was taught; (2) attempts to limit choice in reading materials; and (3) efforts to establish national English language arts standards. Preceding a discussion of these issues is a brief sketch of NCTE's internal workings vis-à-vis the politics of reading instruction up to the time the first NCTE Commission on Reading was appointed.

Brief Sketch of Internal Workings

A professional organization's identity is embedded in its membership, a fact that is seldom more apparent than at a time when that identity is either questioned from the inside or threatened from without. Such was the case for NCTE in 1945, 1971, and 1975—three watershed years in which the organization's political identity in relation to the teaching of reading became especially visible.

As noted earlier, the inclusion in 1945 of "language arts" as a concept in NCTE's lexicon was symbolic of at least some members' desire to delineate an area of the English curriculum separate from subject English for pedagogical and political reasons. With this break came a greater emphasis on how to teach reading in the elementary grades, making NCTE an unrivaled voice on reading instruction until 1955, when the National Association for Remedial Teaching (NART) merged with the International Council for the Improvement of Reading Instruction to form the International Reading Association (IRA). Ruth May Strang, the last president of NART and a founding member of IRA, took the position that "learning to read is a life-time process [and] courses in reading for teachers should include methods of reading throughout the school and college years" (qtd. in Lapp, Guthrie, and Flood 354)—a stance that resonated with Ruth Strickland's presidential address on the need for an articulated English program.

However, aside from a common interest in program articulation, Ruth Strickland and Ruth Strang viewed the teaching of reading from quite different perspectives. It is largely those differences that Robert Ruddell, professor emeritus of language, literacy, and culture at the University of California at Berkeley, believes contributed to his appointment as the first director of

NCTE's Commission on Reading in 1971, shortly after the commission's founding in 1969. Ruddell recalls,

> Many of [NCTE's] leaders up to this time shunned . . . reading, and some even viewed it as such an integral part of the language arts that to focus on reading as a "separate process" was really somewhat sinful. So, in a way [the commission] was a breakthrough for the leadership to recognize the importance of reading as a process that while closely related to "language arts" deserved direct attention. . . . As you may know, my major professor at Indiana was Ruth Strickland. [She] carried a high profile in NCTE but possessed much of the "NCTE viewpoint" described above. I may have been viewed as a hybrid (Leo Fay at Indiana University was my "silent advisor" and a former president of IRA), combining the reading and language arts camps, and this may explain, in part, why I was appointed the first director. (Ruddell)

Whatever the intent of NCTE's leadership in appointing Ruddell, the mere hint of a hybrid beginning for the commission has a familiar ring to it—that, and the fact that federal dollars were in the offing for initiatives that focused on competency-based certification of reading specialists. In a memo to that effect, William Jenkins urged the commission to test its influence on Capitol Hill by circulating a paper on the status of reading instruction among congressional groups and federal funding agencies.

In 1975, Harold L. Herber, at the time a professor of education at Syracuse University and the second director of the NCTE Commission on Reading, wrote a seven-page state-of-the-art paper in support of a federal budget that would include the secondary grades in the National Reading Improvement Program (Title VII). In his testimony before the Senate Appropriations Committee's Subcommittee on Labor and Health, Education, and Welfare, Herber provided evidence that demonstrated the efficacy of professional development programs in which reading specialists work with secondary teachers to integrate reading skills instruction with subject matter (Herber, "Testimony"). (A telephone interview with Emeritus Professor Herber can be found at http://www.ncte.org/centennial/audio.)

The National Reading Panel's Mandates for Reading Instruction

The Commission on Reading's second experience in testing its influence on Capitol Hill was just a beginning. Over the years, the commission would continue to advise NCTE on key issues related to the teaching of reading, but one concern in particular became a lightning rod for response. Authorized by the U.S. Congress in 1997 to bring clarity to what some policymakers viewed as contradictory recommendations from the reading research community, the National Reading Panel (NRP) issued a report that identified five elements of effective reading instruction: phonemic awareness (ability to distinguish and manipulate individual sounds), phonics, fluency, vocabulary, and comprehension (NICHHD, *Summary*). The NRP drew criticism from the start for limiting what counted as research to experimental and quasi-experimental studies only and excluding studies of second language readers (Allington; Alvermann, "Effective"; Yatvin), as well as misinterpreting its own findings in the summary document (Garan).

In 2004, NCTE's Commission on Reading, under the direction of Jane Braunger, then a senior research associate with the Strategic Literacy Initiative at WestEd, initiated a series of written responses that were critical of No Child Left Behind (NCLB) legislation, whose requirements were shaped by the NRP report (Shannon). These responses, along with chapters written by commission members and published in *What Research* Really *Says about Teaching and Learning to Read* (Kucer), advocate in Rigby's words for the "orphaned teaching practices" (17) that the NRP's meta-analysis of experimental research left behind as a result of the panel's decision to ignore a data-rich body of the literature on reading instruction that used qualitative methodologies.

Another offshoot of the NRP report was the Reading First initiative, a federal reading instruction program mandated by NCLB. In its 2002 "Resolution on the Reading First Initiative," NCTE made public its resolve to oppose the federal government's attempt "to define what reading is, to limit what counts as research on reading, and to dictate how reading should be taught in our classrooms" (NCTE, "Resolution"). Reading First's "one size fits all" method of instruction (phonemic awareness, phonics, fluency, vocabulary, and comprehension) conflicted with NCTE's position statement on reading—one that views the reading process as complex and consisting of more than mastering a set of basic skills (NCTE, "NCTE Position Statement"). In the same 2002 resolution on Reading First, NCTE "called on Congress to establish an independent investigatory body to look into the implementation of Reading First" (n. pag.). Congress responded in September 2006 by appointing the U.S. Department of Education's Office of Inspector General to initiate an internal review of alleged conflicts of interest involving consultants hired by the department to conduct professional development in Reading First using commercial reading programs of which they were also the authors. The results of the internal review were such that NCTE issued a statement a year later praising the Inspector General's Office "for doing a conscientious job of identifying blatant noncompliance with the No Child Left Behind Act and for publishing the findings" (NCTE, "Reading First" 1).

Attempts at Limiting Choice of Reading Materials

NCTE was founded in part because of the politics surrounding the issue of who would dictate the contents of reading lists for college-bound high school students. After 1911, with the introduction of more contemporary reading materials into the curriculum, and following the 1944 NCTE–*Reader's Digest* dispute over whether censorship was justifiable during wartime (Gillikin), attempts at limiting teachers' choices of classroom reading material increased to the point that, in 1962, a committee chaired by Edward R. Gordon of Yale University prepared a document that is still regarded as one of NCTE's strongest position statements in its one-hundred-year history. The statement, heralded in 1963 by *The Modern Language Journal* as a bold pronouncement on censorship, also had the backing of the American Civil Liberties Union. "The Students' Right to Read," a nineteen-page pamphlet revised by Kenneth Donelson in 1972, remains NCTE's official response to pressure groups that would censor what they find objectionable in the works of certain authors (including the likes of

Chaucer, Faulkner, Hawthorne, Hemingway, and Shakespeare). More than simply a position statement defending "the teacher's right to assign or recommend controversial material, and the student's right to read such material" (National Federation 71), the document contains a section on how to organize protests when censoring groups seek to indoctrinate the public's thinking. NCTE also publishes Censorship Challenge Reports on a quarterly basis as a way of keeping the membership up to date on the status of actions taken in response to censoring groups (e.g., see Davis).

NCTE's efforts to combat censorship of reading materials continue, although its role in supporting a group of Long Island students in their appeal of a lower court's decision in a book-banning case is perhaps the most well known. In 1980, using funds contributed by several of its affiliates, NCTE filed a friend-of-the-court brief on behalf of *Pico v. Island Trees School District.* The case eventually went to the U.S. Supreme Court, where it was officially known as the *Island Trees School District v. Pico*. In 1982, in a decision based on the First Amendment, the Court ruled that "[l]ocal school boards may not remove books from school library shelves simply because they dislike the ideas contained in these books" (457 US 853). (For more information on this case and NCTE's support of intellectual freedom, see the "Blast from the Past" at http://www.ncte.org/centennial/blastfrompast/freedom.)

Efforts to Establish National English Language Arts Standards

NCTE was a key player, along with the International Reading Association, in the national standards-setting movement of the early 1990s, although the degree to which various groups within NCTE supported this action varied from the start (Mayher, "Reflections"). Yet, according to Patrick Shannon, "only the Commission on Reading was on record as reporting concern over NCTE's involvement" (9). Skepticism reminiscent of the organization's beginnings was directed at the federal government's attempt to regulate the curriculum and teachers' practices. Some of the controversy that surrounded this attempt is captured in the following bricolage of statements from three individuals who had major responsibilities for moving the IRA–NCTE standards project forward. (A fourth individual, representing NCTE, declined to participate in the bricolage.) Their reflections nearly a decade-and-a-half later derive from individual emails I received in response to my request that they describe the controversy surrounding the national standards project as they saw it. Rather than paraphrase their reflections or attribute specific quotations to specific individuals (though I do credit the three individuals in an endnote),[1] I elected to weave their comments in a way that visually depicts, through different fonts, how the entangled social, cultural, and political forces at work one hundred years ago live on.

The first phase of the NCTE/IRA Standards Project started in 1992 with a grant issued by the U.S. Department of Education. There were lots of debates about the purpose and style of the standards, many of them dealing with specificity and "grain size." *There was controversy about the standards but not about the NCTE/IRA joint venture.* The direction was very constructivist. The 1992 NAEP framework had just emerged, even more constructivist than ever. BUT at the same time, the first of the NICHD-funded studies were just starting to hit the professional literature with all the work on brain scans and explicit instruction. The world of reading instruction was changing, but no one seemed to notice that.

After 18 months, the USDOE would not renew the contract, citing insufficient progress *for reasons that are still not clear but seem to have to do with the NCTE/IRA's insistence on equity and access standards.* IRA and NCTE vowed to continue on with their own money, and the officers of the two groups began to play a larger role. There is no doubt that both NCTE and IRA strongly and appropriately resisted the government's efforts to create skill-specific and method-specific standards that could be made easily into mandates and regulations.

There were several attempts to get a document done. *The consensus draft written by a committee of four proved not to be that. At the Spring convention in Minneapolis in 1995, all of the assembled groups rejected the draft—elementary and secondary sections, CEE, and the broader attendees.* Another attempt involved having John Mayher and Michael Kibby work together to produce a draft for review. *While about half of the responses to their draft were very positive, others in NCTE did not welcome it.*

Finally a ghost writer of sorts wrote what was more or less the final draft, which NCTE and IRA published in 1996. But it was a train speeding toward a huge wreck. The press coverage was so brutal that finally NCTE came up with the idea of paying for a small-sized piece in the *New York Times* explaining the two associations' intent with the standards. Over time the standards document has had a positive influence by setting forth some important general principles that can guide curricular and instructional decision making and even policy. Now [July 2009] we are back somewhat to where we were in the early 1990s with interest in national standards.

In acknowledging NCTE's largely failed effort in 1996 to influence national policy in the English language arts arena, John Mayher left open the possibility of re-entering the fray at a later time and, perhaps, succeeding: "As a realist . . . my experience would suggest the prospects are doubtful. But I'm a teacher, and as such I have to go back again to the stone and try, once more, to push it up the hill" ("Reflections" 120). A decade later, NCTE President Kylene Beers expressed much the same sense of forward movement in her open letter to the membership on 28 July 2009, in which she laid out NCTE's strategy for responding to the Common Core State Standards for language arts (K–12) that the Council of Chief State School Officers (CCSSO), in partnership with the National Governors Association, had drafted: "[I]t's obvious that we will have national twelfth-grade exit standards. As of now, 46 states have agreed to adopt them" (Beers, par. 4). While acknowledging disappointment in the CCSSO's failure to consult NCTE initially, President Beers reassured members that by accepting the CCSSO's invitation to respond to the draft document, "we [the NCTE's Executive Committee] are cautiously cooperative. If that cooperative stance proves ineffective, then we will be respectfully vocal with our concerns" (par. 9).

To summarize, the membership of NCTE assumed a politically active stance in making its views known on the teaching of reading during the first one hundred years of its existence. Yet, to close this section without briefly mentioning NCTE's efforts to educate the U.S. Congress on reading-related issues would be a grave injustice. Every April since 2002, NCTE members have traveled to the nation's capitol on Advocacy Day to discuss NCTE resolutions, policy positions, and, since 2006, a formal legislative platform with congressional leaders from their home districts. In 2009, for example, over seventy teachers and teacher educators from elementary through college levels met with their states' congressional leaders to seek support for two pieces of legislation: (1) a comprehensive literacy bill and (2) a House and Senate resolution designating 20 October 2009 as the National Day on Writing (Suppa-Friedman). Support for the Learning and Teaching of English (SLATE), NCTE's grassroots advocacy network, also publishes periodic Action Alerts, providing NCTE members with information about pending legislation.

Research on Reading Instruction

NCTE members' political activism, a focus of the previous section, is a thread that runs through NCTE's goals for research on reading instruction as well. For example, among the four contributions the organization envisions for reading research is this one:

> NCTE will contribute to the development of a broader knowledge base of scientifically valid reading research by encouraging and supporting varied forms of reading research by school and university-based researchers. In the process, NCTE over the next five years will become known as a community where teachers both do scientifically valid reading research and vet it. (NCTE Executive Committee)

"Scientifically valid" knowledge in its narrower definition refers to findings from experimental studies that employ randomized field trials: the very criteria that the National Reading Panel used to exclude qualitative research from its deliberations (NICHHD, *Summary*). In seeking to broaden the definition of what counts as scientifically valid reading research, NCTE went on record in 2007 as opposing efforts to exclude qualitative methodologies that university-based reading researchers and classroom teachers inquiring into their own instructional practices tend to choose when studying reading as an inherent part of the English language arts. In short, NCTE's stance is grounded in the view that reading processes (e.g., decoding, fluency, comprehension, and interpretation) are integral to understanding subject matter (e.g., literature); hence, the need to research the teaching of reading from the perspective of an integrated model of English language arts instruction.

Broadening the definition of scientifically valid research makes room for both quantitative and qualitative methodologies. It also makes possible a context in which to examine NCTE researcher-initiated studies and how over the past century NCTE fostered and rewarded influential research that has contributed to the organization's knowledge base on the teaching of reading.

NCTE Researcher-Initiated Studies

In the early years of NCTE, researchers whose views of the reading process coincided with the psychological models of E. L. Thorndike and William Scott Gray tended to focus on assessing the degree to which certain components of those models (e.g., vocabulary, syntax, comprehension) affected students' ability to interpret what they read. Teachers were advised to teach to the skills that researchers deemed effective, despite the fact that little or no attention was given to the sociocultural factors at play in the larger context in which teachers taught and students learned. Research conducted from this perspective was the basis on which Sterling Leonard developed his *Essential Principles of Teaching Reading and Literature in the Intermediate Grades and the High School* (1922). The preface to this highly influential text, which Leonard authored four years prior to becoming president of NCTE, specified that the book's essential principles intentionally separated "(a) the teaching of reading—mastering the technique of comprehension—from (b) the teaching of literature" (6).

Not all researchers in the early years of NCTE's history designed studies using a psychological model. One notable exception was Dora V. Smith, whom Kenneth Donelson described as "*the* giant among English teachers" ("Ten Teachers" 80; emphasis in original). President of NCTE in 1936, Smith is better remembered for a 1930 survey she developed and administered to seventy-eight junior high school English teachers in seven states to determine how well prepared they were to guide students' reading of books for boys and girls. Out of 230 possible points distributed across questions about the books' characters, animals, and the like, teachers' scores ranged from 21 to 210 (median = 100), with *Penrod* being the only title that every teacher knew. These results led Smith to develop two courses on juvenile and adolescent literature in the College of Education at the University of Minnesota. She insisted that the courses be taught by a methods course instructor responsible for preparing teachers to guide students' reading (as opposed to a professor in the English department). This model of separating the teaching of reading from the teaching of literature became increasingly common across the country.

Influential research that would move the teaching of reading in a different direction began in an era following Lou LaBrant's presidency of NCTE (1954). Throughout LaBrant's seventy-year career as a teacher (she lived to age 102), she spoke vigorously in defense of teaching reading as a part of all subject matter courses, including literature (England and West). A program of research initiated by Harold L. Herber at Syracuse University in the 1960s supported LaBrant's earlier pedagogical insights into the importance of teaching reading in all curricular subjects. With Herber's publication of *Teaching Reading in Content Areas* in 1970, secondary teachers had for the first time a book that provided research-based strategies for simultaneously teaching reading and course content.

The 1970s witnessed yet another innovation in the teaching of reading, this time at the elementary level, based on the work of Kenneth S. Goodman and Yetta M. Goodman at the University of Arizona. Using applied psycholinguistics and a theory of whole language to understand reading, the Goodmans developed a technique known as miscue analysis to show how readers use graphophonic, syntactic, and semantic cues to make meaning of texts (Goodman, "Miscues"). Through this window into the reading process, the deficit model of reading was challenged when teachers understood how speakers of different dialects bring their own linguistic knowledge to bear on making meaning of texts (Goodman, "Ken Goodman"). In 1973, Dorothy S. Strickland published the first empirical study in an NCTE journal that had classroom implications for teaching linguistically different children ("A Program"). By the late 1980s, numerous studies existed of elementary teachers' approaches to reading instruction in what came to be called the whole language movement—with perhaps *Language Stories and Literacy Lessons* (Harste, Woodward, and Burke) one of the best known of those studies.

Meanwhile, researchers interested in the teaching of reading in secondary schools were compiling a rich database of their own. For example, Alan C. Purves and Richard Beach published the first comprehensive review of research on response to literature, which built on earlier NCTE research monographs (e.g., Hoetker). Their review paved the way for later work on how teachers might guide students' reading and discussion of literature (Marshall, Smagorinsky, and Smith), or, alternatively how they might learn from students' social interactions and interpretive readings during peer-led discussions (Lewis).

Beginning in the 1990s through the first decade of the twenty-first century, reading research published in NCTE journals reflected a growing trend among English language arts scholars to situate their work in a sociocultural perspective—one that could accommodate, among many other issues, the increasing presence of popular culture in schools and its political implications for classroom practice. In "Coach Bombay's Kids Learn to Write," for example, Anne Haas Dyson showed how children's uses of pop culture texts could enrich teachers' understandings of the link between students' unofficial peer worlds and reading and writing instruction. In "'The Rose That Grew from Concrete': Postmodern Blackness and New English Education," David E. Kirkland drew from an ethnographic multiyear study to argue that teaching adolescents to critique how texts position them as readers is every bit as important as teaching them to read. Also of note during this period were marked increases in the number of studies that focused on discourse genres, including the teaching of reading through discourses that were culturally relevant for students from nondominant backgrounds (e.g., Gutiérrez and Orellana; Lee) and historical analyses of literary teacher discourses that had parallels in the discourses of teaching reading (e.g., Faust and Dressman).

Not to be overlooked in this centennial celebration of NCTE's promotion of research on the teaching of reading is the fact that two major NCTE publications span several decades of the organization's history. Rush, Eakle, and Berger's *Secondary School Literacy: What Research Reveals for Classroom Practice* is the fourth and most recent volume in a series that was first published in the mid-1950s under the editorship of M. Agnella Gunn. The current volume has *literacy* in its title instead of *reading*—another reminder that reading no longer stands in isolation from the other language arts. Finally, two editions of the *Handbook of Research on Teaching the English Language Arts* (Flood, Jensen, Lapp, and Squire; Flood, Lapp, Squire, and Jensen), both cosponsored by NCTE and the International Reading Association, will be joined by a third edition in, probably, early 2012.

Fostering and Rewarding Research on the Teaching of Reading

NCTE has been proactive in bringing national attention to research on the teaching of reading in ways other than its publications. For example, in 1962, J. N. Hook, then executive secretary of NCTE, was named the first director of Project English, a federally funded program in support of English language arts research. Hook had worked with the Office of Education in the U.S. Department of Health, Education, and Welfare prior to its announcement in 1961 that it would emphasize reading, composition, and related skills through the funding of curriculum study and demonstration centers ("Project English"). Of particular relevance for this chapter were projects devoted to the study of close reading in literature by E. B. Jenkinson and J. S. Hawley at Indiana University (O'Donnell); reading in and out of the English curriculum by M. J. Early at Syracuse University (Seyfert); the appeal of paperback books, newspapers, and magazines among readers with low self-efficacy by E. B. McNeil and D. Fader at the University of Michigan (O'Donnell); and the development of curriculum materials for the elementary school by J. W. Richard Lindemann at the University of Georgia (Slack).

Another avenue for drawing attention to NCTE's support of research is its internal awards and grants program. In an award category that honors teachers' reflective inquiry into their own practice, the Conference on English Education's James N. Britton Award has gone to several scholars for their contributions to the teaching of reading (e. g., Vivian Vasquez in 2005 for her research published in *Negotiating Critical Literacies with Young Children* and Alfred Tatum in 2006 for *Teaching Reading to Black Adolescent Males: Closing the Achievement Gap*). The David H. Russell Award for works of scholarship that have stood the test of time honored Louise Rosenblatt in 1980 for *The Reader, The Text, The Poem: The Transactional Theory of the Literary Work*; Nancie Atwell in 1990 for *In the Middle: Writing, Reading, and Learning with Adolescents*; and Michael W. Smith and Jeffrey Wilhelm in 2003 for *"Reading Don't Fix No Chevys": Literacy in the Lives of Young Men.*

The Promising Researcher Award, established in 1970 by NCTE's Standing Committee on Research, annually recognizes original research in publishable form conducted by a new scholar in the field. Among numerous recipients of this award over the past four decades, the following are representative of both decade and topic: Dorothy Strickland in 1972 for "The Effects of a Special Literature Program on the Oral Language Expansion of Linguistically Different, Negro, Kindergarten Children"; Lee Galda in 1981 for "Three Children Reading Stories: Response to Literature in Preadolescents"; Margaret J. Finders in 1995 for *Just Girls: Literacy and Allegiance in Junior High School*; and Steve Amendum in 2009 for "Federally-Funded Reading Intervention and Reading Growth: Which Features Matter in High Poverty Schools?"

In recognition of prominent figures in American public life who have advanced the cause of reading, the NCTE Literacy Award has honored individuals such as First Lady Barbara Bush (1989), LeVar Burton (1994), Oprah Winfrey (1997), Pearl Cleage (2002), and Gloria Rodriguez (2008). Additional support for research on the teaching of reading is available through NCTE's Cultivating New Voices Among Scholars of Color, a two-year mentoring program for advanced doctoral students and scholars new to the field. Finally, NCTE's Research Foundation funds a number of small grants on a fairly regular basis.

In summary, NCTE's support of research on the teaching of reading has resulted in substantial contributions to the literature over the past one hundred years. Scholarly initiatives to improve reading instruction for students least well served by the dominant culture, while not new in the organization's history, took on added significance during the latter part of the twentieth century, with its shifts in demographics and the federal government's increase in regulatory statutes on teaching reading. As views changed on what counted as reading and which texts were admissible in classrooms, so too did researchers' questions. Reflecting on this body of literature, David Bloome wrote: "By defining literacy as social and cultural practices with social and cultural consequences, [researchers working from an anthropological perspective raised] questions about the validity of definitions of literacy as a psychological process" (52). This theme of new directions for new times is captured in Melanie Sperling and Anne DiPardo's comprehensive review of research on English education and its potential influence on classroom practice. While not specifically focused on the teaching of reading, their 2008 review nonetheless points to some of the same kinds of controversies that Denny Taylor identified in 1998 for reading instruction. Clearly, throughout its existence, NCTE has demonstrated a remarkable capacity for supporting and rewarding researchers who, despite their differences in theoretical and methodological approaches to studying reading instruction, have been unwavering in their goal to influence practice.

Professional Development

Symbolic of NCTE's strength and longevity as an organization is its forward-looking stance on working *with* and *through* the social, cultural, and political forces that are constantly at work shaping (and being shaped by) its active membership. Of particular relevance to this chapter are the ways in which NCTE has contributed to the professional growth of knowledgeable and caring teachers—individuals who participate actively in their own learning by using research that they (and others) produce, and who engage with new technologies to meet the demands of teaching reading in the twenty-first century. To grasp the significance of NCTE's contributions in these two areas, however, a brief overview of the years leading up to the organization's current involvement in professional development is in order.

Setting the Stage

NCTE's reputation for sponsoring self-directed learning through teacher inquiry has resulted in a vast accumulation of resources for teaching reading within an integrated language arts curriculum. In some ways, it could be said that this is a hard-won reputation, given the stresses that have accompanied the field's push for reforms to integrate the English language arts. While some of those stresses are documented earlier in the section on political activism, others remain and perhaps can be told only through the keen (and at times wry) observations of Geraldine Joncich Clifford, a professor of education at the University of California at Berkeley. In tracing the history of NCTE's involvement in reforms aimed at integrating reading and writing instruction, Clifford wryly notes, "Given their classical educations, the first several generations of 'modern' English language arts educators were more given than [my generation] to view pedagogical reform in the terms of epic struggles" (par. 1).

This observation led Clifford to suggest that the overt reaction following the 1936 NCTE publication *A Correlated Curriculum* was more a skirmish than a battle (NCTE Committee on Correlation). Nonetheless, she acknowledges that reform aimed at fixing the fragmented language arts curriculum would have to deal with more than isolated subject matter instruction. For example, the separate worlds of elementary and high school teaching would need bridging, as would the larger debate over excellence versus equity, addressed partially by the federal government's Right to Read program in 1969. (For additional information, see http://www.ncte.org/positions/statements/fedsupportrighttorea.)

By the late 1960s, as Clifford adroitly notes, the inability to sustain the curricular and pedagogical experimentations of Project English, largely through the National Defense Education Act's sponsorship of professional institutes for elementary and secondary teachers (Hook, *NDEA*), brought large-scale efforts directed at integrating the English language arts to a temporary standstill. However, with the advent of mass-marketed personal computers in the mid-1970s and the establishment of smaller professional development networks, such as NCTE's Reading Initiative in 1998, teachers had the means with which to take greater responsibility for their own learning and for locating ideas and materials to teach reading as an integrated language art.

Learning by Participating and Putting Research to Work

Shortly after NCTE's launch of the Reading Initiative in 1998, a group of elementary teachers and teacher educators at the University of South Carolina engaged in a study of teacher inquiry (Stephens, Boldt, Clark, Gaffney, Shelton, Story, and Weinzierl) that enabled them to research their own classroom reading practices as they simultaneously inquired into how they as teachers learned through the inquiry process. Support for learning about learning is still available through the South Carolina Reading Initiative (Stephens, Morgan, Donnelly, DeFord, Young, Seaman, Crowder, Hamel, and Cibic), a statewide staff development program that involves reading teacher educators working in collaboration with classroom teachers to improve reading instruction within an integrated English language arts framework.

Another approach to professional development, one supported by NCTE's Reading Initiative, is CoLEARN, an online resource of course materials for study groups to use in their exploration of teaching strategies, reading assessments, and the like. In making this online resource available to elementary, middle, and high school study groups, as well as to college instructors of literacy methods courses, NCTE's professional development reaches both practicing and prospective teachers. CoLEARN's resources include selected articles and chapters from NCTE publications, online discussions, and invitations to special events hosted by well-known literacy leaders. Clear as to its integrated language arts orientation and the criteria used in selecting its resources, NCTE posts the following message on the CoLEARN website (http://www1.ncte.org/store/learning/116743.htm): "Reading Initiative resources are based on research from sociopsycholinguistics, holistic assessment, school change, and constructivist learning theory" (par. 5).

Collaborations with partner organizations have not diluted NCTE's views on the teaching of reading and a teacher's right to choose reading materials that meet the needs of a specific group of students. Evidence of this commitment to teaching reading within a larger language framework using constructivist pedagogies is visible in ReadWriteThink, a teacher resource site established in 2002 and made possible through the partnership of NCTE, IRA, and the Verizon Foundation (http://www.readwritethink.org/). Kathryn Egawa, the NCTE administrator for the first two years of ReadWriteThink, organized the lesson plans and materials on the website using M. A. K. Halliday's model of language learning (Egawa). Today, visitors can search the site by type of resource, audience, learning objective, and theme.

That ReadWriteThink and the Literacy Coaching Clearinghouse (http://www.literacycoachingonline.org/), founded in 2006 and the product of another NCTE–IRA collaboration, were initiated soon after the No Child Left Behind Act (2001) was signed into law in 2002 is likely no mere coincidence. Nor is it likely that chance played a role in NCTE's decision to publish a policy brief on adolescent literacy (http://www1.ncte.org/library/files/Publications/Newspaper/Chron0907ResearchBrief.pdf), featuring research-based recommendations for effective reading instruction (with implications for teachers, school programs, and policymakers), while discussions were going on in Congress about the proposed Striving Readers legislation (Bills S958 and HR2289). NCTE's political activism reaches deeply into pockets of professional development, whether online or offline.

In fact, offline professional development through an array of conferences and special institutes has been a mainstay of NCTE's efforts to disseminate up-to-date, high-quality research even before that information becomes available in the organization's journals. Of particular relevance for this chapter is a series of eighteen national and regional conferences held in the United States over a five-year period in the 1980s on oral and written language development. "The 'Impact Conferences' as they came to be called," according to Dorothy S. Strickland of Rutgers University, "were proposed by Charlotte Huck in 1977 when she was president of NCTE" (D. Strickland, Message). However, it was not until Yetta M. Goodman and Dorothy S. Strickland were presidents of NCTE and IRA respectively in 1978–79 that funding became available for the conferences. More than a successful collaboration between sister organizations, the Impact Conferences on oral and written language supported NCTE's continuous efforts to bring reading into the language arts fold.

Engaging with Twenty-First-Century Digital Literacies

NCTE's stance on twenty-first-century technologies in relation to the teaching of reading is clear, as indicated in its position statement "The NCTE Definition of 21st Century Literacies." The NCTE Executive Committee approved this widely circulated definition on 15 February 2008 (http://www.ncte.org/positions/statements/21stcentdefinition), and later included it in its 2009 legislative platform. The statement contains new information in one respect: NCTE's support for the digital literacies made possible by advances in new information communication technologies. At the same time, it addresses two age-old questions: What counts as reading? and, hence, How should reading be taught? These are the same questions that drove the founders of NCTE in 1911 to break with traditions of their day, persuaded scholars of the 1960s with a broad sociocultural view of the reading process to part company with those who viewed it more narrowly, and prompted large segments of NCTE's membership in the late 1990s to resist the federal government's attempt to regulate how reading would be taught, and later, what materials would be used for teaching it.

Those echoings aside, what is telling about NCTE's position statement defining twenty-first-century literacies is that it evolved from the membership's demonstrated interest in the new literacies. That interest, in turn, resulted from professional development opportunities and materials made possible by the following NCTE initiatives:

- Pathways for 21st Century Literacies (http://www.ncte.org/pathways/21stcentury), an online program of study for teachers, schools, and districts wanting to examine the potential impact of digital literacies on their curricula
- A 2007 research-based policy brief on twenty-first-century literacies intended for a wide reading audience (http://www.ncte.org/library/NCTEFiles/Resources/Positions/Chron1107ResearchBrief.pdf)

- A 2009 Web seminar entitled "Reading Shakespeare with All Our Students"
- Numerous articles and themed issues on the new literacies (e.g., "Popular Culture and Media Literacy," themed November 2003 issue of *Language Arts*; "Learning through Technology," themed March 2004 issue of *Voices from the Middle*; "New Literacies," themed September 2007 issue of *English Journal*; and "Widening the Audience: Students Reading and Writing Online" in the November 2008 issue of *The Council Chronicle*)

NCTE members have seldom been short on enthusiasm for new ways of opening up the English language arts to new technologies. In the 1940s, for example, Max Herzberg was a high school principal in Newark, New Jersey, when his article "Cinema Syndrome" was published in *English Journal* in 1946. Earlier he had served as NCTE president in 1943 and had chaired the NCTE Committee on Radio and English Teaching. In "Cinema Syndrome," Herzberg expounded at length on the value of motion pictures for teaching students who lacked motivation to read the literature their teachers assigned. To back up his claim that "little doubt exists today that the cinema is as truly one of the language arts as is literature itself" (83), Herzberg offered these words of assurance:

> Some people say, positively and pessimistically: "Motion pictures are theater. Classroom procedures are pedagogy. And never the twain shall meet." I am convinced, however, that the two not only met long ago but that they are destined to an enduring friendship. (86)

Herzberg's claim of more than sixty years ago seems to have been borne out, judging from some of NCTE's professional development resources that depend on image- and performance-based interpretive skills for understanding. A good example appears in the January 2008 issue of *Language Arts*, which features "one of the first scholarly articles in graphic novel format—Gene Yang's 'Graphic Novels in the Classroom,' identified by Yang as 'an essay in panels'" (NCTE, "Blast from the Past" par. 1). Not only does NCTE's membership demonstrate a penchant for the new literacies, but it also seems well positioned to provide leadership in professional development resources that are in step with twenty-first century ways of learning and teaching.

A Brief Coda

Although buffeted by the social, cultural, and political currents of the last one hundred years, NCTE has remained steadfast in its commitment to teaching reading within the English language arts curriculum, not separate from it. At the same time, the membership showed signs of understanding full well that, just as *what* we read and *how* we read changes with the passing years, so too must the way we teach reading. This mix of steadfastness and flexibility is NCTE's trademark. The organization's entangled beginnings will no doubt continue to serve it well throughout the next one hundred years—a time in which reading instruction will change to meet new exigencies, but always within the place it calls home—the English language arts.

Note

1. The following individuals contributed to the bricolage. Their titles reflect the positions they held at the time of the IRA–NCTE standards project:

 Alan Farstrup, Executive Director, International Reading Association

 John Mayher, Professor of English education, Department of Teaching and Learning, Steinhardt School of Education, New York University

 Terry Salinger, Director of Research, International Reading Association

Works Cited

Allington, Richard L. "Troubling Times: A Short Historical Perspective." *Big Brother and the National Reading Curriculum: How Ideology Trumped Evidence*. Ed. Richard L. Allington. Portsmouth, NH: Heinemann, 2002. 3–46. Print.

Alvermann, Donna E. "Effective Literacy Instruction for Adolescents." *Journal of Literacy Research* 34.2 (2002): 189–208. Print.

———. "Exemplary Literacy Instruction in Grades 7–12: What Counts and Who's Counting?" *Literacy Development of Students in Urban Schools: Research and Policy*. Ed. James Flood and Patricia L. Anders. Newark, DE: IRA, 2005. 187–201. Print.

Amendum, Stephen J. "Federally-Funded Reading Intervention and Reading Growth: Which Features Matter in High Poverty Schools?" 2008. MS.

Anderson, Richard C., Elfrieda H. Hiebert, Judith A. Scott, and Ian A. G. Wilkinson. *Becoming a Nation of Readers: The Report of the Commission on Reading*. Washington, DC: National Academy of Education, 1985. Print.

Applebee, Arthur N. *Tradition and Reform in the Teaching of English: A History*. Urbana, IL: NCTE, 1974. Print.

Atwell, Nancie. *In the Middle: Writing, Reading, and Learning with Adolescents*. Upper Montclair, NJ: Boynton/Cook, 1987. Print.

Baker, Franklin T. "High-School Reading: Compulsory and Voluntary." *English Journal* 4.1 (1915): 1–8. Print.

Beers, Kylene. "An Open Letter to NCTE Members about the Common Core State Standards." *National Council of Teachers of English*. NCTE, 28 July 2009. Web. 20 Aug. 2009.

Bloome, David. "Anthropology and Research on Teaching the English Language Arts." *Handbook of Research on Teaching the English Language Arts*. Ed. James Flood, Julie M. Jensen, Diane Lapp, and James R. Squire. New York: Macmillan, 1991. 46–56. Print.

Breck, Emma J. "The Efficient High-School Library." *English Journal* 5.1 (1916): 10–19. Print.

Clifford, Geraldine Joncich. *A Sisyphean Task: Historical Perspectives on the Relationship between Writing and Reading Instruction*. Berkeley: National Center for the Study of Writing, 1987. Technical Report No. 7. *National Writing Project*. Web. 1 Aug. 2009.

Davis, Millie. "Censorship Challenges Comparison Q4 FY09 and Q4 FY08." *National Council of Teachers of English*. NCTE, July 2009. Web. 23 Aug. 2009.

Donelson, Kenneth L. *The Students' Right to Read*. Urbana, IL: NCTE, 1972. *Educational Resources Information Center*. Web. 10 Jan. 2009. ED068990.

———. "Ten Teachers and Scholars Who Influenced the Secondary English Curriculum, 1880–1970." *English Journal* 73.3 (1984): 78–80. Print.

Drury, Judy, and Anne Masters. "School Libraries and the Progressive Movement: A Study of the Role of Librarians in Implementing Progressive Education (1900–1957)." *The Emerging School Library Media Center: Historical Issues and Perspectives*. Ed. Kathy Howard Latrobe. Englewood, CO: Libraries Unlimited, 1998. 17–37. Print.

Dyson, Anne Haas. "Coach Bombay's Kids Learn to Write: Children's Appropriation of Media Material for School Literacy." *Research in the Teaching of English* 33.4 (1999): 367–402. Print.

Egawa, Kathryn. Message to the author. 14 Apr. 2009. E-mail.

England, David A., and B. Jane West. "Lou LaBrant: A Challenge and a Charge." Gerlach and Monseau 141–67.

Farstrup, Alan. Message to the author. 14 Aug. 2009. E-mail.

Faust, Mark, and Mark Dressman. "The Other Tradition: Populist Perspectives on Teaching Poetry, as Published in *English Journal*, 1912–2005." *English Education* 41.2 (2009): 114–34. Print.

Finders, Margaret J. "Just Girls: Literacy and Allegiance in Junior High School." *Written Communication*, 13.1 (1996): 93–129. Print.

Flood, James, Julie M. Jensen, Diane Lapp, and James R. Squire, eds. *Handbook of Research on Teaching the English Language Arts*. New York: Macmillan, 1991. Print.

Flood, James, Diane Lapp, James R. Squire, and Julie M. Jensen, eds. *Handbook of Research on Teaching the English Language Arts*. 2nd ed. Mahwah, NJ: Erlbaum, 2003. Print.

Galda, Susan Lee. "Three Children Reading Stories: Response to Literature in Preadolescents." Diss. New York U, 1980. *DAI-A* 41/06 (1980): item AAT8027440. *ProQuest Dissertations and Theses*. Web. 4 Feb. 2010.

Garan, Elaine M. "What Does the *Report of the National Reading Panel* Really Tell Us about Teaching Phonics?" *Language Arts* 79.1 (2001): 61–71. Print.

Gerlach, Jeanne Marcum, and Virginia R. Monseau, eds. *Missing Chapters: Ten Pioneering Women in NCTE and English Education*. Urbana, IL: NCTE, 1991. *Educational Resources Information Center*. Web. 3 July 2009. ED334590.

Gillikin, Dure Jo. "Angela M. Broening: Implacable Defender." Gerlach and Monseau 97–115.

Goodman, Kenneth S. "Ken Goodman on His Life in Reading." *History of Reading News* 23.2 (2000): n. pag. Web. 28 Mar. 2009.

———. "Miscues: Windows on the Reading Process." 1973. *Language and Literacy: The Selected Writings of Kenneth Goodman*. Ed. Frederick V. Gollasch. Vol. 1. Boston: Routledge, 1982. 93–102. Print.

Goodman, Kenneth S., Patrick Shannon, Yvonne S. Freeman, and Sharon Murphy. *Report Card on Basal Readers*. Katonah, NY: Owen, 1988. Print.

Gray, William Scott. *Studies of Elementary-School Reading through Standardized Tests*. Chicago: U of Chicago P, 1917.*Google Book Search*. Web. 18 Feb. 2009.

Gutiérrez, Kris D., and Marjorie Faulstich Orellana. "The 'Problem' of English Learners: Constructing Genres of Difference." *Research in the Teaching of English* 40.4 (2006): 502–07. Print.

Halliday, M. A. K. *Explorations in the Functions of Language*. London: Edward Arnold, 1973. Print.

Harste, Jerome C., Virginia A. Woodward, and Carolyn L. Burke. *Language Stories and Literacy Lessons*. Portsmouth, NH: Heinemann, 1984. Print.

Hatfield, W. Wilbur. "Modern Literature for High-School Use." *English Journal* 1.1 (1912): 52. Print.

Herber, Harold L. *Teaching Reading in Content Areas*. Englewood Cliffs, NJ: Prentice-Hall, 1970. Print.

———. Telephone interview. 18 Feb. 2009.

———. "Testimony regarding FY 1976 Budget Requests for Elementary and Secondary Education." 9 Apr. 1975. TS. University of Illinois Archives (Record Series 15/73/007, Box 1, File 1), Urbana, IL.

Herzberg, Max J. "Cinema Syndrome." *English Journal* 35.2 (1946): 83–86. Print.

Hoetker, James. *Dramatics and the Teaching of Literature*. Champaign, IL: NCTE, 1969. Print.

Hook, J. N. *A Long Way Together: A Personal View of NCTE's First Sixty-Seven Years*. Urbana, IL: NCTE, 1979. Print.

———. *NDEA Institutes for Trainers of Teachers (Summer 1966).* Washington, DC: US Dept. of Health, Education, and Welfare, Office of Education, Oct. 1966. *Educational Resources Information Center.* Web. 31 July 2009. ED012706.

Huey, Edmund Burke. *The Psychology and Pedagogy of Reading: With a Review of the History of Reading and Writing and of Methods, Texts, and Hygiene in Reading.* New York: Macmillan, 1908.

International Reading Association, and National Council of Teachers of English. *Standards for the English Language Arts.* Newark, DE: IRA; Urbana, IL: NCTE, 1996. Print.

Jenkins, William A. "Political Activities of the NCTE Commission on Reading." 21 Nov. 1972. TS. University of Illinois Archives (Record Series 15/73/007, Box 1, File 2), Urbana, IL.

Kirkland, David E. "'The Rose That Grew from Concrete': Postmodern Blackness and New English Education." *English Journal* 97.5 (2008): 69–75. Print.

Kucer, Stephen B., ed. *What Research* Really *Says about Teaching and Learning to Read.* Urbana, IL: NCTE, 2008. Print.

Lapp, Diane, Laurie A. Guthrie, and James Flood. "Ruth May Strang (1895–1971): The Legacy of a Reading Sage." *Shaping the Reading Field: The Impact of Early Reading Pioneers, Scientific Research, and Progressive Ideas.* Ed. Susan E. Israel and E. Jennifer Monaghan. Newark, DE: IRA, 2007. 347–73. Print.

Latrobe, Kathy Howard, ed. *The Emerging School Library Media Center: Historical Issues and Perspectives.* Englewood, CO: Libraries Unlimited, 1998. Print.

Lee, Carol D. *Signifying as a Scaffold for Literary Interpretation: The Pedagogical Implications of an African American Discourse Genre.* Urbana, IL: NCTE, 1993. Print. NCTE Research Report No. 26.

Leonard, Sterling Andrus. *Essential Principles of Teaching Reading and Literature in the Intermediate Grades and the High School.* Philadelphia: Lippincott, 1922. *Google Book Search.* Web. 1 Mar. 2009.

Lewis, Cynthia. "The Social Drama of Literature Discussions in a Fifth/Sixth-Grade Classroom." *Research in the Teaching of English* 31.2 (1997): 163–204. Print.

Marshall, James D., Peter Smagorinsky, and Michael W. Smith. *The Language of Interpretation: Patterns of Discourse in Discussions of Literature*. Urbana, IL: NCTE, 1995. Print. NCTE Research Report No. 27.

Mayher, John S. Message to the author. 12 Aug. 2009. E-mail.

———. "Reflections on Standards and Standard Setting: An Insider/ Outsider Perspective on the NCTE/IRA Standards." *English Education* 31.2 (1999): 106–21. Print.

National Council of Teachers of English. "Adolescent Literacy: A Policy Research Brief Produced by the National Council of Teachers of English." *National Council of Teachers of English*. NCTE, 2007. Web. 4 Feb. 2010.

———. "Blast from the Past: Graphic Novels." *National Council of Teachers of English*. NCTE, [2009]. Web. 26 Aug. 2009.

———. "The NCTE Definition of 21st Century Literacies." *National Council of Teachers of English*. NCTE, 15 Feb. 2008. Web. 20 Mar. 2009.

———. "NCTE Position Statement on Reading." *National Council of Teachers of English*. NCTE, Feb. 1999. Web. 23 Aug. 2009.

———. "Reading First: NCTE Praises Reading First Audit: Calls for Further Investigation." *Don't Waste Our Times Productions*. DWOT, 25 Sept. 2006. Web. 23 Aug. 2009.

———. "Resolution on the Reading First Initiative." *National Council of Teachers of English*. NCTE, 2002. Web. 23 Aug. 2009.

National Council of Teachers of English Committee on Correlation. *A Correlated Curriculum*. New York: Appleton, 1936. Print.

National Council of Teachers of English Committee on the Right to Read. *The Students' Right to Read*. Champaign, IL: NCTE, 1962. Print.

National Council of Teachers of English Executive Committee. "Reading Research." *National Council of Teachers of English*. NCTE, Nov. 2007. Web. 23 Aug. 2009. Motion 2007:54.

National Federation of Modern Language Teachers Associations. "'The Right to Read': The NCTE Speaks Out on Censorship!" *Modern Language Journal* 47.2 (1963): 70–71. Print.

National Institute of Child Health and Human Development. *Report of the National Reading Panel: Teaching Children to Read (Summary)*. Washington, DC: GPO, 2000. Print. NIH Publication No. 00-4769.

No Child Left Behind Act of 2001. Pub. L. 107–110. 115 Stat. 1425–2094. 8 Jan. 2002. *US Dept. of Education.* Web. 8 July 2009.

O'Donnell, Bernard. "NCTE/ERIC and Project English." *English Journal* 57.6 (1968): 920–25. Print.

Pooley, Robert C. "Pre-Induction Training in English." *English Journal* 33.7 (1944): 355–57. Print.

"Pre-Induction Needs in Language Communication and Reading." *Education for Victory* 2.11 (1943): 1, 16–24. Print. University of Illinois Archives (Record Series 15/71/806, Box 1, File 4), Urbana, IL.

"Project English: An Announcement from the Office of Education, Department of Health, Education, and Welfare." *English Journal* 51.2 (1962): 149–52. Print.

Purves, Alan C., and Richard Beach. *Literature and the Reader: Research on Response to Literature, Reading Interests, and the Teaching of Literature.* Urbana, IL: NCTE, 1972. Print.

Radner, Sanford. *Fifty Years of English Teaching: A Historical Analysis of the Presidential Addresses of NCTE.* Champaign, IL: NCTE, 1960. Print.

Rigby, Ruth E. "A History of the NCTE Commission on Reading Documents: Three Documents That Challenge the Limited Scientific Research Base Given Authority by the National Reading Panel." Kucer 17–26.

Rosenblatt, Louise. *The Reader, The Text, The Poem: The Transactional Theory of the Literary Work.* Carbondale: Southern Illinois UP, 1978. Print.

Ruddell, Robert. Message to the author. 21 Feb. 2009. E-mail.

Rush, Leslie S., A. Jonathan Eakle, and Allen Berger, eds. *Secondary School Literacy: What Research Reveals for Classroom Practice.* Urbana, IL: NCTE, 2007. Print.

Salinger, Terry. Message to the author. 12 Aug. 2009. E-mail.

Seyfert, Warren C., ed. *The English Curriculum in the Secondary School.* Spec. Issue of *Bulletin of the National Association of Secondary School Principals* 51.318 (1967): iii–128. *Educational Resources Information Center.* Web. 3 Aug. 2009. ED015200.

Shannon, Patrick. "Resistance Is Futile?" Kucer 3–16.

Slack, Robert C. "A Report on Project English." *College English* 26.1 (1964): 43–47. Print.

Smith, Dora V. "Extensive Reading in Junior High School: A Survey of Teacher Preparation." *English Journal* 19.6 (1930): 449–62. Print.

Smith, Michael W., and Jeffrey D. Wilhelm. *"Reading Don't Fix No Chevys": Literacy in the Lives of Young Men*. Portsmouth, NH: Heinemann, 2002. Print.

Smith, Nila Banton. *American Reading Instruction*. 1934. Newark, DE: IRA, 2002. Print.

Sperling, Melanie, and Anne DiPardo. "English Education Research and Classroom Practice: New Directions for New Times." *Review of Research in Education* 32.1 (2008): 62–108. Print.

Stephens, Diane, Gail Boldt, Candace Clark, Janet S. Gaffney, Judith Shelton, Jennifer Story, and Janelle Weinzierl. "Learning (about Learning) from Four Teachers." *Research in the Teaching of English* 34.4 (2000): 532–65. Print.

Stephens, Diane, Denise N. Morgan, Amy Donnelly, Diane DeFord, Jennifer Young, Michael Seaman, Karen Crowder, Erin Hamel, and Rebecca Cibic. "The South Carolina Reading Initiative: NCTE's Reading Initiative as a Statewide Staff Development Project." *National Council of Teachers of English*. NCTE, 2007. Web. 10 Apr. 2009.

Strickland, Dorothy S. "The Effects of a Special Literature Program on the Oral Language Expansion of Linguistically Different, Negro, Kindergarten Children." Diss. New York U, 1971. *DAI-A* 32/03 (1971): item AAT7124816. *ProQuest Dissertations and Theses*. Web. 4 Feb. 2010.

———. Message to the author. 6 Feb. 2009. E-mail.

———. "A Program for Linguistically Different, Black Children." *Research in the Teaching of English* 7.1 (1973): 79–86. Print.

Strickland, Ruth G. "What Thou Lovest Well Remains." *College English* 22.5 (1961): 297–304. Print.

Suppa-Friedman, Janice. "Lobbying for Literacy." *SLATE Update* May 2009: n. pag. Web. 9 Aug. 2009.

Tatum, Alfred W. *Teaching Reading to Black Adolescent Males: Closing the Achievement Gap*. Portland, ME: Stenhouse, 2005. Print.

Taylor, Denny. *Beginning to Read and the Spin Doctors of Science: The Political Campaign to Change America's Mind about How Children Learn to Read.* Urbana, IL: NCTE, 1998. Print.

Thomas, Charles Swain. *The Teaching of English in the Secondary School.* Boston: Houghton, 1917. Print.

Thorndike, Edward L. "Reading as Reasoning: A Study of Mistakes in Paragraph Reading." *Journal of Educational Psychology* 8.6 (1917): 323–32. *Google Book Search.* Web. 30 Mar. 2009.

Vasquez, Vivian Maria. *Negotiating Critical Literacies with Young Children.* Mahwah, NJ: Erlbaum, 2004. Print.

Ward, Gilbert O. *The High-School Library.* Chicago: American Library Association, 1913. Print.

Yang, Gene. "Graphic Novels in the Classroom." *Language Arts* 85.3 (2008): 185–92. Print.

Yatvin, Joanne. "Babes in the Woods: The Wanderings of the National Reading Panel." *Big Brother and the National Reading Curriculum: How Ideology Trumped Evidence.* Ed. Richard L. Allington. Portsmouth, NH: Heinemann, 2002. 125–36. Print.

NCTE READING THE PAST. WRITING THE FUTURE. 100 YEARS

A Blast from the Past

Did you know that NCTE has been active in the courts to defend students' right to read? NCTE filed a friend-of-the-court brief on behalf of *Pico v. Island Trees School District*, a landmark case that eventually went to the U.S. Supreme Court and ensured that, as the Court ruled in 1982, "Local school boards may not remove books from school library shelves simply because they dislike the ideas contained in these books."

NCTE Executive Directors

James F. Hosic (1911–1919)

W. Wilbur Hatfield (1920–1953)

J. N. Hook (1954–1960)

James R. Squire (1960–1967)

Robert F. Hogan (1968–1981)

John C. Maxwell (1981–1989

Miles A. Myers (1990–1997)

Faith Z. Schullstrom (1997–2000)

Kent Williamson (2000–present)

Chapter Three

The Teaching of Writing: 1912–2010

Anne Ruggles Gere
University of Michigan at Ann Arbor

This is, of course, an impossible title and an impossible assignment. To write a history of anything requires data, records that document what occurred in the past, so that an author can construct a narrative of events. Even acknowledging that histories are always interpretations, that they do not report what actually happened in the past but are simply records of what writers *say* happened, even this does not make it possible to write a history of writing instruction. The problem is that instruction, especially instruction in writing, remains largely invisible. Teaching at all levels means that an instructor goes into a room with a group of students and closes the door; accounts of what occurs behind that door can vary enormously, depending on who is doing the telling.

Except for the occasional video or classroom observation, there is no documentation of actual teaching. The best we can do is gather related evidence such as books and articles written by teachers or about pedagogical approaches, instructional materials such as textbooks and curriculum guides, or accounts of various interventions and reform movements. Yet none of these materials can be completely relied on. I have observed teachers thoroughly grounded in writing processes—with laminated *prewrite, draft, revise, publish* hanging on classroom walls—push students through one grammar worksheet after another. Instructional materials such as textbooks provide some clues about instruction, but they can be misleading. I still remember, sadly, sitting in a classroom where the teacher was using the first American literature anthology to include Native American literature before the traditional

Colonial selections. As I waited for her to introduce the too-long neglected texts, she flipped past the first section, saying brightly, "We'll start with the Puritans." Curriculum guides produced by and for school districts are similarly unreliable sources of information about what actually occurs in classrooms. Programs of educational reform often circulate at the level of administrators, with only minimal effects on teachers' daily practices. The forces that actually shape instruction are often ephemeral and more difficult to examine. The historical moment, geographical region, material conditions of schools and classrooms, class size, student level, disciplinary context—these and many other factors make writing instruction highly variable. Then, too, writing instruction is not limited to what happens inside classrooms.

In 2004 the National Endowment for the Arts (NEA) published *Reading at Risk: A Survey of Literary Reading in America*, a report based on surveys conducted between 1982 and 2002. During this period, the number of people who wrote outside of school or work increased substantially, from eleven million in 1982 to fifteen million in 2002, or an increase of approximately 30 percent (22). But this fact was overshadowed by concerns about reading. Dana Gioia, then-chair of NEA, described the results in grim terms and summarized the entire report this way: "literary reading in America is not only declining rapidly among all groups, but the rate of decline is accelerating, especially among the young" (vii). According to the report, adults who read novels, short stories, poetry, or plays declined more than 10 percent in two decades, and the steepest decline—more than 25 percent—occurred among those eighteen to twenty-four years of age. Even extending beyond literary reading, there was a 7 percent decline in adults reading any book (ix). Yet the number of writers grew, especially among the eighteen- to twenty-four-year-olds. History shows that those who write outside school and work often receive various forms of instruction from family members, churches, clubs, or, increasingly, online audiences (Gere, *Intimate Practices*; Brandt, *Literacy in American Lives*; Shultz). Accordingly, a history of writing instruction in the United States must look beyond the classroom to consider how writing is taught outside of schools as well as in them.

In the face of limited documentation about classroom practices, rich and complex extracurricular writing, and a cultural bias toward privileging reading over writing, the best I can offer is a highly selective collection of glimpses into some of the factors that may—or may not—have influenced the ways writing has been taught in the United States during the first century of NCTE's existence. At the least, I will avoid portraying the teaching of writing in terms of smooth narratives populated by dominant figures. Instead, I look beyond universals to consider how local circumstances shape writing instruction. I focus on relatively obscure figures as well as more prominent ones, and I reject the goal of identifying best practices in favor of a wider array of pedagogies. To begin, I look at an article by Edwin Hopkins, "Can Good Composition Teaching Be Done under Present Conditions?" published in the inaugural volume of *English Journal*, because it illustrates the problem of writing a history of composition instruction. Then I look across time, from 1912 to the present, at a series of social and political forces, teachers and theorists, and institutions and projects, all of which demonstrate the impossibility of defining precisely either "good composition" or "present conditions."

Hopkins begins his article by answering his own question with a clear *no*, explaining that good composition teaching is impossible because teachers are expected to teach an "appalling" number of students. He goes on to narrate how English composition became a "laboratory subject, but without any material addition to the personnel of its teaching force" ("Can Good" 2). That is, rhetoric, from which composition courses evolved, had focused on oral skills and memorization, which meant that teachers did not need to respond to written texts by students. However, with the transition to a focus on writing came the mandate for teachers to read students' work and confer individually with them about it. In Hopkins's view, the number of students assigned to each composition instructor did not allow for one-to-one conversations between teacher and student. To bolster the case of the writing teacher, Hopkins draws an analogy between the science teacher and the teacher of writing, arguing that the resources, both human and material, for teaching each subject ought to be allocated equitably. The science teacher's need for space and equipment, Hopkins claims, should be balanced with the composition teacher's need for time to respond to a reasonable amount of student writing. Specifically, he asserts that the number of students "for a single teacher in secondary schools should not exceed eighty, and in a college freshman class sixty" (4). Hopkins contrasts his ideal with the actual numbers of students assigned to writing teachers and concludes that "the total labor devolving upon English composition teachers is apparently between 50 and 100 per cent more than the average total of that of any other class of teachers whatever" (4). Throughout the article, Hopkins continues his focus on the working conditions of writing teachers, emphasizing that the number of students assigned to individual teachers has everything to do with what teachers are able to accomplish. An appendix to the article reports on a survey being conducted by a committee of the Modern Language Association (MLA) and invites readers of *English Journal* to participate. This project, cosponsored by NCTE and ultimately known as the Hopkins Report, was designed to document the "appalling" number of students in writing classes. Eventually, 624 secondary school and 345 college teachers responded to the survey, documenting an average of approximately 105 students per teacher (Popken 632, 634).

Hopkins's article and his ongoing campaign to heighten public awareness of the issue of class size in writing instruction clearly raised concerns that mattered to composition teachers then and that continue to matter today. However, this article also exemplifies some of the problems inherent in trying to write histories of composition instruction. The title, "Can Good Composition Teaching Be Done under Present Conditions?" embodies two assumptions—that Hopkins and his readers all know and agree on what "good composition teaching" is and that "the present circumstances" of this teaching can be easily described. Hopkins mentions the laboratory method and teacher–student interactions but does not provide enough detail to give readers a clear idea of what might actually happen in the classroom. Nor does he include an explanation of why the methods he mentions should be considered "good." It is fair to say that the methods Hopkins alludes to were innovative at the time; they represented a significant departure from the more rhetorically based methods of the nineteenth century. But it would have been impossible to identify one set of strategies that would meet the criteria of all writing instructors at the time. Then, as now, multiple approaches to teaching circulated through classrooms, and one teacher's idea of "good" instruction would not necessarily conform to another's. One reason for this is that local context exerts an enormous influence on teaching, and a phrase such as "the present circumstances" implies that local conditions can be described in similar ways across multiple contexts. Hopkins's methods of data collection are predicated on flattening differences across varied sites. While it can be useful to gather and aggregate information about class size from hundreds of schools, noting that teachers have an average of 105 students makes the teacher with 80 students and the one with 130 equally invisible. Claims made in histories of instruction frequently follow similar patterns, privileging one pedagogical approach while minimizing others and reducing contextual variations in order to present a coherent narrative.

Part of the larger context in which Hopkins wrote was shaped by an expansion in writing instruction to serve increasing numbers of students. It was also a context in which the teaching of writing was subject to public scrutiny. The Harvard Reports of 1891 to 1893, written by alumni from nonacademic professions, described incoming college students as unprepared to meet Harvard's standards for writing. These reports had received considerable attention, both within and beyond higher education, and they had helped to make writing instruction a topic of more general interest. *Dial* magazine had published a series of articles describing programs of study in several college English departments in 1894 (Anderson; Cook; Corson; Matthews; Wendell). These descriptions, written by professors at a variety of institutions, including state universities and smaller colleges, provided the general public with detailed information about college courses. Hopkins believed that the public would take great interest in the issue of class size in writing classes, and he was convinced there would be a significant public initiative to improve the working conditions of composition teachers once those conditions became visible to the public. In addition to the 1912 *English Journal* article, he published articles in several other venues and, in 1923, a book that contained a compilation of all the data he had collected. *The Labor and Cost of the Teaching of English in Colleges and Secondary Schools, with Especial Reference to English Composition*, Hopkins hoped, would arouse public outcry about the teaching of writing. But he was wrong about both public interest and initiative regarding class size. The statistics produced by his study did not lead to public expressions of concern about the number of students in writing classes. Despite the public interest in English studies evidenced in articles such as those appearing in *Dial*; despite the growing prominence of English studies; despite the 1894 "Report of the Committee of Ten" (J. M. Taylor), which designated English as the only subject high school students would be required to take for four years, few people outside professional associations such as NCTE expressed concern about class size.

The year 1912 also marked a period of realignment among professional associations. MLA, founded in 1883 as a professional association for English professors as well as those teaching contemporary foreign languages, had begun turning away from questions about teaching. MLA discontinued its pedagogical section in 1902, changing its constitution to emphasize research rather than teaching as its primary function, and the MLA convention began giving more attention to literary research. In part, this shift led to the formation of NCTE and to a realignment of priorities by English instructors. For example, the committee on which Hopkins served had its genesis in the Midwest MLA, but his article, report, and book were all published by NCTE. It was NCTE that took up questions about teaching, especially the teaching of writing, while MLA reports and publications focused more exclusively on research in literature. We can trace this division of foci to the present day, particularly since the Conference on College Composition and Communication (CCCC) is part of NCTE, but it is much more difficult—impossible even—to explain how this particular alignment shaped the teaching of writing.

When Hopkins's article was published in 1912, high school attendance was beginning to increase. In 1890, enrollments totaled 202,963; in 1900, they had risen to 519,251; and in 1912, one million students attended high school. By 1923, when Hopkins's book was published, attendance had grown to over two million, or nearly 30 percent of all fourteen- to seventeen-year-olds. These increases meant ever-larger numbers of students in high school English classrooms (Spring 194). The growth in high school attendance was accompanied by similar expansion in college enrollments. Between 1920 and 1930, the numbers grew from more than two million to more than four million. In addition to the problem of too many students, writing teachers faced the problem of disproportionately low pay, particularly at the college level. As Hopkins documented, "College freshman English composition . . . costs about one-third less than the average for all English subjects" (*Labor and Cost* 21). For example, a total English department budget of $18,000 would devote only $3,000 to the teaching of writing because the salaries of composition instructors were approximately one-third lower than those of their colleagues who taught literature. Since today's composition instructors are similarly underpaid and often occupy less prestigious and secure positions than do literature colleagues in the academy, we can wonder how different the teaching of writing might be if it had been better funded from the start.

Hopkins does not explicitly address issues of gender, but his silence on the subject speaks to the fact that few women were among his colleagues. MLA was a male-dominated group, and nearly all of the founders of NCTE were also male. Those women who achieved some prominence within the organization were often identified through male sponsors. For example, Gertrude Buck, among the first women to receive a PhD in rhetoric and a significant scholar in the field, was usually described as a student of Fred Newton Scott. Not until 1955 was a woman, Louise Pound, elected president of MLA. Women were elected to the presidency of NCTE earlier, with Rewey Belle Inglis in 1929, followed by Ruth Mary Weeks in 1930, Stella S. Center in 1932, Dora V. Smith in 1936, and Essie Chamberlain in 1939. Still, throughout the profession women usually occupied less prestigious positions, which meant they were often writing instructors. As the number of high school teaching jobs opened up, women took an increasing percentage of them. In higher education, women frequently took positions as composition instructors while their male counterparts became professors of literature. Statistics on PhD matriculation and completion show that between 1900 and 1930 only 3 to 5 percent of women in PhD programs completed the degree, whereas more than 15 percent of their male counterparts did. A study conducted in 1929 found that at least 38 percent of all college composition courses were being taught by female instructors, and it seems reasonable to assume that a significant portion of them were women who chose to remain in the academy after failing to complete the PhD (Warner Taylor 22). Gender has been and remains a shaping force in writing instruction. A survey of CCCC members in 2008 found that 64 percent of instructors were female, while only 36 percent were male (Gere, "Initial Report"). Although we can document the fact that composition instruction has been gendered throughout its existence, we can only speculate about how gender has helped to create various contexts for writing instruction.

That Hopkins included both high school and college teachers in his survey reflects the view that continuity exists in the writing instruction carried out by the two types of institutions. Of course, this was, and remains, a contested view. Many markers of division between the two—textbooks, assessment practices, assumptions about writing quality, along with the preparation and status of instructors—contribute to differences in writing instruction between today's high schools and colleges. Yet pedagogical practices including process writing, peer response, and portfolio assessment can be found in both college and high school classrooms. Concerns such as the effects of class size and entities like the National Writing Project and NCTE itself bring instructors at the two levels together in the current moment. It is reasonable to assume that similar sets of differences and similarities characterized high schools and colleges of Hopkins's day. These differences and similarities, however, are difficult to access or assess since the *ways* in which common practices and concerns are enacted vary from one context to another.

The motivating force behind Hopkins's lifelong campaign to reduce the size of writing classes was the support of pedagogies that emphasized considerable one-on-one time between instructors and students, both in grading students' writing and in meeting individually with them to offer comments and suggestions. This attention to fostering dialogue between teacher and student was grounded in a view of writing as creative expression. In the view of theorists such as Percival Chubb and B. A. Hinsdale, writing was not an ability limited to a select few; students could learn to write as long as they had the guidance and criticism of teachers. This emphasis on creative expression was not, of course, the only approach to writing instruction in 1912. Fred Newton Scott and his colleagues acknowledged the importance of creative expression but also emphasized the importance of addressing an audience. This more rhetorical approach positioned the teacher to provide specific strategies rather than simply foster creative expression in writing. In Scott's terms, the goal was to prepare students to write in ways that could contribute to democratic public discourse, always emphasizing, along with Plato, that "any piece of discourse, or mode of communication, is to be measured by its effect upon the welfare of the community" ("Rhetoric Rediviva" 415).

Scott was also responding to what has been called the current-traditional approach to writing instruction, an approach that emphasizes attention to convention and practicality. In the article "Efficiency for Efficiency's Sake," he notes the growing attention to educational efficiency, both among the general public and in a variety of publications, observing that what can be measured with such precision is not the most important part of teaching. With rich sarcasm, Scott then proposes, "if such tests of efficiency are good for pupils and teachers, they are equally good for their superior officers. Why withhold this precious boon from principals, from superintendents, from college presidents?" (41). In "The Undefended Gate," Scott lays out an alternative that strikes him as attractive, taking up the relationship between universities and secondary schools, a relationship he characterizes as feudal. Instead of acceding to the usual (hierarchical) pattern of blaming secondary school teachers and their students for failing to meet university standards, Scott considers social forces that pose challenges for high school teachers. Citing uncultured families, the careless English used by teachers in other fields, and especially daily newspapers, which he analyzes in detail, Scott argues that good writing instruction is undercut by these forces, and without addressing them, no amount of teaching will be effective. This process of identifying social causes of problems in writing instruction, rather than advocating for social efficiency or a focus on the individual writer, offered yet another way to approach writing instruction, but we have little evidence for how it played out in the daily lives of teachers. Chubb, Hinsdale, and Scott all published textbooks promoting their approaches to teaching writing, and a 1917 publication of the U.S. Bureau of Education, *Reorganization of English in Secondary Schools*, articulated and reinforced the social efficiency of the current-traditional perspective (Hosic). Even so, it is impossible to know how these publications were read and used by teachers in grades K–12 and college as they closed their classroom doors and taught writing.

World War I led to many realignments in education, and approaches to the teaching of writing were among them. The war-induced need to develop a stronger sense of national pride and loyalty caused a major shift in English studies. The dominance of British literature in the curriculum was supplanted by an increased attention to American authors as a way of fostering a greater sense of national pride in students. In a general way, composition became linked to the project of affirming nationhood, but writing instructors did not uniformly embrace this idea. One form of resistance substituted the local for the national. An article published in a 1924 issue of *English Journal*, for example, addresses the problem of helping students find topics for writing by describing how investigations of American Indian place names in Michigan can engage students (Clark). This approach can be read as arguing for place-based writing instruction, but of course it is impossible to know if or how writing teachers adopted it in specific contexts. Other educators had more pointed objections to linking composition with nation-building. In a 1926 article, Dora V. Smith objected to focusing writing instruction on patriotic or nationalistic topics, arguing that more personal and imaginative topics would engage students in learning. *Elementary English Review* (renamed *Language Arts* in 1975) became another journal of NCTE in 1924, and its emphasis on students in the elementary grades furthered an agenda that valued specific instructional contexts over a more national perspective. Views like these posed a continuing challenge to advocates of writing for political purposes.

Forces outside classrooms also shaped writing instruction during the early part of the twentieth century. On college campuses, literary clubs that had been founded in the nineteenth century continued to support extracurricular writing because members wrote and presented papers to club members, receiving critical responses to their texts (Gere, *Writing Groups*). The women's club movement also was rooted in the nineteenth century but remained a cultural force in the early 1920s, fostering environments in which women regularly wrote and presented papers. Here, too, it was customary for members to spend many months preparing papers they then presented to the club, often receiving detailed responses to their texts (Gere, *Intimate Practices*). Though we can document that some of these extracurricular writing practices found their way into classrooms, we cannot know the extent or exact shape of instruction that developed from extracurricular writing.

Another external force that shaped writing instruction was testing. Beginning with handwriting scales developed by E. L. Thorndike in 1909, writing became a means of measuring student ability. As the military grew in response to World War I, writing played an increasingly important role in identifying the most intellectually able recruits, thus linking writing and testing. Recruits who were able to write a dictated sentence were sorted into groups for further testing, and literacy skills figured prominently in their assignments (Elliot 58–67). Thus began a long tradition of large-scale testing in the United States, and writing became both the means and the object of much of it.

The move toward large-scale testing was not, of course, limited to the military. The College Board, founded in 1900, led the movement toward large-scale testing for college applicants. By the 1920s, a version of the Scholastic Aptitude Test (SAT) had been developed, and by 1933, psychometricians were convinced that this test could be used to predict college performance (Lemann). A growing interest in scientific procedures fueled the testing movement. With increased industrialization at the end of the nineteenth century, systematic or scientific management became prized, which positioned writing as a skill to be taught in differentiated ways, according to the goals, intelligence, and background of various populations of students. In this view, the most able and advantaged students, those aiming at professional positions, might be encouraged to learn to write in multiple genres, but the less able might be taught to concentrate on forms such as the friendly letter. Testing could help make the distinctions.

Such methods for sorting and placing students were compatible with principles of efficiency and scientific management, and advocates of this approach frequently admonished writing teachers to take a scientific approach to their work. If composition instruction could be made more efficient, complaints and concerns about the quality of writing could be silenced. Even the process of choosing books could, in this view, become more efficient. Mary Marye, author of a 1930 *School Review* article about an evaluation form for selecting composition textbooks for grades 9 and 10, wrote:

> Increased attention is being given to the scientific selection of textbooks in recognition of their importance as an adequate tool in accomplishing a definite purpose in a particular situation, as an influence in training the teacher, and as a determining factor in the content and methods of instruction. The usual "opinion method" of selection, influenced by minor or irrelevant considerations, is giving way to a "data method," based on scientific analysis and measurement according to certain standards. (124)

Marye's article offers a detailed chart based on ten features: appearance, material included, general methods, content of expression, development of expression, effectiveness in motivating vital expression, grammar, punctuation, methods of developing mechanics, and miscellaneous materials—each with multiple subcategories. As her prose indicates, Marye discounted opinion-driven theories in favor of rigorous analysis of data for choosing textbooks. Such attempts to transform teaching into a highly regulated practice undoubtedly had some influence on all dimensions of writing instruction, from the selection of teaching materials to the assessment of student writing, but the extent of this influence remains difficult to assess.

Another outside force that contributed to writing instruction was the child study movement that centered on the work of G. Stanley Hall and emphasized individual expression over social efficiency. In the 1931 article "Teaching the Whole Child," Ruth Weeks, president of NCTE in 1930, argues for intense attention to the feelings and spirits of students. Setting aside the "practical functions of English," she argues that English should help develop the "[w]hole personality for a complete and happy life. . . . The human soul has four faces: thought, feeling, action, and laughter. I think—therefore I am. I feel—therefore I desire. I act—therefore I become more than I am. I laugh—thereby I support the strain of life" (10). This view leads to writing instruction that observes facts, questions "supposed facts for genuineness and truth[,] . . . draw[s] original conclusions, . . . [and applies] theories gleaned from books to one's personal affairs" (11). Implicit in Weeks's approach is the assumption that much composition instruction will focus on writing about literature. She advocates for writing instruction that fosters deeper understandings of literature by outlining a multiple-part strategy that begins by asking what the author has actually said, then turns to questions of the genuineness or truth of the text, and finally examines its generalizability or application to life (11). All of this, according to Weeks, will be aided by writing.

Another assumption in Weeks's pronouncements is that English and writing in particular have much in common with aesthetics in fields such as dance, art, and music and that individual self-expression should be encouraged. This perspective on writing instruction grew out of psychological perspectives that valorized the individual. Influenced by theorists such as Hughes Mearns, who argued that "children speak naturally in a form that we adults are accustomed to call poetry" (65), and Harold Rugg, who advocated for writing that enabled students to give shape to both their external and their internal worlds (Rugg and Shumaker), Weeks and other writing instructors who shared her views advocated for writing as creative expression. In this view, writing can be learned but not necessarily taught. The role of the instructor is to provide occasions and environments that help students learn to write, and writing instruction should enable students to reflect on their experiences, ponder meanings, and develop their imaginations. This approach to writing instruction, like others with which it competed, would have been available to teachers in the 1930s in textbooks as well as in articles such as Weeks's, but it is difficult to know how teachers enacted these principles.

Although each approach to writing instruction had powerful defenders, no consensus developed. Indeed, when NCTE published *An Experience Curriculum in English* in 1935, the monograph contained affirmations of Scott's approach as well as approaches espousing social efficiency and individual expression. Contributors to *An Experience Curriculum in English* did not express concern about its eclecticism. In fact, Wilbur Hatfield, the editor, wrote,

> To attempt to create a single curriculum suited to pupils in environments so different as are to be found in the United States would be folly. The previous experiences and attainments, the capacities, the interests, the present and probably future needs are not the same for children in a city tenement neighborhood, for children in a wealthy suburb, and for children on the farm. Likewise, they are not the same for children in a New Hampshire village and for Mexican-speaking children in Texas. (NCTE Curriculum Commission v)

As Hatfield's explanation makes clear, tensions between various views of writing instruction could be accommodated by focusing on the local. If theorists could not agree among themselves, teachers could look to the specifics of their local context to determine and justify their instructional decisions.

Advocates of these various approaches to writing instruction continued to try to shape the teaching of writing in grades K–12 through the 1930s, but given the multiplicity of views, we cannot claim that any one perspective prevailed. Similarly, writing instruction at the college level was filled with conflicting messages about good composition teaching. Here, too, one response to these conflicts was to defer to the local. Fred Dudley, for example, in a 1939 article in the inaugural issue of *College English*, responded to concerns about the artificiality of writing in the first-year course by offering a number of specific suggestions for staffing and course content, but they were couched in an acknowledgment that their "practicability" would vary with local circumstances. Dudley reinforced this specificity of context by supporting his claims with illustrations from his own institution, Iowa State University. He explained, for example, that his students read articles "connected with campus problems" (24), they write about their "activity in campus organizations" (25), and they make arguments about topics such as "why he is or is not joining a fraternity" or "what he expects from his college course" (25). Dudley also detailed how Iowa State University addressed the issue of writing in disciplines other than English. This version of writing across the curriculum took a variety of locally constructed forms, including having teams of English and other subject matter specialists work together on improving student writing. As David Russell has documented, writing in academic disciplines dates back to the nineteenth century, and writing instruction in these contexts has frequently been locally constructed.

Another example of a local instantiation of composition instruction is that of Theodore Baird at Amherst College in Massachusetts. For nearly thirty years, from 1938 to 1966, Baird directed English 1 and 2, the first-year writing course at Amherst. During that period, over fifty instructors and some 6,000 students came under Baird's influence. Many of the instructors who went on to become professors at other colleges and universities—Walker Gibson at the University of Massachusetts, William Coles at the University of Pittsburgh, Roger Sale at the University of Washington, Richard Poirier at Rutgers University—carried Baird's approaches to teaching with them. As Robin Varnum describes it, Baird's pedagogy centered on conflict; students were encouraged to develop their own voices, but the route to that goal lay in wrestling with others (4). One of the hallmarks of Baird's teaching was his series of topically linked assignments, requiring of students frequent rethinking and revision. Here, for example, are several assignments from 1946 at Amherst College (Varnum 253–54):

1. Write a paper on an action you have repeatedly performed with distinction. Tell exactly how you performed this action on a particular occasion.
2. How did you learn this action? What did you do to learn? Define "learn" in this context.
3. Write a paper on an action you performed once and only once with distinction, an action you performed once but were unable to repeat. Tell exactly how you did it.
4. Rewrite assignment #1.

These assignments, developed by Baird and the other instructors of English 1 and 2, required students to draw on their own experiences and ideas. In English 1, students wrote more than thirty papers in the semester; in English 2, where the papers were longer, they wrote more than twenty compositions, for a total of approximately 24,000 words in the first year. By contrast, students at other colleges wrote approximately 14,000 words (Varnum 24).

Not far from Amherst College, at Dartmouth College, an institution similar in size, student profile, and goals, Albert Kitzhaber taught first-year writing during the 1960s. The first semester of the course, "Literature and Composition for Freshmen," emphasized developing students' capacity to appreciate literature and "develop clear thinking and correct and clear expression" (Kitzhaber 29). The course was organized around the literary works being read, and assignments focused on literary topics such as probing the evil of Richard III in Shakespeare's play or the role of a character in *Antony and Cleopatra*. Instructors at Dartmouth taught two courses (Amherst's taught three), and students wrote approximately 12,000 words. The second-term course, "Freshman Seminar in English," emphasized independent research and also focused on literature. As described by Kitzhaber, the course required students to engage in "independent study . . . [and] use of the library," but their topics had to be approved by instructors, and typical ones looked at literary themes or concepts such as tragedy or historical periods of literature (31–32). The sharp differences between the first-year writing programs at Amherst and Dartmouth illustrate how much local context, and even individual instructors, shaped the teaching of writing.

Larger social and political forces also continued to have a shaping effect on writing instruction. World War II and the accompanying military buildup brought further large-scale testing, the College Board playing a major role in this enterprise while simultaneously continuing its efforts to establish large-scale testing for college admissions. Writing figured prominently in both efforts, thereby continuing the linkage between composition and large-scale testing. At the college level, it was the postwar, GI Bill–supported influx of students into higher education that had the more profound effect on writing instruction. The exponential growth in the number of students requiring a first-year writing course during the late 1940s led to the founding of CCCC in 1950. Established as a group within NCTE, CCCC took as its responsibility a "systematic way of exchanging views and information quickly" among the then approximately 9,000 instructors teaching college composition (Gerber 12). While members of CCCC wanted to learn about successful programs at other institutions, they expressed no desire to identify one "good" theory of composition or to standardize the teaching of writing. Another indication of the emphasis on the local was evident in the urging, for both schools and colleges, that student work be published in local magazines. The lead article in the first issue of *College Composition and Communication* focused entirely on the importance and value of making the writing of first-year students visible to their peers to enhance motivation. Based on a survey of 186 English departments, the article detailed the various ways—projector, school newspaper, mimeograph, bulletin board, library shelf, alumni publication, and undergraduate publication—that student writing could be made available to other students (Wells). The general conclusion that the writing of other students is an important part of a first-year writing course underscores the value attached to the local.

During the 1950s, composition instruction continued to be a site of contest. Those who supported the view that writing is a creative activity argued that this approach offered the best way to achieve excellence in writing. Wilson Thornley, for example, urged the incorporation of more creative writing into the English curriculum, describing it as "a most severe and exacting discipline of the student's mind and spirit" (528), arguing that many educators had "unrealistic and inadequate estimates of creative writing" (530), and proposing that NCTE take leadership in this incorporation. The first volume of the five-volume NCTE Curriculum Series, published between 1952 and 1963, can be read as a response to this urging because it promoted creative approaches to writing instruction (NCTE Commission on the English Curriculum). At the same time, others who were concerned about the Cold War and competition with the Soviet Union urged that writing instruction focus more on expository writing to get things done in the world. In 1961, the NCTE Committee on National Interest published *The National Interest and the Teaching of English*, a document that aimed to position NCTE to receive National Defense Education Act funds, all of which had previously been directed toward mathematics, science, and foreign languages in the post-*Sputnik* era. As a result, funds were provided for the development of Project English, which established curriculum centers at a number of universities. Several centers addressed the teaching of writing, but creative writing did not figure prominently in this project. The focus was on practical expository writing that could communicate effectively and contribute to academic excellence.

Project English's emphasis on writing for academic excellence was not, of course, without its detractors, and one of the most powerful expressions of opposition came from the 1966 Dartmouth Conference, a meeting that brought American and British educators together to discuss, among other things, the teaching of writing. Under the influence of Project English, educators in the United States had been focusing on sequencing the curriculum and framing writing in terms of academic excellence. British educators, by contrast, had developed approaches to writing that emphasized the personal growth of students and encouraged the use of writing processes. The British approach bore some similarity to the earlier American emphasis on creative writing in that it focused on the development of the student rather than on the curriculum. The approach gained considerable prestige as a result of the Dartmouth Conference but also led to increased tension between the two instructional approaches, one emphasizing intellectual growth and the other emphasizing the personal growth of the writer.

Despite the conflicts among various approaches, the teaching of writing continued to flourish and grow. As composition studies moved toward becoming a disciplinary field, an increasingly scientific perspective on writing and writing instruction took shape. The 1963 publication of *Research in Written Composition* (Braddock, Lloyd-Jones, and Schoer) marked the beginning of efforts to study the processes of writing, as opposed to the products of writing that were of most interest to the testing movement. The goals and proposed methodologies of this book were designed to create an empirically based approach to writing instruction. Another pressure on teaching writing came from advocates of classical rhetoric who prompted a reconsideration of rhetoric, with increased attention to invention, which in turn led to more explicit classroom strategies for teaching writing. The publication of Edward P. J. Corbett's *Classical Rhetoric for the Modern Student* (1965) marked a moment when a textbook publisher judged this approach to be economically viable. Corbett's book was not a great commercial success, but it attracted considerable attention from instructors interested in applying rhetorical principles to the teaching of writing. Perhaps the strongest pressure on the teaching of writing resulted from Janet Emig's *The Composing Processes of Twelfth Graders*, published in 1971. This set of case studies answered the call for a more scientific approach to writing instruction—even though it used qualitative rather than quantitative methods—and it offered a description of writing that could be translated into pedagogy for every level, from elementary school to college. Terms such as *prewriting*, *drafting*, and *revising* entered the lexicon of writing instructors, creating the appearance of a unified approach.

Actually, however, teaching writing processes was and is much more varied than the terminology would suggest. Both informal observation and more systematic examination showed that process-based instruction takes many forms. For James Berlin, for example, assuming that "differences in approaches to teaching writing can be explained by attending to the degree of emphasis given to universally defined elements of a universally defined composing process" (765) was wrong-headed. Different approaches to instruction, Berlin claimed, were not prompted by differences in views of composing processes. Rather, varying conceptions of the writer, reality, audience, and language shaped differences in writing instruction. Citing textbooks, scholarly accounts of various theorists, and specific terminology used by advocates of different positions, Berlin described four categories—neo-Aristotelians or classicists, positivists or current-traditionalists, neo-Platonists or expressionists, and new rhetoricians—that characterize varying approaches to teaching writing. Although these categories have been much contested, they illustrate the impossibility of identifying "good" composition instruction because aspects of each can be defined as "good."

In the 1970s, the local context remained, as it had in previous decades, a powerful force for shaping writing instruction. One example of this is the open admissions policy enacted in the City University of New York (CUNY) system. Mina Shaughnessy's "Diving In: An Introduction to Basic Writing," published in 1976, brought open admissions students into full view, and her *Errors and Expectations: A Guide for the Teacher of Basic Writing*, issued the following year, offered a revolutionary pedagogy based on careful attention to the language of the least able students. The context in which Shaughnessy taught had everything to do with the way she approached writing instruction. In the preface to *Errors and Expectations*, she describes the motivation for her work:

> I remember sitting alone in the worn urban classroom where my students had just written their first essays and where I now began to read them, hoping to be able to assess quickly the sort of task that lay ahead of us that semester. But the writing was so stunningly unskilled that I could not begin to define the task nor even sort out the difficulties. I could only sit there reading and re-reading the alien papers, wondering what had gone wrong and trying to understand what I at the eleventh hour of my students' academic lives could do about it. (vii)

Shaughnessy also positions her CUNY students in highly contextualized terms:

> academic winners and losers from the best and worst high schools in the country, the children of the lettered and the illiterate, the blue-collared, the white-collared and the unemployed, some who could barely afford the subway fare to school . . . in short, the sons and daughters of New Yorkers, reflecting that city's intense, troubled version of America. (2)

Shaughnessy's advice about teaching basic writers may have been taken up by instructors from many parts of the country, but clearly it grew out of the local New York City context.

Paralleling the increased attention to the student, whether the basic writers in Shaughnessy's class or the more talented writers who were encouraged to use writing for personal growth, was a greater focus on the teacher of writing. A shaping force in secondary and elementary school writing instruction was the National

Writing Project (NWP), founded in 1974 by James Gray. Starting from the principle that effective teachers could be the best instructors of other teachers, he created a national network of writing project sites that enabled teachers to gather for four-week summer institutes. Although all the sites in the NWP's national network embrace a model that includes the teacher as writer, active learning from the classroom practices of other teachers, and a background in composition studies, the NWP was and still is a federation that acknowledges and affirms the local contexts of individual sites. Teachers who participate in the summer invitational institute may follow the same general pattern of daily writing, workshops, and presentations, but the specific content will vary from site to site, according to local needs. In the thirty-plus years of its existence, the NWP has had an enormous influence on the teaching of writing in the common schools, providing professional development for many thousands of teachers, and yet it has always remained grounded in the local context.

In higher education, instructors in composition also have become increasingly professionalized. Before the 1970s, most of those who taught writing were trained in literature, or occasionally in linguistics or language study. In the final decades of the twentieth century, however, graduate programs in rhetoric and composition began to develop. The proliferation of dissertations and scholarship in the field led to the expansion of publication venues during the 1980s. University presses at Southern Illinois University and the University of Pittsburgh began publishing books by and for composition instructors, and journals such as *Composition Studies* (formerly *Freshman English News*), *Rhetoric Review*, *The Writing Instructor*, and *Written Communication* joined *College English* and *College Composition and Communication* as publications in which composition instructors could place their work. Membership in CCCC grew significantly. In 1974 there were 3,485 members, and in 1994 there were over 8,500.

The emergence of new technologies changed writing instruction for both K–12 and college teachers. Computers and their word-processing programs emerged during the 1980s, and in the ensuing decades they fostered process-based instruction because the new technology made revision much easier. Instead of retyping pages or cutting and pasting text, writers could cut and paste electronically to revise their work. While this digital form eased the process of writing, it also introduced new economic considerations since computerized word-processing systems were expensive, thus barring access for students of modest means. Though access to computers has become more widespread in recent years, broadband access to the Internet, where much writing occurs, remains unevenly distributed in student populations. Research shows that while some students have full-time access to all the resources of the Internet for their writing, others must rely on dial-up or public computers to support their writing; furthermore, students have different levels of comfort with digital technologies ("Are All Youth Digital Natives?"). In this, as in other ways, local contexts shape what students can be expected to accomplish with their writing.

Increased pressure for accountability in education generally began to mount in the early 1990s and continued into the new century. In collaboration with the International Reading Association, NCTE developed *Standards for the English Language Arts*; this document includes several standards focused on writing, among them the following:

4. Students adjust their use of spoken, written, and visual language (e.g., conventions, style, vocabulary) to communicate effectively with a variety of audiences and for different purposes.
5. Students employ a wide range of strategies as they write and use different writing process elements appropriately to communicate with different audiences for a variety of purposes.
6. Students apply knowledge of language structure, language conventions (e.g., spelling and punctuation), media techniques, figurative language, and genre to create, critique, and discuss print and nonprint texts. (IRA and NCTE)

Many states also developed standards for writing instruction and, in keeping with a growing emphasis on student achievement as a measure of effective teaching, these standards usually emphasize what students should learn to do. Not surprisingly, there has been significant variation in standards from one state to another and between state and national standards. Here, as in many other areas of writing instruction, local context contributes to the differences. The federal presence in writing standards and, potentially, in assessment continues to the present. Achieve's American Diploma Project, for example, included standards for writing, and as I write, the Council of Chief State School Officers and the National Governors Association have joined forces to create national high school graduation standards that include core standards for writing.

The emergence of standards has been accompanied by an increase in high-stakes tests of writing. Virtually every state has instituted an assessment program in the common schools that puts writing at the center. The prompts, genres, and rubrics all differ, but it has become increasingly impossible to graduate from high school without succeeding on a state-sponsored writing test. Examples of the variation in the required writing test on the SAT and the optional writing test on the American College Testing Program's ACT, both of which were introduced in 2005, have increased writing's role in assessment. No doubt the teaching of writing has been shaped by these new tests, but it is difficult to ascertain how much and in precisely what ways. Anecdotal reports claim that the genres that appear on a state test are the ones that receive classroom attention, and the emphasis on writing under the pressure of time leads many teachers to incorporate impromptu writing as well as test-taking strategies into the writing curriculum.

At the same time that standards and assessment push toward conformity and reductive approaches to teaching writing, a counterforce at play sees increases in the amount and type of writing being done in the United States. Articles about teaching writing in 2009 include attention to writing for various social networks operating on the Internet as well as for a variety of audiences and purposes. The Internet also provides venues for making students' writing visible to their peers; this new technology offers another means of addressing the long-standing need to enhance motivation by publishing student writing. New understandings of genre as a form of social action have generated renewed interest in incorporating issues of style and language into the teaching of writing. Though the working conditions of writing teachers remain a problem, especially as economic constraints lead to increased class sizes, the teaching of writing outside schools and colleges continues to grow as business and government invest millions of dollars in training employees to write effectively and as self-sponsored groups of writers work together to hone their skills.

The increasingly strong links between writing and the world of work parallel but also extend far beyond the concerns of the social efficiency movement of the 1930s. In the largest sense, writing has always been connected to work, and to commerce in particular. Developed by Sumerians who needed a way to record their business transactions, writing owes its origins to economic systems. In the United States, writing masters in the Colonial period enacted this ontology by teaching only male pupils, since boys were expected to grow up to enter professional or vocational fields that required writing. Girls, in contrast, were taught only reading, since there was no economic reason for them to learn to write. Today the links between writing and the marketplace are less gendered, but they have grown stronger as our economy has shifted away from industrial manufacturing toward service and knowledge economies that emphasize the production and distribution of information. Deborah Brandt argues, based on her recent study of workplace writing, that because of "recent economic, social and technological changes, writing is coming to rival reading as a condition of mass literate experience" (144). Many of today's workers write more than their parents or grandparents did because it is one of the conditions of employment. The proliferation of writing in the workplace has fostered an increase in work-based writing instruction. Business and government currently spend a great deal of money to teach employees how to write effectively. This dimension of writing instruction merits our attention, but it points to an even larger issue that will challenge teachers of writing in the twenty-first century. Brandt puts it this way:

> At least until now school-based writing has functioned largely within the ideological arrangements of a reading literacy; its moral and civic and even economic standing has been garnered indirectly through the high cultural values accorded to reading. But now the equation reverses as the value of reading comes to depend on the transactional status of writing and as literate experience throughout the life span develops increasingly in contexts of commerce, production, competition, private subsidy

> and surveillance. Can mass writing claim a moral authority powerful enough to transform the social institutions that were organized to serve readers over writers? The United States was founded as a nation of readers. How equipped are we for sustaining a nation of writers? (158)

Implicit in Brandt's challenge is the assumption that school-based writing instruction at all levels will need to transform itself in fundamental ways to accommodate the realignments in literacy practices. Brandt argues that it is possible to credit writing with the "perspective taking, reflection, consciousness of language as language," and creativity that has been ascribed to reading (157); however, claiming those dimensions of reading's moral authority will require a profound rethinking of the ways we teach writing, as well as the assumptions that guide that teaching. Strategies for meeting this challenge will, of course, need to take multiple forms because the local conditions vary so widely. Still, the next decades of writing instruction promise to be interesting as well as challenging.

Looking across the first one hundred years of NCTE history, we can see enduring issues and themes as well as the sustaining presence of a professional association that has served and been served by thousands of teachers of writing. It is tempting to end on a note of commonality, but the contests and tensions that have been evident throughout the past century cannot be so easily dismissed. Indeed, the very nature of writing instruction militates against it. From its earliest manifestations, the teaching of writing in this country has been shaped by local contexts, rendering it an activity that cannot be contained within a single paradigm or model. More important, the nature of writing itself, its close connection to the material and economic world, its links to the functional and technological, and its dependence on multiple but partial knowledges—all of these position the teaching of writing as a highly varied practice. A phrase such as "good composition teaching" means many different things, depending on the particular combination of the "present circumstances," and these meanings will continue to proliferate as NCTE moves toward its next centennial.

Works Cited

Anderson, Melville B. "The Instruction in English at Stanford University." *Dial* 16.186 (1894): 167–70. *Online Books Page.* Web. 3 Aug. 2009.

"Are All Youth Digital Natives?" *Berkman Center for Internet & Society.* Harvard U, 5 Mar. 2008. Web. 30 July 2009.

Berlin, James A. "Contemporary Composition: The Major Pedagogical Theories." *College English* 44.8 (1982): 765–77. Print.

Braddock, Richard, Richard Lloyd-Jones, and Lowell Schoer. *Research in Written Composition.* Champaign, IL: NCTE, 1963. Print.

Brandt, Deborah. *Literacy and Learning: Reflections on Writing, Reading, and Society.* San Francisco: Jossey-Bass, 2009. Print.

———. *Literacy in American Lives.* New York: Cambridge UP, 2001. Print.

Chubb, Percival. *The Teaching of English in the Elementary and Secondary School.* New York: Macmillan, 1902. Print.

Clark, A. Bess. "Problem for Composition Teaching." *English Journal* 13.5 (1924): 320–24. Print.

Cook, Albert S. "English at Yale University." *Dial* 16.183 (1894): 69–71. *Online Books Page.* Web. 3 Aug. 2009.

Corbett, Edward P. J. *Classical Rhetoric for the Modern Student.* New York: Oxford UP, 1965. Print.

Corson, Hiram. "English Literature at Cornell University." *Dial* 16.187 (1894): 201–02. *Online Books Page.* Web. 3 Aug. 2009.

Dudley, Fred A. "The Success of Freshman English" *College English* 1.1 (1939): 22–30. Print.

Elliot, Norbert. *On a Scale: A Social History of Writing Assessment in America.* New York: Lang, 2005. Print.

Emig, Janet. *The Composing Processes of Twelfth Graders.* Urbana, IL: NCTE, 1971. Print. NCTE Research Report No. 13.

Gerber, John C. "The Conference on College Composition and Communication." *College Composition and Communication* 1.1 (1950): 12. Print.

Gere, Anne Ruggles. "Initial Report on Survey of CCCC Members." Urbana, IL: NCTE, 12 Jan. 2009. Print.

———. *Intimate Practices: Literacy and Cultural Work in U.S. Women's Clubs, 1880–1920*. Urbana: U of Illinois P, 1997. Print.

———. *Writing Groups: History, Theory, and Implications*. Carbondale: Southern Illinois UP; Urbana, IL: CCCC/NCTE, 1987. Print. Studies in Writing and Rhetoric (SWR) series.

Hinsdale, B. A. *Teaching the Language Arts: Speech, Reading, Composition*. New York: Appleton, 1896. Print.

Hopkins, Edwin M. "Can Good Composition Teaching Be Done under Present Conditions?" *English Journal* 1.1 (1912): 1–8. Print.

———, comp. *The Labor and Cost of the Teaching of English in Colleges and Secondary Schools, with Especial Reference to English Composition*. Chicago: NCTE, 1923. Print.

Hosic, James Fleming, comp. *Reorganization of English in Secondary Schools: Report by the National Joint Committee on English Representing the Commission on the Reorganization of Secondary Education of the National Education Association and the National Council of Teachers of English*. Washington, DC: GPO, 1917. Print. Dept. of the Interior, US Bureau of Education, Bulletin 1917, No. 2.

International Reading Association, and National Council of Teachers of English. *Standards for the English Language Arts*. Newark, DE: IRA; Urbana, IL: NCTE, 1996. *National Council of Teachers of English*. Web. 30 July 2009.

Kitzhaber, Albert R. *Rhetoric in American Colleges, 1850–1900*. Dallas: Southern Methodist UP, 1990. Print.

Lemann, Nicholas. *The Big Test: The Secret History of the American Meritocracy*. New York: Farrar, 2000. Print.

Marye, Mary E. "A Form for Rating Textbooks in English Composition Prepared for the Ninth and Tenth Grades." *School Review* 38.2 (1930): 124–37. Print.

Matthews, Brander. "English at Columbia College." *Dial* 16.184 (1894): 101–02. *Online Books Page*. Web. 3 Aug. 2009.

Mearns, Hughes. *Creative Power: The Education of Youth in the Creative Arts*. 2nd rev. ed. New York: Dover, 1958. Print.

National Council of Teachers of English Commission on the English Curriculum. *The English Language Arts.* New York: Appleton, 1952. Print.

National Council of Teachers of English Committee on National Interest. *The National Interest and the Teaching of English: A Report on the Status of the Profession.* Champaign, IL: NCTE, 1961. Print.

National Council of Teachers of English Curriculum Commission. *An Experience Curriculum in English: A Report of the Curriculum Commission of the National Council of Teachers of English.* New York: Appleton, 1935. Print.

National Endowment for the Arts. *Reading at Risk: A Survey of Literary Reading in America.* Washington, DC: National Endowment for the Arts, 2004. Print. Research Division Report No. 46.

Popken, Randall. "Edwin Hopkins and the Costly Labor of Composition Teaching." *College Composition and Communication* 55.4 (2004): 618–41. Print.

Rugg, Harold Ordway, and Ann Shumaker. *The Child-Centered School.* New York: World Book, 1928. Print.

Russell, David R. *Writing in the Academic Disciplines, 1870–1990: A Curricular History.* Carbondale: Southern Illinois UP, 1991. Print.

Scott, Fred Newton. "Efficiency for Efficiency's Sake." *School Review* 23.1 (1915): 34–42. Print.

———. "Rhetoric Rediviva." *College Composition and Communication* 31.4 (1980): 413–19. Print.

———. "The Undefended Gate." *English Journal* 3.1 (1914): 1–14. Print.

Shaughnessy, Mina P. "Diving In: An Introduction to Basic Writing." *College Composition and Communication* 27.3 (1976): 234–39. Print.

———. *Errors and Expectations: A Guide for the Teacher of Basic Writing.* New York: Oxford UP, 1977. Print.

Shultz, Staci. "Access, Agency, and Agenda: How Online Fan Fiction Communities Sponsor Emerging Literacies." Diss. U of Michigan, forthcoming. Print.

Smith, Dora V. "The Danger of Dogma Concerning Composition Content." *English Journal* 15.6 (1926): 414–25. Print.

Spring, Joel. *The American School, 1642–1985: Varieties of Historical Interpretation of the Foundations and Development of American Education.* New York: Longman, 1986. Print.

Taylor, J. M. "The Report of the Committee of Ten." *School Review* 2.4 (1894): 193–99. Print.

Taylor, Warner. *A National Survey of Conditions in Freshman English.* Madison: U of Wisconsin, 1929. Print. University of Wisconsin Bureau of Educational Research Bulletin No. 11.

Thornley, Wilson R. "The Case for Creative Writing." *English Journal* 44.9 (1955): 528–31. Print.

Varnum, Robin. *Fencing with Words: A History of Writing Instruction at Amherst College during the Era of Theodore Baird, 1938–1966.* Urbana, IL: NCTE, 1996. Print.

Weeks, Ruth Mary. "Teaching the Whole Child." *English Journal* 20.1 (1931): 9–17. Print.

Wells, Edith. "College Publications of Freshman Writing." *College Composition and Communication* 1.1 (1950): 3–11. Print.

Wendell, Barrett. "English at Harvard." *Dial* 16.185 (1894): 131–33. *The Online Books Page.* Web. 3 Aug. 2009.

READING THE PAST. WRITING THE FUTURE.

A Blast from the Past

Did you know that the first NCTE Achievement Awards in Writing were given in 1958? The idea for the program originated with NCTE Past President Paul Farmer; at that time, secondary schools nominated outstanding juniors on the basis of samples of in-class and out-of-class writing as well as a test of the student's "ability to recognize and construct good sentences, recognize effective diction and appropriate stylistic devices, recognize accepted punctuation and spelling, and show an understanding of principles of organization."

Nominees were judged by state committees representing English teachers' organizations and the NCTE Committee on Awards. Winners received a certificate of recognition, "a scroll, plus a recommendation to colleges, universities, and scholarship donors that each winner be granted a college scholarship." Though the winners were announced in the *Bulletin* of the National Association of Secondary School Principals, some of the association's members doubted that "student participation in general essay contests" would improve writing ability. The association nevertheless continued to approve the NCTE Achievement Awards as a scholarship examination.

NCTE Annual Conventions

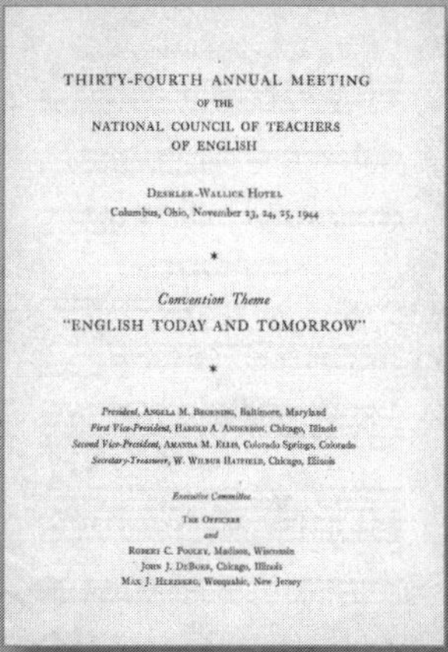

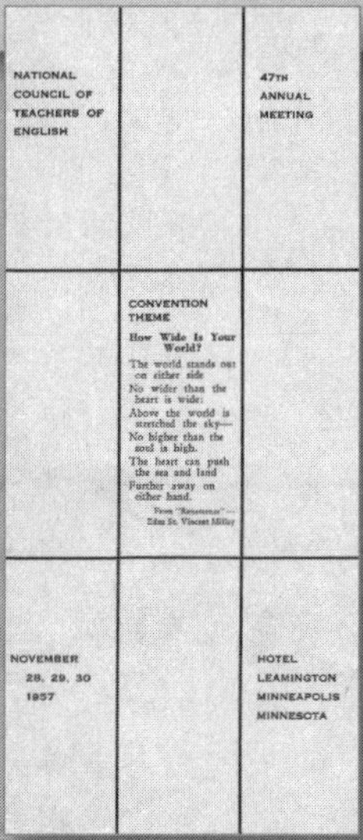

58TH ANNUAL CONVENTION
NATIONAL COUNCIL OF TEACHERS OF ENGLISH
MILWAUKEE WISCONSIN

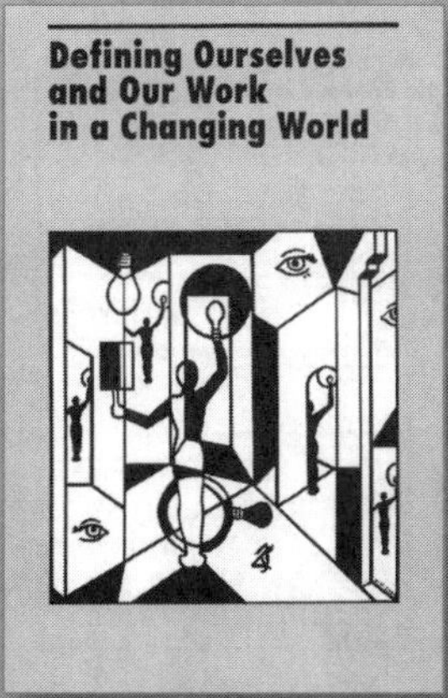

Defining Ourselves and Our Work in a Changing World

The Compleat Teacher:
Bringing Together Knowledge, Experience, and Research
trace the path
inspire
interact
understand
everything we know and do
National Council of Teachers of English

NCTE Governance

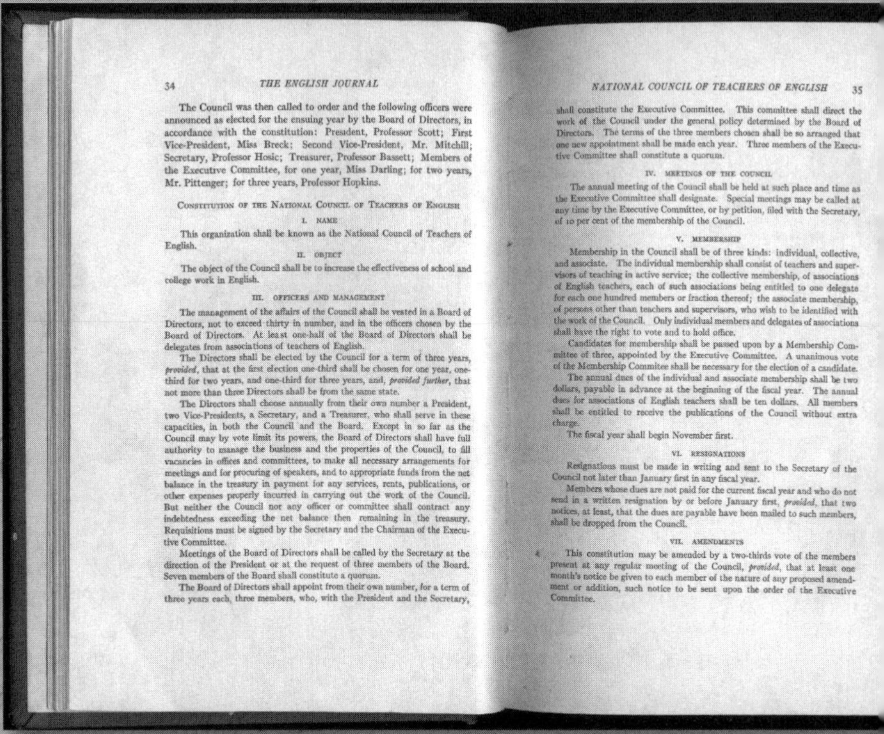

34 *THE ENGLISH JOURNAL*

The Council was then called to order and the following officers were announced as elected for the ensuing year by the Board of Directors, in accordance with the constitution: President, Professor Scott; First Vice-President, Miss Breck; Second Vice-President, Mr. Mitchill; Secretary, Professor Hosic; Treasurer, Professor Bassett; Members of the Executive Committee, for one year, Miss Darling; for two years, Mr. Pittenger; for three years, Professor Hopkins.

CONSTITUTION OF THE NATIONAL COUNCIL OF TEACHERS OF ENGLISH

I. NAME

This organization shall be known as the National Council of Teachers of English.

II. OBJECT

The object of the Council shall be to increase the effectiveness of school and college work in English.

III. OFFICERS AND MANAGEMENT

The management of the affairs of the Council shall be vested in a Board of Directors, not to exceed thirty in number, and in the officers chosen by the Board of Directors. At least one-half of the Board of Directors shall be delegates from associations of teachers of English.

The Directors shall be elected by the Council for a term of three years, *provided*, that at the first election one-third shall be chosen for one year, one-third for two years, and one-third for three years, and, *provided further*, that not more than three Directors shall be from the same state.

The Directors shall choose annually from their own number a President, two Vice-Presidents, a Secretary, and a Treasurer, who shall serve in these capacities, in both the Council and the Board. Except in so far as the Council may by vote limit its powers, the Board of Directors shall have full authority to manage the business and the properties of the Council, to fill vacancies in offices and committees, to make all necessary arrangements for meetings and for procuring of speakers, and to appropriate funds from the net balance in the treasury in payment for any services, rents, publications, or other expenses properly incurred in carrying out the work of the Council. But neither the Council nor any officer or committee shall contract any indebtedness exceeding the net balance then remaining in the treasury. Requisitions must be signed by the Secretary and the Chairman of the Executive Committee.

Meetings of the Board of Directors shall be called by the Secretary at the direction of the President or at the request of three members of the Board. Seven members of the Board shall constitute a quorum.

The Board of Directors shall appoint from their own number, for a term of three years each, three members, who, with the President and the Secretary,

NATIONAL COUNCIL OF TEACHERS OF ENGLISH 35

shall constitute the Executive Committee. This committee shall direct the work of the Council under the general policy determined by the Board of Directors. The terms of the three members chosen shall be so arranged that one new appointment shall be made each year. Three members of the Executive Committee shall constitute a quorum.

IV. MEETINGS OF THE COUNCIL

The annual meeting of the Council shall be held at such place and time as the Executive Committee shall designate. Special meetings may be called at any time by the Executive Committee, or by petition, filed with the Secretary, of 10 per cent of the membership of the Council.

V. MEMBERSHIP

Membership in the Council shall be of three kinds: individual, collective, and associate. The individual membership shall consist of teachers and supervisors of teaching in active service; the collective membership, of associations of English teachers, each of such associations being entitled to one delegate for each one hundred members or fraction thereof; the associate membership, of persons other than teachers and supervisors, who wish to be identified with the work of the Council. Only individual members and delegates of associations shall have the right to vote and to hold office.

Candidates for membership shall be passed upon by a Membership Committee of three, appointed by the Executive Committee. A unanimous vote of the Membership Commitee shall be necessary for the election of a candidate.

The annual dues of the individual and associate membership shall be two dollars, payable in advance at the beginning of the fiscal year. The annual dues for associations of English teachers shall be ten dollars. All members shall be entitled to receive the publications of the Council without extra charge.

The fiscal year shall begin November first.

VI. RESIGNATIONS

Resignations must be made in writing and sent to the Secretary of the Council not later than January first in any fiscal year.

Members whose dues are not paid for the current fiscal year and who do not send in a written resignation by or before January first, *provided*, that two notices, at least, that the dues are payable have been mailed to such members, shall be dropped from the Council.

VII. AMENDMENTS

This constitution may be amended by a two-thirds vote of the members present at any regular meeting of the Council, *provided*, that at least one month's notice be given to each member of the nature of any proposed amendment or addition, such notice to be sent upon the order of the Executive Committee.

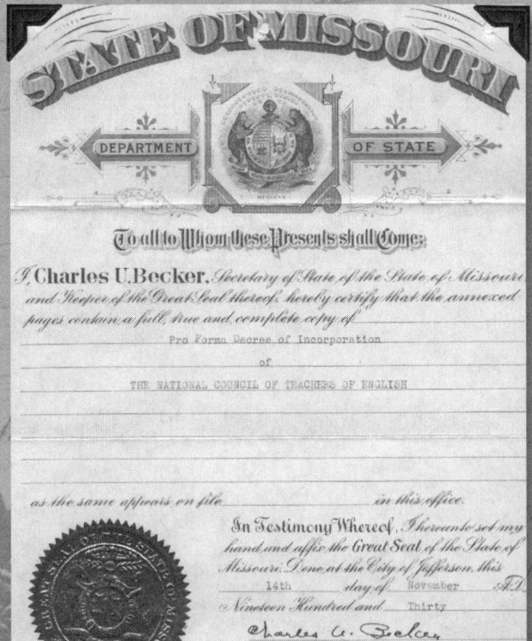

STATE OF MISSOURI

DEPARTMENT OF STATE

To all to Whom these Presents shall Come:

I, Charles U. Becker, Secretary of State of the State of Missouri and Keeper of the Great Seal thereof, hereby certify that the annexed pages contain a full, true and complete copy of

Pro Forma Decree of Incorporation

of

THE NATIONAL COUNCIL OF TEACHERS OF ENGLISH

as the same appears on file in this office.

In Testimony Whereof, I hereunto set my hand and affix the Great Seal of the State of Missouri. Done at the City of Jefferson, this 14th day of November A.D. Nineteen Hundred and Thirty

Charles U. Becker

SECRETARY OF STATE

Chapter Four

Teaching Language

Stephen Tchudi
Chico, California

The National Council of Teachers of English (NCTE) did not have to create a tradition of language teaching from scratch in 1911. It inherited a long and complex history of language instruction, including 2,500 years of schooling in Greek and Latin, a thousand-year-plus evolution of modern English from its Anglo-Saxon roots, a growing body of scholarship on that language's diverse origins, several hundred years of broad agreement on "Standard" or "King's" English, a feisty and distinct emerging American English language and literature, a "Latinate" grammar of English created during the Enlightenment, a long history of teaching two of the three *R*s in the "grammar" schools, and a century of democratization of American public schooling that had created a demand for mother-tongue instruction (Fries, *Teaching of the English Language*; Laird; Marckwardt; NCTE, *Basic Issues*).

The Council also inherited methods of teaching language, many of them emerging from instruction in Latin as well as English. They reflected Enlightenment confidence in learning through rule study (made explicit by Lindley Murray, the leading textbook author of the nineteenth century), parsing (writing out the grammatical characteristics of every word in a passage, including language taken from literary works), the sentence diagram (invented by Alonzo Reed and Brainerd Kellogg as an alternative to parsing), exercises in the correction of "false syntax," and rigorous red-penciling of errors on student themes (Fries, *Teaching*; Goldstein; Liebert; Rivlin; Pollock, DeVane, and Spiller; NCTE Commission on the English Curriculum, *English Language Arts*; Radner).

Those traditions in teaching had firmly ensconced grammar at the center of the language curriculum, coupled with what Sterling Andrus Leonard came to call "the doctrine of correctness" in English usage (*Doctrine of Correctness*). As early as 1914, the NCTE Committee on the Articulation of the Elementary and High School Course in English worried, "Grammar is an educational bug-a-boo, a much terrifying but really harmless mumbo-jumbo. It should be subject to missionary attack. This Committee wishes to be counted among the first of those to take a hand at the rope to pull down this heathen idol" (NCTE Committee on the Articulation 309).

After a century of research, scholarship, and teaching experiences, a good many Council members are still tugging at the rope that might topple formal grammar and the doctrine of correctness, if not as idols, perhaps as a multiheaded creature, a Cerberus or Hydra, a cat of infinite lives that has managed to persist in shaping public perceptions of school and college English instruction.

The Council's history of language study obviously contains much more than the shoutings of a crowd clustered around the statue of grammar. In this chapter, I must necessarily write a good deal about grammar in its various permutations and incarnations, but I don't want grammar to appear to be the only component of NCTE's history of language education. As I examine the one-hundred-year dialectic over language in the annals of NCTE, I explore three major themes, discussing them incidentally within the chronological context of the Council's history. These strands include

- NCTE's ongoing efforts to understand social contexts for schooling and language, including the need to serve diverse student populations while meeting the expectations of the general public, the media, and school governing bodies who seek students' mastery of "Standard" English

- The integration of current or "modern" views of the nature of language itself, including grammars, usage, and sociolinguistics; linguistic scholarship; and the burgeoning volume of knowledge and understanding of the role of language in human consciousness and learning

- Discovery and dissemination of best practices in the learning of language, including both first and second language learners and speakers of a variety of dialects and registers

Other writers in this collection examine in detail the causes that led to the formation of NCTE, but it is important to emphasize that an overarching goal of the Council's founders was to break the stranglehold of college entrance requirements on the schools (Hosic). While much of that debate centered on reading lists and writing practice, the colleges had consistently focused on surface correctness. The Harvard Reports, for example, lambasted the schools for their perceived failures in college preparation, particularly correct writing. Harvard faculty members felt that they must do the work of the lower schools: "In quantity this work is simply appalling; while the performance of it involves not only a constant and unremitted industry, but mental drudgery of the most exhausting nature" (*Report of the Committee on Composition and Rhetoric* 75).

In a widely distributed book, *Freshman English and Theme-Correcting in Harvard College*, Harvard instructors C. T. Copeland and H. M. Rideout explained for the benefit of public and private secondary school teachers how the Harvard model assigned themes daily, weekly, and "fortnightly," all to be rigorously corrected. Just in case teachers didn't get the point, the book included a foldout poster showing a student theme printed in facsimile, with the instructor's detailed corrections overprinted in crimson.

In 1893 the National Education Association's Committee of Ten, in its *Report of the Committee on Secondary School Studies*, had attempted to place correctness in context, saying that "a student may be taught to speak and write good English without receiving any special instruction in formal grammar" (qtd. in Rivlin 8). The committee had also declared that grammar instruction could be "incidental," linked to reading and writing, but it also reinforced older notions of mental discipline from faculty psychology in alleging grammar to be useful in "training of thought." The grammar idol was acknowledged in the Committee of Ten's call for students to be trained in "recognizing the parts of speech" in order to "analyze sentences as to structure and syntax" (Rivlin 6–12).

The inaugural 1912 volume of *English Journal* demonstrates the range of consensus and dissent over issues of grammar and correctness. W. D. Lewis of William Penn High School in Philadelphia rejoiced that "we are using less red ink" on student themes, rejecting the tradition that had led some teachers "to plod our weary way to the waiting midnight lamp and the red ink bottle" (13).

But rebellion against grammar among some teachers caused Charles Swain Thomas, from Newton High School in Massachusetts, to declare, "It is a mistake for the high-school teacher to assume that the teaching of grammar is not his proper function" (85). A gradual decline in the popularity of Latin in the schools led Cyrus Lauron Hooper of Chicago Teachers College to test knowledge of grammar among students entering his program. He found that students who had studied Latin knew more grammar than students who had studied only English grammar, but he noted further that students who had studied German grammar did better than both the English and Latin students. Hooper cautiously concluded that students should have

> either careful training in an inflected language, including careful translation into idiomatic English, or their training in English grammar should be as much as possible after the Latin method of instruction—the constant analysis of sentences as they stand in the paragraph, and always with accuracy of sentence structure. (403)

Much of the concern for language among Council members in the early years was centered on written forms, principally student compositions. Oral language was not taught as the primary form of school English. In fact, before the Council had reached the age of four, some members left the organization, dissatisfied with the way in which speech and its teachers were being treated. Writing on the occasion of the fiftieth anniversary of the Speech Association of America, Giles Wilkeson Gray, former editor of *Speech Association Quarterly*, explained, "Probably the one incident which actually gave, though unintentionally, the basic impulse to the establishment of our organization, was the establishment, in 1910, of the National Council of Teachers of English." He continued,

> In most institutions . . . whatever was being done in the area of speech was actually being carried out under the direction, even the sufferance, of departments of English, which had come to assume a sort of proprietary right over all forms of verbal communication in which the English language was used. Speech had come to be identified with English. Many of those who most strongly advocated this point of view were unable to see any difference between speaking and writing as variant forms of communication. (342)

Speech advocates within the Council had asked for more space at the annual meeting with programs "organized by themselves, for themselves, and devoted to their own problems, about which the main body of the Council knew almost nothing at all, and in which they were not really interested." According to Gray's history, NCTE members were "recalcitrant," and the speech advocates were particularly incensed by an NCTE member who asked, "If a man can write, can he not also speak? Does not the greater encompass the lesser?" Speech teachers at the 1914 NCTE Annual Convention—Gray lists seventeen attendees—passed a resolution withdrawing from NCTE and establishing the "National Association of Academic Teachers of Public Speaking" (342–43).

It would be inaccurate to say that NCTE totally ignored oral English or public speaking. In a 1915 *English Journal* article, Rachel Dithridge, English teacher at Eastern District High School in Brooklyn, described her school's "Speech Improvement Week," explaining,

> Now I wonder that the idea of Speech Improvement Week did not occur to some of us long ago! The increased interest in oral English among all teachers, the insistence on the part of teachers of English that responsibility for speech must be shared by teachers of other subjects, and the recognition accorded the importance of spoken English in educational journals, combine to make this an opportune time for a systematic and united effort toward improved speech. Surely the elocution teacher should lead in this attempt. (465)

The week at Eastern District High School was no minor effort and included workshops and lectures (one by the superintendent of schools, "whose interest in oral language is well known"), graphics prepared by the Poster Club with "brief quotations, emphasizing some important idea in connection with speech," a debate between the boys' and girls' debate clubs, a series of articles in the school newspaper on "various phases of our speech problem," and a "pronunciation match, conducted by the sentence method, devised by the head of our English department" (465–66). Dithridge also emphasized that, at Eastern District High School, "the pupils are largely of foreign parentage and hence the keen consciousness of their need is a constant spur to effort" (465–66).

Nevertheless, it is clear that in the early years of the Council, even as the direct teaching of grammar and usage was being debated, the major focus was on the written word rather than the spoken. Many Council members were concerned not only about the relevance of grammar instruction to speech or writing, but also with the accuracy and precision of the grammars themselves. At the first annual business meeting of the Council, Professor Lewis complained that teachers lacked "uniform nomenclature," that "it is not necessary for our school grammars to carry a mass of unscientific, factitious, make believe phraseology, the residue of an obsolete psychology" (NCTE, "National Council" 37). In the inaugural issue of *English Journal,* C. R. Rounds wrote,

> At the present time, in twenty-five English grammar texts there are ten different names for the use of *good* in the sentence "He is good," and eighteen different names for the use of *red* in the sentence, "We painted our barn red." . . . Is it any wonder that our students do not know English grammar? ("Uniform Grammatical Nomenclature" 53).

Rounds and Lewis were not alone in their concern, and a Uniform Terminology Committee was established and continued as a Council interest for decades. In 1945, Rounds wrote a retrospective on that movement: "[W]hat we want is not a gathering of philologists, but a group of sensible, dependable, practical teachers of grammar well equipped with a sense of humor and a knowledge both of grammar and of how difficult it is for children to grapple with abstractions" ("Historical Sketch" 216). The uniform terminology group was not objecting to—indeed, may not have known about—the Latinate biases of traditional grammar; rather, it wanted order brought out of a perceived chaos in traditional grammar.

Writing in 1913 of the need to make "adjustments" in the teaching of grammar, Lemuel Brown of the Cleveland Normal School recited some traditional values for teaching grammar such as aiding correctness, assisting in the interpretation of literature, and providing "elementary logic" (81). He called for some "formal analysis" in the classroom but added that "drill is how [good English] is learned, especially in the elementary grades preceding formal study" (81). Brown concluded by setting an elevated and ambitious goal for the teacher: "[W]e should be satisfied if our pupils use English idiom as spoken by university presidents and scholars of English" (83). Obviously, Brown's "adjustments" to language study differed very little from the kind of correctness that colleges and textbooks had been advocating, through grammar, for a good deal of the previous century.

Lemuel Brown's essay is interesting, too, for some light it casts on English as a second language, a topic that received far less attention in early Council publications than concerns for the college-bound student. With his assumption that good English idiom was that of scholars and university presidents, Brown had only a paternalistic interest in the problems faced by nonnative speakers. He wrote: "I have among my keepsakes a dear little composition on 'The Coming of the Pilgrims.' The author—and I use the term advisedly—is a dear little girl with snapping black eyes, whose name suggests sunny Italy" (86). Her composition, Brown continued, "seems like some unfortunate quadruped wallowing in black ink," including such "grammatical monstrosities as 'mens' and 'did been'" (86). Despite his apparent horror at her second language English, Brown entered a plea for the teacher not to overwhelm her with corrections that would be discouraging. He held out little hope that she would "develop power" as a writer, "for her cramped surroundings would doubtless be too much for her," but he does suggest that writing practice "will enable her in some measure to escape from the hard and oppressive environment where fate has thrown her, into the free, pure air of imaginative truth" (86–87). Brown leaves little doubt that grammar can be a part of that free, pure air.

Though concerns about admission to college powered many discussions of grammar and usage in the early years of NCTE, some writers nevertheless rejected the perceived elitism of college and literary English and called for practical English studies. In 1913, writing from a businessperson's perspective, R. W. Heath, vice president of the Larkin Company, a mail order business in Buffalo, found "in abundance" books on "the value of words, the elegance of expression, diction, and style." Heath added, "It is not for the business man to speak of these" (172). Rather, he wanted teachers to focus on "simple, good English," and as an incentive, he established a prize for an essay showing how "The Larkin Factory-to-Family Dealing Reduces the High Cost of Living." In assessing winners, Heath would give "one point each for neatness, spelling and punctuation, grammar, and correctness," three points for discussion of the high cost of living, and four points for arguments showing how the Larkin method reduces those costs (172–73). In 1914, Harry O'Brien of the Oklahoma Agricultural and Mechanical College criticized teachers for "going on in the same old rut, teaching farmers how to get culture" (471). He argued that teachers should bypass literary themes to have students describe "the workings of an ensilage cutter or milking machine" or the life history of "a grasshopper or a liver fluke" in plain, clear, correct English (471).

Amid these varying opinions, the Council had no official position on grammar in language instruction. However, founder James Fleming Hosic offered what seems to be a consensus view of the grammar issue in the early years: "English grammar should ordinarily be reviewed in the secondary school" (118). Hosic apparently assumed that grammar was well taught in the elementary schools, a belief that the Committee of Ten had voiced as well. In the secondary school, Hosic wrote, "[C]orrect spelling and grammatical accuracy should be rigorously exacted in connection with all written work" (118). Though he did not call for intensive formal or direct grammar teaching, his statement concerning "spelling and grammatical accuracy" leaves much room for interpretation and could well serve as an umbrella for both grammar proponents and antigrammar groups. Not answered by Hosic's assertions were questions that the Council would struggle with for the next hundred years: How, if at all, does grammar instruction influence student performance? What "grammar," if any, should be taught? What do we mean by "grammar"? What do we mean by "teach"? What is the role of "rules"? What are the responsibilities of English teachers to parents, the colleges, and the general public vis-à-vis language, grammar, and correctness? And perhaps most important: Where does grammar fit into the larger picture of language instruction?

1911–1935: Science and Progressivism

"Johnny laps up the rules, with an example for each, which he may or may not understand," wrote Maurice Moe, of Appleton High School in Wisconsin in 1913,

> but in his composition that week, he leaves a noun in apposition uncomma-ed with blissful unconcern, and when it is returned to him blue-penciled, he guesses that a comma or two is needed and inserts them—but goes on leaving his noun in apposition [to] roam at large. (104)

Moe was part of the movement toward "functional grammar," which came to be the received method in language instruction for much of the next four decades. As described by Harry Rivlin in a 1930 book discussing the movement, functional grammar involved "that application of the knowledge of a grammatical item which will prevent the commission of an error in English or which will assist in the correction of an error already made" (61). Though the focus was still on correctness, the methodology treated correction in context, and grammatical items were taught only as they would directly affect student performance. Rivlin analyzed a number of textbooks as well as statements by NCTE and affiliate groups and noted that analysis and parsing were disappearing, replaced by such functional topics as "use of the present tense to gain vividness" and "variety through the use of phrases and modifiers" (35). Grammar terminology would be introduced only incidentally to help the student function more effectively as a writer.

Functional grammar was also part of the movement toward more "scientific" teaching that grew powerfully in the first half of the century. Signaled by the establishment of the National Society for the Study of Education by John Dewey and others in 1911, the scientific education movement was a curious mix of progressive, experience-based education with tests, measurements, and data gathering. In one of its iterations, the scientific education movement led to E. L. Thorndike's quantification of measurement, including his standardized vocabulary and spelling lists; in another, the science of education also welcomed Alfred Binet's quantifications of intelligence (Binet and Simon).

In a very different way, interest in science led the functional grammarians to examine those elements of grammar that could presumably affect—or "function" in—students' speech and writing. For example, Rivlin argued *against* teaching the use of a "noun as an adjective" as in the phrase, "Chicago gangster," for "there is no grammatical difficulty involved in the use of a noun as adjective" (62). And he saw no point in teaching the idea of the "common" noun as opposed to the "proper" except as a possible "aid in correct capitalization" (62). If an item were intuitive or obvious or shed no light on good English, Rivlin felt, teachers should not bother with it.

In preparing a list of items to teach or not to teach, Rivlin acknowledged linguistic science in the work of Sterling Andrus Leonard of the University of Wisconsin, who published NCTE's first research monograph, *Current English Usage,* in 1932. Drawing on techniques of the new "descriptive" linguistics, Leonard chose *not* to cite examples of usage in the work of classic published authors, as had been the case in much dictionary making and many grammar books. Instead, he assembled a panel of "well known authors, editors, business men, linguists, and teachers" to make judgments about "the propriety of various English usages" (xiii–xiv). In the introduction to the book, NCTE President Ruth Mary Weeks noted that Leonard's research showed a "democratization of usage, giving its approval to such previously denigrated sentences and phrases as '*Who* are you looking for?' 'None *are* expected,' '*Pretty* good,' '*Awfully* old,' and 'I felt *badly*'" (xv). Leonard's work was a bombshell, undercutting prescriptivism and supplying detailed information for the functional teaching of grammar and usage. In a follow-up study in 1938, Albert Marckwardt and Fred Walcott validated and updated the Leonard study and saw their work as a partial response to "much adverse journalistic comment" about Leonard's work, including predictions of "the disintegration of the English language" and doubts about "the sanity of the author" (1).

While being strictly descriptive, Leonard nevertheless employed usage labels of *established*, *disputable*, and the judgmental *illiterate*. Marckwardt and Walcott thought the term *nonstandard* was preferable to *illiterate*, but they supported the perceived value of terms such as *established* and *literary* language. Their advice was that the teacher of English should ask, "[F]irst, how near to correctness and clarity can he bring the average language level of his class; and second, what can he do to lift superior students from mediocrity to elegance in their use of English?" (132). Marckwardt and Walcott suggested "drilling the class" on correct usage and said that the teacher should either engage the "superior" students as tutors or excuse them from drill altogether (133). Regarding grammar, they concluded, "Upon the moot question of how far the study of formal grammar can improve the speech habits of our students the present study sheds little light" (133). Although the question was "moot," they clearly left room for grammar in the curriculum, but called for the texts to "accurately reflect grammar" (133).

Leonard's work was part of a much larger movement in descriptive linguistics. In *The Teaching of the English Language* (1927), linguist Charles Carpenter Fries noted, "On the whole, the schools still perpetuate with very little change an eighteenth century point of view" (Preface). He observed that English instruction occupied a solid place in the curriculum and "enjoys almost unanimous support from both the general community and the school authorities" but that "the schools have not succeeded in their teaching of the English language" (1). After a detailed explication of descriptive approaches to language study, Fries closed his book by emphasizing that

> [t]he study of grammar, therefore, finds its purpose not with "the rules of correct English," but with (1) an apparatus by which to analyze the logical relations of words and word groups within the speech unit we call the sentence, and (2) a description of the means which the English language uses to express grammatical ideas and relationships. (171)

In illustrating how descriptive linguistics could shape pedagogy, Fries told the story of a boy in an English class who was asked to recite the "principal parts of the verb *write*" after making usage errors during an oral presentation. The teacher said to the boy, "In your talk just now you must have spoken without thinking, for you said *had wrote* instead of *had written*." Commented Fries: "Now, as a matter of fact, *to speak without thinking of the forms of language* is exactly what the boy should have done" (111). Fries argued that habit formation, not recitation of the grammar rules, would lead students to improved performance. However, he also noted that "the desire and will to master particular speech habits must have its roots in an understanding of the life and growth of language and a realization of the social meaning and effect of differing sets of language patterns and forms" (157).

How the mix of science, linguistics, progressivism, and democratization worked out in the schools bears further examination. A 1926 article by Chicago Normal School professor Sophia Camenisch begins by observing a "prevailing demand for standards and objectives, for definite measurable progress, and for adaptation to the pupils" ("Some Recent Tendencies" 182). Scientific measurement was, for Camenisch, a means of identifying "minimum-essentials." In grammar and usage, for example, she said, "[T]he thing that is needed and that is wanting even in the best of the progressive courses of study is a well-worked-out sequence of activities perfectly adapted to the growing child" (184). Camenisch declared,

> Topics to be taught for mastery must be drilled on with the right kind of drill. No matter how carefully one teaches the forms of troublesome verbs in the past tense, present participle, perfect participle, third person singular, if there is not sufficient attentive repetition until the form becomes automatic, it has not been handled as an essential. (185)

In a companion article, "A Procedure for Remedial Work in the Mechanics of English," Camenisch outlines a regimen that includes use of "good tests" such as the "Wisconsin tests on sentence recognition and on grammatical correctness" and the "Briggs Form Parallel Tests" for diagnosing student errors. Drill work would be built on test diagnoses, with follow-up using "special drills on mimeographed sheets." A second round of tests would then be given, with "extra work to those who still hope to bring themselves up" ("A Procedure" 517–18).

Sophia Camenisch did not necessarily represent a Council position on these matters, but her writing here and her later work as a member of the language team for *An Experience Curriculum in English* (NCTE Curriculum Commission) suggest that she likely was a spokesperson for teachers attempting to interpret scientific, progressive education pedagogy. Most important, perhaps, is that her amalgamation of measurement, science, habit formation, child-centeredness, and drill turns descriptive linguistics into a formula for teaching, leaving ample room for traditional grammar (perhaps restricted in scope to functional essentials) and teaching for correctness (albeit with usage items identified and validated by language research). And success in English, for Camenisch, seemed to be a middle-class accomplishment, to be aimed at by "those who still care" ("A Procedure" 518).

1935–1940: The Experience Curriculum and Its Exemplars

An Experience Curriculum in English, published in 1935 under the leadership of Wilbur Hatfield and the NCTE Curriculum Commission, is arguably the Council's most consistent, theoretically rationalized, and creative venture into curriculum making. Its language component was crafted with particular care. The curriculum focused on "experience" coupled with "social objectives," and language study was to be integrated into the experiences of reading, writing, listening, and speaking. The topics of grammar and correctness were addressed only in a closing chapter of the publication, in which the authors emphasized the complementary role of language study in English. Skills would emerge through experience-based language use. However, correctness remained as a principal goal, as indicated by the chapter title "Corrective Teaching." Thus, language study—grammar and usage—was reduced to a remedial topic, to be taught in context.

In *An Experience Curriculum in English*, *communication*—the now-preferred term for *English*—was to emphasize "the social nature of language" along with "correct usage" learned through "habit-forming drill" (NCTE Curriculum Commission 133). "Grammar," the commission stressed, "is not . . . presented as a separate discipline—except as an eleventh- or twelfth-grade elective for the philosophically minded." For all students, "only such items of grammar are introduced to serve immediately and importantly in the building of more effective sentences" (135). Thus, while the long-standing concern for correctness remained a central goal of English teaching, functional grammar was carefully positioned to be contextual, limited to essentials, and applied at the point of expression. The commission also showed awareness of the new descriptive usage research, emphasizing that "consistent nagging about the infraction of the many rules of usage, not to mention the countless taboos the purists have set up, is unlikely to produce correctness" (136).

An illustration of a second-grade lesson not only shows how instrumental grammar could be presented but also reveals that, despite the program's emphasis on "experience," the structures of grammar nevertheless continued to shape classroom organization. In this example, the teacher had chosen to teach variety in "subject-predicate-object order" (in fact revealing how grammar, not experience, was providing the organizing principle). She had students manipulate sentences in the SPO pattern, and at an appropriate moment, she casually introduced the concept of the adverb: "[W]e call these expressions that tell when or where adverbs." She then "asks them to make some sentences with adverbs first. . . . [T]he pupils are not given any definitions and do not make any for themselves. They are not required to use the grammar terminology and are not formally tested on the recognition of adverbs" (NCTE Curriculum Commission 228). Most important, the commission emphasized, "*no time at all has been taken to teach [grammar]; it is merely a byproduct of other work that needs to be done*" (228–29). Thus, the dance with grammar was ostensibly to be choreographed around student experience and habit formation, with grammar taught in situ.

The commission was equally cautious in presenting a list of suggested grammatical terms by grade level: "The reader is particularly cautioned against the assumption that because this grammar [list] is presented separately, any grammar is to be taught separately, even for later application" (NCTE Curriculum Commission 229). To emphasize this point, the commission added, "This outline might be omitted entirely without changing the curriculum in the least; it is printed here merely to demonstrate to the skeptical that grammar is being taught—through use" (229).

The grammar agenda for grades 2 through 6—one feels compelled to take a peek at the list even if it was to be incidental—emphasizes "the sentence as a group of words which makes sense," plus such grammatical items as run-ons, fragments, and compound predicates, the last "to secure speed and ease in narrative by combining sentences with the same subjects into sentences with compound predicates" (NCTE Curriculum Commission 231). In grades 7 through 12, the underlying grammatical concepts grew more sophisticated and overt, but the commission ostensibly remained true to the principle of integrated language teaching by showing, for example, how to "reduce formality by substitution of participial phrases for adjective and even adverbial clauses" (231).

A long-standing conflict between sound linguistics and public expectations emerged as *An Experience Curriculum in English* spoke of "the double source of authority": actual use of the language versus "the traditions of authority, classic literature, and grammatical purists" (NCTE Curriculum Commission 248). And the commission's own lingering language elitism emerged from time to time, for instance, in its suggestion that "the more *heinous* or noticeable an error is, the more important is the establishment of its correct correlative" (emphasis added). And despite its disclaimers concerning its list of grammar items, the commission believed that there was an "order of attack" for functional grammar lessons that could be derived from those lists (248). It becomes increasingly clear throughout the book that there was another "double authority" operating within language study itself: one voice that acknowledged an essential unteachability of correctness through formal grammar and a second that argued that functional grammar could provide a basis for effective "corrective teaching."

The conflicts induced by the various dual authorities became more evident in the follow-up volume, *Conducting Experiences in English*, published in 1939 under the leadership of Angela Broening of the Baltimore Schools. The NCTE Commission on the English Curriculum had collected exemplars of experience-based teaching from English teachers all over the United States. The greatest part of the volume was about experiences in reading, writing, and oral language. "Corrective Teaching," the language program, was positioned as the last chapter in the book and ran to only seventeen pages—consistent with the treatment of language in *An Experience Curriculum in English*.

Nevertheless, the exemplars provided in the chapter "Corrective Teaching" are revealing. Broening herself contributed nine of the seventeen pages, describing a systemwide project she had conducted in the Baltimore schools. *An Experience Curriculum in English* had argued for "tests that teach"; Broening found a way to link the science of measurement to language teaching through the newly developed technology of machine-scored diagnostic tests. "To a teacher interested in improvement of learning," she wrote, "there is no greater thrill than the experience of seeing her pupils' reactions to their machine-marked diagnostically coded answer sheets" (NCTE Commission on the English Curriculum 310). Broening used these diagnostic tests as part of a writing assignment; students wrote about something "from their own experience," then were guided in ways of "arranging modifiers correctly . . . using parallel structure . . . [and] subordinating ideas and selecting exact connectives" (323). Other exemplars in the corrective teaching chapter include students' developing spelling lists based on their own writing, finding errors in a silent reading passage to learn about commas, compiling card files of their own usage errors, and discovering "causes of confusion" in popular media and their own writing due to "faulty position of modifiers, lack of parallel structure, incorrect subordination of ideas, vague reference of pronouns, and incorrect or omitted internal punctuation" (322). The grammar idol had morphed, but certainly not been toppled.

The 1940s and 1950s: World War II and Postwar Consolidation

An Experience Curriculum in English never had a full run at curriculum reform, largely because World War II focused the interests of the profession elsewhere. In 1940, John DeBoer published *Educating for Peace* (Jacobs and DeBoer), and shortly after the United States entered the conflict, NCTE President Max Herzberg argued for the usefulness of English in the war effort. Writing for *English Journal*, Herzberg said that the profession must "strengthen the teaching of the more utilitarian forms of expression" (10). Although he believed that "the faculty of vivid description may be useful in military discourse[,] . . . orderliness of arrangement, simplicity of language, and accuracy will be stressed; and all are desirable qualities" (10). NCTE Second Vice President Lennox Grey expressed regret that NCTE had been left out of a key national conference on English and the war. "Early in the war," he wrote, "we heard much talk about ideas and words as weapons and felt that we had much to offer" (13). English teachers should not shy away from using the word *communication* (a word that had been used freely in *An Experience Curriculum in English*), and he cited well-known examples of terse, effective communication: "Sighted sub, sank same" and "Blood, sweat, and tears" (16).

A single issue of the U.S. Office of Education's wartime newsletter, *Education for Victory*, published in 1943, devotes half its pages to the role of English in the war effort, with materials supplied by a committee of NCTE that included Herzberg, Grey, and Robert C. Pooley. The article "Pre-Induction Needs in Language Communication and Reading" takes up the "Language Needs of Soldiers" and provides "Suggestions for Teaching," stressing clear, simple communication. "The standard of usage taught should be that of currently accepted conversational English," the authors declared, for "Army requirements do not necessitate extended study of grammatical rules and other formal aspects of English that go to make up polished literary diction." Usage errors singled out as "fundamental" included "*we was, I seen him, them boys, between you and I,* and others of similar frequency."

Less vital problems such as "*shall* and *will, farther* and *further, can* and *may* and others not generally observed in conversation can be omitted from drill exercises" ("Pre-Induction Needs" 17).

The war was incorporated into English teachers' approaches to grammar and usage. Miriam Booth, English supervisor in Erie, Pennsylvania, argued in 1944 that "[g]rammar can be exciting. Indeed, it must be if teachers of language arts are to compete successfully with thrilling stories of air combat, with the 'Gang Busters,' and with comic books." She continued, "Strangely enough it does compete, and successfully, if it is taught naturally, not artificially" (241). In the manner of functional or instrumental grammar, Booth had her students take a simple, unadorned sentence, "One airplane flew through the cloud in pursuit of another," and helped them see how it could be enlivened through "grammar": "The Spitfire climbed swiftly and dived headlong through the cloud in pursuit of the Heinkel." She added, "Learning the names of these elements as they are used is a natural part of the process" (241). She also described an experience-based project in which students drafted V-mail letters, checked them for dependent, adjective, and adverbial clauses ("These had been taught in the previous units."), and discovered a "new" kind of clause: "Pupils decided to call the new type 'noun' clauses because they perform the work of a noun" (242). After discovering this bit of grammar, the students engaged in drill exercises on clauses, revised their letters using "as many complex sentences as could be worked in logically," and ended the unit by creating a chart showing what they had learned of grammar and usage (242). This was clearly a carefully designed lesson following the language philosophies of *An Experience Curriculum in English*, but it is also indicative of how, despite more than three decades of Council discussions of language learning and habit formation, knowledge of grammar terminology, albeit "discovered" incidentally by the students, was highly valued.

The implicit value of grammar in the language curriculum is also evident in the postwar Commission on Trends in Education of the Modern Language Association (MLA), chaired by linguist and NCTE leader Thomas Clark Pollock. The commission voiced the usual concern that "after ten years of schooling, large numbers of students reach the upper grades of high school without being able to speak, write, or understand English adequately" (Pollock, DeVane, and Spiller 1). It recited a now-familiar list of developments in the "understanding of language," including descriptive as opposed to prescriptive linguistics, the social nature of language learning, spoken language as *the* language, correctness as a secondary aim of language instruction, and the acceptance of American English as something that is not "barbarous" (1–5). However, the commission added that there are "speech forms which are correct and speech forms which are incorrect, and in any community there are definite linguistic standards" (3). Although "knowledge of grammar, even if scientific, does not have automatic functional value" (8), nevertheless "grammar should be taught . . . to contribute directly to the student's ability to use the English language" (21). Further, teachers of functional grammar "should not proceed on the assumption that language study has no principles or technological vocabulary of its own" (21).

Quite another postwar explication of teaching correctness, one less elaborate and far more straightforward, is found in a 1946 *English Journal* essay by John Warriner, head of the English department in Garden City High School on Long Island. In "Hurdling English Mechanics," he wrote, "Much as we desire the satisfaction of seeing our pupils grow in creative power, still we are fearful of sending out of high school many young people whose writing *appears*, even to the most casual reader, full of 'mistakes'" (447–48). (The phrase "creative power" may have been an allusion to a popular, progressive writing book by Hughes Mearns that urged acceptance rather than rigid critiquing of student writing.) Warriner's highlighting of *appears* and *mistakes* acknowledges descriptive usage studies while reminding the reader of the de facto public standard of "correct" English. Warriner and his colleagues created a "hurdle" examination in spelling and mechanics for tenth grade; students who failed were put into an extra three-day-a-week class. As a result, Warriner reported, Garden City High School students came to perform above the mean on the Cooperative English Test. "Students have, in general, shown a great deal of interest in this system," Warriner claimed, "and those who have taken the mechanics course have done so without much grousing" (449). His no-nonsense approach to traditional grammar and usage was to form the foundation for his 1951 *English Grammar and Composition* handbook, which dominated secondary school English textbook sales for a number of years and still serves as a rhetorical foil for advocates of modern linguistics in the classroom. (Though deceased, Warriner is still listed as an author on current editions of language arts textbooks, presumably because of his long-standing sales appeal. See Odell.)

In the early 1950s, the NCTE Commission on the English Curriculum completed a postwar consolidation of theory and practice, launching a curriculum project on a par in depth and complexity with *An Experience Curriculum in English*. The project resulted in the five-volume NCTE Curriculum Series, with books devoted to the "language arts" (the now-preferred term for "English"); elementary, secondary, and college teaching; and the preparation of teachers. Much of the social and experiential focus of *An Experience Curriculum in English* had evolved into a concern for characterizing the individual learner, and grammar and usage were restored to treatment as language elements, not simply as "corrective" tools.

As part of the growing interest in the learner, *The English Language Arts in the Secondary School*, the third volume in the Curriculum Series, opened with a detailed portrait of "adolescents" and their language, including the observation that the teenager (a newish word, sometimes hyphenated as *teen-ager*) "may display marked aggressiveness in speech and a tendency toward constant argumentation" (NCTE Commission on the English Curriculum 17). Secondary students might be expected to "make considerable use of slang and swearing in their speech, since it serves not only to furnish a form of expression for their emotions, but also to attract attention of adults and to show belongingness to their own group" (19). The commission repeated the now-familiar warning that "the teaching of systematic English grammar to a student does not automatically result in his speaking or writing better." However,

> the teaching of grammar cannot be ignored, for through a functional knowledge of the basic structure of the English sentence and the terms used in identifying language forms, an intelligent student can be assisted in the revision of his writing and in the self analysis of recordings of his speech. (359)

To add to the possible confusion created by this call to not-teach-but-teach grammar, the Commission on the English Curriculum strongly stressed "provision for the needs of individuals" (378). It did *not* present a systematic language program, calling instead for "appropriate timing in relation to growth and need" (364), "different approaches for different students" (368), and an "inductive approach" that would allow students to explore the language for themselves (369). For the teacher not highly skilled in such open-ended teaching, it might be tempting just to fall back on the grammar textbook.

The commission also expressed its concern over "the ambiguity of the word grammar" and the "lack of a universally accepted description of English grammar" (NCTE Commission on the English Curriculum, *English Language* 356). It discussed the grammar that was emerging from the descriptive linguists, particularly the structural grammar of Charles Carpenter Fries in *American English Grammar*, explaining how this new approach was solving many of the problems of Latinate grammar by focusing on the nature of phonemes, morphemes, function words, juncture, pitch, structure, pattern, form classes, and levels of usage (385). However, the work of the descriptivists was not the end of the process, and the profession still needed new or more complete grammars.

The 1960s: A New English

In 1962, Thomas Kuhn, a philosopher of science, published *The Structure of Scientific Revolutions*, in which he described how "paradigm shifts" occur in the disciplines. Newtonian physics, he explained, worked quite well for describing physical phenomena until discoveries about the constant speed of light made Newton's formulae incomplete—thus the appearance and acceptance of Einstein's new paradigm explaining relativity. In the 1960s, English teachers quickly adopted the metaphor of the paradigm shift to describe what was happening in their profession.

A series of 1958 Basic Issues conferences, cosponsored by MLA, NCTE, the American Studies Association, and the College English Association, expressed doubts about the effectiveness of the then-current paradigm—the tripod of literature, language, and composition. Their concern reflected public dissatisfaction with American education after the successful Russian launching of *Sputnik* in 1957. "Some hostile critics," the report noted, "have said that if as much student time were spent on any other subject [than English] with so little in the way of results, it would be a national scandal" (NCTE, *Basic Issues* 5). The Basic Issues conferences questioned the apparent disorder of English, especially in accommodating newer mass media such as television, while sustaining conventional concern for print literacy. The conferences thus posed the question, "Can basic programs in English be devised that are sequential and cumulative from the kindergarten through the graduate school?" (7). This question did not come out of the blue, for the "new math" was attracting attention because of its reconceptualizing of that discipline, and in coming years, the disciplines would look to Jerome Bruner's highly respected *The Process of Education*, which called for finding the fundamental structures of disciplines and teaching them in cumulative fashion.

The Basic Issues conferences, like the NCTE Curriculum Series of the 1950s, saw great promise in the work of the structural grammarians: "We must ask whether this new method offers a clue to a better correlation of the knowledge of language structure with writing ability" (NCTE, *Basic Issues* 9). Concurrently, the profession was discovering a book called *Syntactic Structures*, published in 1957 by Noam Chomsky. Largely ignoring the processes of descriptive, structural grammar, Chomsky called for grammars that would reveal how language users could generate an infinite variety of original sentences using a finite set of rules. Chomsky's transformational-generative grammar was quickly seen as something that might fit the bill in the quest for a new English comparable to the new math, though to many teachers Chomsky's work seemed more like math than English. Along with structural grammars, teachers also learned about and puzzled over Kenneth Pike's "tagmemic" grammar, Sidney Lamb's "stratificational" grammar, and M. A. K. Halliday's "systemic" grammar (Laird; Liebert). There was no lack of grammars to offer a new structure for English, but the structural and transformational-generative grammars came to dominate the discussion.

In 1964 the Council's *National Interest and the Continuing Education of Teachers of English* reported that 80.4 percent of teachers surveyed wanted course work in structural or generative grammar (40), while "traditional" grammar was of interest to only 31.1 percent (NCTE Committee on National Interest 42). In a book for parents, *How the "New English" Will Help Your Child*, Michael Shugrue of MLA and NCTE explained,

> While what has occurred in the teaching of language to youngsters is more revolutionary and technical and therefore seems stranger to many parents than new directions in the teaching of composition and literature[,] . . . probably no part of the triad [of literature, composition, and language] needed revision more than the study of language. (48–49)

Shugrue provided parents a primer on structural and transformational grammars and defended linguistic attitudes toward grammar, usage, and correctness against charges of "permissivism" (66).

NCTE also sponsored a book for parents, *The Teaching of Language in Our School*. In the introduction, NCTE Associate Executive Secretary Robert Hogan observed, "Forces are at work to revolutionize the teaching of English" (vii). He added, "The breakdown in communication between specialist and layman is one price we pay for unprecedented advances in knowledge" (x). The author of *The Teaching of Language in Our School*, Miriam Goldstein, provided a detailed presentation of the new linguistics, including a sociolinguistic discussion in the chapter "Bilingualism: Complicating the Two Rs." Goldstein also explained bidialectal approaches to teaching Standard English that would neither shame students nor denigrate their home dialect.

In observing that "[i]ntellectual revolutions . . . are both cause and effect of social revolutions" (45), Goldstein identified a second major stimulus to the "new English": changing attitudes about social class, culture, and race. These changes were catalyzed most notably by the Civil Rights Movement and were reinforced later in the decade by social and political unrest over the Vietnam War.

Earlier Council publications had tended to treat white middle-class students as the norm. The cussing, cantankerous "adolescent" of *The English Language Arts in the Secondary School* (NCTE) does not sound like an urban kid, and if he or she spoke a nonstandard dialect, it was more likely to sound rural than urban, like that of a white youth, not a member of a minority group. By 1965, however, NCTE's *Language Programs for the Disadvantaged: The Report of the NCTE Task Force on Teaching English to the Disadvantaged* showed a distinct awareness of the group it euphemistically, if cautiously, labeled "disadvantaged." Editors Richard Corbin and Muriel Crosby attributed much of the new awareness to John F. Kennedy and the war on poverty. Approaching a delicate subject, Corbin called on the profession to realize that the disadvantaged were primarily "children from America's slums, both rural and urban. These are Puerto Ricans, migrant whites from Appalachia and other economically depressed areas, Mexican 'wetbacks,' and American Indians, but mostly they are Negroes" (6).

Despite their awareness of sociolinguistics, members of the NCTE Task Force on Teaching English to the Disadvantaged took what seems like a patronizing view of the "slum" child, in part because of the influence of language deprivation theorist Carl Bereiter, who alleged that the disadvantaged were deprived of basic concepts and thus of language. Bereiter's influence is clearly revealed in this discussion from the task force: "[O]nce one knows that a box is *big*, he can know that the box is *not little* if he understands "big" and "little" individually as opposites and if he knows the proper use of 'not'" (Corbin and Crosby 67). Critics were quick to point out that no speaker of English lacks either the understanding of or the ability to use the negative in myriad ways, and language deprivation was soon challenged and largely discredited by the whole language movement.

In the more mainstream chapter "A Sustained Program of Language Learning," Walter Loban represented the view that language study should use the child's dialect as a starting point without diminishing or shaming the child, that it should introduce "a barrage of language in different dialects" (Corbin and Crosby 226), and that it should help students inductively understand the consequences of a "nonstandard social dialect" (227). Loban also called for a wide range of oral language activities through records, television, drill tapes, and language laboratories "that would alternate with dramatics, literature, discussion, and writing" (228). Still, the standard dialect *was* a major target: "[B]efore it is too late, teachers should begin to work on some of the more crucial items of usage by means of oral training" (227). It would seem that "crucial" in this case meant that the disadvantaged were, in the end, to master the dialect perceived as necessary for jobs, higher education, and success.

Emerging at this same time was a body of research on the nature of dialects in general and on what initially was called "Negro Dialect" but soon came to be labeled "Black English" by such scholars as J. L. Dillard, William Labov, Walt Wolfram, Roger Shuy, Ralph Fashold, and others (Stoller). In his NCTE book *Discovering American Dialects*, sponsored by the recently created NCTE Commission on Language, Roger Shuy explained that "all people speak a variety of English which can be a dialect" (1). He went on to show how dialects differ from one another in vocabulary, pronunciation, and syntax and that linguists describe rather than legislate dialects and avoid judgmental terminology. J. L. Dillard's *Black English* identified and praised the interesting features of "the language of about eighty percent of Americans of African ancestry" that "is in some ways even more American than other varieties of English spoken in the United States" (ix). Geneva Smitherman's *Talkin and Testifyin: The Language of Black America*, was written, in part, in Black English as a way of pointing out the legitimacy of that dialect (or *any* dialect for that matter) in expressing ideas clearly and forcefully.

Together with new grammars and deepening understanding of dialects and the social bases of language, a third element of the "new English" revolution came from the Anglo-American Seminar on the Teaching and Learning of English of 1966 (the Dartmouth Conference discussed in detail elsewhere in this collection and in Dixon's *Growth through English*). In the United States, the impulse for the new English had originally been a search for more fundamental structures of knowledge following Bruner and the Basic Issues conferences. Dartmouth's "personal growth" model, primarily advocated by the British participants, focused on the child and processes of learning through language. This growth model meshed interestingly with Chomsky's "generative" focus, particularly when coupled with James Britton's explication of Lev Vygotsky and emerging theories of language and cognition (see Pradl). Thus reinterpreted, transformational-generative grammar could supply pedagogical support for progressive, Deweyan, experienced-based learning as well as offering a structure for the new English. Although Dartmouth was seen as another "new" paradigm and was credited largely to the British cousins, its pedagogy was not unrelated to the experiential and social teaching that had been under discussion through most of the Council's first fifty years (Radner).

The 1970s: Extending the New English

Publishers were quick to offer language textbooks based on the new linguistics. In the 1950s, Paul Roberts published *Patterns in English*, a structural grammar, and in the 1960s he issued *The Roberts English Series* based on transformational grammar. Neil Postman wrote *Discovering Your Language*, which focused on descriptivism and language inquiry rather than on mastery of Standard English. Mark Lester wrote a textbook that typified some of the new attitudes toward language; in *Constructing an English Grammar*, he introduced students to the robot, Tobor (*robot* spelled backward), and engaged them in teaching it how to generate an infinite number of sentences with a finite set of rules, in effect creating a model of a transformational grammar. William Strong prepared teaching materials on sentence combining, which uses the principles of transformational-generative grammar to help students build elaborated sentences.

Not all the new grammar textbooks caught on, and traditional textbooks such as Warriner's continued to sell briskly. Nevertheless, as Burt Liebert noted in his 1971 book, *Linguistics and the New English Teacher*, the profession's awakening interest in linguistics led to an expanded language program. Beyond grammar and usage, teachers and their students began to explore general semantics, humor and wordplay in language, dialect discovery, "grammars" of the mass media, advertising analysis, propaganda, euphemism, the "story" of English, language families, linguistic change, and universal languages. Liebert quotes James Sledd, who spoke at a California English conference and declared that linguistics had helped "change the English teacher's self-concept from that of policeman to explorer" (Liebert 261).

The new linguistics also helped teachers see the political nature of language more clearly. Acknowledging George Orwell's "Politics and the English Language," the NCTE Committee on Public Doublespeak was created in 1971 and began chastising public officials for their evasive language, giving out an annual Doublespeak Award that attracted national media interest. And in the 1970s, Council members created two important statements about the relationship of class, politics, and language: one on sexism in language, the second on students' dialects. In 1975 the NCTE Board of Directors adopted *Guidelines for Nonsexist Use of Language in NCTE Publications*, which discussed the debilitating effects of sexist language and offered alternatives. (The reader may have noted that up through the mid-1960s, the Council publications cited here generally used the third-person masculine pronoun to refer to people of both sexes.) Augmenting the guidelines, NCTE published *Sexism and Language* by Alleen Pace Nilsen and colleagues for the NCTE Committee on the Role and Image of Women in the Council and the Committee on Public Doublespeak. The book explained,

> Language plays a central role in socialization, for it helps teach children the roles that are expected of them. . . . Eliminating sexist language will not eliminate sexist conduct, but as the language is liberated from sexist usages and assumptions, women and men will begin to share more equal, caring roles. (182)

The guidelines were not adopted without an interesting controversy that demonstrates the Council's increasing sensitivity to language and politics. Linguist Harold B. Allen submitted a statement to the Board of Directors arguing that the guidelines placed NCTE in the position of censoring the speech and writing of those who would choose to use traditional terms such as *policeman* and *chairman*. Further, he argued, the guidelines violated the realization of linguists that language-in-action, not legislation, determines usage. A long and heated discussion took place at the 1979 Board of Directors meeting, resulting in an affirmative vote of 83 to 55 in support of clarifying the guidelines: the NCTE guidelines were understood not to be binding on either editors or writers, but the Council remained committed to promoting the principles of nonsexist language (NCTE, Board of Directors Meeting Minutes).

A second major resolution linking politics and the English language was passed at the 1974 meeting of the Conference on College Composition and Communication (CCCC), called "Students' Right to Their Own Language":

> RESOLVED, that CCCC affirm the students' rights to their own patterns and varieties of language—the dialects of their nurture or whatever dialects in which they find their own identity and style. Language scholars long ago denied that the myth of a standard American dialect has any validity. The claim that any one dialect is unacceptable amounts to an attempt of one social group to exert its dominance over another. Such a claim leads to false advice for speakers and writers, and immoral advice for humans. A nation proud of its diverse heritage and its cultural and racial variety will preserve its heritage of dialects. We affirm strongly that teachers must have the experiences and training that will enable them to respect diversity and uphold the right of students to their own language. ("Resolutions Passed")

This resolution had grown not only out of the Council's evolving consciousness of issues of race, class, and dialect, but also in opposition to the disputed philosophy of "bidialectalism," which encouraged speakers of nonstandard dialects to master the standard dialect as an alternative to their home dialect and to engage in code-switching as occasions warranted. In 1969, James Sledd had attacked the concept in "Bi-Dialectalism: The Linguistics of White Supremacy," arguing that teachers could not legitimize, linguistically or morally, the concept of bidialectalism, which, he said, pretended linguistic neutrality in offering students a choice of an alternative to their native dialect, while tacitly arguing for the supremacy of standard middle-class English.

The resolution was debated at length by CCCC members. Concerns were variously voiced that the statement would divide membership, that it implicitly endorsed bidialectalism, that it would alienate authors of existing handbooks, that it went too far, that it didn't go far enough, and that it "was unclear about what kind of teacher behavior would result if the implications of the statement were carried out" (Prichard). After its adoption at the 1974 CCCC meeting in Anaheim, "Students' Rights to Their Own Language" received an enormous amount of press—much of it negative and based on journalistic ignorance about language—and it has arguably been the most controversial of policy statements issued by NCTE and its constituent groups. The resolution was published with detailed explanatory material as a special issue of *College Composition and Communication*, and it was reaffirmed, word-for-word, by CCCC in 2002. An expanded bibliography was added in 2006 to update the background research (NCTE, *Students' Right*).

The 1980s and Beyond: Backlash and Response

By no means was there unanimity about the effectiveness of language study under the new linguistic approaches. *Newsweek* fired the opening salvo of what was to become the "back-to-basics" movement in 1975, when journalist Merrill Shiels wrote, "Willy-nilly, the U.S. education system is spawning a generation of illiterates" (58). Selectively using anecdotes from disgruntled parents, professors, and students, and invoking a ten-year decline in SAT verbal scores as evidence, Shiels echoed the kinds of complaints about first-year writing quality among college students that the profession had heard since the Harvard Reports. She declared that English teachers had abandoned any effort to teach students to write "expository English with any degree of structure and lucidity" (58).

Nor did the complaints about the alleged failures of the new English come only from the press. Students and teachers resisted as well. Rebecca Bowers Sipe recalls teaching English in Anchorage, Alaska, in 1972, where Warriner's *English Grammar and Composition* had been replaced by a series of transformational-generative textbooks. At the close of the school year, she reports, teachers would box up their Warriner's and store them secretly "to protect the texts from those who would delight in tossing them out over summer break" (15).

Anna Marie Ferguson of Detroit Cooley High School also objected by making "A Case for Teaching Standard English to

Black Students." In her view, "The riots of the late sixties and their accompanying emphasis on blackness—black studies, black literature, and black dialect—had a marked effect on the teaching of English." Black teachers, she asserted, "knew that they could not sound too correct" for fear of being called "Uncle Toms"; white teachers allegedly "dared not insist on the use of standard English" (38). Ferguson's views certainly did not represent the Council's thinking as reflected in such publications as former NCTE President Charlotte Brooks's *Tapping Potential: English and the Language Arts for the Black Learner* or Marcia Farr and Harvey Daniels's *Language Diversity and Writing Instruction*. Both books offered theoretical positions and practical classroom approaches to reach speakers of nonstandard dialects, who had been ignored or alienated by the educational system. Nevertheless, Ferguson was not alone among English teachers, members of the public, and the press in rejecting language research and NCTE policies, relying instead on anecdotal evidence to declare: "We need to return to teaching standard forms in writing and speaking in the English classroom and to correct, if you will, students' speech and writing" (Ferguson 39).

Challenging the new English from a more developed theoretical stance, in 1980 British high school teacher David Allen published a critique, *Teaching English since 1965: How Much Growth?* His concern was that the new English was leaving less advantaged students speaking and writing what British linguist Basil Bernstein called "restricted" codes. Allen rejected what he perceived to be the new English belief that "all language," both literature and student writing, "is of equal merit" (97). Although Allen's claims were better researched than those of Ferguson, he, like Ferguson, relied largely on impressionism in his description of how the new English had allegedly abandoned standards of quality in speech and writing.

In the United States, the back-to-basics movement found its most detailed articulation in a 1983 report commissioned by Ronald Reagan's Secretary of Education Terrell Bell. *A Nation at Risk* declared that U.S. schools were caught in "a rising tide of mediocrity" (n. pag.). The National Commission on Excellence in Education, authors of the report, initially provided support for English studies: they recommended that all high school students take four years of English, more than any other subject in the curriculum. But their strong emphasis on "standards-based education," accountability, and success measured by standardized test scores had the effect of blunting the kind of language work being advocated by many NCTE members. Within just a few years, virtually every state and many school districts came to institute language standards matched to standardized tests. As often as not, those tests were of the machine-scored variety, leading naturally to standardization of language instruction centering on surface correctness and favoring native speakers of a standard dialect.

To model standards that would be professionally reputable, NCTE collaborated with the International Reading Association to create *Standards for the English Language Arts*. Two of the twelve standards directly describe the language program:

> 6. Students apply knowledge of language structure, language conventions (e.g., spelling and punctuation), media techniques, figurative language, and genre to create, critique, and discuss print and nonprint texts. (3)
>
> 9. Students develop an understanding of and respect for diversity in language use, patterns, and dialects across cultures, ethnic groups, geographic regions, and social roles. (3)

While the standards clearly reflected current research in language and language learning, the effort to satisfy the conservative pressures to focus on basic skills led to ambiguous language that could be used to accommodate an extraordinary range of teaching approaches. For example, under the umbrella of Standard 6, helping students "apply knowledge of language structure," some teachers might continue to teach traditional grammar and usage in textbook fashion. Other teachers, linguistically more progressive, might interpret the same standard as endorsing practices such as student peer editing, which draws on students' "knowledge" of syntax acquired without formal grammar instruction at all. The focus on dialect in Standard 9 certainly shows that the writers were aware of decades of dialect research, yet the phrase "develop an understanding of and respect for diversity in language use" could be employed by groups as diverse as those who argue for students' rights to their own language to those who would "respect" the dialect of the home but nevertheless require students to learn traditional Standard English.

Another standard, Standard 3, was focused primarily on reading but included such linguistic knowledge as "word meaning," "word identification strategies," and "textual features (e.g., sound–letter correspondence, sentence structure, content, graphics)," no doubt reflecting the concerns of International Reading Association members (IRA and NCTE 3). This standard, like Standards 6 and 9, also could be interpreted as supporting a wide range of approaches to teaching, from using conventional phonics and vocabulary drills to teaching reading through whole language, as advocated by such NCTE leaders as Kenneth Goodman and former NCTE President Yetta M. Goodman (Goodman, Hood, and Goodman). Thus, for language study, the *Standards for the English Language Arts* provide less explicit opposition to the back-to-basic forces than many Council members had hoped.

In the 1980s, a backlash had also emerged in the form of the English Only Movement, sparked by former U.S. Senator S. I. Hayakawa. Hayakawa had previously published a progressive book on general semantics—a gospel of the new English, in fact—but he had become linguistically more conservative and began a push to make English the "official" language of the United States, a move that would eliminate multilingual publication of many citizen-vital documents and would pressure schools to eradicate, not accommodate, languages other than English (*U.S. English*).

In a book on the politics of the movement, James Crawford argued that English Only—contrary to its stated purposes of bringing about national unity—was racist, nativist, anti-immigrant, and xenophobic, with those biases masked by a claim of patriotism. In a research summary for the ERIC Clearinghouse on Reading, English, and Communication, Mei-Yu Lu showed that English Only would deny nonnative speakers equal educational opportunity, restrict their linguistic growth, and demean their culture and their home life. In addition to numerous NCTE books and articles protesting the movement and exposing its implicit motives, CCCC adopted a National Language Policy that called for "resources to enable [both] native and nonnative speakers to achieve oral and literate competence" and for "support programs that assert the legitimacy of native languages and dialects." CCCC also sought to "foster the teaching of languages other than English so that native speakers of English can rediscover the language of their heritage or learn a second language" (CCCC, "CCCC Guideline").

The NCTE Commission on Language continues to monitor English Only and antibilingual legislation and policies. In response to the concern that NCTE has for too long ignored second language learners, the 2009 preface to the commission's charge highlights its role in supporting teachers of English language learners:

> NCTE has accepted responsibility for educating its membership so that ELL becomes an intentional part of what we do in every realm, such as policy development, conference proposals, materials, resources, surveys, research briefs, and professional development. NCTE is striving to become the major source of assistance to teachers of English Language Learners. (NCTE Commission on Language)

In the early 1990s, the Oakland, California, Board of Education passed a progressive resolution that teachers should understand *Ebonics*, a term coined to represent what is more commonly called Black English Vernacular or African American Vernacular English. The backlash was immediate, attracting the attention of the national press as well as the Reverend Jesse Jackson, who declared it "an unacceptable surrender, bordering on disgrace" ("Jackson, Oakland" n. pag.). Presumably the surrender was to the forces of white racism that would deny students of color access to what Jackson perceived as mainstream or Standard English. After meeting with the board and ostensibly coming to understand its aims, Jackson apologized for his overreaction. But in a statement that reveals he still did not fully understand the sociolinguistics of upward mobility, Jackson said that the move had his approval because "[t]he intent is to teach these children standard American, competitive English. Because if they cannot read they cannot reason" ("Jackson, Oakland" n. pag.). Thus the outcry over Ebonics had the effect of delegitimizing Black English Vernacular.

CCCC responded with a "Statement on Ebonics," remarking that media reports and commentaries "have been, for the most part, incomplete, uninformed, and in some cases, purposefully distorted." CCCC called for research and training so that teachers, administrators, and parents could come to understand "how educators can best build on existing knowledge about Ebonics to help students to expand their command of the Language of Wider Communication ('standard English')" (n. pag.).

What I've called the "backlash" has pressured teachers to adopt more conservative modes of teaching, focusing on surface language structures that were perceived by the public and legislators as "basic." The No Child Left Behind Act (NCLB) of 2001, championed by George W. Bush and supported by legislators of both parties, continued the push for restricted, "no-nonsense" education in the schools by imposing mandated standardized tests and adequate yearly progress reports that could put underachieving schools on notice and even result in the closing of schools that were perceived to be failing. Council members have responded to NCLB by acknowledging the public's concerns for standards and testing and showing through research in language and pedagogy how those concerns are taken into account.

NCTE has continued to promote strategies that allow teachers to be true to the language as it is while serving the needs of students and the public for "basics." For instance, writing in *English Journal* in 2007, Michelle Crotteau of the Rockingham County Schools in Virginia describes ways of "Honoring Dialect and Culture: Pathways to Student Success on High-Stakes Writing Assessments." Working with speakers of Appalachian dialects, Crotteau showed students facing high-stakes exams how to write from their own experience, had them collect examples of their own dialect, engaged them in oral reading, and introduced Standard English alternatives through oral drill "rather than traditional grammar worksheets" (30). In "Teaching Conventions in a State-Mandated Testing Context," Bonnie Mary Warne from South Anthony, Idaho, explains how she used the principles of transformational sentence combining to encourage students to examine their own dialect and to combine kernel sentences into longer ones that presumably would produce higher test scores. She argues that this approach created "defensible connections between sound writing and an indefensible test" (26). At Stevenson High School in Lincolnshire, Illinois, J. Arias reports creating a series of storytelling, oral language, and game activities that reveal the difficulty of learning a second language (e.g., students tell a story in which "no one can use any words with the letters *i*, *s*, or *n*," which "mimics [the obstacles of] speaking another language") (39). Kenneth Lindblom and Patricia Dunn, former high school teachers now at the State University of New York at Stony Brook, asked their students to analyze the "grammar rants" of media commentators to discover the pundits' views of language; their claims and evidence; and the attitudes and assumptions about socioeconomic class, geography and culture, intelligence, and morality implicit in their speech and writing.

Further, throughout all these discussions about how best to teach language, in particular from the 1960s to the present, not all Council members have agreed that the de-emphasis on grammar has been productive or even based in sound research. A 1996 *English Journal* article by Martha Kolln lamented "the free fall of grammar" in the 1960s, based in part on what she saw as narrowly interpreted research studies that investigated the relationship between language mastery and formal grammar. She felt that the studies had neglected what she and others called "rhetorical" or "contextual" grammar (arguably an extension of the functional grammar movement from the first half of the twentieth century). She noted that the word *grammar* appeared only once on the 1993 NCTE Annual Convention program, and that in a negative context: a presentation on "Beyond Grammar in the Classroom" (27). Kolln, a founder of the NCTE Assembly for the Teaching of English Grammar (ATEG), said, "Our profession has not been well served by the anti-grammar policies based on dubious research and on distorted conclusions and inferences" (29).

Writing in the same issue of *English Journal*, Constance Weaver presented the case for contextual grammar, noting emphatically that this approach did not entail formal grammar instruction, relying, rather, on a variety of strategies, including

> incidental lessons, wherein (for example) grammatical terms are used casually, in the course of discussing literature and students' writing; inductive lessons, wherein students may be guided to notice grammatical patterns and derive generalizations themselves; teaching grammatical points in the process of conferring

> with students about their writing; mini-lessons, which present new and useful information (to a group, a class, or individual)[;] . . . and extended mini-lessons, which typically involve students in trying out or applying the concept, briefly and collaboratively, in order to promote greater understanding. (19)

Back to the Future: Enduring Issues and Concerns

Teachers have no shortage of strategies for responding thoughtfully to the back-to-basics and testing movements, and unquestionably language teaching aims and practices have been steadily refined during the years since the new English appeared, just as they were refined through research in linguistics and pedagogy during the Council's first fifty years (Radner). Nevertheless, the pressures continue, especially with respect to grammar and Standard English. In an editor's note to a 2006 *English Journal* focus issue, "Contexts for Teaching Grammar," Louann Reid quoted a teacher who said, "I know I am not supposed to teach grammar, but the parents and administrators expect me to teach it" (12). The problem here is not so much the expectations of outsiders, which teachers have come to anticipate, but this teacher's feeling that one is "not supposed to teach grammar," implying that the teacher was responding to perceived authorities from *inside* the profession. Reid responds to that teacher, in part, by going back in the Council's history to a statement by Robert Pooley in 1953 on descriptive, thoughtful uses of grammar. Her point seems to be that the Council has had a complex understanding of what one is "supposed" to do about grammar for many years. That knowledge has been elaborated in more recent Council position statements, such as "Guidelines on the Essentials of English" (1982), "NCTE's Position on the Teaching of English: Assumptions and Practices" (1991), and ATEG's "Guideline on Some Questions and Answers about Grammar" (2002).

As we celebrate the Council's centennial, we certainly can regret that the grammar idol has been so difficult to topple. The Council has much more interesting and vital ways to spend its time and energies than in responding to those who want to worship a discredited god. There is far more to language learning and teaching than grammar and correctness, and NCTE can be rightly proud of the role its members have played in developing and accommodating research in an astonishing array of language fields, including, but not limited to, language origins, dialects, registers, international and world languages, mass media, political language, social networking and language communities, literacy across the curriculum, second language learning, the social bases of language, and (inter)cultural communication.

In its "Guidelines on Elementary School Practices: Current Research on Language Learning," issued in 1993, the NCTE Committee on School Practices and Programs, drawing on a draft prepared by NCTE's Assembly for the Teaching of Grammar, gave what stands as an excellent summary statement of the Council's view of language learning and clearly implies a vision for the future:

> Children learn language best when they are intellectually engaged, when they feel comfortable taking risks that learning requires, when they can share their new ideas with others, and when they can take control of, and reflect upon their own learning. (n. pag.)

How best to do that remains the mission of the Council, and the resulting dialectic will be conducted in that quintessential human medium of communication and existence: *language.*

Acknowledgment

I want to extend my deep appreciation to the consultants for this chapter, who provided invaluable guidance from their diverse areas of interest and expertise in language matters: Akua Duku Anokye, Arizona State University; Harvey Daniels, New Mexico State University; Danling Fu, College of Education, University of Florida; Peter Fries, Central Michigan University; Erika Lindemann, University of North Carolina at Chapel Hill; Don Nilsen, Arizona State University; Alleen Pace Nilsen, Arizona State University; Geneva Smitherman, Michigan State University; Susan Tchudi, University of Nevada (emerita); Katie Van Sluys, DePaul University; and Constance Weaver, Miami University, Oxford, Ohio.

Works Cited

Allen, David. *English Teaching since 1965: How Much Growth?* London: Heinemann, 1980. Print.

Allen, Harold B. "A Statement and Proposal for the Board of Directors." 22 Nov. 1979. TS. University of Illinois Archives (Record Series 15/71/001, Box 24, File 7), Urbana, IL.

Arias, J. "Multilingual Students and Language Acquisition: Engaging Activities for Diversity Training." *English Journal* 97.3 (2008): 38–45. Print.

Bernstein, Basil. *Towards a Theory of Educational Transmissions.* London: Routledge and Kegan Paul, 1975. Print.

Binet, Alfred, and Théodore Simon. *The Development of Intelligence in Children.* Baltimore: Williams and Wilkins, 1916. Print.

Booth, Miriam B. "Activating Grammar." *English Journal* 33.5 (1944): 241–45. Print.

Brooks, Charlotte K., ed. *Tapping Potential: English and Language Arts for the Black Learner.* Urbana, IL: NCTE, 1985. Print.

Brown, Lemuel R. "Some Needed Readjustments in the Teaching of English Grammar." *English Journal* 2.2 (1913): 81–92. Print.

Bruner, Jerome. *The Process of Education.* New York: Vintage, 1963. Print.

Camenisch, Sophia Catherine. "A Procedure for Remedial Work in the Mechanics of English." *English Journal* 15.7 (1926): 515–20. Print.

———. "Some Recent Tendencies in the Minimum-Essentials Movement in English." *English Journal* 15.3 (1926): 181–90. Print.

Chomsky, Noam. *Syntactic Structures.* The Hague: Mouton, 1957. Print.

Conference on College Composition and Communication. "CCCC Guideline on the National Language Policy." *National Council of Teachers of English.* NCTE, Mar. 1988, updated 1992. Web. 9 Aug. 2009.

———. "CCCC Statement on Ebonics." *National Council of Teachers of English.* NCTE, May 1998. Web. 9 Aug. 2009.

Copeland, C. T., and H. M. Rideout. *Freshman English and Theme-Correcting in Harvard College.* New York: Silver-Burdett, 1901. Print.

Corbin, Richard, and Muriel Crosby, eds. *Language Programs for the Disadvantaged: The Report of the NCTE Task Force on Teaching English to the Disadvantaged.* Champaign, IL: NCTE, 1965. Print.

Crawford, James. *Hold Your Tongue: Bilingualism and the Politics of "English Only."* Reading, MA: Addison-Wesley, 1993. Print.

Crotteau, Michelle. "Honoring Dialect and Culture: Pathways to Student Success on High-Stakes Writing Assessments." *English Journal* 96.4 (2007): 27–32. Print.

Dillard, J. L. *Black English: Its History and Usage in the United States.* New York: Random, 1972. Print.

Dithridge, Rachel L. "Speech Improvement Week at Eastern District High School." *English Journal* 4.7 (1915): 465–66. Print.

Dixon, John. *Growth through English.* Reading, Eng.: National Association for the Teaching of English, 1967. Print.

Farr, Marcia, and Harvey Daniels, eds. *Language Diversity and Writing Instruction.* New York: ERIC/CUE and IUME; Urbana, IL: ERIC/RCS and NCTE, 1986. Print. ED274996.

Ferguson, Anna Marie. "A Case for Teaching Standard English to Black Students." *English Journal* 71.3 (1982): 38–40. Print.

Fries, Charles Carpenter. *American English Grammar: The Grammatical Structure of Present-Day American English with Especial Reference to Social Differences or Class Dialects.* New York: Appleton, 1940. Print. English Monograph No. 10.

———. *The Teaching of the English Language.* New York: Nelson, 1927. Print.

Goldstein, Miriam. *The Teaching of Language in Our Schools.* New York: Macmillan, 1966. Print.

Goodman, Yetta M., Wendy J. Hood, and Kenneth S. Goodman, eds. *Organizing for Whole Language.* Portsmouth, NH: Heinemann, 1991. Print.

Gray, Giles Wilkeson. "The Founding of the Speech Communication Association of America: Happy Birthday." *Quarterly Journal of Speech* 50.3 (1964): 342–45. Print.

Grey, Lennox. "Communication and War: An Urgent Letter to English Teachers." *English Journal* 32.1 (1943): 12–19. Print.

Hayakawa, S. I. *Language in Thought and Action*. London: Allen, 1952. Print.

Heath, R. W. "The Demands of the Business World for Good English." *English Journal* 2.3 (1913): 171–77. Print.

Herzberg, Max J. "Later May Be Too Late: Role of the English Teacher in Wartime." *English Journal* 32.1 (1943): 8–12. Print.

Hooper, Cyrus Lauron. "The Influence of the Study of Latin on the Student's Knowledge of English Grammar." *English Journal* 1.7 (1912): 393–404. Print.

Hosic, James Fleming. "The Influence of the Uniform Entrance Requirements in English: A Brief Chapter of Educational History, together with a Summary of the Facts so Far Obtained by a Committee of the National Education Association and a List of References." *English Journal* 1.2 (1912): 95–121. Print.

International Reading Association, and National Council of Teachers of English. *Standards for the English Language Arts*. Newark, DE: IRA; Urbana, IL: NCTE, 1996. Print.

"Jackson, Oakland School Board Discuss Ebonics." *CNN.com*. Cable News Network, 30 Dec. 1996. Web. 9 Aug. 2009.

Jacobs, Ida T., and John J. DeBoer, eds. *Educating for Peace: A Report of the Committee on International Relations of the National Council of Teachers of English*. New York: Appleton, 1940. Print.

Kolln, Martha. "Rhetorical Grammar: A Modification Lesson." *English Journal* 85.7 (1996): 25–31. Print.

Kuhn, Thomas S. *The Structure of Scientific Revolutions*. Chicago: U of Chicago P, 1962. Print.

Laird, Charlton. *And Gladly Teche: Notes on Instructing the Natives in the Native Tongue*. Englewood Cliffs, NJ: Prentice-Hall, 1970. Print.

Leonard, Sterling Andrus. *Current English Usage*. Chicago: Inland, 1932. Print. English Monographs No. 1.

———. *The Doctrine of Correctness in English Usage, 1700–1800.* Madison, WI: U of Wisconsin P, 1929. Print. University of Wisconsin Studies in Language and Literature No. 25.

Lester, Mark. *Constructing an English Grammar.* New York: Random, 1973. Print.

Lewis, W. D. "The Aim of the English Course." *English Journal* 1.1 (1912): 9–14. Print.

Liebert, Burt. *Linguistics and the New English Teacher: An Introduction to Linguistics Approaches in Language Instruction.* New York: Macmillan, 1971. Print.

Lindblom, Kenneth, and Patricia A. Dunn. "Analyzing Grammar Rants: An Alternative to Traditional Grammar Instruction." *English Journal* 95.5 (2006): 71–77. Print.

Lu, Mei-Yu. "English-Only Movement: Its Consequences on the Education of Language Minority Children." Bloomington, IN: ERIC Clearinghouse on Reading, English, and Communication, 1998. *Educational Resources Information Center.* Web. 10 Jan. 2009. ERIC Digest. ED427326.

Marckwardt, Albert H. *Introduction to the English Language.* New York: Oxford UP, 1942.

Marckwardt, Albert H., and Fred G. Walcott. *Facts about Current English Usage.* New York: Appleton, 1938. Print. English Monograph No. 7.

Mearns, Hughes. *Creative Power: The Education of Youth in the Creative Arts.* Garden City, NY: Doubleday, 1929. Print.

Moe, Maurice Winter. "Teaching the Use of the Comma." *English Journal* 2.2 (1913): 104–08. Print.

Murray, Lindley. *English Grammar: Adapted to the Different Classes of Learners.* London: Longman, 1811. Print.

National Commission on Excellence in Education. *A Nation at Risk: The Imperative for Educational Reform.* Washington, DC: GPO, 1983. *US Dept. of Education.* Web. 9 Aug. 2009.

National Council of Teachers of English. *The Basic Issues in the Teaching of English: Being Definitions and Clarifications Presented by Members of the American Studies Association, College English Association, Modern Language Association, and National Council of*

Teachers of English from a Series of Conferences Held throughout 1958. Champaign, IL: NCTE, 1959. Print.

———. Board of Directors Meeting Minutes. [22 Nov. 1979] TS. University of Illinois Archives (Record Series 15/71/010, Box 21, File 14), Urbana, IL.

———. "Guideline on the Essentials of English: A Document for Reflection and Dialogue." *National Council of Teachers of English*. NCTE, 1982. Web. 9 Aug. 2009.

———. *Guidelines for Nonsexist Use of Language in NCTE Publications*. Urbana, IL: NCTE, 1976. Print.

———. "NCTE's Position on the Teaching of English: Assumptions and Practices." *National Council of Teachers of English*. NCTE, 1991. Web. 9 Aug. 2009.

———. *Students' Right to Their Own Language*. Spec. issue of *College Composition and Communication* 25.3 (1974): 1–32. Print.

National Council of Teachers of English Assembly for the Teaching of English Grammar. "Guideline on Some Questions and Answers about Grammar." *National Council of Teachers of English*. NCTE, 2002. Web. 9 Aug. 2009.

National Council of Teachers of English Commission on Language. "Commission on Language: Charge." *National Council of Teachers of English*. NCTE, 2009. Web. 9 Aug. 2009.

National Council of Teachers of English Commission on the English Curriculum. *Conducting Experiences in English*. New York: Appleton, 1939. Print.

———. *The English Language Arts in the Secondary School*. NewYork: Appleton, 1956. Print.

National Council of Teachers of English Committee on School Practices and Programs. "Guideline on Elementary School Practices: Current Research on Language Learning." *National Council of Teachers of English*. NCTE, 1993. Web. 9 Aug. 2009.

National Council of Teachers of English Committee on the Articulation of the Elementary and High School Courses in English. "Report of the Committee on the Articulation of the Elementary Course in English with the Course in English in the High School." *English Journal* 3.5 (1914): 303–23. Print.

National Council of Teachers of English Committee on National Interest. *The National Interest and the Continuing Education of Teachers of English: A Report on the State of the Profession.* Champaign, IL: NCTE, 1964. Print.

National Council of Teachers of English Curriculum Commission. *An Experience Curriculum in English: A Report of the Curriculum Commission of the National Council of Teachers of English.* New York: Appleton, 1935. Print.

"The National Council of Teachers of English: Proceedings of the First Annual Meeting, Chicago, December 1 and 2, 1911." *English Journal* 1.1 (1912): 30–45. Print.

National Education Association. *Report of the Committee on Secondary School Studies.* Washington, DC: Bureau of Education, 1893. Print.

Nilsen, Alleen Pace, Haig Bosmajian, H. Lee Gershuny, and Julia P. Stanley. *Sexism and Language.* Urbana, IL: NCTE, 1977. Print.

No Child Left Behind Act of 2001. Pub. L. 107–110. 115 Stat. 1425–2094. 8 Jan. 2002. *US Dept. of Education.* Web. 9 Aug. 2009.

O'Brien, Harry R. "Agricultural English." *English Journal* 3.8 (1914): 470–79 Print.

Odell, Lee, Richard Vacca, Renee Hobbs, and John E. Warriner. *Elements of Language.* Austin, TX: Holt, 2007. Print.

Orwell, George. "Politics and the English Language." *Shooting an Elephant and Other Essays.* London: Secker and Warburg, 1950. Print.

Pollock, Thomas Clark, William C. DeVane, and Robert Ernest Spiller. *The English Language in American Education.* New York: Commission on Trends in Education of the Modern Language Association, 1945. Print.

Postman, Neil. *Discovering Your Language.* New York: Holt, Rinehart, and Winston, 1963. Print.

Pradl, Gordon, ed. *Prospect and Retrospect: Selected Essays of James Britton.* Upper Montclair, NJ: Boynton/Cook, 1982. Print.

"Pre-Induction Needs in Language Communication and Reading." *Education for Victory* 2.11 (1943): 1, 16–24. Print. University of Illinois Archives (Record Series 15/71/806, Box 1, File 4), Urbana, IL.

[Prichard, Nancy S.] Memo to RFH [Robert F. Hogan]. 28 Jan. 1974. TS. University of Illinois Archives (Record Series 15/74/003, Box 2, File 20), Urbana, IL.

Radner, Sanford. *Fifty Years of English Teaching: A Historical Analysis of the Presidential Addresses of NCTE.* Champaign, IL: NCTE, 1960. Print.

Reed, Alonzo, and Brainerd Kellogg. *Graded Lessons in English: An Elementary English Grammar Consisting of One Hundred Practical Lessons, Carefully Graded and Adapted to the Class-Room.* New York: Clark and Maynard, 1886. Print.

Reid, Louann. "From the Editor." *English Journal* 95.5 (2006): 12–14. Print.

Report of the Committee on Composition and Rhetoric to the Board of Overseers of Harvard College. 1892. *The Origins of Composition Studies in the American College, 1875–1925.* Ed. John C. Brereton. Pittsburgh: U of Pittsburgh P, 1995. 73–131. Print.

"Resolutions Passed by Members Present at the CCCC Business Meeting, Anaheim, California. April 6, 1974." TS. University of Illinois Archives (Record Series 15/74/004, Box 1, File 3), Urbana, IL.

Rivlin, Harry N. *Functional Grammar.* New York: Teachers College, 1930. Print.

Roberts, Paul. *Patterns of English.* New York: Harcourt, 1956. Print.

———. *The Roberts English Series.* New York: Harcourt, 1967. Print.

Rounds, C. R. "Historical Sketch of an Attempt to Unify Grammatical Nomenclature." *English Journal* 34.4 (1945): 215–16. Print.

———. "Uniform Grammatical Nomenclature." *English Journal* 1.1 (1912): 52–53. Print.

Shiels, Merrill. "Why Johnny Can't Write." *Newsweek* 8 Dec. 1975: 58–65. Print.

Shugrue, Michael F. *How the "New English" Will Help Your Child.* New York: Association, 1966. Print.

Shuy, Roger W. *Discovering American Dialects.* Champaign, IL: NCTE, 1967. Print.

Sipe, Rebecca Bowers. "Grammar Matters." *English Journal* 95.5 (2006): 15–17. Print.

Sledd, James. "Bi-Dialectalism: The Linguistics of White Supremacy." *English Journal* 58.9 (1969): 1307+. Print.

Smitherman, Geneva. *Talkin and Testifyin: The Language of Black America*. Detroit: Wayne State UP, 1985. Print.

Stoller, Paul, ed. *Black American English: Its Background and Its Usage in the Schools and in Literature*. New York: Dell, 1975. Print.

Strong, William. *Sentence Combining: A Composing Book*. New York: Random, 1973. Print.

Thomas, Charles Swain. "The English Course in the High School: The New England View." *English Journal* 1.2 (1912): 84–94. Print.

Thorndike, Edward. L. *An Introduction to the Theory of Mental and Social Measurements*. New York: Science, 1904. Print.

U.S. English. U.S. English, 2009. Web. 9 Aug. 2009.

Warne, Bonnie Mary. "Teaching Conventions in a State-Mandated Testing Context." *English Journal* 95.5 (2006): 22–27. Print.

Warriner, John E. *English Grammar and Composition*. New York: Harcourt, 1951. Print.

———. "Hurdling English Mechanics." *English Journal* 35.8 (1946): 446–50. Print.

Weaver, Constance "Teaching Grammar in the Context of Writing." *English Journal* 85.7 (1996): 15–24. Print.

READING THE PAST. WRITING THE FUTURE.

A Blast from the Past

Did you know "the reason many students don't retain grammar information is because they can't"? Ann L. Warner raised this key aspect of direct grammar instruction in a 1993 *English Journal* article that noted "only about half the adolescent and adult population reach the highest levels of formal operational thinking" needed to manage grammar in isolation.

NCTE Publications

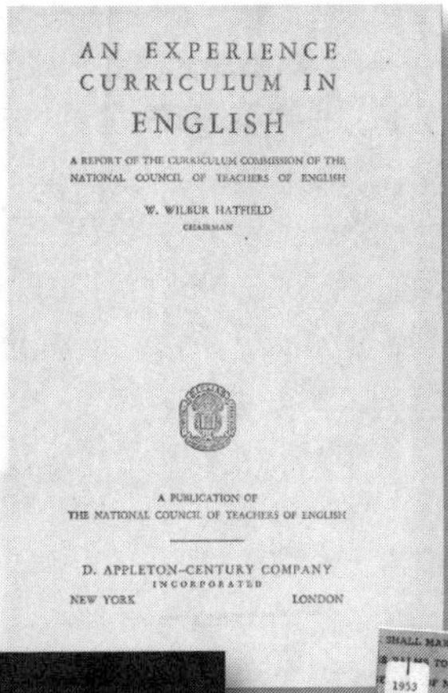

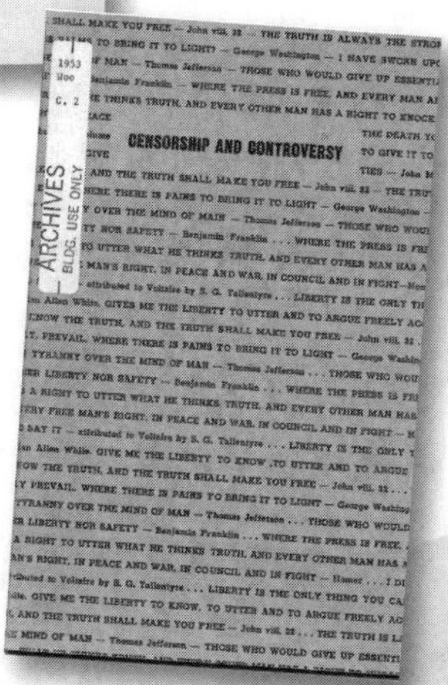

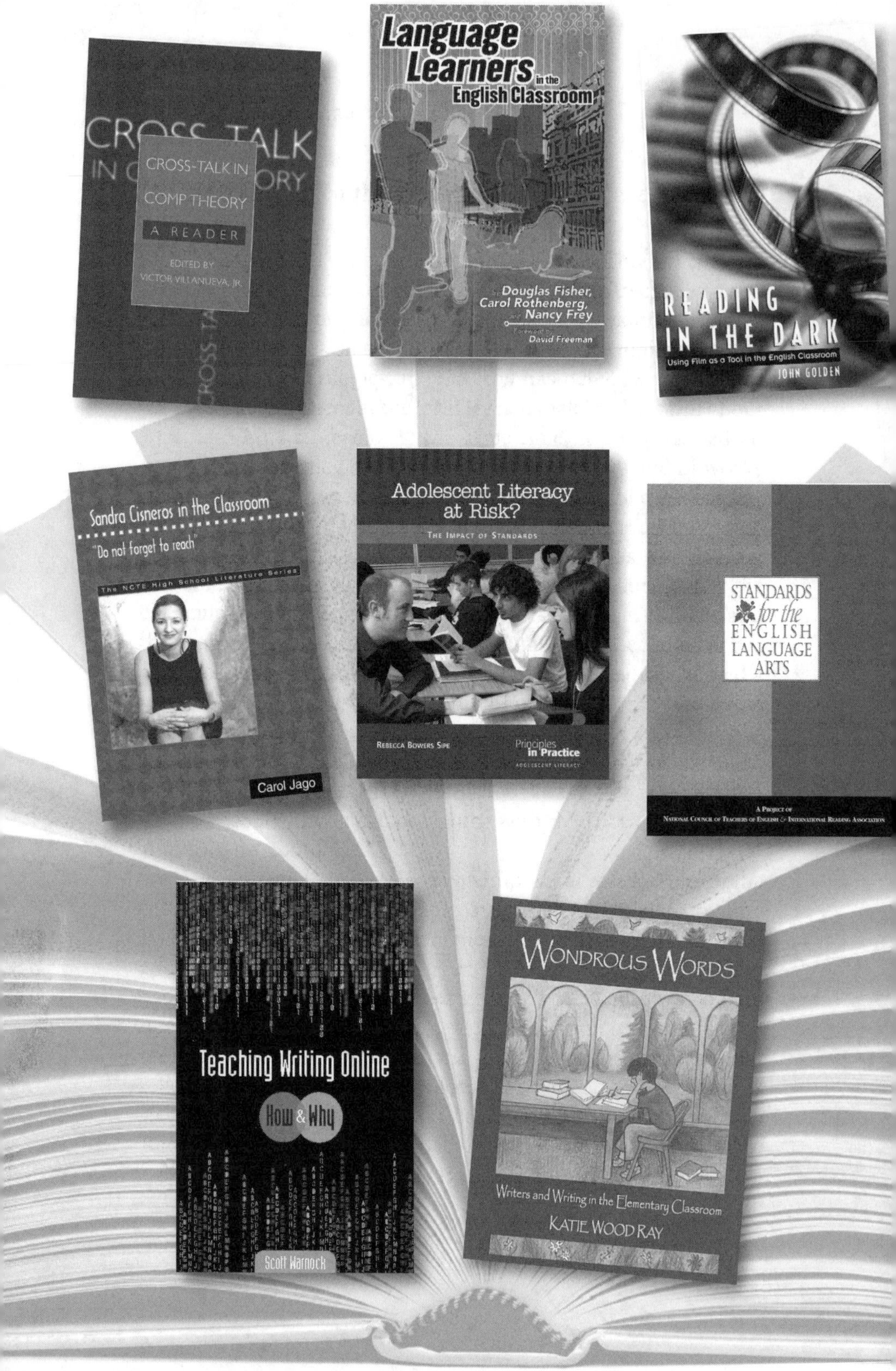
Cross-Talk in Comp Theory
A Reader
Edited by Victor Villanueva, Jr.
Language Learners in the English Classroom
Douglas Fisher, Carol Rothenberg, and Nancy Frey
Foreword by David Freeman
Reading in the Dark
Using Film as a Tool in the English Classroom
John Golden
Sandra Cisneros in the Classroom
"Do not forget to reach"
The NCTE High School Literature Series
Carol Jago
Adolescent Literacy at Risk?
The Impact of Standards
Rebecca Bowers Sipe
Principles in Practice
Adolescent Literacy
Standards for the English Language Arts
A Project of
National Council of Teachers of English & International Reading Association
Teaching Writing Online
How & Why
Scott Warnock
Wondrous Words
Writers and Writing in the Elementary Classroom
Katie Wood Ray

Chapter Five

NCTE and the Teaching of Literature

Arthur N. Applebee, Judith A. Langer,
and Marc A. Nachowitz
University at Albany, SUNY

NCTE was born out of conflicts in the teaching of literature, and though the organization went on to deal with many other issues during the next one hundred years, issues in the teaching of literature continued to be the focus of much of the organization's activity. In this chapter, we look at three broad topics: NCTE's role in defining (1) what gets taught, (2) how it should be taught, and (3) the research base for literature instruction.

What Literature Should Be Taught?

Uniform Lists for College Entrance

The English curriculum at the beginning of the twentieth century was a new and somewhat uncertain enterprise. Institutionalized as a central school subject by the Committee of Ten of the National Education Association (NEA) in 1894, English was an amalgam of loosely related subjects, including reading, analysis, composition, oratory, literary history, rhetoric, spelling, and grammar study. The Committee of Ten was chaired by Harvard President Charles W. Elliot, and the curriculum in English, as in other subjects, was dominated by the wishes of the colleges, then, as now, through a system of college entrance requirements. In English these requirements took the form of a list of books on which college entrance examinations would be based: Shakespeare, Goldsmith, Scott, Irving, Byron, Thackeray, and Macauley were all in place by 1879. These early uniform lists were a relatively predictable mix of American, British heritage, and contemporary works (Applebee, *Tradition* 275–77).

Though the curriculum was dominated by these college entrance requirements, usually addressed through heavily edited school editions of required texts, the student population was undergoing major shifts in the first decades of the century. The public high school, a relatively young institution, was increasingly becoming what the National Joint Committee on English, writing in 1917, would call a "finishing" school, preparing students for life and work, rather than just a "fitting" school, preparing students for college (Hosic 11). Taking on new tasks, including the education of a large immigrant population, educators during the first decade of the twentieth century increasingly placed the school at the center of social reform. Jane Addams, for example, coming directly from her work at Hull House in Chicago, laid the groundwork for such changes in an address to the NEA on the task of educating immigrant children. Rather than providing "evening classes and social entertainments," educators should use the public schools to "bring a fuller life to the industrial members of the community" (111).

The conflict between the goals for college preparation and the demands of the social reformers came to a head in 1910 at the annual meeting of the NEA, when the executive committee of the New York State Association of English Teachers asked for a formal protest against the lists and a thorough revision of college entrance examinations to place emphasis not on "the acquisition of information but [on] the power to read and express" (Hook 13). This led to the appointment of the Committee on College Entrance Requirements to investigate the request. The committee was chaired by James Fleming Hosic of Chicago Normal College, who had already been active in organizing the Chicago English Club (1905) and the Illinois Association of Teachers of English (1908). At the 1911 meeting of the NEA, Hosic in turn obtained a resolution from the English Round Table calling for the establishment of "a national council of teachers of English" (Hunting 556). With that resolution in hand, Hosic organized the first meeting of NCTE in Chicago in December 1911, in order, as he put it in a letter reprinted in the "Proceedings," "by securing concert of action, [to] greatly improve the conditions surrounding English work" (NCTE, "National Council" 31).

Interestingly, though the original New York resolution was brought before the new body for endorsement, the members gathered in Chicago declined to accept it because the New York resolution focused on reform of the entrance examinations rather than their elimination. The members of the new Council preferred eliminating the examinations altogether to relying instead on a system of high school accreditation. Thus, although NCTE was founded as a result of a protest against the uniform lists, the focus was shifted immediately to other ways to strengthen the teaching of English, such as through the new official publication, *English Journal*, and through other publications and committee activities. Although the founders of the Council were primarily concerned with the secondary school, *English Journal* carried some articles on elementary and college instruction, emphases that were strengthened by the adoption of the *Elementary English Review* as a second official journal in 1924 and *College English* as a separate publication in 1939, replacing an earlier College Edition of *English Journal* (1928–1939).

Building Better Booklists

One of NCTE's earliest and most enduring efforts to broaden the range of readings to benefit a wider range of young people was the development of *A List of Books for Home Reading*. The first of these, prepared by an early Council committee chaired by Herbert Bates of Manual Training High School (Brooklyn), was a sixteen-page booklet that sold for a nickel. The original 1913 edition went through eighteen reprintings before being expanded to sixty-four pages in 1923. More than one million copies were sold before a third edition appeared in 1931 (Applebee, *Tradition* 33–34). The Council's efforts to promote wide reading were extensive, including support for the development of school libraries and book lists targeted at both libraries and adult readers. The preparation of such reading lists continued into the twenty-first century, though recent volumes number hundreds of pages with separate editions targeting different age levels (e.g., McClure and Kristo; Brown and Stephens).

Throughout its history, the Council also has taken a leading role in broadening the scope of the literature curriculum beyond the traditional classics, in response both to the evolution of available media and to efforts to broaden the scope of works that are taught to include works from alternative literary traditions. One of its earliest efforts focused on the teaching of drama. The need for such an activity may seem surprising given the emphasis on Shakespeare in the uniform lists, but Shakespeare study was treated as the reading of classic texts. His popularity did little to erode a common conception that there was something salacious about actors and actresses—about, that is, the production of plays. Even Shakespeare was not immune; as late as 1893 the *New England Journal of Education* gave editorial support to a class that had refused to read *Hamlet* in an unexpurgated edition: "The indelicacies of Shakespeare in the complete edition are brutal; they are more than indelicacies, they are indecencies" (Applebee, *Tradition* 22). To support the role of drama in schools, the Council circulated prompt books; published an annotated list, *A List of Plays for High School and College Production*, in cooperation with the Drama League of America; and passed a resolution at its 1918 Annual Convention asking high schools to hire at least one teacher qualified to coach plays (Applebee, *Tradition* 62). The early emphasis on play production also served purposes rooted in progressive ideals to help students develop self-control, presence, cooperative learning, and community effort.

Over the years that followed, the Council gave similar attention to other new genres and media as they emerged: radio productions; photoplays, beginning in *English Journal* as early as 1915 (Hook 55) but becoming a major focus in the 1930s; television; film study; children's literature; adolescent literature; and, most recently, the rich resource of multimedia and Internet productions. In each of these cases, the Council has published a variety of viewpoints, ranging from commentators lamenting the loss of legitimate literature, to teachers using the new genres and media as lures to arouse interest and provide a gateway to "real" literature, to others arguing more boldly for the artistic merit and literary quality of the new works in their own right. If the Council has not actually led the way in these areas of the English curriculum, it has at least provided a consistent forum whereby teachers can learn about new genres and new media and explore their relationships to the traditional curriculum.

Broadening the Canon

Throughout its history, NCTE has used its journals, committee activities, and publication program to broaden the range of books and authors with whom teachers are familiar. As the country moved into World War I, for example, *English Journal* published "Literature in the Light of War" by University of Chicago scholar Percy Boynton. The article was a plea for teaching American literature on the grounds that it could help to make "not only better Americans but better citizens of the world" (86). Arguing for such contemporary or near-contemporary American authors as Frost, Masters, Sandburg, Wharton, Dreiser, and Tarkington, this call was part of a larger movement focusing on American literature and American studies, which in turn led to institutionalizing the American literature course as a near-universal part of the high school curriculum by the end of the 1920s. NCTE continued to bring attention to such authors in the pages of *English Journal* throughout the 1920s. It commissioned Boynton for a series of articles on American Authors of Today that appeared first as *English Journal* articles and later, according to Hook (78), as a well-selling book. The series was announced in an *English Journal* editorial (Hatfield, "Editorial") and noted by the Modern Language Association (MLA) in *PMLA* (27).

NCTE's emphasis on contemporary authors has continued to the present, at times bringing them directly to the pages of its journals, featuring them in convention sessions, publishing serious literary criticism legitimizing them as worthy of academic study, and providing teaching guides and curricular materials to ease the introduction of new works into the classroom. The most recent of these is the NCTE High School Literature Series, which began with a monograph by Carol Jago on Nikki Giovanni and expanded to include a wide range of contemporary authors and texts.

NCTE was also early to recognize the implications of the Civil Rights Movement, and later of feminist and other group-oriented scholarship, for the teaching of literature. In 1941 an NCTE committee chaired by Charlemae Hill Rollins published

We Build Together, an annotated bibliography of children's books about African Americans. This collection emphasized the need for such literature, as well as the criteria for choosing particular selections. The emphasis on criteria was in part a way to reassure teachers that, in broadening the curriculum, they were not abandoning literary merit. Although NCTE's efforts on behalf of minority literature were sidelined by World War II, a Council committee report titled "Pre-Induction Needs in Language Communication and Reading" called for "[l]iterature as the means of creating an understanding of races and cultures leading to tolerance and good will" (23). The Committee on Intercultural Relations, later renamed the Committee on Cultural Relations, was active during this postwar period, supporting an update of Rollins's bibliography and using the pages of *English Journal* and *Elementary English Review* to suggest good reading materials that teachers could use to broaden their work.

As the Civil Rights Movement took hold more firmly, the Council's activities fell more into line with national emphases. A special Task Force on Teaching English to the Disadvantaged looked at education in inner-city, largely minority schools and found it sadly wanting. The program in literature rested on "a shaky foundation," with an emphasis on reading skills and workbook exercises and a consequent neglect of literary materials (Corbin and Crosby 109). The task force's recommendation on the teaching of literature was "that at all levels of instruction, the English curriculum for disadvantaged students include appropriate imaginative literature chosen and presented with these students in mind" (273).

Since the 1960s, the Council has published a wide variety of resources dealing with important authors and texts from many different literary traditions. A selection of titles highlights the breadth and depth of Council activity in this area: Rudine Sims's *Shadow and Substance: Afro-American Experience in Contemporary Children's Fiction* (1982); Anna Lee Stensland's *Literature by and about the American Indian* (1973; revised in 1979); Wayne Martino and Bronwyn Mellor's *Gendered Fictions* (2000); Anne Ruggles Gere and Peter Shaheen's *Making American Literatures in High School and College* (2001); William Spurlin's *Lesbian and Gay Studies and the Teaching of English: Positions, Pedagogies, and Cultural Politics* (2000); Bruce Goebel's *Reading Native American Literature: A Teacher's Guide* (2004); Sherry Finkle and Tamara Lilly's *Middle Ground: Exploring Selected Literature from and about the Middle East* (2008). The High School Literature Series begun by Carol Jago has expanded to include authors as diverse as Alice Walker, Amy Tan, Judith Ortiz Cofer, Langston Hughes, and Sandra Cisneros, among others. Through such publications, the Council has sought to develop a literature curriculum that better reflects the diversity of the United States, as well as the richness of literary traditions from around the world.

The task of broadening the curriculum is not an easy one, however. When the NCTE Task Force on Racism and Bias in the Teaching of English produced a set of criteria for teaching materials in reading and literature in 1970, it complained about a "crippling discrimination" against nonwhite minorities. Specifically, the task force pointed to "the inadequate representation of literary works by members of non-white minorities in general anthologies which serve as basic texts and basal readers" (2). Twenty years later, an NCTE research report noted that 87 percent of the authors included in the most popular junior and senior high literature anthologies were non-Hispanic whites (Applebee, *Literature* 94). The same study found that when selections by authors of color were included, they were considerably less likely to be presented with social or historical background, or to be placed in the context of a literary tradition.

In the nearly twenty years since that report, the major anthologies, at least, have broadened their selections of authors and titles to include more works by women as well as by nonwhite minorities. In the pages of the Council's journals, this broadening has reached beyond the traditional printed page to include multimedia- and Internet-based environments, which for today's students, if not always for their teachers, are at the cutting edge of literary experimentation.

A report from a 2007 leadership and policy summit organized by NCTE's Conference on English Education highlights two dimensions of globalization: the development of new modes of communication that link the world together and support the development of "nonprint literature," and the importance of learning about literatures that originate outside of the traditional British and American literary canon. As the subcommittee on globalization puts it, "With this expanded set of authors and modes of representation, the interpretive responses of students to literature provide a basis to examine identities, relationships, values, and beliefs in terms of local and global contexts" (Alsup and Myers n. pag.). It goes on to caution that such teaching needs to foster "respect" for international authors and discourage responses that focus on "strangeness and exoticism."

The Battle against Censorship

The early teaching of English was shaped in part by a strong ethical tradition, which had twin roots in biblical study and in Matthew Arnold's defense of literature and culture as the bulwark against anarchy. Given the belief that one of the values of literature was the moral messages it conveyed, issues of book selection had to do with what were "appropriate" issues for students at a given age, rather than with defending a teacher's choices against external censorship. Foul language, sexual innuendo, misanthropic values—these were likely to be edited out of even canonical authors such as Shakespeare rather than defended as part of the literature of the times. In this, teachers were working within an ethical tradition stretching back to *The New England Primer* and the McGuffey Readers (Applebee, *Tradition*). As Wilbur Hatfield, the Council's second secretary-treasurer, put it in an *English Journal* editorial in 1926, "while no literature which is ethically unsound should be offered to youth, much may be given that raises no ethical issues" ("We Believe" 715).

Although NCTE publications had long given attention to the appropriateness of particular texts for use in the schools, the threat of external censorship first became a significant problem during the late 1940s, with the rise of McCarthyism and its attacks on incipient communism in virtually all aspects of society. During this period,

> Mark Van Doren, a Roman Catholic, found his books banned as communistic from the library of Jersey City Junior College; some NCTE members lost jobs in California for refusing to

> sign a loyalty oath; *Senior Scholastic* was banned from Birmingham, Alabama, *The Nation* from schools in New York City. (Applebee, *Tradition* 204)

The first reaction from NCTE was to pass a resolution at the 1948 Convention asserting that the principles of the U.S. Constitution should be "completely" upheld in every classroom in the United States. It also established its first Committee on Censorship of Teaching Materials for Classroom and Library, which led in turn to *Censorship and Controversy* (1953), a pamphlet prepared by a blue-ribbon committee that included five NCTE past presidents. The booklet began with a strong condemnation of communism, but went on to attack those who used the perceived dangers of communism "as an excuse for opposing any ideas which they do not like. . . . The techniques and procedures they employ undermine the basic freedoms we cherish" (Hook 169–70).

Although the dangers of McCarthyism were real, professional leaders in the teaching of English continued to be relatively timid in their book selection policies. As late as 1956, a report of the NCTE Commission on the English Curriculum, *The English Language Arts in the Secondary School*, cautioned teachers to avoid books that might disturb youthful minds. This caution was fully consistent with a curriculum that avoided "unexpurgated" texts and that remained within a traditional set of canonical selections. As the profession began to support the teaching of novels that dealt directly with the problems of adolescence, and as a stream of frank new works emerged from World War II, professional leaders began to urge the inclusion of texts whose content might be questioned by particular people or groups. Topics such as racism, coming-of-age with its emerging sexuality, and the brutality of war were to be explored in works of merit, under the guidance of the English teacher. As the emphasis in the curriculum shifted, some communities pushed back. By 1963 a widely cited survey in Wisconsin concluded that the list of censored books would make a "relatively good [reading list] to recommend to high school juniors and seniors" (Burress). Censored titles included the Bible, *Canterbury Tales*, *The Catcher in the Rye*, and *A Tree Grows in Brooklyn*, among many others.

Faced with such problems, the Council began a more vigorous and continuing effort to provide teachers with the support they needed to protect their use of legitimate instructional materials. These efforts included the development of *The Students' Right to Read* (1962), a widely distributed pamphlet that defended that right while also laying out clear procedures and book selection policies that would help schools and teachers deal with the challenges they were likely to face. Schools were urged to adopt formal book selection policies, including procedures for parents to request that their children be allowed to opt out of particular readings, and guidelines for dealing with challenges to specific titles (NCTE Committee on the Right to Read).

Members of the NCTE Headquarters staff have also taken the lead in supporting teachers and schools accused of teaching questionable books, providing procedural advice and sometimes written or personal testimony. One of the first references to Council involvement occurs in a report from a subcommittee on censorship at an NCTE Commission on Literature meeting in 1965. The meeting included some discussion of *The Students' Right to Read* and also of "the extent of the NCTE support behind the scenes for the teaching of the James Baldwin book in a Chicago junior college" (Squire, "Minutes" 8; which Baldwin book was unspecified). Some members argued for more direct support for individual teachers as well as for the preparation of casebooks that would provide more extensive resources than were currently available.

To further strengthen its work in this area, in 1973 the Council joined the American Library Association's efforts in support of the Freedom to Read Foundation, through which a number of interested national organizations are able to pool their resources for greater impact (Hook 239). This pooling of resources has been particularly important as groups with various religious or political positions have developed new networks to support attacks on particular titles and textbooks, sharing resources and strategies with supporters in communities across the nation. The influence and functioning of these efforts have been documented in *What Johnny Shouldn't Read* (DelFattore), published by Yale University Press but distributed by NCTE. Over the years, the Council has taken a stand against the influence of such groups, filing an amicus curiae brief, for example, in the Island Trees (Long Island) censorship case (Suhor). This case began in 1975 when members of the school board obtained a list of objectionable books from Parents of New York United and used it to remove eleven books from the school library. The list included such titles as *The Fixer* by Bernard Malamud, *Black Boy* by Richard Wright, and *Best Short Stories of Negro Writers* edited by Langston Hughes. The case went all the way to the U.S. Supreme Court, which ruled narrowly in favor of the students who had appealed against the removal of the titles.

Charles Suhor, NCTE Deputy Executive Director from 1977 to 1997, points out, however, that such involvement was difficult for the Council, which could easily be seen as

> outside interferers. . . . We thought that writing letters [to school boards] would give us a black eye. . . . The school board or principal would say something nasty about us in the press. But in the early 1990s, Executive Director Jack Maxwell decided that teachers needed the help of an aggressive anticensorship program. Letters tailored to particular cases became routine, and other actions such as collections of rationales for challenged books were effected.

The Council has sponsored a continuing series of publications providing teachers with the materials they need to resist censorship and to justify their book selections, including two CD publications of *Rationales for Challenged Books* (NCTE and IRA; NCTE Anti-Censorship Center).

How Should Literature Be Taught?

The Council's role in the teaching of literature extends far beyond its efforts to broaden the range of works that are taught. Another set of major efforts has focused on the most appropriate approaches to curriculum and instruction.

The teaching of vernacular literature at the end of the nineteenth century was shaped by the desire to demonstrate that literature offered the "mental discipline" of the classical curriculum —that is, that literature offered the internal structure and difficult subject matter necessary to train the "faculties" of memory and reason, just as study of the classical languages had done. The alternative, critics argued, was "mere chatter about Shelley" (Palmer 96). To find that discipline, the teaching of literature in the nineteenth century had turned to two different fields of scholarship: philology on the one hand and literary history on the other. Both fields, however noble their original goals, rapidly deteriorated into minutiae that held little interest for students and little relationship to the content of the literary texts themselves (Applebee, *Tradition*)

When combined with the lists of texts to be studied for college entrance, these emphases led to the development of annotated editions of school texts; these were in widespread use by the 1880s. One of the earliest was William Rolfe's 1867 American edition of Craik's *Julius Caesar*. This edition, which set a pattern for the many that followed, contained "an Introduction, The History of the Play, The Sources of the Plot, Critical Comments on the Play (26 pages), the play itself (102 pages), Notes (82 pages!), and an Index of Words and Phrases Explained" (Mersand 279–80).

By the time the Council was organized in 1911, many of the same teachers and scholars who were rebelling against the uniform college entrance lists were also looking for alternative ways to organize and teach the curriculum in literature. They drew from a variety of sources to justify their search. One major influence was the child study movement and the work of G. Stanley Hall, who urged that rather than mental discipline, the curriculum should recapitulate the history of the culture, aligning with what he believed were the normal stages of child development. Another was the progressivism of John Dewey and his emphasis on the interrelationships between education, the community, and the nature of the child.

Organizing the Curriculum

Against this backdrop, one of the first committees appointed by the Council was charged with studying alternative types of organization for high school English. Its findings, published in *English Journal* in 1913, demonstrated once again that the curriculum in literature was determined by the uniform lists. Rather than separate types of organization, the committee reported a "remarkable uniformity" in the English curriculum (NCTE Committee on Types of Organization 593).

Although the early years of the Council were dominated by concerns with high school English, the Council did pay some attention to the elementary school as well. The early NCTE Committee on the Articulation of the Elementary and High School Courses in English surveyed teachers, principals, and superintendents about the teaching of English in the last three years of elementary school and the first year of high school, finding in general a lack of articulation and considerable overlap in the works being taught. The committee agreed that books should be selected "primarily for their appeal to the pupils' sympathies and interests" (NCTE Committee on the Articulation 319); those most frequently reported for the elementary grades were "*The Christmas Carol*, *The Courtship of Miles Standish*, *Evangeline*, *The Lady of the Lake*, *The Legend of Sleepy Hollow* and *Rip Van Winkle*, *Snowbound*, *Tales from Shakespeare*, *Julius Caesar*, *The Merchant of Venice*, *The Great Stone Face*, *The Man without a Country* and *Heidi*" (309).

Reorganizing the Teaching of English: The First Attempt

Even as these Council committees made their reports, a much larger effort was underway to reconfigure the curriculum in English. This was the work of the National Joint Committee on English, cosponsored by NCTE and the NEA's Commission on Reorganization. The Joint Committee on English was chaired by James Fleming Hosic of Chicago Normal College, who was also the Council's first secretary-treasurer and founding editor of *English Journal*.

When the *Reorganization of English in Secondary Schools* (Hosic) appeared in 1917, it provided a coherent and comprehensive restatement of the new shape of English instruction in general and literature in particular, recapitulating a variety of arguments that teachers and scholars had been making over the preceding decade (cf. Applebee, *Tradition*). The report began by affirming the independence of the high school curriculum from the dictates of the colleges. It argued for "a considerable range" of course content adapted to the needs of varying groups of students, coupled with "a reasonable uniformity of aims and a body of common culture" (Hosic 26). The aims of such study were "skill in thinking, high ideals, right habits of conduct, healthy interests, and sensitiveness to the beautiful attainments to be coveted by all" (Hosic 26). Rather than a formal discipline, English was to be viewed as "social in content and social in method of acquirement, [structured around] expressional and interpretative experiences of the greatest possible social value to the given class" (Hosic 27). This did not mean an abandonment of the classical canon, however, for it was precisely that canon that had such social value.

The *Reorganization Report,* as it came to be known, was quite specific about the content of the curriculum in literature, laying out grade-by-grade lists of books for classroom study, as well as for individual reading. The distinction was one already adopted by the uniform lists, but it fit comfortably with the new goals of providing a "considerable range" of work as well as ensuring a "common culture."

The specific sequencing of work followed closely the recommendations of G. Stanley Hall in his work *Adolescence* (1904). The eighth and ninth grades were the place for "stirring narrative" (69), including the myths and legends of Greece and Rome as well as modern adventure novels by Sir Walter Scott and Robert Louis Stevenson. The tenth grade dealt with "serious questions of right and wrong" (64); the eleventh, with "the relations of men and women to each other," but only in the context of the "high ideality" of *Idylls of the King* and *Silas Marner* (70). Only in the twelfth grade would students confront a traditional study of literature that presented a chronologically organized history of American and British literature (70–71). Echoes of this parsing of the high school curriculum continue in American schools to the present day.

According to J. N. Hook, during the 1920s "almost every public high school and many private ones were affected by [the *Reorganization Report*] to some degree in philosophy, in course content and arrangement, and in increased attention to student needs" (47–48).

Toward an Experience Curriculum

The Joint Committee on English established a pattern that has continued throughout the Council's history, in which issues in curriculum and instruction would emerge out of larger social and professional movements, be taken up by individual teachers and scholars in Council journals and conferences, and then be reconciled and given authoritative form and substance through the work of a major Council committee or commission.

The years following the *Reorganization Report* were filled with a variety of attempts to provide teachers with new ways of organizing curriculum and instruction in literature (Applebee, *Tradition*). As early as 1918, NCTE began publishing literary maps and other materials to enliven the teaching of literature and to highlight local authors. More important, teachers began to share their experiments with new ways of organizing the curriculum as they struggled to move beyond the uniform lists to a more coherent organization. Articles in *English Journal* explored methods of individualizing instruction, such as Helen Parkhurst's Dalton (Massachusetts) plan, which involved negotiating individual contracts for work to be done to achieve an A, B, or C grade over a given period. Others explored "mastery units," popularized by Henry C. Morrison. As in the Dalton plan, students could proceed at their own pace through such units until they achieved mastery of the intended outcome.

Both the Dalton plan and mastery units were ultimately criticized by Council leaders for their emphasis on individualism at the expense of social interaction around the literature that students read, as well as for their tendency to trivialize knowledge by focusing on things that could be easily observed and quantified. The approach that became most popular, and that fit best with the metaphor of experience in the *Reorganization Report*, was the project method, proposed by William Heard Kilpatrick of Columbia University's Teachers College. The project method emphasized purposeful activity, which in turn "brings satisfaction and thus forges the necessary bonds between stimulus and response" (69). The benefit of the project method, as it was taken up by teachers of English, was that the emphasis on purposeful activity made experience and education virtually synonymous. As Kilpatrick put it, "The best way in which I can now conceive the curriculum itself is as a series of experiences in which by guided induction the child makes his own formulations. Then they are his to use" (310).

By 1929, at the urging of NCTE President Ruth Mary Weeks, the Council was ready once again to tackle the issue of how to organize the curriculum. Whereas the *Reorganization Report* had been guided by the Committee of Thirty, the NCTE Curriculum Commission appointed by Weeks had 175 members with expertise across all levels, kindergarten through college. W. Wilbur Hatfield, secretary-treasurer of the Council, was chair.

The major report of the commission, *An Experience Curriculum in English* (1935), sought to provide the concrete guidance on curriculum and instruction that the *Reorganization Report* had lacked. The curriculum as a whole was organized around "units" of up to three weeks duration, themselves organized into experience strands, within which units were "arranged like broad easy stair steps in a reasonably steady progression of intellectual difficulty and social maturity" (Hatfield, "Preface" viii). Each unit had a "primary objective" that laid out the overarching goal for the unit and "enabling objectives" that focused on knowledge and skills that students might need to acquire in order to meet the primary objective. Literary study was grouped within a variety of strands, presented separately for grades K through 6 and 7 through 12, that were by this point very traditional, with titles such as Enjoying Action and Suspense (K–6) , Solving Puzzles (e.g., mystery stories, 7–12), Sifting the Radio Programs (K–6), and Enjoying Photoplays (7–12). And while the work that was proposed had moved a long way beyond the historical and philological roots of literary study, *An Experience Curriculum* still lacks a methodology for engaging students very deeply in the works they are studying.

In spite of these shortcomings in the treatment of literature, *An Experience Curriculum* had a widespread impact on textbooks and courses of study across the country (Applebee, *Tradition* 122). According to Hook (111), it sold over 25,000 copies in the first few years after publication, an average of several copies for each school system then in existence. It remained in print until the

1960s. Although the NCTE Curriculum Commission published at least three other volumes—one on college English, another illustrating what the experiences of the first report looked like in action, and a third on correlating curriculum across subject areas—none of these had the impact of *An Experience Curriculum*.

The Curriculum Revisited in the Post-War Era

The forces that shaped *An Experience Curriculum in English* were interrupted by World War II, when goals for education narrowed around the development of patriotism and of the skills and values that could support the war effort. The Council responded quickly, with the Executive Committee approving the report "The Role of the English Teacher in Wartime" just three weeks after Pearl Harbor (Hook 133). The report asserted the traditional values of literature in helping students develop a "sense of what it is that America is fighting for by developing an understanding of democratic ideals and by stimulating devotion to them." And it went on to claim that "[t]he teaching of English in wartime will concern itself also with the needs of the individual for social and personal adjustment" (Hook 134).

While the patriotism in the first assertion echoes similar emphases during and after World War I, the second reflects a general movement during the war and postwar era toward "life adjustment," fitting the curriculum around the needs and interests of the adolescent. The movement began within the Progressive Education Association, was taken up by the Educational Policies Commission of the NEA in a series of reports during the 1940s, and was given the unfortunate label of "life adjustment" by the U.S. Office of Education (Applebee, *Tradition* 143–44). As it affected the teaching of literature, this movement added impetus to the teaching of adolescent literature dealing with the immediate "needs and interests" of adolescent youth and shifted the focus in curriculum and instruction toward discussions of "life problems."

The Council's response to these issues was again to establish a (slightly renamed) Commission on the English Curriculum. Appointed in 1945, this time under the direction of Dora V. Smith, a past president of NCTE and professor of education at the University of Minnesota, the commission produced during the 1950s three reports on English language arts in elementary and secondary schools and, during the 1960s, a report on college English and one on teacher education.

These volumes again emphasized the "unit" as the basic tool for organizing curriculum, but what was meant by a unit was that "varied activities in the language arts are developed around a central theme or purpose" (NCTE Commission on the English Curriculum, *The English Language Arts* 69). Given the general emphasis on life adjustment, literature in the secondary school was dealt with in a section called "Meeting Youth's Needs through Literature." The elementary school volume treated reading and literature together, mixing discussions of mass media with children's literature in discussing "The Contribution of Reading and Literature to Personal Development" (NCTE Commission on the English Curriculum, *Language Arts for Today's Children* 5). The volumes lacked clear guiding principles for what should be taught, relying on generalizations about growth curves and the characteristics of children at different ages. However, any number of activities could be justified as being more complex or meeting a need, and all types of activities were offered. In spite of these shortcomings, the volumes were in step with their times and were generally favorably received (Applebee, *Tradition* note 68, 183). They were also the last Council effort to specify a comprehensive curriculum; in later years, the organization preferred to focus on broad standards or alternative models for the curriculum, or to offer unit plans that focused on specific topics.

Literature after Sputnik

The launch of *Sputnik* in 1957 changed everything in education. Criticisms of progressivism, which had been building throughout the 1940s and early 1950s, suddenly captured the public and professional imagination. Congress responded with the National Defense Education Act (NDEA) of 1958, which provided funds to strengthen the teaching of mathematics, science, and modern foreign languages but allocated no monies for improving the teaching of English.

The Council reacted unusually swiftly. In the professional arena, it cosponsored a series of conferences on Basic Issues in the Teaching of English. The conferences, supported by Ford Foundation funding, agreed that English must be regarded as a "fundamental liberal discipline" (NCTE, *Basic Issues* 7), a far cry from the emphasis on life adjustment in the reports that the NCTE Commission on the English Curriculum was still issuing. For the teaching of literature, this meant that the basis of curriculum would lie in the characteristics of the discipline, a specific body of knowledge with its own internal logic, rather than in the needs and interests of the student or the preferences of a local community.

In the political arena, the Council addressed the shortcomings of the NDEA by establishing the NCTE Committee on National Interest, chaired by a newly appointed NCTE executive secretary, James R. Squire. *The National Interest and the Teaching of English* (1961) made no attempt to deal with the subtle debates within the profession; instead, it argued strongly for the importance of English instruction to the welfare of the nation, coupled with clear evidence of inadequacies in instruction. Although the report was reprinted in full in the *Congressional Record*, expansion of the NDEA was blocked in the U.S. House of Representatives after being approved in the Senate. This first report was followed by a second in 1964, *The National Interest and the Continuing Education of Teachers of English*, and in that same year Congress finally opened up NDEA funding to the teaching of English.

The first National Interest report did help garner congressional approval in 1961 for the inclusion of English in the Cooperative Research Program (originally approved in 1954), an action that led to Project English, a program administered by the U.S. Office of Education. J. N. Hook, Squire's predecessor at NCTE, was named as first coordinator. Although Project English was not specifically an NCTE activity, U.S. Office of Education staff conferred frequently with leaders of NCTE and related professional organizations. The directors of curriculum study centers and basic research studies that were supported by Project English also were active in NCTE and reported on their efforts in NCTE journals and publications. These projects contributed to a post-*Sputnik* realignment of the curriculum around English as a tripod (the disciplines of language, literature, and composition) that differed greatly from the emphases in the pre-*Sputnik* era (cf. Applebee, *Tradition* 198–204; Shugrue).

Beyond the Academic Model

The Council's emphasis on a completely academic model for the teaching of literature was relatively short-lived, as attention shifted back toward programs that would be more socially relevant and more responsive to the psychology of the child rather than to the structure of the discipline. The catalyst within the Council was the Anglo-American Seminar on the Teaching and Learning of English, or Dartmouth Conference, a monthlong gathering of teachers and scholars from Australia, Canada, the United Kingdom, and the United States. The conference was a transformative experience for many of the American participants; although they arrived as proponents of a discipline-based model, they found their presuppositions about teaching and learning challenged by the different practices and values of their peers from other countries.

In addition to its effects on participants, the conference led to two widely cited reports, one from an American perspective (Muller) and the other from a British point of view (Dixon). Dixon's title, *Growth through English*, captured the spirit of the model toward which Council leaders began to move. For the teaching of literature, this meant more emphasis on personal responses to literature, more emphasis on drama and creative dramatics, and more concern with the interrelationships between literature, talk, and writing.

There were many competing trends during this period, however, and the metaphor of growth had to compete with continuing calls for attention to cultural heritage as well as with a back-to-the-basics movement often coupled with a press for behavioral objectives. The Council's journals and publications continued to present all sides of these issues, but it is fair to say that in its official positions and major statements, the organization became increasingly liberal. Behavioral objectives were addressed by the Council's Commission on the English Curriculum at the 1969 Annual Convention and published in 1970 as *On Writing Behavioral Objectives for English*, edited by John C. Maxwell and Anthony Tovatt. The general tenor of this book is perhaps best captured by the title of James Moffett's convention session, "Misbehaviorist English" (Hook 244–45).

When the NCTE Commission on the English Curriculum turned to the larger issue of the curriculum as a whole in that same year, it did not even attempt a reconciliation of the competing views within the profession, instead laying out three competing models for the curriculum from prekindergarten through college (Mandel). The three were built around personal growth, cultural heritage, and the development of specific language competencies. These were presented by different authors, without an attempt to compare their strengths and weaknesses. Unlike earlier efforts to provide model curricula to lead the profession forward, this report seems to have had very little impact.

Constructing a New Paradigm

Beginning in the 1970s but intensifying in the 1980s and 1990s, theories of language teaching and learning were increasingly "constructivist" in orientation. With diverse roots in linguistics, psychology, sociology, and philosophy, constructivist approaches share a view of knowledge as an active construction built up by the individual learner acting within a social context that shapes and constrains what is learned but does not determine it in an absolute sense. Constructivist approaches emphasize that learning is most effective when it takes place in the context of activities that are meaningful and engaging for the learner; that "errors" may in fact be reflections of systematic, if not fully mature, stages of learning; and that learning is a social rather than an individual process.

James Britton, from the University of London Institute of Education, was a British representative at the Dartmouth Conference who played a major role in introducing American teachers and scholars to the implications of constructivist theories of language learning. A background paper he prepared for Dartmouth and that later was published by the Council traced out the implications for the teaching of literature. In a statement that had to be startling to advocates of a disciplinary model of English, Britton shifted the focus to engagement with the ideas and issues in literature with a small *l*. Rather than knowledge of literary history or literary criticism, he argued, the most important outcome of literary study should be "a legacy of past satisfactions" (5).

Early versions of constructivist approaches in Council publications and conferences focused on "process approaches," particularly in the teaching of writing. As early as 1971, the Council published Janet Emig's dissertation, *The Composing Processes of Twelfth Graders,* a landmark study that was more influential for its demonstration that writing did involve a process than for the particular ways in which that process was described. But Britton's Dartmouth pamphlet had already begun sketching out what a similar orientation might mean for the teaching of literature (and it is not incidental that Emig spent time with Britton's research group at the University of London while completing her dissertation).

Early versions of constructivism were captured by the English Coalition Conference, a three-week effort by NCTE, MLA, and five other groups to find some common ground in the teaching of language. Their 1989 report (Lloyd-Jones and Lunsford) is firmly within a constructivist tradition, emphasizing the active nature of learning and the interplay of skills and content "in a dynamic process of practice and assimilation" (xxiii). Although the conferees arrived at considerable agreement about goals and directions in English teaching, the report fails to offer clear guidelines for the teaching of English language arts in general or the teaching of literature in particular. Caught in a reaction against prescriptive lists of content to be taught—the scope and sequence charts of school programs as well as the cultural literacy of advocates such as E. D. Hirsch—the conference found no broader principles to offer. Instead, the report presents a variety of alternatives and options for elementary, secondary, and college programs that do not coalesce to provide a sense of unity and direction for the curriculum as a whole. Guidelines for literature at the secondary level, for example, included: "Study a variety of complete works of literature, as well as a wide variety of other texts, such as student writing, television, advertising, video, specialty magazines, film, and technical reports" and "Invite students to read deeply in our diverse literary tradition, including writing by men and women of many racial, ethnic, and cultural groups" (Shea). In offering such platitudes rather than a clear vision, the coalition report suffers from some of the same problems that plagued the earlier reports from the NCTE Commission on the English Curriculum.

In the last decade of the twentieth century and the first of the twenty-first, exploration of constructivist models has evolved from the relative simplicity of process models focusing on individuals to more complete sociocognitive models that focus on the ways in which learning is shaped in interaction with the social context within which it takes place (Langer, "A Sociocognitive View"). One focus of that exploration has been the federally sponsored Research and Development Center for the Learning and Teaching of Literature (which has since evolved into the Center on English Learning and Achievement) at the University at Albany. From the center's beginning in 1987, Council officers actively supported its activities, served on its national advisory board, provided space on its convention programs, and published its work.

Under the direction of Arthur Applebee, Judith Langer, and Alan Purves, the center set out to explore the state of literature instruction and to develop new approaches to curriculum, instruction, and assessment that would better align with constructivist frameworks. Langer, for example, conducted a lengthy series of studies on the nature of literary understanding and the instructional contexts that could best enrich its development. She described these highly effective learning contexts as "envisionment building classrooms" (*Literature Instruction*; *Envisioning Literature*). Applebee began with a study of current practices in the teaching of literature (*Literature*), followed by a reconceptualizing of curriculum around ongoing "conversations" about issues that would challenge and engage students ("Toward Thoughtful Curriculum"; *Curriculum*). Purves, after developing an array of assessment instruments that would better describe literature achievement from a constructivist perspective ("Testing Literature"), went on to address the complex issues involved in incorporating multicultural literature as an integral rather than an incidental part of a comprehensive literature program (Cruz, Jordan, Meléndez, Ostrowski, and Purves). Other colleagues at the center used similar constructivist frameworks to explore the nature of effective teaching and learning in elementary school classrooms (Allington and Johnston; Allington, Johnston, and

Day; Pressley, Allington, Wharton-McDonald, Block, and Morrow). Many of these studies were published in NCTE books and journals.

Even as Council members were exploring constructivist paradigms, others were working to incorporate into school classrooms perspectives from developments in literary theory. A large part of this effort is reflected in the work to broaden the canon, discussed earlier in this chapter. Another part, however, involves familiarizing teachers with developments in other areas. *Transactions with Literature* (Farrell and Squire) pays tribute to Louise Rosenblatt and her transactional theory of literature. *A Teacher's Introduction to Reader-Response Theories* (Beach) summarizes strengths and weaknesses of a variety of approaches characterized as reader response, including Rosenblatt's work. Other books in the NCTE Teacher's Introduction Series focus on philosophical hermeneutics (Crusius) and postmodernism (Linn). *Understanding Others* (Trimmer and Warnock), *Changing Classroom Practices* (Downing), and *Literature and Lives* (Carey-Webb) explore the impact of cultural and cross-cultural studies. *Critical Encounters in High School English* (Appleman) demonstrates how a variety of different versions of critical theory can play out successfully in the school classroom, offering students powerful tools for making sense of what they read. *Gendered Fictions* (Martino and Mellor) and *Lesbian and Gay Studies and the Teaching of English* (Spurlin) explore the implications of various forms of gender studies for the teaching of literature. Together with conference sessions and journal articles, publications such as these have helped to meld constructivist approaches to instruction with developments in literary theory and scholarship.

Confronting the Standards Movement

Even as scholars and teachers were exploring constructivist paradigms in Council publications and conferences, the movement for "systemic reform" was having an impact on classrooms across the country. The movement has complex roots. It includes a conservative tradition emphasizing "liberal education," with roots in the Great Books program of Mortimer Adler as well as the cultural literacy of E. D. Hirsch. But it also includes a social justice agenda, driven by a recognition that many schools, particularly those serving the urban poor, have been failing for decades to break the cycle of poverty and low achievement (Smith and O'Day).

Systemic reform emphasizes bringing all components of the educational system into alignment in the service of common goals: curriculum, assessment, teaching materials, and teacher education. For this alignment to take place, it is necessary to be clear about what students should know and be able to do in each subject area at every grade level; these are the standards around which the other parts of the instructional system can then be aligned. The National Council of Teachers of Mathematics developed a widely cited set of standards in 1989, and other subject areas soon felt the pressure to follow suit.

NCTE, in collaboration with the International Reading Association (IRA), took up the challenge in 1991 with a request for federal funding to develop a set of voluntary national standards in the English language arts. Funding followed the next year, and the standards project got underway with Janet Emig as project chair and the Center for the Study of Reading at the University of Illinois as the coordinating organization. The constructivist orientation of the Council's leadership, however, soon came into conflict with the expectations of the U.S. Department of Education, which was looking for a comprehensive inventory of knowledge and skills in the various areas of the English language arts. After two years of meetings involving an extensive group of teachers and scholars, federal funding was withdrawn. But rather than let the project collapse, NCTE and IRA decided to complete their work on their own.

Standards for the English Language Arts (1996) is a very different document from the one standards advocates might have envisioned. Rather than detailed lists of what students should know and be able to do at a variety of grade levels, the document offers twelve standards that apply across grades and contexts. Although literature has a place in many of the standards, it is singled out in Standard 2: "Students read a wide range of literature from many periods in many genres to build an understanding of the many dimensions (e.g., philosophical, ethical, aesthetic) of human experience" (IRA and NCTE 3). As a goal for English instruction, this is difficult to argue with, but as a framework for laying out a curriculum or designing an assessment, it does not take a teacher very far. And that of course was the intention of the standards writers. As the prologue to the list of twelve standards puts it, "[T]he standards provide ample room for the innovation and creativity essential to teaching and learning. They are not prescriptions for particular curriculum or instruction" (3). Instead of prescriptions, the document offers a series of eighteen vignettes organized by grade level but offered without interpretive commentary. These were chosen to "illustrate a variety of classroom practices and projects, in which students' perspectives, interests, and needs shape classroom discussion, writing projects, and curriculum choices" (66). The text contains no citations, but the document has a thirteen-page appendix of resources for teachers, available from one or the other of the sponsoring organizations.

If the standards document was more a defense of the richness and complexity of language and literacy than a guide to curriculum or assessment, the issues in curriculum and assessment raised by the standards movement have continued to be addressed at Council conferences and in its publications. Indeed, *Standards for the English Language Arts* was accompanied by a series of Standards in Practice publications targeted at specific grade levels, and the Council's website now provides extensive curriculum and professional development materials that teachers can use to move from this vision toward more concrete guidance about approaches to curriculum and instruction. The rich materials available on the Web are not linked to the *Standards* document, however.

In the little over a decade since *Standards for the English Language Arts* was issued, the Council has continued to explore the role of English in a twenty-first-century world. In 2008 the NCTE Executive Committee adopted two position statements on twenty-first-century literacies, for example, acknowledging the rapid changes that have taken place in the technologies through which literacy can be expressed and endorsing their place and importance within the English classroom (NCTE, "NCTE Definition," "21st Century Curriculum"). These statements treat these literacies primarily as new ways of communicating and socializing and do not address their relevance to literature instruction. A working group on literature from a 2007 Conference on English Education leadership and policy summit looked more directly at these issues. The working group, convened by Richard Beach of the University of Minnesota and Hephzibah Roskelly of the University of North Carolina at Greensboro, argued that in the twenty-first-century, literature

> needs to be defined to include a range of multimodal and digital texts associated with popular culture: manga novels, comic books, digital poetry/storytelling, mixed media drama productions, etc. As has always been the case with children's literature, these texts combine print and visual images in ways that serve to engage young audiences accustomed to multimodal media texts. (Beach and Roskelly n. pag.)

The working group also recognized that in these new environments texts were increasingly linked in very immediate but also nonlinear ways, creating new kinds of relationships and cross-referencing. Such explorations of the changing nature of literary culture will be a necessary part of redefining a literature curriculum for the twenty-first century.

A Research Base for Literature Education

Research has had a place in NCTE activities since its original Committee on Types of Organization of High-School English surveyed principals about the ways in which the curriculum was organized. For much of the early history, however, the research that was reported in Council journals and publications dealt with other, more easily studied aspects of the English curriculum—particularly language and communication skills that could justify the teaching of English in terms of its value and use in everyday life. By essentially ignoring the teaching of literature, studies such as *The Place of English in American Life* (Clapp) allowed literature to avoid the extreme functionalism that sometimes threatened to take over other aspects of the curriculum.

By the 1930s, the Council had established a Committee on Research to heighten teachers' awareness of studies relevant to their teaching, but there was a continuing competition for resources (journal pages and conference slots) between research and practice—so much so that a group of prominent scholars, many of whom were active in NCTE, founded an independent National Conference on Research in Elementary School English in 1932; the conference was broadened to include all levels in 1937 (Petty 5). During this period, the Council did publish Stella S. Center and Gladys Persons's *Teaching High-School Students to Read* (1937). The experiment explored in this work took place in New York City during the Great Depression, replacing the regular English class with a reading school that emphasized reading comprehension using a variety of materials graded for difficulty. Although literary texts were included in the project, so too were workplace "types," and the emphasis was clearly on reading rather than literature.

Not until the 1960s, with James Squire in the role of executive secretary, did research related to the teaching and learning of literature begin to play a major role in the Council's activities, in part as a result of renewed attention to research on all aspects of English. Thus a new NCTE Research Foundation was underway by 1962, with enough resources to provide small grants for teachers and scholars. The following year the Council established the David H. Russell Research Award; the third award in the series was the first related to literature, going to Wayne Booth of the University of Chicago for his *Rhetoric of Fiction*. Also in 1963, the Council launched a research report series; the second volume, *The Responses of Adolescents While Reading Four Short Stories* (1964), was a revision of Squire's 1956 doctoral dissertation at the University of California at Berkeley. Among other findings, this study demonstrated the many dimensions of response and their development over time and suggested that instruction needed to take this process of evolving understanding into account.

Thus began a long series of publications investigating various aspects of literature teaching and learning. Coupled with articles published in the journal *Research in the Teaching of English*, launched in 1967, the NCTE research report series began the process of providing an empirical base for decisions about curriculum and instruction in literature and other aspects of the teaching of English. One of the most influential early strands of this research focused on response to literature. James Wilson's *Responses of College Freshmen to Three Novels* (Report No. 7; 1966), looked at the effects of teaching on patterns of response. But the publication that provided the methodology to allow this tradition of research to blossom was Alan Purves's *Elements of Writing about a Literary Work* (Report No. 9; 1968). Purves was a professor of English at the University of Illinois who had earlier worked at the Educational Testing Service. His monograph offered a system for analyzing responses to literature, using categories that ranged from such literary devices as allusion and irony to general statements such as "thematic importance" and came complete with coding rules and reliability estimates. Purves's system of analysis was picked up rapidly by other researchers interested in literature education and response to literature, providing a useful tool that could be adapted to describe oral or written response, patterns of instruction, and curricular emphases in individual classrooms as well as in national cultures (Applebee, "Elements of Response").

The Council's most ambitious look at curriculum and instruction during Squire's tenure as executive secretary was the National Study of High School English Programs, directed by Squire and Roger Applebee, a high school department chair brought from Rochester, New York, to co-direct the study. With funding from the U.S. Office of Education, teams of teachers and scholars visited 168 high schools chosen for their outstanding programs in English; the results of these visits were published as *High School English Instruction Today* (Squire and Applebee).

In one sense, the National Study was intended as the Council's way to reform curriculum and instruction by example; it sought to "ascertain the ways in which strong schools are already achieving important results in English" (Squire and Applebee, *High School* 1). In fact, it documented both strengths and weaknesses in the programs it visited and set the stage for a variety of later efforts to strengthen the profession. The study did find that the teachers in these schools were better prepared and more professionally active than their peers surveyed earlier for the *National Interest* studies (54–56). Yet even with that preparation, observations of more than 1,600 classes showed that recitation and lecture dominated; discussion accounted for less than a quarter of class time observed (Table 22, 299). Reflecting the rapid move away from life adjustment, over 50 percent of the teachers rated "close textual study" as of "great importance" in the teaching of literature, but classroom observations suggested that teachers were having trouble translating this into effective classroom practice, particularly with students in the lower tracks (102–06). The study also found that the selections chosen for study were more distinctly literary than during the life adjustment period, but there was also evidence of self-censorship and a deliberate de-emphasis of major twentieth-century works (102). Studying the adequacy of school library collections as well as texts chosen for classroom study, observers found one memorable collection with six biographies of William Faulkner but none of his works (188).

The National Study highlighted some issues in content and approaches in the teaching of literature but failed to provide any strong alternatives to then-current approaches. That task fell to a follow-up study of instruction in the United Kingdom. Again directed by Squire and Applebee and using many of the same procedures, *Teaching English in the United Kingdom* (1969) provided a radical alternative to the teaching of literature as it was evolving in American schools.

In contrast to the American emphasis on the discipline, with its internal structure and body of knowledge, the emphasis in the United Kingdom was "centered on the pupil—*his* interests, *his* response, *his* view of the world" (Squire and Applebee, *Teaching English* 52). The role of subject matter was to provide the experiences through which students extended their linguistic and cognitive skills by applying them in new contexts. The goal of teaching, as James Britton of the University of London put it, was "to refine and develop responses the children are already making" (4). Rather than engaging in highly structured discussion, teachers in the United Kingdom stressed "improvised drama, imaginative writing, personal response to literature, and a large amount of informal classroom discussion" (Squire and Applebee, *Teaching English* 52). In an echo of what Squire had described in NCTE Research Report No. 2 (*Responses*), students' initial responses were understood to be tentative and developing rather than complete and well formulated. Unlike their American counterparts who ended discussion with consensus and a summing-up, the British teachers were more comfortable relying on the educative effects of the process of discussion itself.

The American observers, fresh from the self-censorship they had observed in successful American programs, were also startled at the diversity of texts available to British teachers. Even *Lady Chatterley's Lover* found its place in the reading lists for one of the classrooms they observed (Squire and Applebee, *Teaching English* 95), a book they were unlikely to find in a school library in the United States.

The Council's activities in the 1960s provided a lasting institutional base for supporting research that could help in the development of more effective teaching and learning of literature and other aspects of the English language arts. The research report series has published other widely cited studies of literature teaching and learning, including James Hoetker's *Students as Audiences* (No. 11; 1971); Ann Terry's *Children's Poetry Preferences* (No. 16; 1974); F. André Favat's *Child and Tale* (No. 19; 1977); Arthur Applebee's *Literature in the Secondary School* (No. 25; 1993); Carol Lee's *Signifying as a Scaffold for Literary Interpretation* (No. 26; 1993); James Marshall, Peter Smagorinsky, and Michael Smith's *The Language of Interpretation* (No. 27; 1994); and Lesley Mandel Morrow's *Motivating Reading and Writing in Diverse Classrooms* (No. 28; 1996).

Other publications also have contributed to a research base for making recommendations for the teaching of literature, including Purves and Beach's *Literature and the Reader* (1972), synthesizing research on the teaching of literature, and two editions of the *Handbook of Research on Teaching the English Language Arts* (Flood, Jensen, Lapp, and Squire [1991]; Flood, Lapp, Squire, and Jensen [2003]), with chapters on responding to literature, reading preferences, the teaching of literature, and voluntary reading.

At the same time, the David H. Russell Research Award has been an effective vehicle for highlighting relevant works from the broader scholarly tradition, sometimes by authors active in NCTE and at other times drawing in new people. In addition to Wayne Booth, authors of other works especially relevant to the teaching of literature have included James Britton (for lifetime achievement), Louise Rosenblatt (for *The Reader, the Text, the Poem*), Robert Scholes (for *Textual Power*), James Moffett (for *Storm in the Mountains*), and Arthur Applebee (for *Curriculum as Conversation)*. At the same time, the Promising Researcher Award has nurtured young scholars who have typically gone on to take active roles in Council activities, ensuring a continuing place for research and scholarship.

NCTE's Legacy in the Teaching of Literature

NCTE has played a major role in shaping the teaching of literature over the past one hundred years. From its genesis in challenges to the lists of books provided for college entrance examinations to the nascent debates on the definition of literature amidst twenty-first-century technologies, the Council has defended the role of professional judgment at the local level in making decisions about what and how to teach. At the same time, it has provided an open forum for informed discussion of new works and of works from underrepresented literary traditions. Whether advocating for the inclusion of drama in 1913 or literature dealing with gay and lesbian issues in the 1990s, the Council's publications and conferences have been a positive force in ensuring that the curriculum in literature reflects the diversity of the country and the world. At the same time, the forums that the Council has provided through its publications and conferences have played a vital role in the professional growth of individual teachers across the nation. Jean E. Brown, now of Rhode Island College, spoke for many others when she described the Council as her "lifeline" as a beginning teacher in the desert Southwest: "For the teachers who are isolated, you can commune with the *Journal* and know that you are not alone."

The Council has also played an important role in helping the profession assimilate new ideas about curriculum and instruction in literature as they emerge from the larger educational and social context. During the past one hundred years, the general pattern has been to support a healthy debate and expression of sometimes opposing views in the Council's publications and conferences and then, as a consensus begins to emerge, to sponsor a synthesis that reflects a new conventional wisdom. This pattern was particularly clear for the first half of the century, with the *Reorganization Report* being followed by *An Experience Curriculum in English*, and that in turn by the Commission on the English Curriculum publications of the 1950s. The Dartmouth Conference yielded a similar synthesis in Dixon's *Growth through English*, though the debate in that case played out among the differing national perspectives represented at the conference rather than over a more extended period in the Council's publications and conferences.

Since the 1960s, perhaps because the external pressures on schools in general and literacy instruction in particular have been so strong, the Council's policies and position statements have been less comprehensive—defending a vision of the teaching of literature that values engagement with compelling human issues rather than one that focuses on an easily measurable list of knowledge and skills. But there has been no attempt to develop a model of a new curriculum in English in general or literature in particular, and seemingly no desire to create one.

Finally, the Council over the past one hundred years has provided a home for systematic research on the learning and teaching of literature. The varied nature of the Council's membership—including classroom teachers, district leaders, teacher educators, literacy researchers, and literary critics and scholars—can generate conflicting priorities and interests, but this diversity also ensures a necessary bringing together of individuals with different expertise around common issues of how we can best teach and our students best learn. And from that rich interaction comes a history of improvement in the teaching of English in general and literature in particular, reflected in the pages of the Council's books and journals, on the floor of its conferences, and on the discussion boards, webpages, and wikis of the Council and its constituent groups today.

Acknowledgments

Special thanks are due to a number of our colleagues who, during extensive telephone interviews, generously shared their insights into the influence of NCTE on the teaching of literature. These include Richard Beach, Rudine Sims Bishop, Jean E. Brown, Carol Jago, Teri Lesesne, Sarah Robbins, and Charles Suhor.

Works Cited

Addams, Jane. "Foreign-Born Children in the Primary Grades." *National Educational Association Journal of Proceedings and Addresses of the Thirty-Sixth Annual Meeting Held at Milwaukee, Wis., July 6–9*. Chicago: U of Chicago P, 1897. 104–12. Print.

Adler, Mortimer J. *How to Read a Book: The Art of Getting a Liberal Education*. New York: Simon, 1940. Print.

Allington, Richard L., and Peter H. Johnston. *Reading to Learn: Lessons from Exemplary Fourth-Grade Classrooms*. New York: Guilford, 2002. Print.

Allington, Richard L., Peter H. Johnston, and Jeni Pollack Day. "Exemplary Fourth-Grade Teachers." *Language Arts* 79.6 (2002): 462–66. Print.

Alsup, Janet, and Jamie Myers. "Globalization and English Education." *National Council of Teachers of English*. NCTE/CEE, [2007]. Web. 13 June 2009.

Applebee, Arthur N. *Curriculum as Conversation: Transforming Traditions of Teaching and Learning*. Chicago: U of Chicago P, 1996. Print.

———. "The Elements of Response to a Literary Work: What We Have Learned." *Research in the Teaching of English* 11.3 (1977): 255–71. Print.

———. *Literature in the Secondary School: Studies of Curriculum and Instruction in the United States*. Urbana, IL: NCTE, 1993. Print. NCTE Research Report No. 25.

———. "Toward Thoughtful Curriculum: Fostering Discipline-Based Conversation." *English Journal* 83.3 (1994): 45–52. Print.

———. *Tradition and Reform in the Teaching of English: A History*. Urbana, IL: NCTE, 1974. Print.

Appleman, Deborah. *Critical Encounters in High School English: Teaching Literary Theory to Adolescents*. New York: Teachers College, 2000. Print.

Bates, Herbert. *A List of Books for Home Reading*. Chicago: NCTE, 1913. Print.

Beach, Richard. *A Teacher's Introduction to Reader-Response Theories*. Urbana, IL: NCTE, 1993. Print.

Beach, Richard, and Hephzibah Roskelly. "Introduction to the Draft Report: The What, Why, and How of Teaching Literature." *National Council of Teachers of English*. NCTE/CEE, [2007]. Web. 1 Feb. 2009.

Booth, Wayne C. *The Rhetoric of Fiction*. Chicago: U of Chicago P, 1961. Print.

Boynton, Percy H. "Literature in the Light of the War." *English Journal* 7.2 (1918): 77–86. Print.

Britton, James N. "Response to Literature." *Response to Literature: The Dartmouth Seminar Papers*. Ed. James R. Squire. Champaign, IL: NCTE, 1968. 3–10. Print.

Brown, Jean E. Telephone interview with Marc Nachowitz. 2 Feb. 2009.

Brown, Jean E., and Elaine C. Stephens, eds. *Your Reading: An Annotated Booklist for Middle School and Junior High*. 11th ed. Urbana, IL: NCTE, 2003. Print.

Burress, Lee A., Jr. *How Censorship Affects the School*. [Oshkosh]: Wisconsin Council of Teachers of English, 1963. Print.

Carey-Webb, Allen. *Literature and Lives: A Response-Based, Cultural Studies Approach to Teaching English*. Urbana, IL: NCTE, 2001. Print.

Center, Stella S., and Gladys L. Persons. *Teaching High-School Students to Read: A Study of Retardation in Reading*. New York: Appleton, 1937. Print.

Clapp, John Mantle, ed. *The Place of English in American Life: Report of an Investigation by a Committee of the National Council of Teachers of English*. Chicago: NCTE, 1926. Print.

Corbin, Richard K., and Muriel E. Crosby, eds. *Language Programs for the Disadvantaged: The Report of the NCTE Task Force on Teaching English to the Disadvantaged*. Champaign, IL: NCTE, 1965. Print.

Crusius, Timothy W. *A Teacher's Introduction to Philosophical Hermeneutics*. Urbana, IL: NCTE, 1991. Print.

Cruz, Gladys, Sarah Jordan, José Meléndez, Stephen Ostrowski, and Alan C. Purves. *Beyond the Culture Tours: Studies in Teaching and Learning with Culturally Diverse Texts*. Mahwah, NJ: Erlbaum, 1997. Print.

DelFattore, Joan. *What Johnny Shouldn't Read: Textbook Censorship in America.* New Haven, CT: Yale UP, 1992. Print.

Dixon, John. *Growth through English.* Reading, Eng.: National Association for the Teaching of English, 1967. Print.

Downing, David B., ed. *Changing Classroom Practices: Resources for Literary and Cultural Studies.* Urbana, IL: NCTE, 1994. Print.

Drama League of America Committee on Plays for Secondary Schools and Colleges, and NCTE Committee on Plays for Schools and Colleges. *A List of Plays for High School and College Production.* Chicago: Drama League of America; Chicago: NCTE, 1916. Print.

Emig, Janet. *The Composing Processes of Twelfth Graders.* Urbana, IL: NCTE, 1971. Print. NCTE Research Report No. 13.

Farrell, Edmund J., and James R. Squire, eds. *Transactions with Literature: A Fifty-Year Perspective.* Urbana, IL: NCTE, 1990. Print.

Favat, F. André. *Child and Tale: The Origins of Interest.* Urbana, IL: NCTE, 1977. Print. NCTE Research Report No. 19.

Finkle, Sherry L., and Tamara J. Lilly. *Middle Ground: Exploring Selected Literature from and about the Middle East.* Urbana, IL: NCTE, 2008. Print.

Flood, James, Julie M. Jensen, Diane Lapp, and James R. Squire, eds. *Handbook of Research on Teaching the English Language Arts.* New York: Macmillan, 1991. Print.

Flood, James, Diane Lapp, James R. Squire, and Julie M. Jensen, eds. *Handbook of Research on Teaching the English Language Arts.* 2nd ed. Mahwah, NJ: Erlbaum, 2003. Print.

Gere, Anne Ruggles, and Peter Shaheen, eds. *Making American Literatures in High School and College.* Urbana, IL: NCTE, 2001. Print. Classroom Practices in Teaching English Vol. 31.

Goebel, Bruce A. *Reading Native American Literature: A Teacher's Guide.* Urbana, IL: NCTE, 2004. Print.

Hall, G. Stanley. *Adolescence: Its Psychology and Its Relations to Physiology, Anthropology, Sociology, Sex, Crime, Religion and Education.* New York: Appleton, 1904. Print.

Hatfield, W. Wilbur. "Editorial: Our Own Reading." *English Journal* 11.6 (1922): 369. Print.

———. "Preface." *An Experience Curriculum in English: A Report of the Curriculum Commission of the National Council of Teachers of English*. New York: Appleton, 1935. v–xii. Print.

———. "We Believe." *English Journal* 15.9 (1926): 715–16. Print.

Hirsch, E. D., Jr. *Cultural Literacy: What Every American Needs to Know*. Boston: Houghton, 1987. Print.

Hoetker, James. *Students as Audiences: An Experimental Study of the Relationships between Classroom Study of Drama and Attendance at the Theatre*. Champaign, IL: NCTE, 1971. Print. NCTE Research Report No. 11.

Hook, J. N. *A Long Way Together: A Personal View of NCTE's First Sixty-Seven Years*. Urbana, IL: NCTE, 1979. Print.

Hosic, James Fleming, comp. *Reorganization of English in Secondary Schools: Report by the National Joint Committee on English Representing the Commission on the Reorganization of Secondary Education of the National Education Association and the National Council of Teachers of English*. Washington, DC: GPO, 1917. Print. Dept. of the Interior, US Bureau of Education, Bulletin 1917, No. 2.

Hunting, W. J. "Department of Secondary Education Secretary's Minutes: English." *Addresses and Proceedings of the National Education Association* 49 (1911): 555–56. Print.

International Reading Association, and National Council of Teachers of English. *Standards for the English Language Arts*. Newark, DE: IRA; Urbana, IL: NCTE, 1996. Print.

Jago, Carol. *Nikki Giovanni in the Classroom: "The Same Ol' Danger but a Brand New Pleasure."* Urbana, IL: NCTE, 1999. Print.

Kilpatrick, William Heard. *Foundations of Method: Informal Talks on Teaching*. New York: Macmillan, 1925. Print.

Langer, Judith A. *Envisioning Literature: Literary Understanding and Literature Instruction*. New York: Teachers College, 1995. Print.

———, ed. *Literature Instruction: A Focus on Student Response*. Urbana, IL: NCTE, 1992. Print.

———. "A Sociocognitive View of Literacy Learning." *Research in the Teaching of English* 19.4 (1985): 325–37. Print.

Lee, Carol D. *Signifying as a Scaffold for Literary Interpretation: The Pedagogical Implications of an African American Discourse Genre.* Urbana, IL: NCTE, 1993. Print. NCTE Research Report No. 26.

Linn, Ray. *A Teacher's Introduction to Postmodernism.* Urbana, IL: NCTE, 1996.

Lloyd-Jones, Richard, and Andrea A. Lunsford, eds. *The English Coalition Conference: Democracy through Language.* Urbana, IL: NCTE; New York: MLA, 1989. Print.

Mandel, Barrett J., ed. *Three Language-Arts Curriculum Models: Pre-Kindergarten through College.* Urbana, IL: NCTE, 1980. Print.

Marshall, James D., Peter Smagorinsky, and Michael W. Smith. *The Language of Interpretation: Patterns of Discourse in Discussions of Literature.* Urbana, IL: NCTE, 1994. Print. NCTE Research Report No. 27.

Martino, Wayne, and Bronwyn Mellor. *Gendered Fictions.* Urbana, IL: NCTE, 2000.

Maxwell, John C., and Anthony Tovatt, eds. *On Writing Behavioral Objectives for English.* Urbana, IL: NCTE, 1970. Print.

McClure, Amy A., and Janice V. Kristo, eds. *Adventuring with Books: A Booklist for Pre-K–Grade 6.* 13th ed. Urbana, IL: NCTE, 2002. Print.

Mersand, Joseph. "The Teaching of Literature in American High Schools: 1865–1900." *Perspectives on English.* Ed. Robert C. Pooley. New York: Appleton, 1960. 269–302. Print.

Modern Language Association. "American Bibliography for 1923." *PMLA* 39.1 (1924): 1–47. Print.

Moffett, James. *Storm in the Mountains: A Case Study of Censorship, Conflict, and Consciousness.* Carbondale: Southern Illinois UP, 1988. Print.

Morrow, Lesley Mandel. *Motivating Reading and Writing in Diverse Classrooms: Social and Physical Contexts in a Literature-Based Program.* Urbana, IL: NCTE, 1996. Print. NCTE Research Report No. 28.

Muller, Herbert J. *The Uses of English.* New York: Holt, 1967. Print.

National Council of Teachers of English. *The Basic Issues in the Teaching of English: Being Definitions and Clarifications Presented by*

Members of the American Studies Association, College English Association, Modern Language Association, and National Council of Teachers of English from a Series of Conferences Held throughout 1958. Champaign, IL: NCTE, 1959. Print.

———. "The NCTE Definition of 21st Century Literacies." *National Council of Teachers of English*. NCTE, 15 Feb. 2008. Web. 1 Mar. 2009.

———. "21st Century Curriculum and Assessment Framework." *National Council of Teachers of English*. NCTE, 19 Nov. 2008. Web. 1 Feb. 2009.

National Council of Teachers of English, and International Reading Association. *Rationales for Challenged Books*. Urbana, IL: NCTE, 1998. CD-ROM.

National Council of Teachers of English Anti-Censorship Center. *Rationales for Challenged Books*. Vol. 2. Urbana, IL: NCTE, 2005. CD-ROM.

National Council of Teachers of English Commission on the English Curriculum. *The English Language Arts in the Secondary School*. New York: Appleton, 1956. Print.

———. *Language Arts for Today's Children*. New York: Appleton, 1954. Print.

National Council of Teachers of English Committee on Censorship of Teaching Materials for Classroom and Library. *Censorship and Controversy*. Chicago: NCTE, 1953. Print.

National Council of Teachers of English Committee on the Articulation of the Elementary and High School Courses in English. "Report of the Committee on the Articulation of the Elementary Course in English with the Course in English in the High School." *English Journal* 3.5 (1914): 303–23. Print.

National Council of Teachers of English Committee on National Interest. *The National Interest and the Continuing Education of Teachers of English: A Report on the State of the Profession*. Champaign, IL: NCTE, 1964. Print.

———. *The National Interest and the Teaching of English*. Champaign, IL: NCTE, 1961. Print.

National Council of Teachers of English Committee on the Right to Read. *The Students' Right to Read*. Rev. ed. Champaign, IL: NCTE, 1962. Print.

National Council of Teachers of English Committee on Types of Organization of High-School English. "Types of Organization of High-School English." *English Journal* 2.9 (1913): 575–96. Print.

National Council of Teachers of English Curriculum Commission. *An Experience Curriculum in English: A Report of the Curriculum Commission of the National Council of Teachers of English*. New York: Appleton, 1935. Print.

"The National Council of Teachers of English: Proceedings of the First Annual Meeting, Chicago, December 1 and 2, 1911." *English Journal* 1.1 (1912): 30–45. Print.

National Council of Teachers of English Task Force on Racism and Bias in the Teaching of English. "Criteria for Teaching Materials in Reading and Literature." 26 Nov. 1970. TS. University of Illinois Archives (Record Series 15/73/008, Box 1, File 4), Urbana, IL.

National Council of Teachers of Mathematics. *Curriculum and Evaluation Standards for School Mathematics*. Reston, VA: National Council of Teachers of Mathematics, 1989. Print.

National Education Association Committee of Ten. *Report of the Committee of Ten on Secondary School Studies, with the Reports of the Conferences Arranged by the Committee*. New York: American Book, 1894. Print.

Palmer, D. J. *The Rise of English Studies: An Account of the Study of the English Language and Literature from Its Origins to the Making of the Oxford English School*. London: Oxford UP, 1965. Print.

Petty, Walter T. *A History of the National Conference on Research in English*. Urbana, IL: NCTE, 1983. Print.

"Pre-Induction Needs in Language Communication and Reading." *Education for Victory* 2.11 (1943). Print. University of Illinois Archives (Record Series 15/71/806, Box 1, File 4), Urbana, IL.

Pressley, Michael, Richard L. Allington, Ruth Wharton-McDonald, Cathy Collins Block, and Lesley Mandel Morrow. *Learning to Read: Lessons from Exemplary First-Grade Classrooms*. New York: Guilford, 2001. Print.

Purves, Alan C. *Elements of Writing about a Literary Work*. Champaign, IL: NCTE, 1968. Print. NCTE Research Report No. 9.

———. "Testing Literature." *Literature Instruction: A Focus on Student Response*. Ed. Judith A. Langer. Urbana, IL: NCTE, 1992. 19–34. Print.

Purves, Alan C., and Richard Beach. *Literature and the Reader: Research in Response to Literature, Reading Interests, and the Teaching of Literature*. Urbana, IL: NCTE, 1972. Print.

Rollins, Charlemae Hill. *We Build Together: A Reader's Guide to Negro Life and Literature for Elementary and High School Use*. Chicago: NCTE, 1941. Print.

Rosenblatt, Louise M. *The Reader, the Text, the Poem: The Transactional Theory of the Literary Work*. Carbondale: Southern Illinois UP, 1978. Print.

Scholes, Robert. *Textual Power: Literary Theory and the Teaching of English*. New Haven, CT: Yale UP, 1985. Print.

Shea, George B., Jr. "The English Coalition Conference: Secondary." *National Council of Teachers of English*. NCTE, 1989. Web. 1 Feb. 2009.

Shugrue, Michael F. *English in a Decade of Change*. New York: Pegasus, 1968. Print.

Sims, Rudine. *Shadow and Substance: Afro-American Experience in Contemporary Children's Fiction*. Urbana, IL: NCTE, 1982. Print.

Smith, Marshall S., and Jennifer O'Day. "Systemic School Reform." *The Politics of Curriculum and Testing: The 1990 Yearbook of the Politics of Education Association*. Ed. Susan H. Fuhrman and Betty Malen. London: Falmer, 1991. 233–67. Print.

Spurlin, William J., ed. *Lesbian and Gay Studies and the Teaching of English: Positions, Pedagogies, and Cultural Politics*. Urbana, IL: NCTE, 2000. Print.

Squire, James R. "Minutes of the Commission on Literature." Champaign, IL: NCTE, 1965. Print.

———. *The Responses of Adolescents While Reading Four Short Stories*. Champaign, IL: NCTE, 1964. Print. NCTE Research Report No. 2.

Squire, James R., and Roger K. Applebee. *High School English Instruction Today*. New York: Appleton, 1968. Print.

———. *Teaching English in the United Kingdom: A Comparative Study*. Champaign, IL: NCTE, 1969. Print.

Stensland, Anna Lee. *Literature by and about the American Indian: An Annotated Bibliography*. 2nd ed. Urbana, IL: NCTE, 1979. Print.

Suhor, Charles. Telephone interview with Marc Nachowitz. 8 Jan. 2009.

Terry, C. Ann. *Children's Poetry Preferences: A National Survey of Upper Elementary Grades*. Urbana, IL: NCTE, 1974. Print. NCTE Research Report No. 16.

Trimmer, Joseph, and Tilly Warnock, eds. *Understanding Others: Cultural and Cross-Cultural Studies and the Teaching of Literature*. Urbana, IL: NCTE, 1992. Print.

Wilson, James. *Responses of College Freshmen to Three Novels*. Champaign, IL: NCTE, 1966. Print. NCTE Research Report No. 7.

NCTE READING THE PAST. WRITING THE FUTURE. 100 YEARS

A Blast from the Past

Did you know that NCTE once sponsored a committee to compile an "annotated list of literary shrines" so that members taking car trips could locate and visit famous writers' homes? The NCTE American Literary Landmarks Committee was formed in 1965 and for years gathered and compiled what was described as a "prodigious" amount of material. The literary shrines list, however, was never published. Despite the committee members' work, the co-chair had the only copy of the materials and would not release it. After years of requests, letters, and phone calls, none of which he answered, the project was abandoned and the committee disbanded in 1975.

NCTE Journals

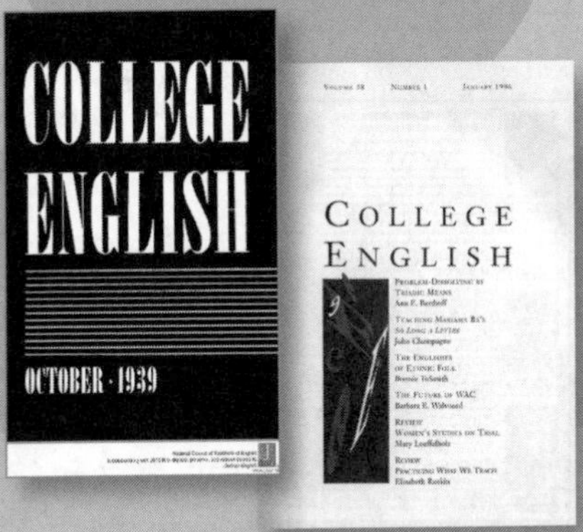

College
Composition and Communication
THE OFFICIAL BULLETIN OF THE CONFERENCE ON COLLEGE COMPOSITION AND COMMUNICATION
CONTENTS
Volume 41 Number 3
October 1990
College
Composition and
Communication
The Idea of Expertise
The Logic of Unconventional Reading
Student and Professional Errors
Ken Kesey on Collaboration
The Wyoming Resolution—
100 Ways to Make It a Reality
Conference on College Composition and Communication
National Council of Teachers of English
COLLEGE
COMPOSITION
AND
COMMUNICATION
O Wind, If Winter Comes,
Can Spring Hope Eternal?
Number One
February 1981
English
Education
The Conference on English Education
National Council of Teachers of English
English
Education
ENGLISH LEADERSHIP
CEL
Quarterly
IN THIS ISSUE
Integrating Technology
INSIDE
Teaching
English
in the
Two-Year
College
TE
TYC
FEATURE HIGHLIGHTS
Ideas for the Future of TYCA
Rhetoric of Race: Critical Pedagogy without Resistance
The Textbook's the Thing: Re-Emphasizing Creative Nonfiction in First-Year Composition
Just Not Enough Time: Accelerated Composition Courses and Struggling ESL Writers
Forum, the Newsletter for Issues about Part-Time and Contingent Faculty
Volume Twenty-Seven
Number Four
May 2000
TEACHING ENGLISH
IN THE TWO-YEAR COLLEGE
T
E
T
Y
C
Talking Points
Beliefs into Practice

Chapter Six

Teaching Multimodal/Multimedia Literacy

Mary T. Christel
Adlai E. Stevenson High School, Lincolnshire, Illinois

with Sandy Hayes
Becker Middle School, Becker, Minnesota

When charter members of the National Council of Teachers of English (NCTE) established a professional organization to support advancements in the teaching of reading, writing, and speaking, the notion of "multimodal literacy" would have been the proverbial pipe dream in the spectrum of skills required of a literate student. In 1911 the phonographic recording, the motion picture, the radio program, and, of course, print journalism, constituted the major available forms of mass media for classroom study. Early in the twentieth century, educators fretted about what was appropriate for the general student population and what constituted functional and accomplished literacy. Little of that discourse centered on the role that mass media played in developing fully literate students, and if there was any mention of something such as motion pictures, the discussion tended to praise the high art of canonical literature over the low-brow appeal of popular culture. Most of all, arguments advanced the proposition that students needed to cultivate the skills and taste to appreciate high literary art in order to recognize popular culture's tendency to appeal only to the lowest common denominator. A closer, historical examination of the evolution of media education yields considerable evidence that the Council carefully considered how the growth of mass media over a century required new and evolving skills to understand what exactly constituted being a fully literate individual.

With an eye to developing some "real life skills," the study of newspapers and journalistic writing received serious attention in the 1910s and 1920s. In "Anything New in High-School English?" M. Ida Williams, as early as 1915, addressed that question by examining the importance of studying newspapers and magazines. This approach encouraged students to become critical consumers of information from newspapers, and later from periodicals, based on the need for information as well as entertainment. Students needed to recognize that it was not enough to take a newspaper at face value; they also needed to apply informed criteria to judge a newspaper's value: "First, which are the best newspapers in the United States; second, what are the standards by which a newspaper should be judged?" (Tourison 192). Attention also turned to engaging students in the production of journalistic writing by creating school newspapers and magazines. Early proponents of newspaper production such as Russell Paine encouraged student journalists to see that they were writing for a clear and immediate purpose that had utility beyond earning a grade. The lessons of media production would in turn help them be better critics of the reporting they read in newspapers. In later decades, the Council and other bodies articulated "media literacy" principles that included the importance of giving students the opportunity to produce their own media texts, so this early interest in media production is significant.

Not surprisingly, the use of recordings and a study of music appreciation also reached into the English language arts classroom. A record player was certainly an available form of media technology in the classroom during the 1910s and 1920s. At that time, the back matter of many issues of *English Journal* featured advertisements for RCA Victor phonographs as well as for recordings of music and the spoken word suitable for the classroom. By 1938 the NCTE Committee on Phonograph Recordings of Poets urged the Council to finance a recording series that featured W. H. Auden, Vachel Lindsay, and Langston Hughes, among others, reading from their own works. This Council initiative lasted through the 1950s and included the Masterpieces of Literature series that featured readings of prose works. Readers of *English Journal* also discovered articles that offered suggestions for how music could be paired with the study of poetry or used to inspire written compositions. A. Laura McGregor presented "A Lesson Series: The Correlation of Music and Literature," which matched great works of classical music to the study of Longfellow's "The Building of the Ship." The presence of these audio texts in the classroom anticipated the greater availability of archived radio programs for academic study in the 1930s and 1940s.

In the 1930s, motion pictures or "photoplays" did not make their way into the English classroom as quickly as recordings did, because available projection technology for educational purposes was limited. Furthermore, "movies" as a form of popular culture left educators to wonder if they had a place in the classroom at all. The Council, however, focused its attention on the impact of motion pictures as a powerful and popular form of entertainment with great potential to enthrall students during their leisure time. As early as 1932, William Lewin prepared for *English Journal* "Standards of Photoplay Appreciation," and then in 1934 published a monograph, *Photoplay Appreciation in American High Schools*, which reported on his carefully designed study to measure how students' critical viewing skills could be developed: "The plan of the experiment was to set up, in pairs, equivalent groups of students for the purpose of comparing the reactions of instructed and uninstructed classes and measuring differences in appreciation" (Lewin, *Photoplay Appreciation* 9). The study involved 1,851 students in grades 8 through 12 from thirty-one schools in twenty-eight cities across the country. Fifty-seven movie theaters provided 14,000 free admissions to those students. Once the "instructed" and "uninstructed" students viewed a particular film, they answered a set of questions that elicited their opinions about the quality of the photoplay and then prompted them to provide a literary analysis focusing on plot, characterization, and theme. Lewin theorized that "desirable ideals and attitudes can be developed through the discussion of well-selected current photoplays" (8). His study yielded pedagogy to help students uncover the artistic, literary merit of the best of current cinema and encouraged schools to form relationships with local movie theaters to allow student screenings. The influence of Lewin's work lasted well into the 1960s.

The type of programming offered by commercial movie theaters became the topic of a resolution adopted at the 1935

NCTE Annual Convention. Developed by the NCTE Committee on Photoplay Appreciation, the resolution denounced the "double billing" of films not equally suited in content and themes to student audiences ("Our Capital Convention" 151). Even Julian Brylawski, vice president of the Motion Picture Theater Owners of America, supported this criticism of film marketing. The resolution also supported "the efforts of increasing thousands of teachers to raise the level of American taste in movies by mass education" ("Our Capital Convention" 151). Even though the showing and studying of films was slow to come to most English classrooms, NCTE nevertheless attempted to help students cultivate their tastes in popular culture during their leisure time.

Reports from the 1935 Convention also reveal that the Council was encouraging "experimentation" in teaching English, with an eye to integrating magazines such as *Atlantic Monthly* into creative writing instruction. Esther Irene Layton from William Chrisman High School in Independence, Missouri, made a presentation entitled "An Experimentation with Magazines," which promoted the critical reading and analysis of *Scholastic*, *Current Literature*, *Magazine World*, and *Modern Literature*. Alfred Dashiell, managing editor of *Scribner's Magazine*, observed, "Students should learn that culture is not spelled with a capital letter, but is something which the whole mass of us create" ("Our Capitol Convention" 147). This Convention marked a critical moment in the Council's recognition of the powerful influence of mass media. Bringing media texts into the classroom for careful analytical study could supplement, rather than replace, standard works traditionally belonging to English language arts curricula.

Later in the 1930s, two important voices emerged to provide guidance for teachers and urge appreciation for media study in the English language arts. Walter Ginsberg centered his attention on the presence of film in the classroom. He noted that teachers in the late 1930s were "excitedly aware of technological advances already affecting the great expressional and interpretive areas of life with which our English teaching is concerned" ("Technology and Teaching" 439). Ginsberg understood that such enthusiasm needed pedagogical focus, so his work outlined quality resources available to teachers, including a variety of films edited to suit the classroom in terms of content and length. A highly cooperative partnership had formed between film producers and educators such as Ginsberg, and they promoted the view that "the human values of the democratic way of life will be made vivid" through the study of appropriate motion pictures ("Technology and Teaching" 442). Teachers, then, had a rationale and resources for making film analysis a richer experience for their students.

The second significant voice during this period belonged to Hardy R. Finch. Finch conducted a survey for NCTE that further "testified" to the growing impact of what was still considered the "new medium" of film (Child 706). Finch identified "two hundred schools throughout the United States . . . engaged in the production of films"; the combined efforts of these programs had produced "a total of more than 373 films" (Finch 365). Finch conceded that many of these films were novice efforts, but he also concluded that "a number of films . . . are quite professional in their procedures" (365). He reviewed a number of "'school newsreels' or 'publicity' films . . . [that] foster better relationships between the school and community" (368) as well as student-produced "guidance" or "teaching films" promoting healthy leisure activities or offering self-help advice on grooming and first aid (370). For Finch, socially responsible subject matter seemed more important than the aesthetic appeal of filmmaking. Finch concluded his survey with a seven-point rationale for producing films in English classes, a rationale that is cited in subsequent *English Journal* articles outlining filmmaking programs.

Eleanor D. Child, for example, a classroom teacher in Greenwich, Connecticut, took Finch's seven-point rationale to heart. As a teacher and the director of her school's audiovisual department, she was able to use the school's formidable filmmaking resources to train her students in basic filmmaking. They filmed each football game and created newsreels for the parent–teacher association. One student "earned money during the summer producing a 2,200-foot color film for the local recreation board" (Child 712). Finch's and Child's efforts to bring media production into the schools illustrated not only that media consumers could become media producers but also that the experience had both academic and community service applications.

In the 1940s, some teachers boldly examined the role that mass communication played in developing literate students and full participants in a democratic society. By 1946, Mildred C. Schmidt of University School in Columbus, Ohio, proposed, "let us drop the 'English' and call ourselves 'communication' teachers" (159). She contended, "Our modern student learns through the radio, the screen, the daily press, and books—all the way from the comics to the twenty-five-cent book or the Book-of-the-Month Club selection. A few learn through our finest books" (159). She argued that the study of texts from popular culture would help students engage the issues and events relevant to their present experience. She emphasized "[h]ow comics and present radio programs promote and continue stereotyped characters and ideas and how such serials keep abreast of the times and national thinking" (160). That students attended films, read comic books, and listened to radio serials could be used to examine how the messages conveyed in media "set up values and behavior patterns, sketched a nationality for use, and gave us common understandings" (160). Schmidt recognized that rich, relevant—and teachable—texts did not appear only between the covers of vetted textbooks.

As the notion of what constituted a "teachable text" evolved, the dramatic presence of radio in the daily lives of Americans drew the attention of many classroom teachers. In 1937, Max J. Herzberg, chair of the NCTE Radio Committee, published a pamphlet that surveyed the objections leveled at radio programming, especially that it was "poor in quality and vulgar in tone" (3). Radio, many believed, had "come to interrupt our daily lives too much" (4). Herzberg's pamphlet reprinted articles from *English Journal* that provided a means of studying radio to assess the quality of news and entertainment. By the early 1940s, distribution of quality radio recordings for classroom study became easier to access. Radio networks, especially CBS and NBC, employed education directors who made materials available to teachers and who conducted studies about how these materials were used in actual classrooms along the East Coast. In addition to his work with film, Walter Ginsberg developed materials for teachers. He detailed efforts by Teachers College at Columbia University, the radio networks, the U.S. Office of Education, and record companies to provide quality recordings of radio programs as well as pedagogical strategies for using them effectively with students ("Recordings"). Teachers also benefited from more expanded examples of media study that regularly appeared in *English Journal.* John C. Raymond and Alexander Frazier wrote about their use of daytime serials as laboratory material to model increasingly sophisticated media literacy lessons; "[t]he purpose of this project was to help young persons develop insight into the reasons for popularity of one field of radio literature through a variety of experiences" (563). Raymond and Frazier's study of soap opera content also extended to the sponsorship of those programs by businessmen more interested in successful commerce than in quality programming. Recognizing the importance of both the media text and its commercial context, teachers such as Raymond and Frazier focused not only on the aesthetics of radio programming but also on its appeal to audiences and its aim of promoting products and services to its devoted listeners. Raymond and Frazier also invited a journalism class to respond to this course of study by writing in response to the following question: "Is the study of radio's daytime serials a justifiable school experience?" (563), an assignment that asked students to evaluate the place of media study in their academic experience.

Having developed over three decades meaningful relationships with professional media producers and NCTE members, the Council in 1946 established the Radio Award Project to celebrate the achievements of the media. At the time, "The Committee on Radio and Photoplays of the National Council of Teachers of English . . . felt a deep sense of responsibility toward the promotion of a project which would stimulate discrimination in radio-listening among the students of English throughout the country" (Novotny 149). The Radio Award Project not only resulted in NCTE's developing necessary criteria for recognizing a series of radio programs and formats for their outstanding achievements, but it also generated classroom lesson ideas and handouts that helped teachers build thoughtful instruction around radio texts. Rather than assuming a stance critical of various forms of popular culture, the Council recognized ways in which radio made positive contributions not only to society but also to the classroom.

On the other hand, the impact of mass media in the 1940s was not always seen as a positive or enriching influence. The comic book "craze" (Dias 142) took the brunt of such criticism. Today, the analysis of graphic novels has been "sanctioned" at the very least as a way to reach reluctant or deficient readers, but it was not always so. Even as recently as the 1980s and 1990s, some educators decried such texts as low culture or not significantly challenging in developing reading skills. In 1946, Earl Dias tackled this perception in "Comic Books—A Challenge to the English Teacher." Dias summarized the results of a survey of comic book content that had been conducted by the Child Study Association. The survey classified "comic magazines" and uncovered the canny marketing strategies that kept a stream of monthly issues in the hands of young readers. Dias allowed that reading comics on particular topics—pirates, for example—might lead students to pick up a more canonical work such as *Treasure Island*. He also anticipated the eventual acceptance of comic books when he speculated warily, "It appears . . . that comic books are here to stay a while and the English teacher must do his part to solve the problems that these publications create" (145). The concerns that Dias voiced were probably representative of the views of teachers across the country who felt ill-equipped to experiment with these new kinds of texts or questioned how they could enrich the standard English language arts curriculum.

If Earl Dias thought that the popularity of comic books was an obstacle to students' reading "serious" literature, he certainly could not have anticipated the impact that the expanding media environment would have on English education. In an address to the High School Section during the 1951 NCTE Annual Convention, William D. Boutwell, editor of *Scholastic Teacher*, articulated the challenges that the growing volume of media present in American students' lives created for English language arts education. In "What Can We Do about Movies, Radio, Television?" Boutwell imagined a typical teacher, not unlike Earl Dias, who lamented the allure of comic books over classic literature and who was easily daunted by the prospect of integrating a fledgling media literacy program into a 1950s classroom along with reading, writing, and grammar instruction. Boutwell reminded NCTE of its contributions to media education through the efforts of the NCTE Commission on the English Curriculum, which urged "study of all three of these new giants"—movies, radio, and television ("What Can We Do" 134). Boutwell observed that the Council had committees on radio and motion pictures; it cooperated with the Motion Picture Producers Association of America in issuing edited versions of feature films for classroom use; and it had published *What Communication Means Today* (1944) ("What Can We Do" 133–34). In response to the question, "Has this effort to widen the English program reached the classroom?" Boutwell noted that "courses in radio now appear in high schools in twenty-five states" and "[i]n 1949 some five thousand students took such courses" ("What Can We Do" 134). In his estimation, NCTE members needed to take advantage of these resources and trends. He goaded his audience into taking action by reminding them that these media powerhouses were not going away and would have increasingly greater impact on the individual and on society. He offered a series of suggestions to bring together NCTE, school districts, the Federal Communications Commission, and producers of media to engage students in the analysis of media that would produce more discriminating consumers and better citizens. Boutwell envisioned making "a suitable place in the course of study or in separate courses for all three of the newest media" ("What Can We Do" 136). Boutwell's speech marks a point at which media education needed to be more systemically integrated into the English language arts curriculum, providing students with the tools to avoid becoming passive consumers of media in both their emerging and familiar forms.

In the 1950s, television came to the forefront of media educators' concerns, and NCTE made its position clear on the role it should play in the lives of literate students. Though the Council continued to present its Radio Award in 1951, honoring NBC Theater for the second year in a row, members also approved a resolution to "urge that the Federal Communications Commission reserve and in due time allot at least 20 percent of available television channels to educational institutions" ("The Milwaukee Meeting" 111). In 1955 another resolution asked "the National Council of Teachers of English to urge local groups of English teachers to seek the cooperation of studios and producers in continuous efforts to upgrade the quality and value of T-V programs" ("A Helpful Convention!" 114). Together with these key resolutions, a clear commitment to cultivating quality programming led the Council to present an award for television drama in 1955. The criteria for that award involved selecting a program "contributing most to classroom teaching from September 1954 to May 1955" (Forsdale and Sterner 520). The announcement of the award signaled the Council's desire to promote the analysis of television programming from a critical perspective, even though "most television drama cannot be viewed in the classroom [and] will have to be examined in home viewing" (Forsdale and Sterner 520). During the pre-VCR era, teachers' inability to bring these texts into the classroom prevented the easy integration of television into media instruction, but the Council recognized the emerging impact of television on students' lives outside of the classroom, even when classroom study of the medium proved difficult.

Even so, a good deal of audiovisual equipment did become a staple of classroom instruction in the 1950s. Filmstrips, 16 mm films, and recordings enhanced students' experience of the study of literature as companies such as Coronet Films began producing educational materials. Audiovisual collections in local and university libraries grew as well. *English Journal* routinely published articles that advised teachers about the availability and quality of newly released titles. In March 1955, Richard Braddock, an assistant professor from Iowa State Teachers College, shared a list of short-subject films suitable for classroom use in "Films for Teaching Mass Communication"; he included a brief synopsis, the address of the distributor, and the rental cost. In "Using Visual Aids in Teaching English," Thomas Cauley presented a list of films available from various social, governmental, and for-profit organizations grouped according to theme or topic: "Getting Along Socially," "Straight, Unbiased Thinking," "Solving Personal Problems" (317–18). Classroom teachers and audiovisual specialists also responded with great candor to the frustrations and rewards of using the technology. John T. Muri observed, "Some teachers have the feeling that it 'does not pay' to spend very much money for delicate machinery that will get [rough] treatment in the classroom" ("Use" 34). Muri also addressed issues of time and educational value: "Many feel that they cannot afford the time necessary to give their students the proper background for listening so as to make the exercise a lesson and not just recreation" (35–36). Articles such as Muri's reveal an awareness that technology and media texts should not be introduced frivolously into the curriculum, even though teachers had greater access to the equipment produced in the hardware and software boom of the 1950s.

The influx of media texts promoted a desire for more careful study of their impact on schoolchildren. In "National Trends in Teaching High School English," Arno Jewett, specialist for language arts in the U.S. Office of Education, offered a review of research and data accumulated from classroom visits as well as observations based on a survey of "197 local and county courses of study, plus twenty state syllabi" (327). Jewett identified fifteen key trends, one of which focused on the impact of television, and he noted, "Now that television has taken from twelve to fifteen hours of teenagers' leisure time at home each week, it is moving into the classroom" (329). Jewett was able to document that "closed circuit experiments in teaching English by TV to high school pupils [were] being carried on" across the country and in the Seattle, Detroit, and Chicago areas (329). Jewett wondered about the effectiveness of delivering information to students through this electronic medium: "How well does it provide for pupil activity and learning by doing?" (329). By the late 1950s, the television set had moved into some classrooms, closed-circuit instruction providing some educational programming produced by local learning institutions and the forerunners of public television.

English Journal kept up with these trends in media education and provided a rich and ongoing resource for the use and analysis of magazines, films, radio, and television in the English classroom. Thomas Kevin Ryan's survey of articles published in *English Journal* between 1911 and 1960 reveals the contributors' attitudes toward media education and ways in which media texts were approached in the classroom. As a whole, the articles of this period presented four principal uses for media in English instruction:

- as tools of instruction for other components of English curriculum;
- as subjects for scholarly study;
- as materials for which discriminating judgments must be developed; and

- as materials which could provide enjoyment and information according to personal tastes. (1–2)

English Journal writers, though, "chose to view the mass media materials as tools for the more efficient and more effective teaching of literature, language or composition, or as a new medium which they analyzed by literary standards" (3). Ryan notes that articles favored "media use by a six to one margin." The contributors who tended to be least in favor of media education were NCTE officers. For them the "media was viewed as a gateway through which inimical forces of immorality might easily enter the minds of young people" or "instill in youth a lowering of standards of excellence in social behavior" (2). These critics also pointed to media exposure's "eroding the intellectual framework of the nation" and believed that "mass media should be given to the less capable students who really weren't worth much more" (2). Media education would continue to have both supporters and critics as it made steady inroads into the English language arts curriculum throughout the 1960s and as more and more Council-produced resources became available.

By 1960, NCTE began publication of the journal *Studies in the Mass Media*, edited by Joseph Mersand and issued eight times a year from October to May. The journal was a successor of sorts to William Lewin's *Photoplay Studies,* which was published by the National Education Association from 1935 to 1940 and which produced over 300 film guides (Mersand, "By Way of Introduction" 3). Lewin hoped that NCTE "would take over the title and properties of these guides and continue them as an official publication" of NCTE (Mersand, "By Way of Introduction" 3). *Studies in the Mass Media* expanded the scope of Lewin's *Photoplay Studies* to embrace all forms of mass media, though each issue focused on a single medium, including photoplay (film), television, recordings, books, radio, journalism, and drama in live festival performances, most notably of Shakespeare's works. A typical issue ran twenty pages and featured a study guide for an upcoming television program or film. The guides included a plot synopsis, an examination of the adaptation process, behind-the-scenes production information, background reading, study questions, and classroom activities. The materials that focused on television commonly promoted the study of "specials" from the Hallmark Hall of Fame series. The publication also supported NCTE's ongoing commitment to producing recordings for the classroom by offering a guide in the May 1961 issue for *Lucyle Hook Reads Emily Dickinson for NCTE*, a recording of 67 poems (Muri, "Study Guide"). Regular contributors such as Hardy R. Finch and John T. Muri, proven experts in media education, were familiar to readers. Ads featured study guides for motion pictures that supplemented the wealth of practical classroom ideas in each issue. Though *Studies in the Mass Media* amassed 1,700 subscribers in the United States and abroad, it ceased publication after thirty-two issues. In "Vale," published in the final issue, Mersand claimed, "The termination of *Studies in Mass Media* . . . does not mean that the National Council of Teachers of English will discontinue its interest in the better utilization of mass media [as] [t]his interest has been traditional with the Council almost since its inception" (20).

Despite publications such as *Studies in the Mass Media* and the increasing diversity among types of media relevant for classroom study, film studies continued to maintain a high profile. However, a 1963 report by Stuart Selby drew attention to what seemed to him a lack of progress in that aspect of media education. Selby recalled "NCTE's rather extensive commitment to film education in the period from 1932 to 1942" and observed that "screen education has been a continuing Council concern for many years" (426). Fresh from attending a conference on screen education in Oslo, Norway, Selby surveyed various approaches to film education in European school systems, especially in Britain, Norway, and the Netherlands. While he "strongly concur[ed] that instruction in the visual media should be a vital part of every person's education today" and recognized that there had been a "gradual increase in film and television instruction in the United States at the college and university level" (428), Selby also noted that "few writers in various Council publications ever discussed the teaching of film as anything requiring special knowledge or talent" (428). This failing, according to Selby, may have been a result of "insufficient respect for the film even among many who advocate its introduction into the classroom" (428). Selby held up the British Society for Education in Film and Television (SEFT), founded in 1950, as a model organization that "develops and shares materials and curricula for screen education, including classroom exercises, general articles on the screen," and other materials to help member teachers develop the skill, confidence, and expertise to integrate film education into the classroom. Selby hoped that "NCTE or the NEA could provide the encouragement and financial support which a fledgling film teachers' group would require until it matured" to develop something similar to SEFT in the United States (429). Despite Selby's complaints, NCTE's interest in all types of media education did not appear to be stagnating. In the 1960s, the Council supported many committees working to integrate media studies into the English language arts curriculum, and these groups recognized a need for books that provided theoretical and practical resources. Several NCTE book publications of the period merit further discussion.

NCTE produced *The Motion Picture and the Teaching of English* (1965) with a grant from Teaching Film Custodians, "a nonprofit corporation (established in 1938) which [sought] to enrich education by making available film material" (Sheridan, Owen, Macrorie, and Marcus ix) from commercial film studios. NCTE and Teaching Film Custodians had previously developed a selection of film excerpts and study guides to expand the resources available to classroom teachers. Unlike earlier materials that had focused on a "literary" analysis of motion pictures, *The Motion Picture and the Teaching of English* provided readers with the knowledge base and pedagogy to examine the grammar and syntax of a film, including shot composition, editing, sound, and mise-en-scène. This text served as an important foundation for later books focusing on film analysis by Ralph Amelio and William Costanzo.

The fledging area of television studies benefited from the publication of two books in the 1960s. The NCTE Committee on the Study of Television turned to Neil Postman to create a rationale and a methodology for analyzing television programs. In *Television and the Teaching of English* (1961), Postman sought to raise awareness of the influence of television by suggesting that a teacher regularly could post information regarding programs of interest for students to consider, and then eventually form a student committee to carry on such research and notification.

To address the careful "study" of television, Postman suggested making a "special assignment" of television viewing at home that would result in classroom discussion. By encouraging television viewing as part of homework assignments, Postman expressed concern about students' access to the family set and about assigned viewing encroaching on family viewing time. He also wondered if parents would recognize television viewing as a legitimate academic endeavor. Nevertheless, though the assignment might be "superficial" in nature, Postman saw value in a "teacher demonstrating to his students, even if in a brief and broad effort, that the content of television can be as relevant to the classroom as many things from books or stage" (84).

In 1966, Patrick D. Hazard shared Postman's concerns and tried to address the inherent artistic and intellectual values of some television programming. Hazard edited *T.V. as Art: Some Essays in Criticism*, a collection of essays developed from the Television Festival held at the 1965 NCTE Annual Convention in Cleveland. The essays advocated selective viewing and the study of broadcast television, which revealed aspects of the medium that could have great social, intellectual, and artistic merit. He and his contributors felt that it was incumbent on teachers "to encourage a new generation of creators to make television closer to our first expectations for the medium" (6). The essays expanded on Postman's rudimentary pedagogy by taking up televised political campaigns, episodic dramas, television films, and children's programming. Both *T.V. as Art* and *Television and the Teaching of English* effectively prepared for the careful study of television programming as part of a comprehensive approach to media education and media literacy.

In 1962 the NCTE Committee on the Use of Mass Media published *Using Mass Media in the Schools*. This book took a comprehensive look at teaching not a single form of mass media, but films, radio, television, newspapers, recordings, and books. In the book's preface, "A Call for Pioneers," editor William D. Boutwell rallied English educators to action, just as he had in his 1951 speech to the High School Section. He designed the book to address his central question, "what attitude should I [an English teacher] take toward the mass media?" (vii), recognizing that "[t]he mass modes of communication have become important institutions in American life" (vi). Sections of the book categorized "The Anatomy of Mass Media," focused on "What Educators Can Do," and finally presented "What Teachers Are Doing." This book embraced the notion that English language arts curricula should be concerned with analyzing a variety of media, not just film.

During an era of expanding elective courses in the late 1960s and early 1970s, media education flourished at the secondary level for the first time. Some English educators and researchers did not consider electives a positive trend, a view John K. Crabbe gave voice to in the *English Journal* article "Those Infernal Electives." Crabbe warned that becoming bored by conventional approaches to English education at the secondary level was no excuse for allowing the college model of "specialty" courses to become the driving force behind reshaping the curriculum. Out of boredom or not, however, the electives landscape grew and included both film appreciation and production courses. Ralph Amelio, a mainstay of NCTE's media education committees and frequent convention presenter, contributed two important books to the development of film courses, *Film in the Classroom: Why Use It, How to Use It* (1971) and *The Filmic Moment: Teaching American Genre Films through Extracts* (1975). Both books are based on Amelio's work in developing and teaching a film elective course at Willowbrook High School in Willowbrook, Illinois. The contentious discourse on the role of expanding electives provided an opportunity to look more closely at media education, and experts such as Amelio offered accessible resources to develop and refine the necessary pedagogy.

In 1974, *English Journal* devoted most of its October issue to the teaching of media, providing an expanded platform for assessing its position in the English language arts. Herb Karl's editorial presented a comprehensive definition of what it meant to be "media literate": "Just as surely as every person has a right to read, so too has every person a right to know what he is being told and sold through the electronic media" (7). Concerned about the public's inability effectively and consciously to deconstruct advertising, news, and entertainment programming, Karl consideed media education vital, given the current media landscape, and defines the concerns of media education: "Here are two possible

—by no means original—approaches: media study and media doing. Media study involves the careful analysis of the content of a specific medium with some attention paid to the 'character' of that medium"(8). "Media doing," or media production, had been lurking in various classrooms and curricula since the 1920s, when teachers recommended that students produce newspapers to understand how to evaluate good reporting. Karl promoted an integrated philosophy of media education that would take in as much of the media environment as a semester or yearlong course could reasonably cover and that meshed with the instructor's ability to amass the materials and strategies to cover them. "The ultimate goal of media literacy," Karl concluded, "is a population (old and young) capable of judging whether electronic media are humanizing or dehumanizing contemporary civilization"(9). "Media literacy is not a luxury. It's a necessity" (9). In 1975, NCTE adopted a resolution on media literacy to "promote sophisticated media awareness at the elementary, secondary and college levels" and "to encourage teacher education programs which will enable teachers to promote media literacy in students" (NCTE, "Resolution on Promoting" n. pag.). The resolution also encouraged NCTE to develop relationships with other organizations that study the mass media and its impact on individuals and their society. (For a historical discussion of the profession's interest in nonprint media as reflected in the cover-to-cover contents of NCTE journals from 1961 to 1978, see Suhor.)

By the 1980s, a generation of teachers and media specialists was entering the profession having grown up with an 8 mm camera at their disposal. They had experienced the thrill of both media production and impromptu exhibition of their efforts in conjunction with more conventional experiences in the English language arts classroom. James Morrow contended, "The fusion of discipline and delight that marked my own teenage filmmaking persuades me that 'media literacy,' by which I mean both critical viewing and creative production, deserve to infuse classrooms of the eighties" (48). He argued that such media literacy initiatives "need not be synonymous with fancy technology [or] fat budgets" (48). Morrow's willing and eager generation of teachers, who understood the importance of media literacy, would still have to convince many veteran teachers and administrators that this skill was a vital component of the English language arts curriculum as the pedagogical pendulum swung "back to basics" in the 1980s.

Technology continued to present teachers with new options in the 1980s. VCR players appeared with greater regularity in classrooms, but prepackaged films and bootlegged copies of broadcast television shows created an even greater need for teachers to consider how, when, and why they used nonprint media. In the past, when 16 mm prints of films had been rented from off-campus sources, their arrival might dictate when they were shown; films were screened to conform with the return date rather than with a pedagogically sound "teachable moment" in a unit. Videotape, however, allowed for film screenings at the optimum time and in increments not necessarily tied to the length of a reel of film. The rewind feature of a VCR also allowed for rescreening key scenes more conveniently than was possible with slot-loading projectors. Surprisingly, teachers didn't necessarily break from long-established paradigms of screening a film all the way through, with little attention to rescreening segments or using film in a more flexible manner. As the saying goes, "old habits die hard."

In December 1981, the editors of *English Journal* featured an article by Harold M. Foster, "Electronic Media: Teaching Television Literacy." This article provided focused theoretical insight into the value of teaching "television literacy" as well as a practical system for analyzing a television episode:

> The structural elements, editing, movement, composition, color, lighting, and sound comprise the language of this new literacy and are used by television and filmmakers to produce a strong emotional response—made that much stronger because of the lack of awareness in those being manipulated. (71)

Because the VCR allowed teachers to bring episodic television into the classroom, this kind of pedagogical guidance was welcome and necessary. Foster provided a range of classroom activities that involved conducting panel discussions, reading reviews, and writing essays—all based on the analysis of television programming. All of these activities were natural to the English classroom and promoted the basic skills of reading, writing, thinking, listening, and speaking.

To promote media literacy, a film festival emerged in the 1980s as a regular fixture at the NCTE Annual Convention. Previous conventions intermittently had hosted screenings of films and even a "television festival" that spanned three days at the 1965 Cleveland Convention. But the idea for developing a permanent, annual festival came from Carole Cox. She explains:

> I was invited to be on the NCTE Committee on Film Study in Language Arts (1983–86) and also invited to Chair the NCTE Children's Literature Assembly committee to revise the NCTE publication, *Films and Filmstrips for Language Arts* by Jill May. For the latter, I was given a committee that was interested in film but had little experience in using film in the classroom. I brought children's films and a projector to our meetings at the conventions and developed a protocol for reviewing films. . . . It was from the experience of showing these children's films with members of my committee that I got the idea of a film festival for all levels.

The Annual Convention continues to feature a daylong screening of films that over the years has benefited from the contributions of Harold "Hal" Foster, Andrew Garrison, Cynthia Lucia, Greg Harris, and Mary T. Christel. The festival not only has presented film screenings but also has given attendees the opportunity to interact with the filmmakers, among them Frederick Marx, one of the directors of *Hoop Dreams*, and Connor McCourt, nephew of Frank McCourt and director of *The McCourts of Limmerick*. The NCTE Commission on Media eventually adopted the festival as one of its ongoing projects to ensure that it would continue after Carole Cox's long tenure as chair ended in 1997.

During this period of greater interest in media literacy, William Costanzo was instrumental in developing policy statements that coincided with his involvement in NCTE committee and commission work. He recalls,

> My first leadership role within the NCTE was to chair the Committee on Film Study from 1983 to 1986. Among other things, we published a *Report on Film Study in American Schools*, which appeared in 1988 (ERIC). I was also appointed to the NCTE Commission on Media, which I later directed (1987–90)

> and which prepared *Visual Media for English Teachers: An Annotated Bibliography* at the end of my tenure. (Message)

By the early 1990s, it was time for an updating of Hal Foster's book *The New Literacy: The Language of Film and Television* (1979), and Costanzo's *Reading the Movies* (1992) became a strong seller for NCTE, leading the field through the 1990s. Costanzo recalls how that book came about: "NCTE's first film book began as the suggestion of Charles Suhor, former deputy director, who thought that the ideas presented in my workshops would reach more teachers in the form of a paperback" (Message). Costanzo subsequently published *Great Films and How to Teach Them* (2004), which expanded and enriched the set of strategies presented in his first volume.

The growing grassroots interest in teaching media literacy prompted an informal meeting of interested teachers at the NCTE Annual Convention in St. Louis in 1987 and again the next year in Baltimore. These meetings led to the formation of a special interest group, the Assembly on Media Arts. At that time, there was no regular means for bringing together Council members and convention attendees who were vigorous proponents of media literacy or who were merely curious and looking for direction and support. The Assembly on Media Arts was founded with a nominated, rotating membership to foster and sustain interest in media literacy education. Richard Fehlman, who served as the newsletter editor and president of the assembly, remembers his early involvement:

> One of the activities I enjoyed was the [Assembly-sponsored] sharing session, An Hour of Practical Ideas and Methods for Teaching Media Literacy in English Class, on Saturday afternoon during NCTE conferences. Teachers were encouraged to come and share ideas about in-class activities that "worked," that is, had a firm theoretical base about why theirs was a valuable learning experience. (Message)

The Assembly on Media Arts provided an annual venue for sharing ideas and advancing media education. It also published a quarterly newsletter, *Media Matters*, primarily edited by Laurence

(Ben) Fuller. Fuller saw the newsletter as a vital aspect of the Assembly's mission:

> [B]y editing four issues annually of *Media Matters* I published a number of articles [and] book reviews by people like Roy Fox, David Randall, Bruce Rockwood, Rich Fehlman, et al., which helped keep the membership informed of what was going on. I also included offprints of articles and lesson plans from a variety of British and American publications and convention presentations with each mailing, thereby giving an international perspective to the subject.

The Assembly on Media Arts continues to sponsor this annual gathering at the Annual Convention, a gathering that recently has become an occasion for presenting NCTE's Media Literacy Award. Though the newsletter has been replaced by an online message board and blog to maintain increased contact with members, this special interest group continues to keep the interests of media alive in the Council as emerging trends in twenty-first-century literacy create more opportunities to examine the role that media education has played and continues to play in the English language arts curriculum.

Responding to vigorous efforts on the part of assembly leadership, NCTE participated in sponsoring in two summer conferences in the early 1990s that centered on media literacy. William Costanzo remembers the first gathering, held in 1992 in Philadelphia:

> The most exciting event for me was NCTE's first national conference, focused specifically on media education, held at the Annenberg School for Communication. . . . This was a chance to bring together those within the Council who shared a special interest in media and English—a convention of our own. In addition to offering two days of panels, demonstrations, book fair, and personal exchanges, the event actually made money. (Message)

In the summer of 1994, NCTE cosponsored a conference with the National Telemedia Council at the University of Wisconsin at Madison. This experience brought together media experts from the United States, Canada, and Australia. Despite the continuing interest in media literacy, economic realities have significantly restricted further special interest conventions.

NCTE's Commission on Media, established in 1979, encouraged the recognition of media literacy as part of the full spectrum of English language arts skills. Though the commission participated in drafting *Standards for the English Language Arts* (1996), published by the International Reading Association and NCTE, for some longtime advocates media literacy received too little attention in the early drafts. As director of the Commission on Media at that time, Carole Cox and her colleagues saw a need to revise the document:

> The only mention of media had to do with second language learners, suggesting that teachers tape record something and send it home. . . . Not only was it not a useful media activity, it was clear whoever wrote it knew nothing about teaching English learners, sending recording equipment home (where English may or may not be spoken), or privacy laws. We brought this to the attention of the Standards team, made suggestions for meaningful use of media, and the final Standards certainly reflect a more inclusive approach to media. In fact, two "new" language arts [viewing and visually representing] were added to the traditional four: listening, speaking, reading, and writing. . . . [Those media-related skills] are now included in every discussion of language arts [and] language arts and literacy textbooks for pre-service teachers.

Under Cox's guidance, the commission integrated media analysis and production into the final draft of *Standards for the English Language Arts* as well as into the supporting examples designed to show how each standard can be successfully integrated.

Even though *Standards for the English Language Arts* eventually reflected the importance of cultivating media literacy skills across the English language arts curriculum, a need to legitimize and defend their integration still lingered. In the late 1990s, several articles published in *English Journal* responded to *Standards for the English Language Arts* and grappled with including media literacy experiences within existing curricula, not just segregating them into specialty electives. Richard Fehlman enumerated a series of principles or beliefs in "Viewing Film and Television as Whole

Language Instruction." Responding to the first draft of the *Standards for the English Language Arts*, Fehlman pointed out that the document "has no consistent references to viewing, something practiced in our culture with an intense and valued regularity, more so, I would surmise, than any of the other language skills" (43). At the height of the whole-language movement, he posed a provocative question: "How whole is language education which does not include instruction about viewing?" (43).

In "Media Literacy Does Work, Trust Me," Ellen Krueger argued that *Standards for the English Language Arts* should provide a powerful means to legitimize the natural integration of media literacy skills and activities. Her article describes how she used *Guidelines for the Preparation of Teachers of English Language Arts* (1996), published by NCTE's Standing Committee on Teacher Preparation and Certification, to explain that media literacy was crucial to the development of the full spectrum of skills necessary to be literate on the eve of the twenty-first century. Even with the added attention to media literacy in *Standards for the English Language Arts* and in *Guidelines for the Preparation of Teachers of English Language Arts*, media literacy teachers and specialists felt particularly embattled at this late stage in the evolution of media education. Even so, Krueger ended on a note of optimism, "I don't think teachers should fear or avoid using media; the activities I've outlined require no advanced degree in media education nor technical expertise in media production. Teachers should also not view media as a mere complement to reading a play or a novel" (20). Media texts, Krueger and Fehlman asserted, need to be viewed on their own terms and not as an "add on."

By 2001, NCTE publications had created a high profile for teaching film, that enduring staple of media literacy instruction for English teachers. William Constanzo published *Great Films and How to Teach Them* (2004), and though his 1992 *Reading the Movies* was out of print, the twelve film study guides in that book were made available on CD. John Golden contributed *Reading in the Dark: Using Film as a Tool in the English Classroom* (2001) as well as *Reading in the Reel World: Teaching Documentaries and Other Nonfiction Texts* (2006). All three of these books sold quite well, demonstrating that classroom teachers and teacher educators desired resources to help them integrate film studies into the curriculum in thoughtful ways.

In 2007, NCTE media-themed publications that didn't strictly focus on film analysis made their debut. James Bucky Carter's edited volume, *Building Literacy Connections with Graphic Novels: Page by Page, Panel by Panel*, showcased the dramatic change in attitudes toward the teaching of graphic texts, first decried when the "comic book craze" emerged in the 1940s. *Lesson Plans for Creating Media-Rich Classrooms*, edited by Mary T. Christel and Scott Sullivan, offered twenty-seven lessons that focused on both the analysis and the production of media texts from Pulitzer Prize–winning photos, video games, advertising, and reality television to print and broadcast news. These publications expanded the range of media literacy resources that emerged from articles and presentations appearing in various Council journals and during the Annual Convention.

Moving into a new century demanded that the Council as a whole, and the media literacy community in particular, consider the direction that media literacy needed to take. The focus on the cusp of the twenty-first century was on the Internet. Convention sessions and journal articles reviewed software, annotated useful websites, directed teachers to resources to help students analyze and evaluate Internet sites, explained Boolean logic and hypertext, and promoted activities such as WebQuests. *Literacy* became a noun in search of an adjective, sporting modifiers such as *information, critical, visual, new, multi-, multimodal, multimedia, digital, technological, out-of-school*, and *21st century*.

Exploring technological and media literacies in a 2002 *English Education* article, Meg Callahan observed,

> Technological literacy and media literacy have often been considered distinct topics within and beyond the field of English education. Technological literacies have been most frequently associated with information seeking and composition-processes, while media literacy has primarily highlighted analysis of media texts. Recent scholarship has begun to challenge this simple dichotomy. Media literacy proponents recommend production as a critical element in understanding the constructed nature of all texts. Not until recently, however, have educators had access to the sorts of digital editing programs that allow the seamless

> integration of multiple modes of text from multiple sources. The infusion of this kind of technology into media literacy provides a kind of balance between analysis and production that more traditional English courses seek between reading and writing. (61)

NCTE resolutions and policy statements chronicle the evolving understanding of "new literacies" and the increasing importance of creating and composing. William Kist of Kent State University, author of *New Literacies in Action: Teaching and Learning in Multiple Media* (2004), explains,

> An important moment for the organization was in 2003 when NCTE passed the resolution that was cowritten by Nancy McCracken, David Bruce, and myself on nonprint composition. This was an important statement that was ratified by the membership, demonstrating the value that the organization has placed on nonprint reading and writing. (Message)

NCTE's "Resolution on Composing with Nonprint Media" called for a broadened concept of literacy and for integrating multimedia composition into the English language arts curriculum. In response, the NCTE Executive Committee in 2005 developed a position statement on multimodal literacies. Framed as a series of declarations and authored by NCTE Executive Committee members Randy Bomer, Shari Frost, Sandy Hayes, Doug Hesse, Dickie Selfe, Jackie Swensson, and Joanne Yatvin, the statement presented a broad definition of multimodal literacies and outlined the implications for teaching and learning (see NCTE, "Position Statement on Multimodal Literacies").

This work positioned NCTE advantageously for the Web 2.0 revolution. With ever-cheaper and user-friendly cameras, voice recorders, audio production and video editing software, a proliferation of Web 2.0 creative tools, and free hosting sites such as Google and YouTube, the possibilities for creating and publishing high-quality multimedia products in classrooms exploded. The NCTE Commission on Media and NCTE members continue to profile what these new literacies mean in the classroom. NCTE journals and convention sessions feature examples of innovative and effective practices. The ReadWriteThink website contains nearly one hundred lesson plans on media literacy. In 2004 the Partnership for 21st Century Skills, an organization of policymakers and business and education leaders, asked NCTE to illustrate the Partnership's framework of skills, including information and media literacy skills, with exemplars of student work that utilized information and communication technology. In 2008, NCTE volunteers updated this "literacy map" to reflect the Partnership's expanded twenty-first-century skills framework and to illustrate the possibilities created by the proliferation of new tools. NCTE also began to gather digital images of effective teaching practices involving multimodal literacies, posting videos of the classroom work of 2007 Media Literacy Award–winner Abigail Kennedy on the NCTE website and in Pathways professional development course work. Members also began posting vignettes and student work from their own classrooms on the NCTE Ning.

In February 2008, the NCTE Executive Committee adopted its own "Definition of 21st Century Literacies." Within days, positive reaction hit the blogs, from guru Will Richardson to people living as far away as Scotland and Australia. In the ensuing year, the definition was highlighted by other professional education groups, discussed in blogs and on Nings, and even quoted in a blog post detailing how the Twitter "coverage" of the 2009 Iranian elections met all the standards contained in the NCTE definition. In November 2008, the Executive Committee expanded on the definition by adopting the NCTE "Framework for 21st Century Curriculum and Assessment," which gave teachers guidance in developing and assessing the skills and abilities students need to participate fully in the global community.

With so much activity and attention on the growing presence of media literacy instruction in the Council and in the profession at large, the time seemed right to recognize excellence in media literacy instruction. The Media Literacy Award, conferred by the NCTE Commission on Media, recognizes exemplary, sustained, innovative, and collaborative classroom instruction focused on media literacy principles. Jean Biebel of Wauwatosa East High School in Wisconsin received the first award, presented at the Annual Convention in Nashville in 2006.

The 2003 NCTE "Resolution on Composing with Nonprint Media" also had called for preservice, inservice, and staff development programs focused on new literacies, multimedia composition, and a broadened concept of literacy. Grounded in NCTE's "Position Statement on Principles of Professional Development" approved by the Executive Committee in 2006, NCTE's professional experiences have shown considerable diversity. They include, for example, *Engaging Media-Savvy Students*, a kit of resources for teaching multimodal literacies through popular culture and technology. In 2007, NCTE pioneered *Pathways for Advancing Adolescent Literacy*, its first online collaborative professional development course, which features a thread on twenty-first-century literacies. In 2008, *Pathways for 21st Century Literacies* was launched, coinciding with the special Institute for 21st Century Literacies held in Indianapolis. This interactive institute explored emerging trends in twenty-first-century curriculum, instruction, and assessment in the context of the NCTE's "Definition of 21st Century Literacies." Faculty for the institute included Kathleen Blake Yancey, Helen Barrett, Elizabeth Beagle, Kylene Beers, Patsy Hall, Sandy Hayes, William Kist, Ernest Morrell, Michael Neal, and Fran Sharer. NCTE Web seminars were launched in 2008. Not only have many of these seminars dealt with twenty-first-century literacies, but like Pathways, the seminars themselves utilize digital learning environments and model collaborative, multimodal pedagogy.

NCTE Annual Conventions, especially those in 2007 and 2008, also have provided opportunities for showcasing new literacies. The Commission on Media–sponsored Gallery of New Media made its debut at the 2007 Convention in New York, continuing with five gallery sessions and several daylong installations in 2008 in San Antonio. The San Antonio Convention also introduced Tech-on-the-Go interactive presentation kiosks. And of course, future convention sessions will continue to a provide a rich mix of resources: presentations that push theoretical and philosophical thinking, that provide a thoughtful research base, and that showcase both emerging and exemplary classroom practices.

Though NCTE has done much to understand and advance notions of what it means to be media literate and fully literate as a student and as a teacher in the twenty-first century, more remains to be done. In the May 2009 article "A Call for New Research on New and Multi-Literacies" in *Research in the Teaching of*

English, Elizabeth Birr Moje poses research questions that still need answers: What is the distinction between media and literacies? How does their interrelationship make the distinction difficult? How do media, literacies, cognitive practices, and social practices overlap? In what ways are they separate? What is the distinction between new, old, and multiple literacies? What is the likelihood that old texts, media, and literacies will be replaced by new ones? And, perhaps most vital, "[w]hatever the *outcome*, it seems important to start attending more explicitly to the question of what new and multimedia *do* for learners, particularly if we want to influence policies that shape access to new media, texts, and literacy instruction" (358).

Influencing policy on twenty-first-century literacy instruction may be the next bold work of NCTE and the Commission on Media. In 2007, groundwork was laid at the forward-thinking 21st Century Literacies Impact Conference, organized by NCTE with support and sponsorship from the Partnership for 21st Century Skills, Apple, and the Verizon Foundation. This conference, held on the University of California's Berkeley campus, brought together leaders from science, social studies, and mathematics education organizations, the International Reading Association, and the National Writing Project; policy advocates and policymakers from organizations such as the Alliance for Excellent Education, the George Lucas Education Foundation, and the U.S. Department of Education; members of the Partnership for 21st Century Skills such as Oracle, Microsoft, and Riverdeep; and members of the NCTE Commission on Media and other media literacy groups such as the Center for Media Literacy and the American Association of School Libraries. In this two-day conference, participants shared perspectives on the new literacy skills students need, on the kinds of professional development necessary to support teachers, and on the policies, partnerships, and collaborations that will be needed to make these shifts happen.

The 20 October 2009 National Day on Writing, with its attendant opening of the National Gallery of Writing, may be another opportunity to create the collaborations and perspectives that can influence policy. At this writing, the National Gallery opening is still weeks away, but opportunities already abound for examining attitudes and responses in blogs; the NCTE Ning; online news articles; Facebook; and a compelling online video, *Who Is a Writer: What Writers Tell Us* (Bowden and Vandenberg). The writing submitted to the National Gallery promises a richness and diversity that will encourage visitors to reflect on the differences, intersections, and complexities of "new" and "old" literacies; on the reasons why people compose; and on the choices they make in creating specific compositions. In this hoped-for variety, we may all gain insight into how emerging media can be used to extend and enhance literacy instruction, insights that may help gauge where students are situated in twenty-first-century literacies and how future policies can be shaped to support them.

Celebrating a centennial is a time to look both backward and forward. As Jeffrey D. Wilhelm reflects,

> Teaching involves both preserving past literacies and embracing new ones. We need to model how literate people evolve with the times and are able to critique the times. In this way, we can be a profession that both reaches into the past and into the future. In the past, we find the resources to understand the present. By embracing present literacies, we can help our students reach into their rapidly changing futures. The credibility we gain by embracing new literacies in student lives will only help us do so. (48)

A century ago the founders of NCTE could not have imagined the powerful forces of mass media and digital communication that would shape how, why, and what we currently teach under the umbrella of "English," "language arts," or "communication studies." These innovations have stimulated fierce discussion of funding inequities, the digital divide that plagues educators seeking to bring students the most up-to-date tools and instruction. It is not enough, at the beginning of the twenty-first century, to put a pen, some paper, and a printed text in the hands of students, but it is also difficult to imagine how emerging technologies and new understandings will have changed the teaching and learning of the English language arts when some future author writes the history of media education during NCTE's second century.

Works Cited

Amelio, Ralph. *The Filmic Moment: Teaching American Genre Film through Extracts*. Dayton, OH: Pflaum, 1975. Print.

———. *Film in the Classroom: Why Use It, How to Use It*. Dayton, OH: Pflaum, 1971. Print.

Boutwell, William D., ed. *Using Mass Media in the Schools*. New York: Appleton, 1962. Print.

———. "What Can We Do about Movies, Radio, Television?" *English Journal* 41.3 (1952): 131–36. Print.

Bowden, Darsie, and Peter Vandenberg. *Who Is a Writer? What Writers Tell Us*. National Conversation on Writing. Council of Writing Program Administrators' Network for Media Action, 2007. Online video.

Braddock, Richard. "Films for Teaching Mass Communication." *English Journal* 44.3 (1955): 156–67. Print.

Callahan, Meg. "Intertextual Composition: The Power of the Digital Pen." *English Education* 35.1 (2002): 46–65. Print.

Carter, James Bucky, ed. *Building Literacy Connections with Graphic Novels: Page by Page, Panel by Panel*. Urbana, IL: NCTE, 2007. Print.

Cauley, Thomas. "Using Visual Aids in Teaching English." *English Journal* 43.6 (1954): 316–19. Print.

Child, Eleanor D. "Making Motion Pictures in the School." *English Journal* 28.9 (1939): 706–12. Print.

Christel, Mary T., and Scott Sullivan, eds. *Lesson Plans for Creating Media-Rich Classrooms*. Urbana, IL: NCTE, 2007. Print.

Costanzo, William. *Great Films and How to Teach Them*. Urbana, IL: NCTE, 2004. Print.

———. Message to Mary T. Christel. 9 Dec. 2008. E-mail.

———. *Reading the Movies: Twelve Great Films on Video and How to Teach Them*. Urbana, IL: NCTE, 1992. Print.

Cox, Carole. Message to Mary T. Christel. 9 Jan. 2009. E-mail.

Crabbe, John K. "Those Infernal Electives." *English Journal* 59.7 (1970): 990–1004. Print.

Dias, Earl J. "Comic Books—A Challenge to the English Teacher." *English Journal* 35.3 (1946): 142–45. Print.

Fehlman, Richard H. Message to Mary T. Christel. 4 Jan. 2009. E-mail.

———. "Viewing Film and Television as Whole Language Instruction." *English Journal* 85.2 (1996): 43–50. Print.

Finch, Hardy R. "Film Production in the School—A Survey." *English Journal* 28.5 (1939): 365–71. Print.

Forsdale, Louis, and Alice Sterner. "A Television Award." *English Journal* 43.9 (1954): 520–21. Print.

Foster, Harold M. "Electronic Media: Teaching Television Literacy." *English Journal* 70.8 (1981): 70–72. Print.

———. *The New Literacy: The Language of Film and Television*. Urbana, IL: NCTE, 1979. Print.

Fuller, Laurence B. Message to Mary T. Christel. 8 Dec. 2008. E-mail.

Ginsberg, Walter. "Recordings for High-School English." *English Journal* 29.2 (1940): 134–40. Print.

———. "Technology and English Teaching." *English Journal* 28.6 (1939): 439–48. Print.

Golden, John. *Reading in the Dark: Using Film as a Tool in the English Classroom*. Urbana, IL: NCTE, 2001. Print.

———. *Reading in the Reel World: Teaching Documentaries and Other Nonfiction Texts*. Urbana, IL: NCTE, 2006. Print.

Hazard, Patrick D., ed. *T.V. as Art: Some Essays in Criticism*. Champaign, IL: NCTE, 1966. Print.

"A Helpful Convention!" *English Journal* 44.2 (1955): 110–14. Print.

Herzberg, Max J., ed. *Radio and the English Teacher: Suggested Units for Courses of Study, Classroom Procedures and Projects, and a Bibliography*. Chicago: NCTE, 1937. Print.

International Reading Association, and National Council of Teachers of English. *Standards for the English Language Arts*. Newark, DE: IRA; Urbana, IL: NCTE, 1996. Print.

Jewett, Arno. "National Trends in Teaching High School English." *English Journal* 46.6 (1957): 326–29. Print.

Karl, Herb. "Guest Editorial: Media Literacy: The Right to Know." *English Journal* 63.7 (1974): 7–9. Print.

Kist, William. Message to Mary T. Christel. 5 Dec. 2008. E-mail.

———. *New Literacies in Action: Teaching and Learning in Multiple Media*. New York: Teachers College Press, 2004. Print.

Krueger, Ellen. "Media Literacy Does Work, Trust Me." *English Journal* 87.1 (1998): 17–20. Print.

Lewin, William. *Photoplay Appreciation in American High Schools*. New York: Appleton, 1934. Print.

———. "Standards of Photoplay Appreciation." *English Journal* 21.10 (1932): 799–810. Print.

McGregor, A. Laura. "A Lesson Series: The Correlation of Music and Literature." *English Journal* 13.7 (1924): 489–93. Print.

Mersand, Joseph. "By Way of Introduction." *Studies in the Mass Media* 1.1 (1960): 3. Print.

———. "Vale." *Studies in the Mass Media* 4.8 (1964): 19–20. Print.

"The Milwaukee Meeting." *English Journal* 40.2 (1951): 109–12. Print.

Moje, Elizabeth Birr. "A Call for New Research on New and Multi-Literacies." *Research in the Teaching of English* 43.4 (2009): 348–62. Print.

Morrow, James. "Media Literacy in the 80s." *English Journal* 69.1 (1980): 48–51. Print.

Muri, John T. "A Study Guide to Poems of Emily Dickinson." *Studies in the Mass Media* 1.8 (1961): 3–20. Print

———. "The Use of Recordings in High School English Classes." *English Journal* 46.1 (1957): 32–39. Print.

National Council of Teachers of English. "The NCTE Definition of 21st Century Literacies." *National Council of Teachers of English*. NCTE, 15 Feb. 2008. Web. 7 Sept. 2009.

———. "NCTE Framework for 21st Century Curriculum and Assessment." *National Council of Teachers of English*. NCTE, [2008]. Web. 7 Sept. 2009.

———. "Position Statement on Multimodal Literacies." *National Council of Teachers of English*. NCTE, Nov. 2005. Web. 7 Sept. 2009.

———. "Position Statement on Principles of Professional Development." *National Council of Teachers of English*. NCTE, Nov. 2006. Web. 5 Feb. 2010.

———. "Resolution on Composing with Nonprint Media." *National Council of Teachers of English*. NCTE, 2003. Web. 7 Sept. 2009.

———. "Resolution on Promoting Media Literacy." *National Council of Teachers of English*. NCTE, 1975. Web. 17 Aug. 2009.

National Council of Teachers of English Standing Committee on Teacher Preparation and Certification. *Guidelines for the Preparation of Teachers of English Language Arts*. Urbana, IL: NCTE, 1996. Print.

Novotny, Lillian. "NCTE Radio Awards Project." *English Journal* 35.3 (1946): 149–52. Print.

"Our Capital Convention." *English Journal* 24.2 (1935): 137–52. Print.

Paine, Russell. "Journalism and the 'Reality Stimulus.'" *English Journal* 14.3 (1925): 193–201. Print.

Postman, Neil. *Television and the Teaching of English*. New York: Appleton, 1961. Print.

Raymond, John C., and Alexander Frazier. "Daytime Serials as Laboratory Material." *English Journal* 38.10 (1949): 563–67. Print.

Ryan, Thomas Kevin. Preface. "Mass Media and the Secondary School: An Examination of the Attitudes of the National Council of Teachers of English, 1911–1960, toward Five Selected Mass Media as Expressed in *The English Journal*." Diss. Ball State U, 1971. Print.

Schmidt, Mildred C. "Teaching Communication Today." *English Journal* 35.3 (1946): 159–61. Print.

Selby, Stuart. "International Progress in Screen Education." *English Journal* 52.6 (1963): 426–29. Print.

Sheridan, Marion C., Harold H. Owen, Jr., Ken Macrorie, and Fred Marcus. *The Motion Picture and the Teaching of English*. New York: Appleton, 1965. Print.

Suhor, Charles A. "A Study of Media in Relation to English." Diss. Florida State U, 1981. Print.

Tourison, Eleanor. "The Newspaper of Today." *English Journal* 16.3 (1927): 192–99. Print.

Wilhelm, Jeffrey D. "One Last Thought: The Evolution of Literacy." *Voices from the Middle* 10.3 (2003): 48. Print.

Williams, M. Ida. "Anything New in High-School English?" *English Journal* 4.7 (1915): 439–44. Print.

NCTE READING THE PAST. WRITING THE FUTURE. 100 YEARS

A Blast from the Past

Did you know that NCTE convention sessions hit the airwaves in 1934? On 30 November, CBS and NBC broadcast two fifteen-minute radio programs coast to coast. The first featured Stanford University philosophy professor Edwin A. Starbuck's convention address, "Some New Techniques for Judging Literature"; the second broadcast saw the editors of *Scribner's, Collier's,* and *English Journal* discuss the topic "What Is Good English Today?"

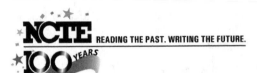

NCTE Resolutions

1939

THEREFORE BE IT

RESOLVED, That American schools imperatively need a large and immediate increase in the supply of books and current periodicals, not only such materials as may be used in unison study by whole classes, but even more the wide variety of books of all sorts which should be available to satisfy and broaden individual interests; and BE IT FURTHER

RESOLVED, That school administrators and supervisors be urged to increase several fold the provision for adding to and administering the supply of fiction, general reading, and periodicals in sc

1945

WHEREAS, we the members of the Committee on Intercultural Relations believe that no individual should be denied his civil rights because of race or religion; and WHEREAS, we believe that no member of the National Council of Teachers of English should be denied any privileges of the Council because of race or religion; BE IT RESOLVED, that the Board of Directors of the National Council of Teachers of English request the Executive Committee to hold annual meetings of the Council only in those cities in which hotels, particularly the headquarters hotel, accord members of the Council rooms and dining room service regardless of race or religion.

ter some discussion the RESOLUTION was ADOPTED.

2001

FINAL VERSION OF RESOLU

Resolved, that the National Council of Teacher's of English publicly commend teachers, staff, and administrators

- For their courage in leading students near the World Trade Center to safety and for their professionalism as they continue to work with students in extraordinarily difficult circumstances;
- For assuming responsibility in similar instances where students' safety and well being were threatened; and
- For providing opportunities for students in the United States and throughout the world to interpret these events.

1953

WHEREAS a committee of the NCTE has prepared a pamphlet entitled *Censorship and Controversy* which has been carefully read and criticized by an NCTE committee, approved by the Council Director of Publications, and published by the Council; be it

Resolved, That the NCTE commend the work of the Committee on Censorship and Controversy and reaffirm the following positions taken by the Committee:

1. The National Council of Teachers of English reasserts the freedom to teach. It believes that freedom to teach is closely bound to the freedoms to listen, to speak, to write, and to read. In reasserting all these freedoms, it again reaffirms its loyalties to American democracy.
2. The NCTE believes that freedom to teach includes freedom to examine and to dissent

1973

RESOLVED, the NCTE urge all members to support passage of the Equal Rights Amendment in those states where it has not yet been ratified by writing to their representatives, urging their colleagues to write their representatives, and making the amendment a subject of discussion in their classes.

1969

ON ENDING THE VIETNAM WAR

BACKGROUND: This organization of teachers has concerned itself for years with its professional aims: improving the teaching of English at all lev situations. But at this particular moment in history, a strictly profess is not enough. The Council sees in the Vietnam War not only a educational objective but a threat to the very culture it is expecte young people for. Be it therefore

Resolved, That the Council officially express its abhorrence of the and its desire to see this divisive conflict ended; and that this resol to the President of the United States and all the members of the fe ment who are directly concerned with decisions on the war in Viet

2002

FINAL VERSION OF RESOLUTION 1:

Resolved, that the National Council of Teachers of English support the tradition of local and state control of English language arts curriculum, instruction, and assessment, and oppose the use of the No Child Left Behind Act to mandate a "short list" of professional development providers or commercial products in reading.

Be it further resolved that NCTE call upon Congress to commission knowledgeable, independent professionals to critique the currently promoted research base for the Reading First Initiative, specifically the National Reading Panel report.

NCTE Award Programs

Chapter Seven

Working toward Social Justice in the Classroom, School, and Community

Carol D. Lee
Northwestern University

Anika Spratley
Johns Hopkins University

Social justice issues affecting education in the United States have been persistent across the twentieth and into the twenty-first centuries (Ladson-Billings; Williamson, Rhodes, and Dunson). Such issues include, but are not limited to, structural inequalities limiting opportunities to learn for youth from minority and low-income communities. Structural inequalities have been both de jure and de facto, including segregation in housing and schooling, differences in educational resources (e.g., teacher quality, per-pupil funding, building-level resources), and differences in access to a rigorous curriculum (Darling-Hammond; Haycock, Barth, Mitchell, Wilkins, and Somerville). In this history, race/ethnicity and class have been highly correlated; that is, communities of color have and continue to be disproportionately lower income (National Urban League). In part because race/ethnicity and class have been so intertwined with social justice inequalities, issues of language variation have served as markers of difference and deficits. Thus, attitudes about language and assumptions about ability have served as a lens through which curriculum, assessment, and teacher training have been filtered. These attitudes also have informed programs of educational research. The work of English language arts instruction has been a pivotal focus for social justice debates around language and learning, including attendant assumptions about how language and ability may be connected. In the context of English language arts instruction, these debates concern the language of instruction, the kinds of texts that should be taught and to whom, and how reading, speaking, and writing should be assessed.

In the first decades of the twentieth century, debates over the aims of K–12 education were prevalent (Tyack; Woodson). Until around 1930, only a small percentage of the population attended, let alone graduated from, high school, particularly among low-income populations. However, African Americans, who would have been less than fifty years out of enslavement by the early twentieth century, had made unprecedented achievements in literacy and school enrollment (Bond; DuBois and Dill). In the first two decades of the twentieth century, several broad themes were emerging that represented very different conceptions of the role of education and of relations between ability, assessment, and the content of instruction. One theme focused on Euro-centered classical knowledge in preparation for college admission as a primary function of the high school curriculum. These efforts were articulated in the so-called Eliot Report of the Committee of Ten of the National Education Association (1894). The Eliot Report included a conference on the teaching of English as a subject. The report recommended attention to English grammar and vocabulary study based on studies in Latin, French, and German, stating "philological and rhetorical studies as 'necessary if the pupil is to be brought into anything but the vaguest understanding of what he reads'" (Graff 99). The report was specific with regard to allocating time not only to specific subjects but also to specific topics within subjects. By 1894 the National Conference on Uniform Entrance Requirements in English had met to draft a list of texts to be used for college admission examinations (Applebee, *Tradition and Reform* 30–31). This Euro-classical orientation to literary texts and language in the English classroom represented one important aspect of the cultural ecology in which the National Council of Teachers of English (NCTE) was born. In fact, one important impetus for the establishment of NCTE was the proposition that classroom teachers, rather than an elite group representing university interests, should make decisions regarding curriculum requirements in English.

At the same time that these debates regarding an appropriate literary canon and the role of language study were swirling, a movement focused on conceptions of ability and the role of assessments was also in play. By 1905 in France, Alfred Binet had developed what were considered scientific measures of ability. Binet's intent had been to identify students who needed special help but not to sort them into groups. However, by 1916 psychologists in the United States had taken up the idea of measurable innate intelligence. Louis Terman and colleagues at Stanford University had developed a version of the Binet test for use in the United States, and by 1917 the U.S. Army Alpha and Beta tests served as the precursor to the ubiquitous IQ tests in U.S. schools. By the 1920s and 1930s, IQ tests were commonly being used in schools for the purpose of determining which students should receive what kind of curriculum. The legacy of these efforts continues in the use of tracking and in the substantive differences in curricular rigor available to different groups of students (Hilliard).

A third movement during this same period is probably best epitomized by Dewey's publication of *Democracy and Education* (1916) and the establishment of the Progressive Education Association in 1917. A progressive educational philosophy focused on learning through experience and exploration stood in contrast to behaviorist theories of learning, with their scientific assessments of innate ability. Dewey said, "What the best and wisest parent wants for his own child, that must the community want for all of its children. Any other ideal for our schools is narrow and unlovely; acted upon, it destroys our democracy" (Dewey, *School and Society* 7). The progressive movement emphasized learning by doing.

We point out these three movements in education for several reasons. First, they represent the intellectual environment in which NCTE was born in 1911. While NCTE was established as a direct response to efforts to prescribe the English curriculum from outside the profession, over its history many of the responses to social justice issues that we discuss in this chapter fundamentally evolved from the tensions across these three movements: the Euro-classical orientation, the IQ and attendant assessments, and the progressive education movement. These tensions involve the question of an English canon at all levels of instruction, the role of language in instruction, and how text selection and a focus on language interact in assessments, with consequences for opportunities to learn, especially for students from ethnic minority and low-income communities. These specific tensions come into direct focus within NCTE from the 1960s forward, largely because participation by minorities within NCTE before that time was minimal, but also because political and social movements heightened both public and professional interest in issues of educational equity (Karenga). These issues of educational equity perhaps were most intense in English language arts classrooms for two principal reasons: first, the focus on the explicit exploration of language, and second, the fact that reading and writing serve as gatekeepers for learning across content areas. Interestingly, this gatekeeping function was noted in the Eliot Report on the study of English as a subject in 1894.

We organize this chapter around three social justice themes: (1) the role of language in instruction, (2) the selection of texts, and (3) building capacity for addressing the needs of historically underserved students. We discuss the role of NCTE policy statements, task forces, organizational structures, and initiatives in responding to these issues of social justice entailed in the teaching of the English language arts.

The Role of Language in Instruction

We are indebted to Geneva Smitherman's "The Historical Struggle for Language Rights in CCCC" for much of the information in this section (Message to Lee; Message to Spratley). The 1928 NCTE President Charles Carpenter Fries stated that schools should offer language instruction that makes students aware of other important dialects in American language, not just the standard dialect, so that students can move from one social level to another (Radner). Issues of language in instruction include both dialect variation and English as a second language. The role of language variation in education has a long history in the United States. The Eliot Report described earlier called for attention to European classical rhetoric as a tool for teaching written communication as well as textual analysis. As European immigrants entered the United States in large waves during the 1920s and 1930s, one movement favored eliminating home languages, viewing mastery of English as a gatekeeper for upward mobility and assimilation; other movements favored including ethnic languages of immigrant communities in school. For example, communities in Wisconsin with predominantly German populations included German along with English instruction (Tyack).

NCTE and its affiliates have been central to these dialogues since NCTE's inception. When the Conference on College Composition and Communication (CCCC) was just two years old, a heated debate was published across several issues of *College Composition and Communication*, the journal of CCCC. Linguist Donald J. Lloyd in 1951 wrote a scathing reply to Kenneth L. Knickerbocker's critique of linguistic forms that were considered by some to be colloquialisms (e.g., "Who did you meet?" vs. "Whom did you meet?"). Lloyd's critique was then responded to by Martin Steinmann Jr. The debate largely centered on the role of linguistics as a scientific discipline documenting language variation and change, as against the role of schooling in reifying presumptions about a "correct" English. While these debates did not focus on ethnic language variation, they did embody distinctions based on class. Publications in *College Composition and Communication* focused largely on the implications of class-based language variation for teaching usage and written composition. As Smitherman notes, "In this early period, those students were typically not students of color but were rural and/or working class Whites" ("Historical Struggle" 10). Lloyd stated, "The assertion or implication that the language of a person who uses none of these expressions is superior on that account is a professional error which no English teacher should commit in print, and no editor should permit him to make" (10). While many articles in *College Composition and Communication* in the 1950s argued for respecting dialects of the working class, there was still a tendency to view school as a site for replacing nonstandard English. As Harold Allen stated in a 1952 report published in *College Composition and Communication*, "Preparing the Teacher of Composition and Communication–A Report," teachers should "help students to substitute one set of language practices for another set, and to develop new practices which they previously have not had to use" (11).

By the 1960s and early 1970s, however, the political climate had changed, and debates over language and the academy shifted dramatically (Smitherman, *Talkin and Testifyin*). This was not only the height of the Civil Rights Movement but also the beginnings of the Black Power movement, the Chicano movement, the American Indian Movement, the anti–Vietnam War movement, and the feminist movement. During the 1968 CCCC Annual Convention in Minneapolis, Dr. Martin Luther King, Jr., was assassinated. In response to the assassination and long-standing observations by many scholars of color that issues of race and ethnicity were not being addressed in either CCCC or NCTE, in terms of topics but also in terms of who was making presentations, a shift in the internal politics of NCTE took place. At that 1968 meeting, Ernece B. Kelly gave a speech that was later published in *College Composition and Communication* as "Murder of the American Dream." Smitherman describes Kelly's speech: "In this brief but powerful work, Kelly reproached CCCC for the lack of Black representation in the program, rebuked the organization for the exclusion of Black intellectual and literary products in anthologies, and took it to task for the way it was dealing with Black language" ("Historical Struggle" 14). In response to Kelly's challenge, she was asked to coedit a special December 1968 issue of *College Composition and Communication*. This was the first issue of that journal to feature several African American writers, among them Ernece B. Kelly, Sarah Webster Fabio, and James A. Banks. This transition in CCCC had a direct influence on the decision to establish the Black Caucus of NCTE and CCCC in 1970. Ernece B. Kelly was active in those efforts, including the publication of the *Students' Right to Their Own Language* policy, issued in 1974 (NCTE). By the 1960s and 1970s, with an increasing Latina/Latino immigrant population, debates over bilingualism reemerged. During this same period, there was increased attention to African American English (AAE).

Linguists were examining the structure of AAE, and sociolinguists were examining its rhetorical features and pragmatic functions (Dillard; Hoover; Labov, *Language in the Inner City*;

Paznik; Smitherman, "The Black Idiom"). At the same time, there were heightened efforts in education to represent AAE as an impediment to learning to read and compose (Hess and Shipman; Bereiter and Engelmann). Some educational researchers sought to test the hypothesis that AAE impeded reading comprehension by designing what were called dialect readers (Baratz; Stewart). The conclusion from these studies was that AAE did not impede children's abilities to learn to read (Rickford and Rickford). Despite these findings, a number of reading programs were developed to help nonstandard-dialect-speaking children learn to read based on the hypothesis that their language was inferior. DISTAR, which eventually became what we now refer to as direct instruction, is perhaps the best known of these programs.

By the 1970s, CCCC had taken an active stand in this debate. Over a two-year period from 1972 to 1974, from the work of a small committee to the CCCC Executive Committee, a brief policy position was expanded into a document that synthesized the linguistic research base and focused on fifteen persistent questions with which educators wrestled. It is not an accident that by this time, the racial and ethnic composition of key working committees influenced the fact that this issue came before the organization. Geneva Smitherman, Ernece B. Kelly, and Sarah Webster Fabio are a few of the scholars of color who have been directly responsible for CCCC's and NCTE's progressive positions with regard to dialect variation. Following CCCC's lead, in 1974 NCTE voted on a "Resolution on the Students' Right to Their Own Language" at the annual business meeting in New Orleans. This resolution called for teachers to be trained to understand and respect dialect differences and for NCTE to help disseminate knowledge about how to help students learn about language variation and to become proficient in their ability to speak and write no matter what dialects they speak. The resolution stated, "Resolved, that the National Council of Teachers of English affirm the students' right to their own language—to the dialect that expresses their family and community identity, the idiolect that expresses their unique personal identity . . ." (NCTE, "Resolution"). However, the 1974 NCTE resolution differed in several significant ways from the CCCC resolution (Smitherman, "Historical Struggle"). The NCTE resolution acknowledged the value of dialect variation but called for schools to teach the conventions of "written edited American English," the latter a position that CCCC consciously did not take. The CCCC position statement argued for the right and appropriateness of maintaining dialect variation and claimed a role for dialect variation in school-based writing and speaking (Smitherman, "The Blacker the Berry"; Ball; Lee, "Signifying"). However, in 2003, at the Annual Convention in San Francisco, NCTE members voted to reaffirm the 1974 CCCC position statement. Indeed, there are powerful examples of scholars—many of whom have been active in CCCC concerning issues of language variation—whose academic writing incorporates strategic uses of dialect variation. These include Geneva Smitherman, Elaine Richardson, and Keith Gilyard, among others. Table 7.1 below includes a sampling of some of the monographs on Black English and dialect variation that have been published by NCTE.

This roller coaster debate over language variation and literacy shifted again in the 1980s, epitomized by the 1983 article by Thomas J. Farrell published in *College Composition and Communication*, "IQ and Standard English," in which he stated, "I am hypothesizing that learning the full standard deployment of the verb 'to be' [in contrast to the habitual "be" used in African American English, as in "I be" rather than "I am"] is integral to developing Level II thinking because the deployment of that verb played a part in the development of abstract thinking in

TABLE 7.1 NCTE Books on Dialect Variation

1965 –	Richard Corbin and Muriel Crosby, eds. *Language Programs for the Disadvantaged: The Report of the NCTE Task Force on Teaching English to the Disadvantaged*
1970 –	William Labov. *The Study of Nonstandard English*
1974 –	Bernice E. Cullinan. *Black Dialects and Reading*
1985 –	Charlotte Brooks, ed. *Tapping Potential: English and Language Arts for the Black Learner*
1993 –	Carol D. Lee. *Signifying as a Scaffold for Literary Interpretation: The Pedagogical Implications of an African American Discourse Genre*
2006 –	Rebecca S. Wheeler and Rachel Swords. *Code-Switching: Teaching Standard English in Urban Classrooms*
2009 –	Jerrie Cobb Scott, Dolores Y. Straker, and Laurie Katz, eds. *Affirming Students' Right to Their Own Language*

ancient Greece" (479). Farrell's argument was rebutted by Karen Greenberg: "Not only is this chain of reasoning circular, it is nonsensical" (455). By 1996, the Oakland, California, Board of Education came under national attention and indeed attack for voting to focus on AAE in language arts instruction (Perry and Delpit). The national debate was hotly contested. Yet CCCC again took a bold stand, reiterating its 1974 position. In 1998, CCCC adopted the "CCCC Statement on Ebonics," which recognized that Ebonics, a "systematic and rule-governed" linguistic system, was not an "obstacle to learning." "The obstacle lies in the negative attitudes toward the language, lack of information about the language, inefficient techniques for teaching language and literacy skills, and an unwillingness to adapt teaching styles to the needs of Ebonics speakers" (n. pag.). The statement also called for additional research on how educators can build on existing knowledge about Ebonics and help students expand their command of the "Language of Wider Communication."

The United States is a country of immigrants—with the exception of the Native Americans who were the original inhabitants of this land. This means that issues regarding a percentage of the population for whom English is not the first language have been at play from the beginning. Because mandatory, public primary education did not really take hold in the United States until the early part of the twentieth century, public debates over the language of instruction have been persistently intense. Public policy and attitudes toward bilingual education have shifted based on the political standing of particular immigrant groups. For example, in 1839 Ohio passed a state law that allowed German–English instruction if requested by parents. At the turn of the twentieth century, roughly 4 percent of children in elementary schools were receiving some part of their instruction in German. In 1847, Louisiana passed a similar law for instruction in French and English; in the New Mexico Territory in 1850, the law called for Spanish and English. Other states allowed instruction in Norwegian, Italian, Polish, Czech, and Cherokee ("History of Bilingual Education" n. pag.). In contrast, in 1864 Congress passed a law prohibiting Native American children from being taught in their native languages. With the advent of World War I, fears arose about whether maintaining foreign languages influenced political loyalties. As a consequence, movements to require English Only instruction began to develop. Thus, with increasing levels of immigration from western and eastern Europe in the 1920s and 1930s, English Only became a badge of Americanization.

The political convergence of the Civil Rights Movement with the political longings of a number of historically nondominant groups influenced bilingual education in the United States. As detailed in the "History of Bilingual Education," the Bilingual Education Act was passed in 1968, providing funding for school districts to incorporate native language instruction. In 1974 a class action suit (*Lau v. Nichols*) was brought before the U.S. Supreme Court, which ruled that failing to make special provisions for students whose native language is not English was a violation of the 1964 Civil Rights Act. In that same year, the Equal Educational Opportunities Act was passed, prohibiting discrimination in education on the basis of race, ethnicity, sex, or national origin, and in 1975 the National Association for Bilingual Education was established. In 2002 the Bilingual Education Act was replaced by the English Language Acquisition, Language Enhancement and Academic Act (Title III of the No Child Left Behind Act), requiring that schools report adequate yearly progress for English language learners. This body of legislation has provided a legal framework for attention to the needs of English language learners, although debates over how to address those needs continue.

Attention to dialect variation has gone hand in hand with attention to bilingualism and has been a sustained focus of NCTE and its affiliates since the 1970s. Another important legacy of the *Students' Right to Their Own Language* is the 1988 "CCCC National Language Policy." This policy was a direct response to what were at the time evolving efforts across states to adopt English Only policies. As Dell Hymes notes, "The United States is a country rich in many things but poor in knowledge of itself with regard to language" (v). California was the first state in recent history, in 1986, to enact an official English Only policy. CCCC responded by establishing a Language Policy Committee in 1987 that continues to work today. Smitherman, who played such an important role in *Students' Right to Their Own Language*, also has served to spearhead the work of the Language Policy Committee since its inception. The committee monitors

English Only and antibilingual legislation and policies, promotes language diversity awareness, and disseminates information on language diversity to educational practitioners and policymakers. The three major goals of the "CCCC National Language Policy" are to accomplish the following:

1. To provide resources to enable native and nonnative speakers to achieve oral and literate competence in English, the language of wider communication.
2. To support programs that assert the legitimacy of native languages and dialects and ensure that proficiency in one's mother tongue will not be lost.
3. To foster the teaching of languages other than English so that native speakers of English can rediscover the language of their heritage or learn a second language. (CCCC, "CCCC Guideline")

Several features distinguish this language policy. First, it does not position the maintenance of language diversity as a social good only for English language learners. Rather, it states that enabling the development of competence in more than one national language, as well as being adaptive in the use of more than one dialect of English, are important as outcomes in their own right. Second, this policy statement has also been instrumental in changing the language used to describe what has traditionally been called *Standard English*, a term laden with value judgments about correctness. Instead, the policy statement uses the phrase "English, the language of wider communication," which has evolved into "English of wider communication." This phrase captures a pragmatic function of a particular version of English but does not privilege it above others.

The intensity of the English Only movement, however, continued. In 1998, California approved Proposition 227, which required that all instruction be in English only. In 2000, Arizona passed a similar law. Since the 1980s, twenty-six states have enacted some version of English Only statutes. Since the early 1970s, NCTE, including CCCC, has passed some thirteen resolutions explicitly addressing the need for bilingual education. Most notable have been the "Resolution on English as a Second Language and Bilingual Education" (1982), the "Resolution on

English as the 'Official Language'" (1986), the "Resolution on Bilingual Education" (1999), and the "CCCC Guideline on the National Language Policy" (1988). In 1988, CCCC issued a policy statement against English Only legislation that was being considered in a number of state legislatures. By 1991, CCCC Chair Donald McQuade had sent a letter to U.S. senators urging them to endorse the CCCC National Language Policy.

In addition to policy statements, NCTE has developed a number of publications and professional development resources and services to provide teachers with support for leveraging the language resources of English language learners. In addition, in 2004 NCTE established the James R. Squire Office of Policy Research in the English Language Arts. Led by Anne Ruggles Gere of the University of Michigan, the Squire Office develops and disseminates policy briefs, recommendations for teachers and policymakers, and summaries of research on key topics, including a policy brief on English language learners (2008). In addition, NCTE's English as a Second Language Assembly provides a formal space for teachers and researchers focusing on bilingualism and literacy to meet. Helping English language learners has also become a strategic policy goal for the entire organization (see http://www.ncte.org/governance/ELL), prompting such initiatives as the creation of a Pathways professional development program for teachers of English language learners.

In addition to concerns about bilingualism and dialect variation, NCTE also has addressed other language-related issues of social justice. In 1975, responding to a proposal from NCTE's Women's Committee, the organization issued a policy statement against the use of sexist language and developed a document, *Guidelines for Nonsexist Use of Language in NCTE Publications.* NCTE also supported passage of the Equal Rights Amendment (Twenty-Eighth Amendment to the U.S. Constitution) and, for a time, held its Annual Convention only in states that had ratified it.

Thus, through explicit policy statements, publications, and professional development activities of the organization and many of its affiliates, conferences, and special interest groups—in particular, CCCC, the Black Caucus, and the Latina/o Caucus—NCTE has played a pivotal role in helping to shape attitudes, policies, and practices with regard to the role of language variation in giving students at all levels of schooling the opportunity to learn to read, write, and speak. One of the figures who has been central in these efforts from the 1970s forward within NCTE has been noted sociolinguist Geneva Smitherman, who says,

> Over the years, NCTE and CCCC have been involved in promoting social justice around issues of language, the language arts curriculum and/as related to race/ethnicity. This involvement has taken the form of books, journal publications, organizational policies, convention panels, programs, and support for "special interest" groups. (Smitherman, Message to Spratley)

The Selection of Texts

Learning to read with understanding a range of texts is at the heart of English language arts teaching. For that reason, controversies around text selection have been part of the conversations in the field for some time. Gerald Graff describes the historical influences on the conception of a literary canon for the secondary school curriculum: "In 1894, representatives to the National Conference on Uniform Entrance Requirements drafted a list of texts to be set for college entrance examinations in English" (99). Such examinations had the effect of dictating texts to be taught in U.S. high schools. Arthur N. Applebee's *Literature in the Secondary School: Studies of Curriculum and Instruction in the United States* (1993) analyzes the selection of literature in English language arts secondary classrooms. Here and in an earlier report, *A Study of High School Literature Anthologies* (1991), Applebee found that literature anthologies at the middle and high school levels continue to be dominated by white authors from the European American and European literary traditions. While the last thirty years have seen an increase in nonwhite authors (American and in other parts of the world), the percentages are still small, and selections representing noncontemporary periods are even more restrictive. We raise the issue of text selection in our discussion of social justice because the debates over the school canon have typically focused on access to texts and opportunities to learn, particularly for students from low-income and nondominant communities. The Eurocentric literary canon has been presumed to embody higher-order knowledge and to provide access to higher-level learning. Language practices and everyday knowledge and experiences of students from nondominant groups have been viewed as impediments to such learning. (See Lee, *Culture, Literacy, and Learning* for a contrasting argument.)

NCTE has weighed in explicitly on this debate consistently over the past sixty years. In 1950, NCTE President Mark Neville stated, "Books for study should be selected in the light of their appeal to pupils' emotional and intellectual maturity, their cultural heritage, and teacher interest" (260). One of NCTE's earliest efforts to address the cultural heritage of African American students was a list of books published in 1941, Charlemae Hill Rollins's *We Build Together: A Reader's Guide to Negro Life and Literature for Elementary and High School Use.* This was an annotated bibliography of children's books for both elementary and high school students, books that included realistic portrayals of black people as well as criteria for selecting texts with African American characters and storylines. NCTE published three editions of the volume, in 1941, 1948, and 1967 (Rollins; Willett). By 1970, in the midst of cultural empowerment movements within African American, Latina/Latino, Native American, and Asian American communities, heated debates over the content of literature anthologies and the lack of literature by nonwhite authors were taking place, not only within the profession broadly speaking but also within NCTE directly.

With the assassination of Dr. Martin Luther King, Jr., 1968 was a turning point, both for society and for NCTE and CCCC. In the May 1968 issue of *College Composition and Communication*, editor William F. Irmscher affirmed that the current cultural and political environment placed a "new demand" on CCCC (105). Though Ernece B. Kelly was deeply affected by Dr. King's murder, characterizing it as a "tragedy for Black people and white people as well," ("Murder" 107), she nevertheless agreed to chair the NCTE Task Force on Racism and Bias in the Teaching of English. Other early members of the task force were simultaneously involved in the development of the Black Caucus and the Chicano (now Latina/o) Caucus of NCTE: José Carrasco,

Carlota Cárdenas Dwyer, James Lee Hill, Adolfo McGovert, and Felipe Ortego. Even though we discuss the selection of texts, language diversity, and capacity-building separately in this chapter, within NCTE attention to these issues has always been deeply intertwined. In 1970, Nancy Prichard was the assistant executive secretary of NCTE. As the task force was coming into being, Kelly and Prichard exchanged letters about the work they hoped to accomplish. In her response to Prichard, Kelly identified the following goals for the task force:

- The TF will assess the nature and breadth of the phenomenon of the continuing development of texts and tests which discriminate against cultural and racial groups.
- The TF will chart short- and long-range plans for acting on this two-pronged problem of bias.
- The TF members will involve themselves actively in the implementation of these plans on their local levels; this does not rule out members forming satellite groups to operate on a national level. (Kelly, Letter 2)

The NCTE archives at the University of Illinois at Urbana–Champaign include collections of African American, Native American, Latina/Latino American, and Asian American literature, pamphlets, bibliographies, and curriculum guides gathered by the task force to examine in order to make recommendations for schools. The task force also met with publishers to urge greater and more authentic inclusion of literature from non-European authors in school anthologies. An outgrowth of these efforts was the 1979 edition of Scott Foresman's *America Reads*, for which title task force member Carlota Cárdenas Dwyer served as an editor (Kirklighter). In 1970 both CCCC and NCTE adopted "Criteria for Teaching Materials in Reading and Literature," developed by the Task Force on Racism and Bias in the Teaching of English. That original statement was revised in 1978 and reissued as "Guidelines on Non-White Minorities in English and Language Arts Materials." The statement was written as a "positive response to the educational objective and the social and cultural concern that the truth and reality of our nation's history and literature be embodied in its texts and other teaching materials, and that includes the fact of the racial and ethnic diversity of its peoples" (Kelly, *Searching* xv). The document identified pervasive problems in school literature curricula and textbooks: misrepresentation of the range of texts (e.g., authors, genres, character types) by authors from diverse ethnic communities; common stereotyping of nonwhite characters; and commentaries that " depict inaccurately the influence of nonwhite minority persons on literary, cultural, and historical developments in America" (Kelly, *Searching* xvi). The criteria document also included recommendations for book editors and publishers as well as for teachers and administrators.

Since 1970, NCTE has voted on a number of resolutions to expand the range of literature taught in our schools and represented in anthologies, as well as resolutions promoting a deep understanding of literature across multiple cultural traditions. These resolutions include but are not limited to the following:

- Resolution on Items Testing Competence in Black Literature on Qualifying and Certifying Examinations (1970)
- Resolution on Preparing Teachers with Knowledge of the Literature of Minorities (1972)
- Resolution on Preparing Effective Teachers for Linguistically Different Students (1974)
- Resolution on Multicultural Curriculum Materials (1975)
- Resolution on Native American Literature (1978)
- Resolution on Ethnic Minorities in Teaching Materials (1985)
- Resolution on the Availability of Literature by Minority Writers (1986)
- Resolution on the Study of Literature (1987)
- Resolution on Literature-Based Reading Instruction (1988)
- Resolution on Scripted Curricula (2008)

These resolutions reflect NCTE's long-standing commitment to expanding the canon of literary texts taught in our schools and demonstrate NCTE's understanding of the impact of such diversity for civic life.

Building Professional Capacity for Addressing Diversity as a Goal of Social Justice

The opportunity to learn is at the center of social justice in education and is deeply influenced by the knowledge base, beliefs, and dispositions of teachers. The teaching of English language arts is particularly well suited for addressing issues of social justice for at least two reasons. First, literature offers a forum for interrogating the human condition, including how humans relate to one another. Second, writing promotes self-reflection, a disposition that can promote civic consciousness in a democracy.

Since its inception, NCTE has sought to build professional capacity into the teaching of the language arts by providing forums for research in and on teaching practices and venues for language arts teachers to develop professional communities. These efforts have looked both outward and inward. The outward focus has included making resources widely available to the profession through publications, presentations at the annual and regional conventions, and a range of professional development opportunities. The content of many of these efforts has addressed the range of social justice issues we have discussed in this chapter.

At the same time, there have been challenges over the years in addressing diversity within the organization. Diversity in the leadership of NCTE is important for charting the direction of the organization in addressing issues of social justice in education. From time to time, however, tensions have developed around the diversity of Council leadership, the inclusion of topics on diversity and social justice in Council initiatives and programming, and the involvement of presenters from diverse backgrounds on convention programs. These internal tensions, which have reflected issues within the broader society, have been evident since the early days. As Jacquelyn Jones Royster discusses elsewhere in this volume, blacks began to attend NCTE in 1929, and NCTE faced challenges in hosting its annual conventions in cities in the South with segregated facilities. As Royster also notes, NCTE has taken bold steps to resist policies of segregation. At the same time, as the membership of NCTE became more ethnically diverse, a number of groups began to feel the need for a space to address their interests explicitly. These efforts led to the establishment of the Latina/o Caucus in 1968, the Black Caucus in 1970, the Asian/Asian American Caucus in 1995, the Caucus for American Indian Scholars and Scholarship in 1997, and the Jewish Caucus in 2002. These caucuses provide forums for community-building and networking, even as they address representation on the annual program of practitioners/scholars and topics addressing diversity, representation within the leadership of NCTE and CCCC, policy positions taken by the organization, and literacy research that addresses the needs of diverse learners. As was the case with many of the language issues discussed in the first section of this chapter, CCCC has often been the site where such efforts took shape and then were taken up by NCTE.

The Black Caucus was formed in 1970 at the CCCC Annual Convention in Seattle. At its inception, the caucus called for "a pool of names of competent Black scholars to be used for future programs of both CCCC and NCTE" (qtd. in Gibbs 101). Marianna White Davis, at that time an English professor at Benedict College in South Carolina, spearheaded the call to establish a Black Caucus. Other early leaders who have continued to play significant roles within the caucus, NCTE, and CCCC include Ernece B. Kelly, Geneva Smitherman, Vivian Davis, James Hill, and Sandra Gibbs. In fact, any discussion of NCTE's attention to issues of diversity must acknowledge the pivotal and long-term role played by Sandra Gibbs in the several official positions she held in NCTE. Gibbs, former senior program officer for federal relations and an NCTE staff member from 1973 to 2007, provided important support for both the Black and Chicano (now Latina/o) Caucuses. The Black Caucus has been involved in a number of the significant resolutions adopted by both NCTE and CCCC. It has also played an important role in the election of African Americans to leadership roles within both organizations, including four African American presidents of NCTE and eight of CCCC.

One of the activities of the Black Caucus to evolve with widespread impact has been the African American Read-In. The African American Read-In was established in 1989 out of collective efforts by the NCTE Black Caucus under the leadership of Jerrie Cobb Scott of the University of Memphis, who went on to become its national director. Introduced at a Black Caucus meeting through its Issues Committee, the African American Read-In is a national campaign during Black History Month (February) to encourage students to read African American literature. NCTE provides a staff liaison and other support for the Read-In, which takes place in schools, churches, libraries, bookstores, and community organizations around the country. It provides a host of resources to promote the reading of African American literature through reading lists, lesson plans, podcasts, and presentations by noted African American authors. More than a million young readers took part in the Read-In in 2009.

The Latina/o Caucus began in 1968 as the Chicano Teachers of English, with a leadership that included Felipe de Ortego y Gasca, Carlota Cárdenas Dwyer, Jose Carrasco, Kris Gutiérrez, and Roseann González (Gutiérrez; González). As with the early leadership of the Black Caucus, these persons were intimately involved in a number of NCTE and CCCC task forces and initiatives related to diversity, including the Task Force on Racism and Bias in the Teaching of English, established in 1970. By 1980 the name was changed to the Chicano Caucus and then finally to the Latina/o Caucus. The birth of the Latina/o Caucus shared much with the Black Caucus. The early leadership in both groups was intimately involved in NCTE and CCCC activities concerned with diversity and equity in the profession at large, in opportunities to learn for students of color, and for presence within the organization. It was largely out of efforts within the Latina/o Caucus to diversify the topics and presenters on the NCTE Annual Convention program that the Rainbow Strand of convention programming came into being. Proposed by Roseann González and Kris Gutiérrez at a program planning meeting in Urbana, the Rainbow Strand was later taken up in 1987 as an official part of the annual meeting. Thereafter, the Rainbow Strand was directed and coordinated by Sandra Gibbs. For many years, the Black Caucus and the Latina/o Caucus co-hosted a cultural activity at the Annual Convention, featuring community-based students of color and activities by culturally diverse performers. This joint cultural activity was always well attended and provided NCTE with a community presence in the host cities where conventions were held. This regular convention event also provided opportunities for networking among scholars with direct interests in diversity, language, and literacy. Over the years, the caucuses have provided opportunities for NCTE members to become engaged in the official workings of NCTE beyond attending or presenting sessions at the annual meetings. The caucus structure has enabled any number of special interest groups to organize around issues related to social justice in education.

The evolution of these caucuses within NCTE provides a lens through which to understand ongoing tensions within the organization with regard to the representation of people of color among its venues and leadership. These tensions were born out of frustrations in the late 1960s and early 1970s that fueled a number of resolutions and task forces. Among these was the Task Force on Involving People of Color in the Council, begun in 1975 as the Minority Affairs Advisory Committee. Reports calling for increased minority representation within NCTE leadership, programs, and publications were produced in 1975, 1976, 1980, 1981, 1985, 1986, 1987, and again in 1996. After meeting in Washington, DC, in 1995, the task force issued in 1996 a report criticizing NCTE for not making sufficient progress on the cumulative recommendations that had been made over a twenty-year period. The 1995 task force included NCTE members who had been active members and leaders of the various caucuses and was chaired by Charlotte Brooks, a past president of NCTE who led the Black Caucus project that produced the publication *Tapping Potential.*

The report recommended increased presence of minority staff at NCTE Headquarters, a process for increasing minority representation on NCTE ballots, and methods for enhancing minority representation in the annual program and for helping new members better understand the structure and operations of NCTE. Task force members also developed a vision statement for greater involvement of people of color in the Council, which was adopted by the NCTE Executive Committee on 19 April 1996 (NCTE Task Force on Involving People of Color in the Council). The report of the task force is available at http://www.ncte.org/library/NCTEFiles/Involved/Volunteer/Elections/Report_from_the_Task_Force_on_Involving_People_of.pdf.

Most recently, in 2007 the NCTE Executive Committee appointed a Task Force to Advance and Support Members of

Color. The group issued a report highlighting progress made by NCTE in its programs, publications, organizational structures, and policies and offering seventeen far-reaching recommendations for reform and growth. Among the goals established in the report are doubling the membership of people of color within the next five years, strengthening mentoring and paths to leadership for NCTE members of color, increasing the involvement of NCTE members and leaders of color in the Annual Convention, evaluating Council practices as they affect members of color, and establishing various awards to recognize the contributions of people of color to the Council and the profession. The NCTE Executive Committee adopted and fully funded the report's recommendations "as important steps towards becoming a more inclusive, influential Council" (NCTE Task Force to Advance and Support Members of Color 3).

One of the ways in which NCTE has taken up the challenge to involve people of color has been the establishment of the Cultivating New Voices Among Scholars of Color (CNV) program. CNV was established in 2000 by the NCTE Research Foundation as a result of a conversation between Peter Smagorinsky, Arnetha F. Ball, and Carol Lee at an editorial meeting for *Research in the Teaching of English*. Smagorinsky was then a trustee of the foundation and took the recommendation up for a vote. CNV is a mentoring program for emerging literacy scholars of color, typically either advanced graduate students, new assistant professors, or teachers new to researching their practice. Senior NCTE scholars mentor these emerging professionals over a two-year period, helping them manage the dissertation process, the job search, networking, publishing, proposal writing, learning about NCTE, and investigating issues of cultural and language diversity in literacy education. Since 2000, forty-four fellows have been funded. There are many indicators of the success of this program in terms of outcomes for fellows, as measured by dissertation completion; tenure-track positions; earning tenure; awards from organizations such as CCCC, the American Educational Research Association, and the National Association for Multicultural Education; research funding; and work in communities and schools to support equity (Enciso). In addition, CNV fellows have gone on to assume leadership roles within NCTE, including the current director of CNV, Valerie Kinloch, a fellow in the first CNV cohort. NCTE, through CCCC, also sponsors the Scholars for the Dream Travel Award, initiated in 1991, and the Tribal College Faculty Fellowship. These programs provide travel awards for promising scholars of color to attend and present at the CCCC Annual Convention.

In addition to building capacity for researchers and teachers prepared to address issues of social justice in literacy education, NCTE's Research Foundation established funding for teacher research. These research grants are often aimed at increasing opportunities to learn. As Patricia Enciso states, "since 2004, the Research Foundation has invested . . . in collaborative (school-community-university) research, grants in aid, and teacher research grants that outline as part of their goals a stated interest in improving the conditions of literacy education for youth who have been and continue to be marginalized and underserved by the district, state and federal education policies and practices" (2).

NCTE has also recently established a Commission on Social Justice in Teacher Education Programs through its Conference on English Education (CEE). The commission at the time of this writing is being led by former CNV fellow David Kirkland. The work of the commission is

> grounded in the belief that it is impossible to make sense of the field of English language arts without using gender, race, and class as central categories of description and analysis. The challenge before the Commission is to develop and uncover models of teaching that are flexible enough to capture and reflect the ways these elements function together; to determine how teachers in English language arts see themselves and others; and to delineate the opportunities for transformation, constructive growth, and change in their profession. (CEE 1)

Conclusion

The history of NCTE in many ways has mirrored the history of debates in education over language and literacy as well as the most pressing issues of social justice that we have faced as a nation. In addition to issues of race, ethnicity, and language diversity highlighted in this chapter, NCTE has addressed youth with special needs as well as issues of sexual orientation, class, and war and peace as these play out in providing opportunities to read, write, and speak in ways that support academic learning. NCTE has provided a forum for contesting ideas and nurturing community among a range of literacy scholars and practitioners. These contests have been engaging and often heated, but always informative. We look forward in the next one hundred years to continued growth in our profession in ways that expand opportunities to learn and build on the diverse strengths that all our youth bring to acts of reading, writing, and speaking in school, and indeed in life.

Works Cited

Allen, Harold B. "Preparing the Teacher of Composition and Communication—A Report." *College Composition and Communication* 3.2 (1952): 3–13. Print.

Applebee, Arthur N. *Literature in the Secondary School: Studies of Curriculum and Instruction in the United States.* Urbana, IL: NCTE, 1993. Print. NCTE Research Report No. 25.

———. *A Study of High School Literature Anthologies.* Albany, NY: Center for the Learning and Teaching of Literature, 1991. Print.

———. *Tradition and Reform in the Teaching of English: A History.* Urbana, IL: NCTE, 1974. Print.

Ball, Arnetha F. "Cultural Preference and the Expository Writing of African-American Adolescents." *Written Communication* 9.4 (1992): 501–32. Print.

Baratz, Joan C. "A Bi-Dialectical Task for Determining Language Proficiency in Economically Disadvantaged Negro Children." *Child Development* 40.3 (1969): 889–901. Print.

Bereiter, Carl, and Siegfried Engelmann. *Teaching Disadvantaged Children in the Pre-School.* Englewood Cliffs, NJ: Prentice, 1966. Print.

Bond, Horace Mann. *The Education of the Negro in the American Social Order.* New York: Octagon Books, 1966. Print.

Brooks, Charlotte K, ed. *Tapping Potential: English and Language Arts for the Black Learner*. Urbana, IL: NCTE, 1985. Print.

Conference on College Composition and Communication. "CCCC Guideline on the National Language Policy." *National Council of Teachers of English*. NCTE, Mar. 1988, updated 1992. Web. 22 Aug. 2009.

———. "CCCC Statement on Ebonics." *National Council of Teachers of English*. NCTE, May 1998. Web. 22 Aug. 2009.

Conference on English Education. "Commission on Social Justice in Teacher Education Programs." *National Council of Teachers of English*. NCTE, n.d. Web. 23 Aug. 2009.

Corbin, Richard, and Muriel Crosby, eds. *Language Programs for the Disadvantaged: The Report of the NCTE Task Force on Teaching English to the Disadvantaged*. Urbana, IL: NCTE, 1965. Print.

Cullinan, Bernice E., ed. *Black Dialects and Reading*. Urbana, IL: ERIC/RCS and NCTE, 1974. Print.

Darling-Hammond, Linda. *Equality and Excellence: The Educational Status of Black Americans*. New York: College Entrance Examination Board, 1985. Print.

Dewey, John. *Democracy and Education: An Introduction to the Philosophy of Education*. New York: Macmillan, 1916. Print.

———. *The School and Society*. 1899. *Google Book Search*. Web. 22 Aug. 2009.

Dillard, J. L. *Black English: Its History and Usage in the United States*. New York: Random, 1972. Print.

DuBois, W. E. Burghardt, and Augustus Granville Dill. *The Common School and the Negro American*. Atlanta: Atlanta UP, 1911. Print.

Enciso, Patricia. *NCTE Research Foundation Report on a Sustained Investment in Diversity and Equity*. Urbana, IL: NCTE, 2007. Print.

Farrell, Thomas J. "IQ and Standard English." *College Composition and Communication* 34.4 (1983): 470–84. Print.

Gibbs, Sandra E. "Black Caucus of the National Council of Teachers of English and Conference on College Composition and Communication." *Organizing Black America: An Encyclopedia of African American Associations*. Ed. Nina Mjagkij. New York: Garland, 2001. 101. Print.

González, Roseann. Message to Carol D. Lee. 8 May 2009. E-mail.

Graff, Gerald. *Professing Literature: An Institutional History*. Chicago: U of Chicago P, 1989. Print.

Greenberg, Karen. "Responses to Thomas J. Farrell, 'IQ and Standard English.'" *College Composition and Communication* 35.4 (1984): 455–60. Print.

Gutiérrez, Kris. Message to Carol D. Lee. 8 May 2009. E-mail.

Haycock, Kati, Patte Barth, Ruth Mitchell, Amy Wilkins, and Jan Somerville, eds. *Ticket to Nowhere: The Gap between Leaving High School and Entering College and High Performance Jobs*. Spec. issue of *Thinking K–16* 3.2 (1999): 1–31. Print.

Hess, Robert D., and Virginia C. Shipman. "Early Experience and the Socialization of Cognitive Modes in Children." *Child Development* 36.4 (1965): 869–86. Print.

Hilliard, Asa G., III. "Back to Binet: The Case against the Use of IQ Tests in the Schools." *Contemporary Education* 61.4 (1990): 184–89. Print.

"History of Bilingual Education." *Rethinking Schools* 12.3 (1998): n. pag. Web. 1 Oct. 2009.

Hoover, Mary Rhodes. "Community Attitudes toward Black English." *Language in Society* 7.1 (1978): 65–87. Print.

Hymes, Dell H. Foreword. *Language in the USA*. Ed. Charles A. Ferguson and Shirley Brice Heath. New York: Cambridge UP, 1981. v–ix. Print.

Irmscher, William F. "In Memoriam: Rev. Dr. Martin Luther King, Jr., 1929–1968." *College Composition and Communication* 19.2 (1968): 105. Print.

Karenga, Maulana. "Afrocentricity and Multicultural Education: Concept, Challenge, and Contribution." *Toward the Multicultural University*. Ed. Benjamin P. Bowser, Terry Jones, and Gale Auletta Young. Westport, CT: Praeger, 1995. 41–61. Print.

Kelly, Ernece B. Letter to Nancy S. Prichard. 10 Mar. 1970. TS. University of Illinois Archives (Record Series 15/73/008, Box 1, File 3), Urbana, IL.

———. "Murder of the American Dream." *College Composition and Communication* 19.2 (1968): 106–08. Print.

———, ed. *Searching for America*. Urbana, IL: CCCC/NCTE, 1972. Print.

Kirklighter, Cristina. "Let Us Remember the Histories of Those Who Have Preceded Us." *Somos Primos*. Society of Hispanic Historical and Ancestral Research, May 2009. Web. 22 Aug. 2009.

Knickerbocker, Kenneth L. "The Freshman Is King, or Who Teaches Who?" *College Composition and Communication* 1.4 (1950): 11–15. Print.

Labov, William. *Language in the Inner City: Studies in the Black English Vernacular*. Philadelphia: U of Pennsylvania P, 1972. Print.

———. *The Study of Nonstandard English*. Champaign, IL: NCTE, 1970. Print.

Ladson-Billings, Gloria. "From the Achievement Gap to the Education Debt: Understanding Achievement in U.S. Schools." *Educational Researcher* 35.7 (2006): 3–12. Print.

Lee, Carol D. *Culture, Literacy, and Learning: Taking Bloom in the Midst of the Whirlwind*. New York: Teachers College, 2007. Print.

———. "Signifying as a Scaffold for Literary Interpretation." *Journal of Black Psychology* 21.4 (1995): 357–81. Print.

———. *Signifying as a Scaffold for Literary Interpretation: The Pedagogical Implications of an African American Discourse Genre*. Urbana, IL: NCTE, 1993. Print. NCTE Research Report No. 26.

Lloyd, Donald J. "Darkness Is King: A Reply to Professor Knickerbocker." *College Composition and Communication* 2.1 (1951): 10–12. Print.

National Council of Teachers of English. *Guidelines for Nonsexist Use of Language in NCTE Publications*. Urbana, IL: NCTE, 1976. Print.

———. "Resolution on the Students' Right to Their Own Language." *National Council of Teachers of English*. NCTE, 1974. Web. 8 Aug. 2009.

———. *Students' Right to Their Own Language*. Spec. issue of *College Composition and Communication* 25.3 (1974): 1–32. Print.

National Council of Teachers of English Task Force on Involving People of Color in the Council. "1996 Report from the Task Force on Involving People of Color in the Council." *National Council of Teachers of English*. NCTE, 1996. Web. 23 Aug. 2009.

National Council of Teachers of English Task Force on Racism and Bias in the Teaching of English. "Criteria for Teaching Materials in Reading and Literature." 26 Nov. 1970. TS. University of Illinois Archives (Record Series 15/73/008, Box 1, File 4), Urbana, IL.

———. "Guideline on Non-White Minorities in English and Language Arts Materials." *National Council of Teachers of English*. NCTE, 1978. Web. 22 Aug. 2009.

National Council of Teachers of English Task Force to Advance and Support Members of Color. *Final Report of the NCTE Task Force to Advance and Support Members of Color*. September 2007. Print.

National Education Association Committee of Ten. *Report of the Committee of Ten on Secondary School Studies, with the Reports of the Conferences Arranged by the Committee*. New York: American Book, 1894. Print.

National Urban League. *The State of Black America 2009*. New York: National Urban League, 2009. Print.

Neville, Mark. "For Mortal Stakes." *College English* 12.5 (1951): 256–63. Print.

Paznik, Jane. *The Artistic Dimension of Black English: A Disclosure Model and Its Implications for Curriculum and Instruction*. Diss. Columbia U Teachers College, 1976. Ann Arbor: UMI, 1976. Print.

Perry, Theresa, and Lisa Delpit, eds. *The Real Ebonics Debate: Power, Language, and the Education of African-American Children*. Boston: Beacon, 1998. Print.

Radner, Sanford. *Fifty Years of English Teaching: A Historical Analysis of the Presidential Addresses of NCTE*. Champaign, IL: NCTE, 1960. Print.

Rickford, John R., and Angela A. Rickford. "Dialect Readers Revisited." *Linguistics and Education* 7.2 (1995): 107–28. Print.

Rollins, Charlemae Hill. *We Build Together: A Reader's Guide to Negro Life and Literature for Elementary and High School Use*. Chicago: NCTE, 1941. Print.

Scott, Jerrie Cobb, Dolores Y. Straker, and Laurie Katz, eds. *Affirming Students' Right to Their Own Language: Bridging Language Policies and Pedagogical Practices*. New York: Routledge; Urbana, IL: NCTE, 2009. Print.

Sledd, James. "Bi-Dialectalism: The Linguistics of White Supremacy." *English Journal* 58.9 (1969): 1307+. Print.

Smitherman, Geneva. "The Black Idiom: What the English Curriculum Bees Needin." *Arizona English Bulletin* 15.3 (1973): 76–78. Print.

———. "'The Blacker the Berry, the Sweeter the Juice': African American Student Writers." *The Need for Story: Cultural Diversity in Classroom and Community.* Ed. Anne Haas Dyson and Celia Genishi. Urbana, IL: NCTE, 1994. 80–101. Print.

———. "The Historical Struggle for Language Rights in CCCC." *Language Diversity in the Classroom: From Intention to Practice.* Ed. Geneva Smitherman and Victor Villanueva. Carbondale: Southern Illinois UP; Urbana, IL: CCCC/NCTE, 2003. 7–39. Print. Studies in Writing and Rhetoric (SWR) series.

———. Message to Anika Spratley. 21 Mar. 2009. E-mail.

———. Message to Carol D. Lee. 2 May 2009. E-mail.

———. *Talkin and Testifyin: The Language of Black America.* Boston: Houghton Mifflin, 1977.

Steinmann, Martin Jr. "Darkness Is Still King: A Reply to Professor Lloyd." *College Composition and Communication* 2.2 (1951): 9–12. Print.

Stewart, William A. "On the Use of Negro Dialect in the Teaching of Reading." *Teaching Black Children to Read.* Ed. Joan C. Baratz and Roger W. Shuy. Washington, DC: Center for Applied Linguistics, 1969. 156–219. Print.

Tyack, David B. *The One Best System: A History of American Urban Education.* Cambridge, MA: Harvard UP, 1974. Print.

Wheeler, Rebecca S., and Rachel Swords. *Code-Switching: Teaching Standard English in Urban Classrooms.* Urbana, IL: NCTE, 2006. Print.

Willett, Holly G. "We Build Together: Charlemae Rollins and African American Children's Literature." *American Educational History Journal* 31.1 (2004): 51–57. Print.

Williamson, Joy Ann, Lori Rhodes, and Michael Dunson. "A Selected History of Social Justice in Education." *Review of Research in Education* 31.1 (2007): 195–224. Print.

Woodson, Carter Godwin. *The Mis-Education of the Negro.* 1933. Washington, DC: Associated, 1969. Print.

NCTE Headquarters

Workroom, Chicago
Normal College
(1911–1912)

211 W. 68th Street,
Chicago, Illinois
(1926–1953)

508 S. 6th Street, Champaign, Illinois
(1960–1971)

1111 W. Kenyon Road, Urbana, Illinois
(1971–present)

Chapter Eight

In the Service of Student Learning: Literacy, Assessment, and the Contributions of NCTE

Kathleen Blake Yancey
Florida State University

Like other histories, the history of literacy assessment during the twentieth century and into the twenty-first is one that can be understood in several ways. We might consider, for example, significant figures, including leaders of the National Council of Teachers of English (NCTE), and the roles they have played in shaping assessment practices—or resisting practices seemingly at odds with supporting students. Alternatively, we might approach the century chronologically, moving through "periods" of assessment activity as the century progressed. But since no single history of a phenomenon can be credible, we have instead *histories*, created and constructed from primary documents, secondhand accounts, and multiple personal narratives. According to Samuel Wineberg, whose twenty-year research program has focused on how history is made, three material practices are critical to the making of history: (1) corroborating diverse accounts as represented in the materials; (2) verifying the credibility of the accounts and their authors; and (3) contextualizing the materials appropriately, according to the time of their creation and their contemporaneous culture.

Given this definition of history making, on the basis of multiple kinds of textual material and through the practices outlined by Wineberg, I provide simultaneously two accounts of NCTE's role in the development of literacy assessment during the last one hundred years. The first account is located in a set of six *moments* when NCTE forwarded literacy assessments congruent with NCTE values, and the second in four *themes* apparent across those moments. These moments collectively portray NCTE's role in *advocating for* and helping to create assessments in support of learners and learning, as well as *speaking against* measures that truncate learning or stigmatize students. A second historical account, reading across these six moments, is thematic, focusing on what I call refrains: themes that sound more quietly or more loudly from time to time, but that seem built into all literacy assessment efforts. These refrains are four in number:

- The call for efficiency as America increases its commitment to mass education
- The tension between scientific measurement and a concern for the development of students
- The role of labor, both for the teacher in responding to student work and for the student, first, in inscribing text and later, in composing
- A provision of funds for assessment trumping funds for learning, a provision that collectively expresses a distrust of both teachers and students

What is presented here does not pretend to be either an exhaustive or comprehensive history or a definitive theory of assessment. But together these moments and these themes begin to sketch out a layered history of NCTE's role in literacy assessment during the last one hundred years.

Moment One: Assessment as an Exercise in Science

The first moment occurred at the same moment that NCTE was founded, in the early part of the twentieth century, when both reading and writing became connected to the technology of testing so prolific even (perhaps never more than) today. Such testing included "writing specimens," for example, and "scales" for scoring. Moreover, in publishing the work of the founders of these technologies such as Edward L. Thorndike, NCTE provided a forum that at once informed teachers without endorsing the author's claims, and it did so while also presenting alternative approaches.

The first year of NCTE's *English Journal*, ending with the December 1912 issue, includes James Fleming Hosic's editorial that comments on the year: "With this issue the *English Journal* completes volume one" (638). In remarking on NCTE's beginnings, "The Closing Year" sounds the four themes that have consistently informed the teaching of English and its assessment, regardless of the many versions "English" has taken: speech, language arts, composition, literature, or, later, media and twenty-first-century literacies. At the same time, as Patti Stock reminds us in this volume, in 1911, when NCTE was in formation, so too was the very young "profession" of English. Thus, as we will see, in this *English Journal* editorial both the issues *of* the time and the issues that would resonate *over* time are identified and interconnected, especially as related to assessment.

> Beginning on a hopeful note, "The Closing Year" observes that the year's record is one of remarkable activity and hopeful progress. The *Journal* itself has found a large and sympathetic audience, and it has served as the medium for many writers and varied themes. All that its sponsors hoped for has come to pass and more besides. (Hosic 638)

The editorial then proceeds to identify reasons that teachers, presumably under the NCTE banner, might make common cause, among them (1) the need for teachers to determine the content of the curriculum, (2) the need for professional preparation for teaching, and (3) the need to retain teachers, thus addressing the current problem of "impermanence." Central to these issues are the labor of English teaching and the absence of adequate support: "English has been put forward during several decades as the central subject of the curriculum, and has been so administered as to demand immense labor of the most exacting character, without at the same time receiving adequate provision in equipment and teaching staff" (Hosic 638). (In fact, in the first issue of *English Journal*, Vincil Carey Coulter's article, "Financial Support of English Teaching," includes data-based analysis—provided both verbally and visually in tables and graphs—documenting the amount of support science and English teachers received, with the science teachers better off by a wide margin.)

Connected to the idea of support is the idea of efficiency, a topic of great importance to the culture at large, and a point about which the editorial writer is all too aware.

> It is interesting and stimulating to see how the efficiency crusade, which is sweeping over all fields of business and industry, is gaining ground among educators. As a matter of fact, a quiet succession of investigations has long been going on in the schools, and Mr. Taylor's illuminating discussion of the number of pounds of pig-iron a laborer can carry in a day was far antedated by numerous school and college investigations. Nevertheless, the efficiency wave is so big that it seems to have swept everything along in its course, with the result that analogies from business efficiency are often falsely carried over into fields where they have no place. Mr. Birdseye's "college scrap heap" (in the *Reorganization of Our Colleges*) was as fallacious in the way he referred to it as was some years later the efficiency measure of a college professor in terms of "student hours." (Hosic 640)

From the beginning of NCTE, "analogies . . . falsely carried over" were identified and called into question; thus, the virtue of business efficiency, located in "pounds of pig-iron," is precisely the wrong model for education. At the same time, Hosic expresses confidence that a different kind of efficiency, one connected to the testing then being developed through science, can benefit the teaching of English:

> The construction of a concrete scale of measurement by Professor Thorndike and Mr. Hillegas seems, as a piece of scientific work, to be as Professor Michelson's determination of the length of a meter through the measurement of light-waves. Whatever way you look at it, there seems to the inquirer to be no gainsaying that "differences equally often noticed are equal, unless the differences are either always or never noticed." There is no getting away from this generalization. The establishment of a measurement of composition representing the rankings of several hundred carefully selected judgments is therefore a monumental and dignified achievement. (641)

A more scientific assessment, grounded in the Thorndikean testing science of the time, isn't a small good, but a good both "monumental and dignified." Put differently, such assessment is both as rigorous and precise as the measurement of a physical phenomenon, such as light waves, and yet also dignified in a humanistic way.

Moreover, science can contribute to the professionalization of English teaching more generally, precisely by "testing the results of English teaching."

> Much is to be gained, no doubt, by the use of more exact and scientific methods of testing the results of English teaching than those now in use. Progress is so slow as change must come through mere shifting of opinion. Demonstration is more convincing than argument, and it appeals strongly to those trained in modern methods of thought. Many who have long scoffed at "pedagogy" are now visibly impressed by "experimental education." It seems clear that *English Journal*, in company with other magazines of like character, must in the interests of its constituency, devote large space to the scientific as opposed to the purely theoretical and inspirational. (Hosic 640)

Here, demonstration, science, and experimental education all point the way to a new teaching of English, and *English Journal,* and thus by implication NCTE, "must . . . devote large space to the scientific," which necessarily means that the "purely theoretical and inspirational" will receive less.

In this single editorial appear the four themes that at once characterize the moment of NCTE's founding and the tensions surrounding assessment that likewise characterize the next hundred years. What's more: these themes work together. Thus, we see efficiency and labor as twin concerns: a call for efficiency is at odds with an understanding of the value of English education, particularly in the context of inadequate working conditions and inadequate support. We see an optimism about the contributions that a more scientific, humanistic approach to assessment might offer that will persist across the years but that will not be shared. And we see a concern for teacher professionalism that is at the center of NCTE, now and over time, and a hope that assessment can contribute to it.

Moment Two: Assessment as "Growth in the Power of Individuals"

A second moment occurred during the 1930s when NCTE supported the "experience" curriculum, one that in foregrounding the child was at odds with mass testing, especially the new multiple-choice tests, which ironically called upon fairness as a raison d'être.

Some argue that the fairness issue connected with mass testing began long before the 1930s, and they tend to cite Horace Mann's 1845 argument that teachers should test students not in speech but on paper, in part to serve the interest of fairness (Odell, *Traditional Examinations*). Mann had observed that teachers' evaluations of students' oral presentations were uneven and thus unfair; tests of writing, which could be reviewed more consistently, provided a remedy for this problem. It wasn't until what Michael Neal calls the "technology of testing"—located in the key terms of testing, especially *validity* and *reliability*; in the procedures of testing; and in the scoring of tests—began to be developed that large-scale and mass testing commenced. C. W. Odell's 1928 *Traditional Examinations and New-Type Tests* illustrates well what such tests could mean. This volume runs to well over 450 pages, prescribing best practice for all kinds of what we have come to know as objective or standardized tests, including "traditional" (essay), recall, "multiple answer," completion, and matching tests. Several chapters are given over to the logic and distribution of "marking systems," and even the chapter on alternative tests includes only true-false and yes-no tests. In sum, while the intent may be humane and the motive fairness, the effect is uniform and numerical.

At the same time, another volume authored by Odell demonstrates that much of what was needed for authentic assessment of student learning was *already* understood. He observes in *Educational Measurement in High School* that, for example, the "appreciation" so central to the teaching of literature is nearly impossible to test (91) and that many tests of English composition "have been labeled tests of English composition, but they are rather tests of language and grammar" (114). Perhaps most interesting, testing expert Odell articulates the distinction between standards and scales as assessment tools and as mechanisms for professional development:

> One of the chief values of the use of composition scales [scoring guides] lies in the development of standards in the minds of teachers. The writer does not recommend that teachers employ composition scales for rating every theme to which they assign a mark. He does, however, most emphatically believe that they should become familiar enough with the best of such scales that, partly as result of actually using them[,] . . . they should have built up in their minds more definite and satisfactory standards of pupil achievement. (116)

In contrast to this systematic approach to educational assessment, however, is that proposed by W. Wilbur Hatfield. Given the title of one article describing it, "The Ideal Curriculum," we shouldn't be surprised that his approach is as moral as it is educational. Put differently, it is education as moral good:

> The very word "curriculum," which in Latin meant racing-horse or race course, suggests vigorous activity—wholehearted, joyous, outreaching activity. The runners, as St. Paul puts it, "press toward the mark for the prize": they are animated by a desire, not a fear. And the mark that St. Paul mentions is not a figure in a teacher's grade book but a goal which gives direction to the racers' efforts. (182)

In this model of education, given the student's desire, "marks" are almost superficial. In practical terms, what Hatfield advocates for is a Deweyian, integrated curriculum whereby "life experiences [are] adapted to schoolroom circumstances" (183):

> The backbone of the ideal curriculum . . . is a sequence of life-experiences constantly increasing in complexity and subtlety. The muscle of such a curriculum is provided by the elements of skill, the mastery of which spreads and deepens as the pupil progresses. The items set down in its "materials" column [that is part of a curricular matrix] can be no more than suggestive. The appraisals must be measures of growth of power in life-experiences rather than formal tests. Its ultimate purpose is the production of individuals capable of serving their society and of enjoying their world. (191)

Here, of course, Hatfield argues quite specifically against "formal tests" because, in his view, "appraisals" of growth are more appropriate. Education, as the rhetoric of Hatfield's explanation suggests, occurs as a "natural" development; accordingly, a systematic approach would be inappropriate in that it would interfere with a naturally occurring phenomenon.

In this moment, then, we see two differing views of assessment at odds with each other, one located in a systematic approach linked to standards and scales, the second located in natural experiences, everyday genres, and the teacher–student relationship.

Moment Three: The Lay Reader Program

A third moment occurred during the late 1950s and early 1960s when NCTE refused to endorse the so-called Lay Reader Plan, also called the Rutgers Plan and the Diederich Plan. This plan—funded through the Ford Foundation, the federal government, and local school districts and coordinated by the Educational Testing Service (ETS)—paid housewives a piecework rate for grading student writing assignments. In refusing to support this effort, NCTE affirmed both the role of the professional teacher and the pedagogical importance of providing formative assessment to the student.

The Lay Reader Plan was more than its name suggests. As explained by Paul B. Diederich of the ETS, it was in fact a new curricular design, keyed to skills development, to considerable reading, and to considerable writing that would receive response. Skills development was delivered via the well-known *English 2600* (1973), a textbook of self-correcting grammar exercises based on Skinnerian principles (Blumenthal), while the reading curriculum, forecasting the popular reading workshop approach launched some twenty-five years later, assigned students to very large sections (of two hundred students) where they could read without interruption self-chosen books from a given inventory.

The centerpiece of the curriculum, however, was composition. Here, students would compose "themes," weekly at least but possibly more often, that would receive response, because a new reader, one who would relieve teachers of the "burden" of correcting student work, would be provided: a college-educated homemaker who would be paid a piecework rate—typically twenty-five cents per text—to "correct" each theme. According to Diederich, this labor was easy to come by: "housewives of the average community" were "pathetically eager to undertake this work at almost any price that the community can afford" (231) and, once employed, would provide the response that would make possible this part of the curriculum.[1]

The pages of *English Journal*, where this plan was announced in 1960, fairly bristled with discussion of it during the next two years (see Burke; Doherty). A librarian from Rutgers wrote in to say, for example, that the plan was *not* a Rutgers plan at all, that Rutgers had merely provided a place for teachers, with the support of the Ford Foundation, to design the curriculum (Shaw). A teacher who had participated in this new curriculum also wrote, his intent to defend the new practice:

> I had no problems with my lay reader, a former English department head in a small town in Pennsylvania. She was very conscientious and dependable. At first, I rather nervously read over every paper that she graded. It was several weeks before she actually began to save my time and my energy as I began to admit that she was a fair grader. We had several conferences in which I marked a dozen or so papers to show her the points I wanted emphasized. After we smoothed over the points of friction, I was amazed at how many more themes of quality my students were writing. Heretofore, I had found it impossible to correct and grade a theme-a-week without working far into the night each weekday and spoiling my weekends. Now for the first time in over twenty years of teaching high school English, I was doubling and at times tripling the number of composition assignments. (Logan 486)

But of all the issues at play—including the feasibility of the plan; the relationship of reading to success in college; the critique that the plan catered to college-bound students while ignoring other students—two linked issues stood out: first, the assessment of student work by nonprofessionals; and second, the deleterious effect of the plan on teacher professionalism. Articulating this critique, Paul Krueger, a doctoral student with credentials as a former chair of a high school English department, noted that since the best response to writing is contextualized within a relationship, typically that between a student and a teacher, it didn't seem possible that an unfamiliar reader could offer the quality of response provided by an English teacher. In reply to this specific critique, a lay reader—also published in *English Journal*—defended the anonymity of such a reader as "all to the good":

> He can then be unprejudiced enough to judge the writing, not the children. Our school sends its themes to the lay readers with numbers instead of names. The children do not know who the readers are. We have no personal contact at all. This system has worked beautifully. As one little girl said at the end of her personal letter assignment, "Don't worry about anyone else seeing this. Ladies who don't know us correct our papers." (Kolker 54)

Apart from the irony of personal letters having "Ladies who don't know us" as readers and referring to them with the masculine pronoun even though every one of them was required to be a female housewife, this approach to assessment is clearly indebted to the scientific model, in which standard prompts, uniform times, and blind readers are the gold standard. Echoing advocates of the experience curriculum, Krueger presents a different view of assessment, one distinctly located in the personal relationships of the classroom, and, as important, he speaks as a practicing teacher. In doing so, he also speaks to the collective of teachers in sounding a note of caution:

> In turning over to a lay person the responsibility for evaluating composition, one of the most important aspects of teaching English, we are making an admission, it seems to me, that not only can't we do the job for which we have been hired, but that a lay person, without special training, can teach composition as well as we who have had special training. In recent years we have been pleading with state certification agencies to stiffen the requirements for the certification of English teachers, *especially as they regard advanced instruction in composition and its techniques*. Yet, with the lay reader program, we assume that even less training is necessary and turn over the evaluation of themes to lay people, many of whom have had even less training in composition than teachers who are already in need of more training. (531; emphasis in original)

In other words, Krueger rightly understands that the larger *effect* of a lay reader program is to deprofessionalize teachers, an understanding that the then-executive director of NCTE shared, if behind the scenes.[2]

Having read the announcement of the program some three years earlier in the *ETS Newsletter*, J. N. Hook shared the broad outlines of it with the NCTE Executive Committee, suggesting that it was "an experiment that we may want to watch, both because of its possible values and because of its possible dangers." In her reply, Luella B. Cook, chair of the NCTE Committee on Evaluation, replaced the assessment context with another, that of fostering the learning of the student while at the same time meeting the needs of many students: "It's the same old argument, isn't it—or related to it—between individualizing instruction and teaching the masses. We need both—in differing amounts and in different situations and geared to each other" (Letter). At the same time, Cook also defined the issue as a contest between teaching and assessment—"Perhaps the center of the controversy lies in a confusion between subjective and objective appraisal, or between teaching values and judgmental values" (Letter)—and promised to take the issue up with her committee at the Annual Convention.

In the end, nothing came of the Lay Reader Plan, perhaps in part because, when asked, Hook chose not to support it and in part because of the way it redefined teaching. Put in today's terms, in the Lay Reader Plan, response—which is a kind of formative assessment—was "outsourced" to well-meaning lay readers, an approach that anticipates current outsourcing such as electronic rating schemes promoted by testing companies, as well as the use of such electronic raters to relieve the teacher of the "burden" of response. Similarly, the tutoring services of commercial vendors such as SmartThinking respond to the same "need."

Krueger's point about the appropriate role of the personal in assessment is also prescient: this is an issue that becomes central in portfolios and threatens to scuttle them. As portfolio assessment developed, measurement experts wanted to know how to employ portfolios, given that their authors are not masked but textually identified. Living at the intersection between teaching and assessment, this issue becomes especially poignant when the portfolios go digital. Research on electronic portfolios demonstrates that, to engage students and enhance learning, portfolios should not only *not* be masked, but, rather, they should be *personalized*; that is, they should include the full identities of the students inside the portfolio (Cambridge, Cambridge, and Yancey).

In sum, the episode of the Lay Reader Plan allowed NCTE to decide on a principle of teacher professionalism, forecasting the role of teacher response as central to student learning both then and into the future. As important, in the pages of *English Journal*, the Lay Reader Plan itself was allowed to compete in the marketplace of ideas, where because of teacher professionals and NCTE members such as Paul Krueger, it mercifully expired.

Moment Four: An Assessment Bridging the Divide

A fourth moment occurred during the time of the 1970s and 1980s, which by turns seemed the best and most questionable of times. Put differently, it was a time when teacher-initiated portfolio projects linked curriculum and assessment to support student learning. It was a time when NCTE spoke out on the legitimacy of students' own language and on the need for teacher education curriculum to align with the curriculum for students and with the assessments linked to that curriculum. It was, however, also a time marking the beginning both of resistance to bad testing and of advocacy for more humane assessment of student work.

As Anne Ruggles Gere notes in this volume, the 1970s saw a shift to what has been called process pedagogy, based in large part on the findings of researchers such as Donald Graves in elementary classrooms, Janet Emig in high school classrooms, and Sondra Perl in postsecondary classrooms. Observing and interviewing student writers, these teacher-researchers learned *from* students how composing works, and collectively, these studies and others like them provided a new curriculum for composing located in new practices: invention, drafting, peer review, reflection, revising and rewriting, and publishing. During this time, new assessment practices also developed from this process-rich model of composing, most influential among them the portfolio. With a portfolio—a collection of writing, selected from an archive and reflected on by the student—writers and their various audiences could literally see development over time and achievement across texts. These portfolios—which included the by-now traditional curricular areas of reading, writing, and literature—demonstrated the power of NCTE and teachers more generally to serve two often-conflicting interests: accountability and student development.

Three examples illustrate the work of teachers in bringing together a new curriculum, process pedagogy, and progressive assessment during this time. The first, the 1992 NCTE volume *Portfolios in the Writing Classroom* (Yancey), illustrated in the voices of teachers and in the examples of authentic classroom practice how middle school, high school, and college teachers could use portfolios both as a resource for curriculum and as a mechanism for assessment located in two equally valued dimensions: development and accomplishment. Its major contribution, in this context, was threefold: (1) it demonstrated that development and accomplishment were not at odds with each other; (2) it showed that to foster learning and accurately assess student work, portfolios, because of their multiple samples, constituted the best option; and (3) it included students' own reflections in the assessment.

The second example, the Heinemann collection edited by Donald H. Graves and Bonnie S. Sunstein, *Portfolio Portraits* (1992), showcased innovative language arts curricula, especially in kindergarten through grade 12 classrooms, as suggested by chapter titles such as "Portfolios in First Grade: A Teacher's Discoveries," "A Fifth-Grade Class Uses Portfolios," and "Eighth Grade: Finding the Value in Education." Here, teachers were not only *not* resisting assessment, but they were also developing new evaluative models that legitimized their classroom values.

A third and final example, an article by Linda Leonard Lamme and Cecilia Hysmith appearing in *Language Arts*, "One School's Adventure into Portfolio Assessment" (1991), narrated the account of teachers in a single school coming together to review students' portfolio texts in order to decide how well the curriculum was working for students and how it might work better. In this example, we see how teachers, moving outside their classrooms, could collaborate on their own assessment-based research directed toward improving the curriculum.[3]

At the same time that portfolio assessment was being introduced, a second reform effort tied to assessment also began, this one focused on reforming the literature curriculum by changing the tests that influenced that curriculum, both the tests certifying teacher competence and the tests shaping student knowledge. Put differently, this effort—which focused not on writing and portfolios but on literature—took a systematic approach in linking curriculum, assessment, and teacher professionalism. During the 1960s, as the teaching of writing shifted from a product to a process approach, the literary canon was experiencing a similar transformation. Put simply, it broke apart: literature by authors of different ethnicities, especially African Americans, as well as literature by women, began appearing in classrooms. Aware that, at some level, what gets assessed is both what is valued and what is *systematically* taught, NCTE in 1970 passed a resolution advocating that works by authors of "Black Literature" be assessed in the ways that other professional competencies were evaluated.

In its preamble, the 1970 "Resolution on Items Testing Competence in Black Literature on Qualifying and Certifying Examinations" cited "a long and continuing neglect of African and Afro-American literature in the secondary schools" as a motivation for the resolution, noting that NCTE activity itself—the "recent inclusion of workshops in African and Afro-American literature by the National Council of Teachers of English"—evidenced "a new recognition and belief in presenting Black literature to secondary school students as a meaningful and important aspect of the study of literature" (par. 1). Accordingly, the preamble argues, NCTE must address the professionalization of teachers in this area, which of course is certified by tests. The resolution itself reads:

> Resolved, that as long as tests are administered, items designed to test and examine competence in Black literature be included in all forthcoming editions and revisions of the literature sections of all teacher certification and recertification examinations, all English achievement tests, and the Graduate Record Examination; and that these test items be included neither as

> options nor as supplementary items but as integral parts of these examinations. (par. 2)

Two points are especially worth noting. First, the resolution recognizes the relationship of all the components in the system—from "English achievement tests" and the GRE to "certification examinations"—and claims that they must all be aligned: with Black literature as an *integral* part of each assessment. Second, the resolution holds only as long "as tests are administered." In other words, the resolution isn't in favor of testing per se, but rather of testing *all* the parts of the curriculum that a teacher should know, including Black literature. In this moment, then, interest in assessment wasn't limited to writing; it included various areas of the language arts, and it included practice as well as policy.

The third trend occurring during this time, however, was located not in confidence about ways to reform curriculum and assessment, but rather in anxiety about teacher control in the classroom, especially when it came to externally mandated tests. From 1970 until 1977, no fewer than twelve resolutions keyed to assessment were adopted by NCTE's Board of Directors. Some, such as the "Resolution on Supporting Secretary Califano's Positions on National Testing" (1977) and the "Resolution on Including Speaking and Listening in National Assessment of Educational Progress (NAEP) Assessments" (1973), supported policies or leaders outlining more progressive views of assessment. More commonly, however, motions such as the "Resolution on Legislatively Mandated Competency-Based Testing" (1977) argued against proposals seeming to call teacher professionalism and competence into question. Just as important, this set of resolutions was the first of a wave of resolutions against harmful testing practices that continues today.

This moment in the history of literacy assessment, like the ones leading to it, had an inherent duality. NCTE was claiming the right both to define literacy assessments in new, innovative, and progressive ways and, in some cases, to conduct such assessments. At the same time, NCTE expressed its concern that, in the public arena, state and national policy was moving in more regressive ways.

Moment Five: Standardization Returns and the Role of Public Policy

A fifth moment shaping NCTE's values with respect to assessment occurred with the increase in standardized tests. As we have seen, this moment began in the 1970s, picked up traction in the 1980s and into the 1990s, and increased in velocity with the No Child Left Behind Act of 2001. In several ways—including multiple resolutions, the NCTE report *The Impact of the SAT and ACT Timed Writing Tests* (2005), and efforts to inform Congress about needed changes in federal laws—NCTE has acted to alert both profession and country about differences between good and bad assessments, about what assessments should include as well as exclude, and about how assessments not only measure but also construct both learning and students. And during the 1990s, assessments were inextricably linked to standards in a new effort for NCTE as it sought to create standards for language arts.

Standards were not new for NCTE: from its beginnings, NCTE had included members with an interest in standards. As James M. Powers from Salem Public Schools in Oregon put it in a 1912 issue of *English Journal,*

> I wish that we could get ourselves out of this maze, and that some standards could be set up whereby the students and teachers might be made to feel that they are beginning somewhere; that they are traveling along some well-recognized path; and that they are heading for some goal worth the while to reach. (50)

And through the years, various NCTE members and leaders advocated for standards that would, they believed, help students. In 1960, for example, Luella B. Cook, the 1956 president of NCTE, explored what standards might mean in "The Search for Standards" (1960). Noting the tension between competing aims of teaching, she neatly synopsizes the struggle we see in 1912—and now, in 2009, as I write this chapter:

> Two different concepts of teaching responsibility clash unceasingly in our minds: the concept of growth and development

> of the individual, as subjectively measured against time and his native capacity; the concept of actual accomplishment, as objectively measured against specific criteria of excellence. Both concepts are valid and deserve our allegiance. The problem which confronts us is to determine the manner in which each of these concepts should operate in relation to the other at each of the three levels of education: elementary, secondary, and college. (321)

Cook's remedy is "first of all a concept of standards which will operate for all levels of ability, which will hold in high esteem the job well done, regardless of its size" (325). Quality, according to Cook, "applies to small things as well as to large things. In our efforts to recapture our concern for quality let us not be lured into a worship of quantity" (325). Here we again see the tension between a scientific notion of quantity as defined by its contrast with the "small things" of teaching.

Still, it wasn't until the 1990s that NCTE took up the "standards issue" in earnest, collaborating with the International Reading Association (IRA). As explained by Ben Nelms, this effort hoped to "meet the times' call for articulation of agreed-upon principles for the content area" and to provide "national consensus on the nature of English and the needs of teachers and students in the field" (49). As explained by NCTE itself, the standards were complementary: "designed to complement other national, state, and local standards and [to] contribute to ongoing discussion about English language arts classroom activities and curricula" (NCTE, "NCTE/IRA Standards" par. 1). In other words, the standards—for example, that "[s]tudents use spoken, written, and visual language to accomplish their own purposes (e.g., for learning, enjoyment, persuasion, and the exchange of information)"—were not a set of stand-alone directives, but rather a set of twelve curricular statements intended to be in dialogue with other such statements.

Equally important, by definition what these standards were *not* was highlighted. They were not, for example, "prescriptions for particular curriculum or instruction" (IRA and NCTE 3), nor were they to be considered as separate or discrete items. As a statement of what should be taught, they were keyed both to assumptions about literacy development and to the resources students needed to succeed in developing as accomplished readers and writers, including the following:

- All students must **have the opportunities and resources to develop the language skills** they need to pursue life's goals and to participate fully as informed, productive members of society.
- These standards assume that **literacy growth begins before children enter school** as they experience and experiment with literacy activities—reading and writing, and associating spoken words with their graphic representations.
- They **encourage the development of curriculum and instruction** that make productive use of the emerging literacy abilities that children bring to school.
- These standards provide ample room for the **innovation and creativity essential to teaching and learning.**
- These standards are **interrelated and should be considered as a whole. . . .** (NCTE, "NCTE/IRA Standards" par. 2; emphasis in original)

Many NCTE members were not altogether happy about the NCTE standards, regardless of how prescriptive or not they may be: quite the reverse. Very often, teachers didn't resist the standards per se so much as what seemed to follow them so relentlessly: assessments, especially reductive assessments. The pages of all the NCTE journals were filled with critiques, titled variously, but all concerned about the tests that would follow: "Teaching in the Time of Testing: What Have You Lost?" (McCracken and McCracken), "Teaching in a World Focused on Testing" (Buckner), and "Stories from the Shadows: High-Stakes Testing and Teacher Preparation" (Watson et al.). Likewise, numerous resolutions spoke against reductive tests of isolated skills associated with standards in general, tests whose importance increased under No Child Left Behind.

The negative connection between standards and assessment, however, was probably nowhere better expressed than by P. L. Thomas in *English Journal*'s "Standards, Standards Everywhere, and Not a Spot to Think" (2001), summarized here:

> Standards and standardized testing are well-intentioned beasts that value the whole over any of its parts. Reading and writing are individual acts at the most intimate level of evolving understanding and learning. In effect, state or national standards, along with high-stakes testing, are wholly incompatible with authentic reading and writing instruction by teachers and authentic reading and writing by students.
>
> The standards movement reduces student understanding; reading and writing are acts of expanding understanding. The English classroom is the central place where teachers and students must begin to champion and embrace the unpredictable and chaotic nature of coming to know this world through language.

The standards movement continues even today; in fact, in 2009, with the election of Barak Obama and a newly Democratic Congress, it seems to have taken on new energy. This time, however, the renewed focus on standards is not organized by teachers, but by a collection of interested parties, including the National Governors Association, testing agencies such as the American College Testing Program (ACT), and reform-oriented organizations such as Achieve. NCTE, which has been asked to comment on these new standards as applied to language arts (the Common Core English Language Arts State Standards), is proceeding cautiously. Led by NCTE Past President Randy Bomer, a blue-ribbon group—including teachers such as NCTE Executive Committee member Jennifer Ochoa and past Executive Committee members Diane Waff and Doug Hesse—has provided a review (NCTE, *Report*). As of this writing, however, the outcome of this most recent standards initiative is unknown. What is known is that, according to U.S. Secretary of Education Arne Duncan, these standards will lead to new assessments. How *new* these assessments will be—in terms of design, student opportunity, and teacher participation—is very much an open question.

This last point, about how new an assessment might be, is made especially salient by one of NCTE's notable achievements in the last decade: pointing out how old and regressive the "new" 2005 Scholastic Aptitude Test (SAT) of writing actually is. The College Board introduced this test—which includes a multiple-choice test of grammar and usage for about two-thirds of the student's score and a thirty-five-minute writing prompt for the remainder—in large part as a response to a perception that the University of California system would no longer require SAT scores of college applicants (Yancey, "Writing Assessment"). An NCTE task force appointed by then-NCTE President Randy Bomer and led by Robert Yagelski provided a critical review of this new "writing" test. Summarized in *The Impact of the SAT and ACT Timed Writing Tests: A Report from the NCTE Task Force on SAT and ACT Writing Tests* (2005), the "four areas of concern related to the potential impact of the new timed writing component of the SAT" (2) include

1) Concerns about the validity and reliability of the test as an indication of writing ability.
2) Concerns about the impact of the test on curriculum and classroom instruction as well as on attitudes about writing and writing instruction.
3) Concerns about the unintended consequences of the uses of the writing tests.
4) Concerns about equity and diversity. (2)

The report, according to NCTE Executive Director Kent Williamson, generated more attention than any other such document and has played a major role in hastening what is clearly a decline in national use of the test for college admissions. As of this writing, more than 700 colleges have gone SAT-optional (or given it up altogether), including some elite schools such as Smith College and Wake Forest University. Perhaps more important, without including SAT scores in the admissions process, these colleges are enrolling classes of students that are both more diverse and at least equally impressive as those admitted when SAT scores were required. The *Impact* report, in other words, provided an impetus for change that is consistent with NCTE values.

This fifth moment, then, can be characterized as a study in contradiction. Embracing a set of standards keyed to description rather than prescription, NCTE found both acceptance of and resistance to them from its members while it spoke out eloquently against one of the most common tests used in the country.

Moment Six: Digital Technologies and New Assessments

A sixth and final defining moment of NCTE engagement with literacy assessment involves the role that digital technologies are playing in transforming literacies as we know them and what that means for assessment practices. NCTE was the first and is still the only literacy organization that has provided a definition of twenty-first-century literacies. At this moment, it is in the process of helping enact that definition by articulating a curricular framework, with assessment implications, that will provide for the future of literacy instruction and its appropriate assessment.

The context for this work is rich with challenges, but two deserve special mention. First, the kinds of texts being produced—from multimedia compositions to blogs to tweets—proliferate so quickly and diversely that it's difficult to know what their common features might be and thus how to evaluate them. Second, given the historical impulse for efficient assessment, it isn't clear what role, if any, is appropriate for automated scoring. As we consider these questions, however, national policy as framed by the assessment world is in effect redefining writing as a material practice. In the 2011 National Assessment of Educational Progress (NAEP), eighth and twelfth graders will compose at the keyboard, tapping resources of the word processor such as formatting, boldfacing, and italicizing and using spellcheckers and grammar checkers as part of their composing processes (National Assessment Governing Board). In other words, these students are being positioned as digital composers.[4]

NCTE has already begun to address these issues connected to digitality and networked composing, both incrementally and more generally. The incremental approach is demonstrated, for example, in the adoption in 2007 of "Principles and Practices in Electronic Portfolios" by the Conference on College Composition and Communication (CCCC). Because of its focus on best practices as well as principles, this statement identifies CCCC and NCTE more broadly as an organization that can provide guidance for new texts, in this case for digital portfolios. More specifically, the CCCC statement identifies eight dimensions associated with the purpose, role, preparation, and use of electronic portfolios in a writing program. Each dimension is then followed by suggestions for supportive practices that should be extended to students by four groups of stakeholders: (1) composition faculty, (2) writing program directors, (3) technology staff, and (4) administrators. In addition, the position statement includes a full set of resources to help teachers, including examples of e-portfolios, a bibliography on them, and a set of relevant sources for reflection. In providing this comprehensive set of sources, the position statement moves beyond merely stating a position to *providing*, in this case, resources so that attention is given both to assessment and to the context in which it occurs.

In 2008, anticipating the shifts in reading and writing motivated by digital technologies and networking of various kinds, NCTE moved beyond important but incremental actions to address more comprehensively the literacy needs of the twenty-first century. NCTE began by approving a formal and comprehensive definition of twenty-first-century literacies:

> Literacy has always been a collection of cultural and communicative practices shared among members of particular groups. As society and technology change, so does literacy. Because technology has increased the intensity and complexity of literate environments, the twenty-first century demands that a literate person possess a wide range of abilities and competencies, many literacies. These literacies—from reading online newspapers to participating in virtual classrooms—are multiple, dynamic, and malleable. As in the past, they are inextricably linked with particular histories, life possibilities and social trajectories of individuals and groups. Twenty-first century readers and writers need to:
>
> - Develop proficiency with the tools of technology
> - Build relationships with others to pose and solve problems collaboratively and cross-culturally
> - Design and share information for global communities to meet a variety of purposes
> - Manage, analyze and synthesize multiple streams of simultaneous information
> - Create, critique, analyze, and evaluate multi-media texts

- Attend to the ethical responsibilities required by these complex environments (NCTE, "NCTE Definition" n. pag.)

But almost as quickly—within five months—NCTE also developed frameworks for both curriculum and assessment. Regarding assessment, NCTE recognized that evaluation practices "need to take into consideration both traditional components and elements that may be different for 21st century student work" (NCTE, "NCTE Framework" n. pag.). Traditional elements include, according to this statement, dimensions such as "effectiveness of the work in achieving its purpose; impact of the work on the audience; creativity or aesthetics demonstrated in the final product; and creativity, initiative, and effectiveness demonstrated in solving problems." The second category, "Newer elements of assessment of 21st century student learning," includes features such as

> potential interaction with and impact on a global audience; students' selection of tools or media that most effectively communicate the intention of the product; students' level of ethical and legal practice as they remix products; and level of ethics and safety exhibited in students' online behavior. (NCTE, "NCTE Framework" n. pag.)

Taken together these frameworks function as a heuristic not only for the assessment of texts but also for the design of assignments, and they position NCTE as a leader in both activities.

In surveying this new landscape, NCTE has taken care to note the challenges these new literacies bring to schools. For example, the frameworks observe that "students' greater proficiency with tools or formats than the teacher . . . may generate outcomes not anticipated in an assessment rubric," and that "technology glitches beyond students' control that negatively impact the quality of the final products" can also confuse any assessment activity (NCTE, "NCTE Framework" n. pag.). The realism of these concerns, of course, is at least in part attributable to the role that NCTE teachers living in real classrooms played in the frameworks' development.

This sixth and last moment, then, is one located in ambiguity but also in promise, with national standards and potential national assessments looming while NCTE leads the nation in highlighting how digital literacies are transforming the lives of students, teachers, and the public at large.

Conclusion

Histories, made variously, are necessarily incomplete. In Deborah Brandt's award-winning *Literacy in American Lives* (2001), the history of literacy comes alive through the interviews of native informants, everyday people who recount their memories of writing and, especially, of reading. In Norbert Elliot's award-winning *On a Scale* (2005), a social history of assessment is narrated through theory, other histories, and primary documents, especially those housed at the Educational Testing Service. Here, I've focused on NCTE's contribution to the dialogue around, and the practice of, literacy assessment by constructing that story in part through assessment literature, but largely through a set of NCTE primary documents—the pages of its journals and its books; letters of an NCTE executive director and president; and a set of task force reports and resolutions composed by numerous teachers across a broad span of time. Even so, given the scope of this chapter, this history is, of course, also incomplete, filled with missing moments that others in new histories will overlap, fill in, and interpret.

Still, we can make some observations. At the beginning of the twentieth century, teachers came together in NCTE because of their concern for the literate lives of children and a commitment to supporting those lives. From the beginning, classroom practice was at the heart of NCTE's concerns, and where classroom practice was important, assessment wasn't far behind—for the public, for politicians, for educational reformers, for students, for teachers, and, certainly, for NCTE. As we have seen, the issues so important in the early decades of NCTE's history—the national call for increased efficiency regardless of the enterprise; the tension between scientific measurement and a concern for the development of students; the role of labor and the ways that this labor is part of professional life, regardless of how badly funded; and the continuing theme of funds for assessment robbing funds for learning—haven't in these one hundred years been resolved.

Far from it. Indeed, one conclusion this history suggests is that these themes sound all too familiar.

At this moment in assessment history, however, NCTE seems to be taking a new tack in addressing the assessment of literacy. Put in the jargon of the twenty-first century, we might say that NCTE is multitasking. On the one hand, NCTE continues to provide important public critique of flawed assessment practices, as it did in 2005 with the NCTE Task Force on SAT and ACT Writing Tests. On the other hand, as in the case of the 2008 twenty-first-century literacies resolutions, NCTE is identifying and outlining issues attending the future of literacies, in the process providing a heuristic for addressing them. At the current moment in assessment, then, NCTE is, as the title of this volume suggests, looking both backward and forward, not only to read the past but also to write the future.

And not least, bound up in all of this assessment activity of a hundred years is a consistent, abiding effort to serve the needs of students through the efforts of humane literacy assessments constructed as central to the practices of diverse literacies.

Notes

1. This characterization of the housewives is a study of its time. It's a truism that tests construct students, but it's also the case, as this example suggests, that in the making of tests and other assessment activities, test-makers construct other stakeholders as well, and in this case, housewives are constructed as pathological. As Norbert Elliot points out, in describing this effort in the *Harvard Graduate School of Education Association Bulletin* (1961), Diederich described these "neurotic" homemakers as inveterate shoppers who would, given this invitation, respond similarly: "A part-time job working as readers of essays would bring them out like bargain-day at Macy's" (Elliot 190). The rhetoric of assessment here, in terms of the comparison of reviewing student work and shopping, is worth examination.

2. Norbert Elliot, emphasizing its value as "an economic model" supporting increased class size through a locally controlled "contextualized based system," sees the Lay Reader Plan quite differently from NCTE leaders such as J. N. Hook, whose concerns focused on the relationship of formative assessment to student development and teacher identity and professionalism. See Elliot, *On a Scale*, pp. 190–92.

3. Other notable efforts during this time included the NCTE volume edited by Charles R. Cooper and Lee Odell, *Evaluating Writing: Describing, Measuring, Judging* (1977), which raised questions about various mechanisms for scoring essays (e.g., holistic and primary trait). For a consideration of the relationship between the assessment of essays and of their wave-like chronology, see Yancey, "Looking Back as We Look Forward."

4. Several NCTE members and two NCTE presidents participated on the Steering Committee or Planning Committee for the 2011 NAEP, including Bobbi Houtchens, Carol Jago (2010 NCTE president), Sandra Murphy, Carl Whithaus, and Kathleen Blake Yancey (2008 NCTE president).

Works Cited

Blumenthal, Joseph C. *English 2600: A Programmed Course in Grammar and Usage*. 4th ed. New York: Harcourt, Brace Jovanovich, 1973. Print.

Brandt, Deborah. *Literacy in American Lives*. New York: Cambridge UP, 2001. Print.

Buckner, Aimee. "Teaching in a World Focused on Testing." *Language Arts* 79.3 (2002): 212–15. Print.

Burke, Virginia M. "A Candid Opinion on Lay Readers." *English Journal* 50.4 (1961): 258–64.

Cambridge, Darren, Barbara Cambridge, and Kathleen Blake Yancey. *Electronic Portfolios 2.0: Emergent Research on Implementation and Impact*. Sterling, VA: Stylus, 2009. Print.

Conference on College Composition and Communication. "Principles and Practices in Electronic Portfolios." *National Council of Teachers of English*. NCTE, Nov. 2007. Web. 30 Aug. 2009.

Cook, Luella B. Letter to J. N. Hook. 25 Feb. 1958. TS. University of Illinois Archives (Record Series 15/71/001, Box 2), Urbana, IL.

———. "The Search for Standards." *English Journal* 49.5 (1960): 321–35. Print.

Cooper, Charles R., and Lee Odell, eds. *Evaluating Writing: Describing, Measuring, Judging*. Urbana, IL: NCTE, 1977. Print.

Coulter, Vincil Carey. "Financial Support of English Teaching." *English Journal* 1.1 (1912): 24–29. Print.

Diederich, Paul B. "The Rutgers Plan for Cutting Class Size in Two." *English Journal* 49.4 (1960): 229–66. Print.

Doherty, Eugene N. "The Princeton Township Lay-Corrector Program." *English Journal* 53.4 (1964): 273–305. Print.

Duncan, Arne. "States Will Lead the Way toward Reform." *US Dept. of Education*, 14 June 2009. Web. 30 Aug. 2009.

Elliot, Norbert. *On a Scale: A Social History of Writing Assessment in America*. New York: Peter Lang, 2005. Print.

Emig, Janet. *The Composing Processes of Twelfth Graders*. Urbana, IL: NCTE, 1971. Print. NCTE Research Report No. 13.

Graves, Donald H. *Writing: Teachers and Children at Work*. Exeter, NH: Heinemann, 1983. Print.

Graves, Donald H., and Bonnie S. Sunstein, eds. *Portfolio Portraits*. Portsmouth, NH: Heinemann, 1992. Print.

Hatfield, W. Wilbur. "The Ideal Curriculum." *English Journal* 21.3 (1932): 182–91. Print.

Hook, J. N. Letter to the NCTE Executive Committee. 9 July 1957. TS. University of Illinois Archives (Record Series 15/71/001, Box 4), Urbana, IL.

[Hosic, James Fleming.] "The Closing Year: The Efficiency Wave." *English Journal* 1.10 (1912): 638–41. Print.

International Reading Association, and National Council of Teachers of English. *Standards for the English Language Arts*. Newark, DE: IRA; Urbana, IL: NCTE, 1996. *National Council of Teachers of English*. Web. 30 Aug. 2009.

Kolker, Harriette Buckner. "Some Answers to Some Questions on the Lay Reader Program." *English Journal* 52.1 (1963): 51–54. Print.

Krueger, Paul H. "Some Questions on the Lay Reader Program." *English Journal* 50.8 (1961): 529–33. Print.

Lamme, Linda Leonard, and Cecilia Hysmith. "One School's Adventure into Portfolio Assessment." *Language Arts* 68.8 (1991): 629–40. Print.

Logan, Edgar. "The Diederich Plan Revisited." *English Journal* 53.7 (1964): 484–87. Print.

McCracken, Nancy Mellin, and Hugh Thomas McCracken. "Teaching in the Time of Testing: What Have You Lost?" *English Journal* 91.1 (2001): 30–35. Print.

National Assessment Governing Board. *Writing Framework for the 2011 National Assessment of Educational Progress*. Pre-publication edition. Iowa City, IA: ACT, Fall 2007. National Assessment Governing Board. Web. 30 Aug. 2009.

National Council of Teachers of English. *The Impact of the SAT and ACT Timed Writing Tests: A Report from the NCTE Task Force on SAT and ACT Writing Tests*. Urbana, IL: NCTE, 2005. Print.

———. "The NCTE Definition of 21st Century Literacies." *National Council of Teachers of English*. NCTE, 15 Feb. 2008. Web. 30 Aug. 2009.

———. "NCTE Framework for 21st Century Curriculum and Assessment." *National Council of Teachers of English*. NCTE, [2008]. Web. 30 Aug. 2009.

———. "NCTE/IRA Standards for the English Language Arts." *National Council of Teachers of English*. NCTE, n.d. Web. 30 Aug. 2009.

———. *A Report of the NCTE Review Team on the July 2009 Draft of the Common Core English Language Arts State Standards*. 15 Sept. 2009. TS.

———. "Resolution on Including Speaking and Listening in National Assessment of Educational Progress (NAEP) Assessments." *National Council of Teachers of English*. NCTE, 1973. Web. 30 Aug. 2009.

———. "Resolution on Items Testing Competence in Black Literature on Qualifying and Certifying Examinations." *National Council of Teachers of English*. NCTE, 1970. Web. 30 Aug. 2009.

———. "Resolution on Legislatively Mandated Competency-Based Testing." *National Council of Teachers of English*. NCTE, 1977. Web. 30 Aug. 2009.

———. "Resolution on Supporting Secretary Califano's Positions on National Testing." *National Council of Teachers of English*. NCTE, 1977. Web. 30 Aug. 2009.

Neal, Michael. *Writing Assessment and the Digital (R)Evolution of Texts and Technologies*. Forthcoming 2010. Print.

Nelms, Ben F. "Reconstructing English: From the 1890s to the 1990s and Beyond." *English Journal* 89.3 (2000): 49–59. Print.

Odell, C. W. *Educational Measurement in High School.* New York: Century, 1930. Print.

———. *Traditional Examinations and New-Type Tests.* New York: Century, 1928. Print.

Perl, Sondra. "The Composing Processes of Unskilled College Writers." *Research in the Teaching of English* 13.4 (1979): 317–36. Print.

Powers, James M. "More Simple and Definite Standards." *English Journal* 1.1 (1912): 50. Print.

Shaw, Ralph R. "Riposte." *English Journal* 50.2 (1961): 137–38. Print.

Thomas, P. L. "Standards, Standards Everywhere, and Not a Spot to Think." *English Journal* 91.1 (2001): 63–67. Print.

Thorndike, Edward L. "Notes on the Significance and Use of the Hillegas Scale for Measuring the Quality of English Composition." *English Journal* 2.9 (1913): 551–61. Print.

Watson, Patricia A., et al. "Stories from the Shadows: High-Stakes Testing and Teacher Preparation." *Language Arts* 79.3 (2002): 216–25. Print.

Williamson, Kent. Personal conversation with the author. 8 May 2009.

Wineberg, Samuel S. "Historical Problem Solving: A Study of the Cognitive Processes Used in the Evaluation of Documentary and Pictorial Evidence." *Journal of Educational Psychology* 83.1 (1991): 73–87. Print.

Yancey, Kathleen Blake. "Looking Back as We Look Forward: Historicizing Writing Assessment." *College Composition and Communication* 50.3 (1999): 483–503. Print.

———, ed. *Portfolios in the Writing Classroom: An Introduction.* Urbana, IL: NCTE, 1992. Print.

———. "Writing Assessment and Its Reward Function: A Brief Historical Review and a New Agenda." *Race and Racism in Writing Assessment.* Ed. Asao Inoe and Mya Poe. Carbondale: Southern Illinois UP, forthcoming 2010. Print.

NCTE 100 YEARS READING THE PAST. WRITING THE FUTURE.

A Blast from the Past

Did you know that literature scholar and educator Louise Rosenblatt characterized 1956 as "a critical hour for the teaching of literature in the schools of America"? Her 1956 *English Journal* essay, "The Acid Test for Literature Teaching," reflected her concern that teachers had created students who "are anxious to have the correct labels—the right period, the biographical background, the correct evaluation." For Rosenblatt, "Literature provides a *living through*, not simply knowledge *about*."

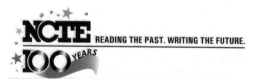

NCTE Affiliates and Assemblies

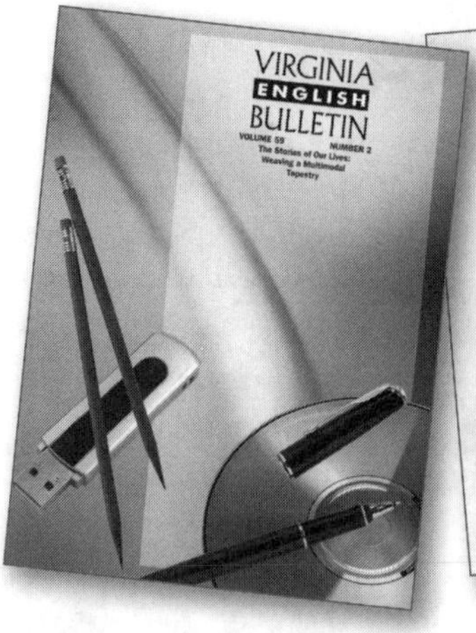
VIRGINIA
ENGLISH
BULLETIN
VOLUME 59
NUMBER 2
The Stories of Our Lives:
Weaving a Multimodal
Tapestry

The Nebraska
English Journal
"I teach because..."
VOL. 51.1
SPRING 2008

Volume 36
Winter 2009
Number Two
THE
ALAN
REVIEW
JIM THORPE
SONNY'S WAR
WARRIOR ANGEL
Out of the Pocket

SEP 17 2009
NEW JERSEY COUNCIL OF TEACHERS OF ENGLISH
NEW JERSEY
ENGLISH JOURNAL
2009

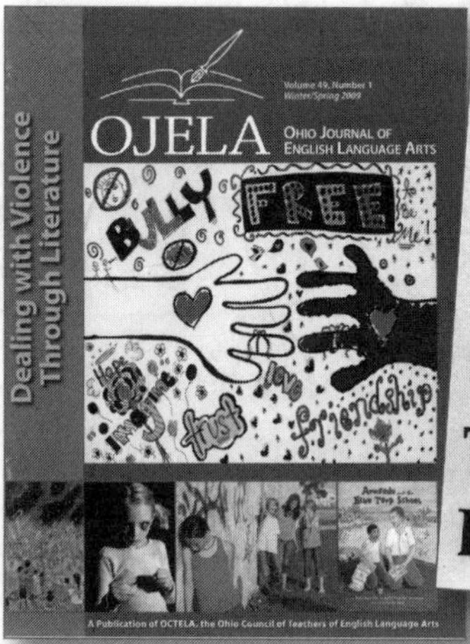
Volume 49, Number 1
Winter/Spring 2009
OJELA
OHIO JOURNAL OF
ENGLISH LANGUAGE ARTS
Dealing with Violence
Through Literature
BULLY
FREE
friendship
A Publication of OCTELA, the Ohio Council of Teachers of English Language Arts

NEATE
Volume 107 Number 2
Spring 2008
Teacher As Writing
Mentor
The
Leaflet

Oregon English Journal
Theme:
Education and Hope:
Teaching in Hard Times
octe
Volume XXXII, Number 1
Spring 2010

UTAH ENGLISH
JOURNAL
2002
GO FOR THE GOLD!
Winning Ideas for
English/Language Arts
GOLD

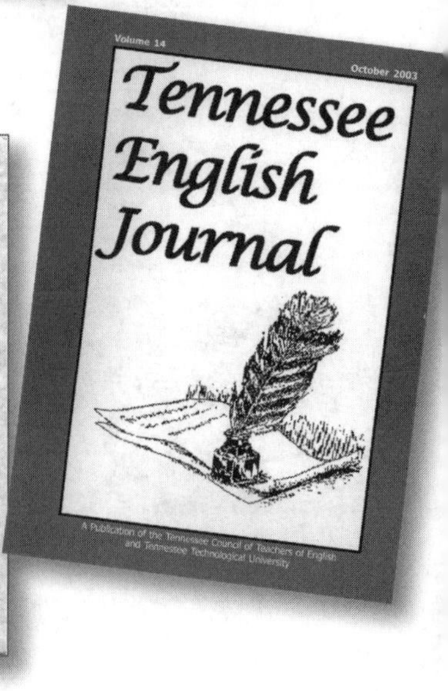
Volume 14
October 2003
Tennessee
English
Journal
A Publication of the Tennessee Council of Teachers of English
and Tennessee Technological University

Chapter Nine

NCTE and the Preparation of English Language Arts Teachers: Learning to Do Good Work Well

Patricia Lambert Stock
Michigan State University

The scholarly discipline English and the school subject English are relative newcomers to the academic scene. Harvard, Oxford, and Cambridge Universities did not establish professorships of English until 1876, 1904, and 1911, respectively (Parker); and it is generally understood that the school subject English was defined and established as a required part of the secondary school curriculum in America as a result of the work of the 1892 Committee of Ten appointed by the National Education Association (NEA). All who have written about the establishment of English studies tell us that, although subject English is young, its antecedents—among them a range of studies and practices including grammar; logic; rhetoric; oratory; philology; literature, sacred and profane; composition; spelling; penmanship—date back some 2,000 years (Applebee; Miller; Palmer; Squire, "The History"). In part, these multiple roots and sprouted branches of "English" have shaped the primary, secondary, and tertiary questions that have concerned teachers of English and their teachers across the past century: (1) What is English? (2) How is English best taught and learned? (3) How are teachers of English best prepared for their professional work?

While my concern in this essay is with how English teachers and teacher educators associated with the National Council of Teachers of English (NCTE) have prepared themselves and their colleagues to teach subject English, kindergarten through university, that concern cannot be unbraided from their work to establish and define the subject during the century in which "English" and NCTE emerged and developed together. Across the century, a tripod metaphor to define English studies—language, literature, and composition—was established and proved resilient in the postsecondary teaching of English. In the 1892 report of the Committee of Ten's Conference on English held at Vassar College, constitutive elements of the school subject English—the only subject the committee recommended for study by all students across all four years of high school—were defined as competencies: the ability to understand the expressed thoughts of others, to express one's own thoughts, to develop a taste for and extend one's reading of "good" literature (NEA Committee of Ten 46–47). From the outset, this distinction between postsecondary and secondary school teachers' conceptions of "English," and whether and how those conceptions should or might be brought into alignment, has proved to be a major concern of those interested in answers to the questions, What is English? How is English best taught and learned? and How are teachers of English best prepared for their professional work? Distinctions and alignments have also shaped when, with whom, and how NCTE has addressed these questions.

In his important essay "A History of the Preparation of Teachers of English," Alfred Grommon, fifty-seventh president of NCTE, observes that the makeup and procedures of NEA's Committee of Ten set a pattern for the kind of collaborative work in which NCTE has engaged during the past one hundred years to address issues of concern to English educators and the broader society ("A History" 487). And while the Council has shifted its attention across the century from the first, to the second, to the third of the field-shaping questions, it has addressed each of them always reciprocally. During the early years of the twentieth century, as Council members focused on defining the newly established subject English, they did so in order to support one another's work to teach the subject purposefully and meaningfully to all students. Beginning in the late 1920s, in light of the emerging work of learning theorists and philosophers of education, when English educators turned their attention to designing curricula and instructional practices, they imagined one another offering those curricula and engaging students in those practices. And, in the last half of the century, when the Council concerned itself directly with issues of teacher preparation, in terms and venues determined as much by public interest and public opinion as by developing professional understandings, it did so in concert with renewed efforts to define subject English. In this essay, I revisit a century of committees, commissions, and conferences working within contemporary contexts in order to draw attention to NCTE's first century of work—in partnerships with interested others—to prepare and influence the preparation of teachers of the English language arts and to address the constitutive questions that have shaped the field of English education.

Groundwork for the Preparation of English Language Arts Teachers

Although NEA committees were not convened primarily to address issues of teacher preparation, those established after the Committee of Ten commented, in passing, on what qualified individuals to become teachers and how those individuals should be prepared for their work, just as the Committee of Ten had. These NEA committees carried forward and initiated terms for conversation about teacher preparation that can be found in the discourse shaping the preparation of English language arts teachers even today. For example, reports of the NEA Committees of Twelve and Fifteen offered visions of teacher preparation that recommend the selection of teachers with strong personal qualities, scholarly dispositions, and ability in instruction and discipline, and—in the case of secondary and normal school teachers—with specialized training for their work. Anticipating practices that are now commonplace, a subcommittee report of the Committee of Fifteen recommended a postgraduate year of training for teachers and supervised field placement (NEA Committee of Twelve 77–78; NEA Committee of Fifteen 34–35). At a time when the typical elementary school teacher had less than the equivalent of a high school education (Lucas 50), these committees—in addition to echoing society's centuries-old concern for the moral reliability of those to whom we entrust our young people—recommended that teachers' preparation include purposeful professional as well as general education experiences. In

1907, in keeping with thinking at the time, the NEA Committee of Seventeen advanced a program of preparation for secondary school teachers that emphasized the study of classical languages and literatures, preparation considered essential for secondary and postsecondary teachers of English for years to come. For the next half-century, in studies dealing with a variety of issues that concerned educators, these and other committees and task forces inched their way toward framing and exploring questions focusing on the preparation of elementary, secondary, and postsecondary school teachers of particular academic subjects and disciplines in the United States. Within NCTE this work began in the context of English language arts teachers' efforts to answer the question, What is English?, in light of the diverse students who would be required to study the subject.

Defining "Subject" English

During the early years of the twentieth century, after an 1894 National Conference on Uniform Entrance Requirements in English developed a catalog of readings required for college admission, the secondary school English curriculum was designed to prepare students for postsecondary English studies. Books on the teaching of the English language arts written by college and university faculty became primary vehicles for preparing school teachers of English whose job it would be to guide their students through this curriculum.[1] As teachers of English began to come together in clubs and associations to discuss and support one another's professional work, they questioned the efficacy of an "English" curriculum designed exclusively to prepare students for postsecondary studies. This was especially true in those cities where growing numbers of immigrant families were settling. With broader visions of subject English in mind, these teachers joined together with like-minded college and university faculty to establish the National Council of Teachers of English in 1911. While their primary purpose in coming together was to ensure that subject English would be defined with all students, not just those college-bound, in mind, and would include composition and language studies as well as literature studies, from the outset they embraced the challenge of teaching one another what and how to teach the subject they were calling into being.

Across these years, as NCTE worked with other organizations to refine definitions of subject English and how it might best be taught and learned, the Council's conferences and the published scholarship of its leaders became the primary means by which kindergarten-through-university teachers of English prepared themselves for their professional work. One month after the Council was established, *English Journal*—founded, owned, and edited by James Fleming Hosic, NCTE's first secretary-treasurer—began publishing work written for and aimed at enriching the professional practice of teachers of English at all levels of instruction. Most of the articles that made their way into *English Journal* were based on presentations that teachers offered one another in NCTE conferences and conventions and were aimed at presenting teaching ideas and practices for peer review and community use, or to put it another way, at developing a scholarship of teaching the English language arts.

At the same time, textbooks written by NCTE leaders widely influenced the teaching of English and served as sources for teachers' knowledge of their subject, a practice for teacher preparation that was repeated midcentury in composition studies, another discipline conceived and nurtured in NCTE. The wisdom of some of these texts—*The Teaching of English in the Elementary and Secondary School* (1903) by George R. Carpenter, Franklin T. Baker, and the Council's first president, Fred Newton Scott, for example—was groundbreaking at the time and speaks instructively to teachers even today. Alfred Grommon credits Scott with issuing in this textbook the earliest stipulation that teachers of English in America should know American as well as English literature, and with arguing for rhetorical approaches to the teaching of language and literature rather than decontextualized ones that focus on "correctness" ("Teachers" 385). Perhaps because Scott was the first and second president of NCTE and perhaps because he was also a past president of the Modern Language Association of America (MLA), his understandings of subject English were particularly influential ones. Also influential at the time was the thinking of scholars such as John Dewey and G. Stanley Hall, whose work addressed the relationships between child development, schools, and society and provided teachers of English, like those who established NCTE, theoretical and philosophical arguments for the curriculum, instruction, and schools they envisioned to meet the needs of the diverse students in their classrooms.

One way in which NCTE worked to define "English" and how it would be taught was in partnership with NEA. During the second decade of the twentieth century, NEA undertook the task of reorganizing subject matter and instruction in American high schools. James Fleming Hosic, whose active and influential membership in NEA is described in Jacqueline Jones Royster's chapter in this volume, chaired the NEA–NCTE National Joint Committee on the reorganization of English in the American high school. While the 1917 report issued by the committee did not recommend significant changes in the content of the English curriculum, it did redefine goals for the teaching of English in terms that revealed the influence of the child development movement and progressive-era thinking (Hosic). The report also recognized the teacher to be the most important factor in the high school English curriculum. And although it was careful to acknowledge that what constituted the best preparation for that teacher had not been widely or thoroughly considered, the committee did sketch a vision of the teacher of English as someone who had studied literary types, read widely in American as well as English literature, been trained in oral and written composition and in principles of education, and practiced teaching under supervision (Hosic 149).

Teaching and Learning Subject English

In 1929, less than twenty years after the founding of NCTE and just over a decade after release of the report of the NEA–NCTE Joint Committee, NCTE established the Curriculum Commission. In taking upon itself the task of developing a "pattern curriculum," an illustrative curriculum for the teaching of English, kindergarten through graduate school, NCTE drew attention to the

Council's membership, allowing, in fact requiring, it to imagine the teaching of English across all levels of schooling. Following the practice of earlier NEA committee work, NCTE's Curriculum Commission invited other interested professional groups to join its deliberations. In 1935, when the Council published the commission's report, *An Experience Curriculum in English*, discussed at length in Stephen Tchudi's chapter in this volume, one of the document's appendixes, "Teacher Education in English," called for the adoption of an experience curriculum in programs designed to prepare teachers of English language arts. Echoing earlier NEA committees' emphasis on the importance of carefully selecting students preparing to become teachers of English, the report also recommended four-year, four- to five-year, and five-year programs of study for elementary, junior high school, and high school teachers of English, respectively—this at a time when 25 percent of high school teachers had not completed four years of college (Lucas 50).

Alfred Grommon tells us that research conducted during the 1930s, when NCTE published *An Experience Curriculum in English*, particularly research into the teaching of English in public schools conducted by Dora V. Smith, twenty-fifth president of the Council, constituted "a benchmark in the development of programs for the education of teachers of English for elementary and secondary schools" ("Teachers" 389; see also D. Smith, *Evaluating Instruction in English*; D. Smith, *Evaluating Instruction in Secondary School English*; D. Smith, *Instruction*). According to Grommon, Smith's research, coupled with the wide respect she enjoyed in the profession, made her the logical choice to direct a second (and slightly renamed) Commission on the English Curriculum, established by the NCTE Executive Committee in 1945. Conceiving its charge broadly and once again involving representatives of other interested organizations and agencies, over the next twenty years NCTE's Commission on the English Curriculum published five influential studies: *The English Language Arts* (1952), *Language Arts for Today's Children* (1954), *The English Language Arts in the Secondary School* (1956), *The Education of Teachers of English for American Schools and Colleges* (Grommen; 1963), and *The College Teaching of English* (Gerber, Fisher, and Zimansky; 1965).

When it appeared in 1963, *The Education of Teachers of English for American Schools and Colleges*, the fourth of the commission's five reports, was the most definitive study of the preparation of teachers of English in the United States undertaken to date. In the editor's introduction to the volume, Alfred Grommon explains that the report's findings and recommendations are integrally connected to the vision of the teaching of English presented in the commission's three previously published reports. Taken together the reports of the NCTE Commission on the English Curriculum—produced during a period of dramatic change in America and American education—tightly braided the Council's commitment to effective preparation of teachers of the English language arts with its commitment to a meaningful, purposeful English language arts curriculum and with instructional practices and working conditions in which English language arts might be taught and learned by all children.

Public and Professional Attention Turns to Teacher Preparation

Across the 1940s, 1950s, and 1960s, forces beyond as well as within the field of education directed public interest and professional attention to the preparation of teachers. One force that took shape in a number of publications was aimed at reforming high school curricula widely regarded as composed of shallow life-adjustment tasks into which rich courses of study recommended by progressive education theorists had been narrowed. Among these publications were studies that spoke influentially to academics. For example, two reports published by Harvard University argued that secondary school education in America had become too practical and vocational. These reports called for a reemphasis on ethical and cultural studies and great books, and for the study of English as a discipline, not a set of competencies, to be exercised in the service of other learning (Harvard University Committee; Joint Committee). Similar arguments, published in books written by influential public intellectuals,[2] found broad public support in 1957 when the USSR successfully launched *Sputnik*. Calls from within and beyond the profession for renewed academic rigor in American education took shape in legislation in 1958, when the U.S. Congress passed the National Defense Education Act (NDEA), providing funds for research in math, science, and foreign language education and for the professional development of teachers of these subjects. Although research into the teaching of English and for English teachers' professional development was not funded by the NDEA until 1964, work sponsored by foundations and professional associations to reform the English curriculum and make the teaching of English more rigorous began before that.

In 1958 the Ford Foundation funded four conferences to address Basic Issues in the Teaching of English. Cosponsored by NCTE, MLA, the College English Association (CEA), and the American Studies Association (ASA), the Basic Issues conferences paved the way for what proved to be a particularly productive decade of cooperative work between these groups. The most significant recommendations emerging from the Basic Issues conferences called for the secondary school English curriculum to mirror the tripod model in place in university English departments and for the study of English language, literature, and composition to be "sequential and cumulative," from kindergarten through graduate school (NCTE, *Basic Issues*). The first major effort to develop this academic curriculum was conducted by the Commission on English, established by the College Entrance Examination Board (CEEB) in 1959. During the five years of its work, this commission, composed of a group of distinguished English educators that included NCTE's Executive Secretary James R. Squire, not only advanced the conception of the secondary school English curriculum that had emerged in the Basic Issues conferences but also conducted a series of six- to eight-week summer institutes in which 868 secondary school English teachers earned graduate credit for studying current work in language, literature, and composition with distinguished university faculty. This university–school professional development model, also used in NDEA summer institutes, is generally regarded as the most important outcome of the CEEB Commission on English.

When the CEEB Commission on English released its 1965 report, *Freedom and Discipline in English*, eleven of the commission's fourteen recommendations focused on teacher preparation, teacher certification, and teaching conditions. By that time, work was already underway to draw national attention to the importance of subject English. In 1960, NCTE members attending the annual business meeting had directed the Council's

> Executive Committee to inform the Congress of the United States and the United States Office of Education of the compelling need for an extension of the National Defense Education Act of 1958 to include English and the humanities as a vital first step toward improving instruction in English and of stimulating program development in this important area. (Hook 195)

Twelve months later, the NCTE Committee on National Interest, chaired by Executive Secretary Squire, released a report documenting the working conditions and preparation of teachers of English in the nation's schools, a report that became part of the *Congressional Record* of the U.S. Congress. Supporting an action agenda to be undertaken on a national scale, *The National Interest and the Teaching of English* (1961) reported that 90 percent of American students were enrolled in English, that the demand for teachers exceeded the supply by 27 percent, and that of those actually teaching secondary school English, 40 to 60 percent lacked even the minimum level of preparation for a college major (33). Specifically, the report called for national support to achieve seven interrelated goals:

- To focus instruction in English upon the study of language, literature, and composition
- To educate teachers of English to the developmental and sequential nature of the study and to institute a national program for encouraging articulation of English studies throughout the school years
- To improve present preparatory programs for teachers of English
- To improve the preparation of practicing teachers of English
- To improve the services and supplies available to teachers of English
- To recruit and prepare more teachers of English. (3)

The report also described projects that would help achieve the goals, among them these:

- A widespread program of national institutes for elementary and secondary teachers
- University scholar/schoolteacher collaborations
- Supervisory services in state and local school districts and coordination of them
- Regional centers for study and demonstrations
- Conferences of college and university personnel concerned with the education of teachers of English
- Large-scale experimental projects focusing especially on linguistic materials in the teaching of English
- Conferences on critical problems in the teaching of English such as teaching English in culturally depressed communities
- Research basic to the teaching of English.

Following release of the report, the U.S. Office of Education allocated funds for Project English. Chaired by J. N. Hook, NCTE's former executive secretary, the project took shape in many activities called for in *The National Interest and the Teaching of English*: curriculum study centers, basic research projects, demonstration centers, and a series of conferences. One of these conferences, held in Allerton Park, Illinois (1962), led to the development in MLA of the Association of Departments of English (ADE). Although the Council's first National Interest report focused attention on the need for stronger preservice education for teachers of English, it did not result in NDEA's funding institutes for summer and yearlong professional development; however, a second report did.

Composed of compelling numbers and arguments for English teachers' inservice education, *The National Interest and the Continuing Education of Teachers of English* (1964) observed, for example, that only 50 percent of the teachers surveyed for the report had majored in English, that 30 percent had not taken a course in English in the preceding ten years, and that more than 50 percent were not required to demonstrate evidence of professional growth in their subject area (4–5). This second report called for professional development institutes for English teachers—institutes that the NDEA subsequently funded from 1965 to 1968—by drawing attention to the beneficial impact of earlier institutes for teachers sponsored by the CEEB Commission on English (ix). The report also called for consultant and supervisory assistance and for inservice educational opportunities for elementary and secondary school teachers to be provided at both the state and local levels (ix).

When NCTE conducted the survey, questionnaire, and documentary research issued in its two National Interest reports, it did so to inform a concerned public citizenry about serious deficiencies in English instruction and in the preparation of teachers of English. While the recommendations in these reports described venues and circumstances needed for well-designed teacher preparation programs, the vision for the substance and conduct of those programs, under development in the Council for a number of years, was to be found in the fourth report of the Commission on the English Curriculum. *The Education of Teachers of English for America's Schools and Colleges* (Grommon), a collection of twelve essays published in 1963, offered recommendations for the initial and continuing preparation of teachers of elementary, secondary, and college English. A teacher shortage of crisis proportions[3] as well as public concern about the quality of education in the late 1950s and early 1960s provided NCTE groups such as the Committee on National Interest and the Standing Committee on Teacher Preparation and Certification opportunities to call productively for public support and funding for English teachers' preparation. But it was the NCTE Commission on the English Curriculum that developed its fourth report to influence the shape, substance, and quality of that preparation.

In effect, *The Education of Teachers of English for American Schools and Colleges* advanced earlier calls for high standards for the selection of candidates for teacher education programs and for professional preparation of teachers of English, K–12. Convinced that the education of teachers of English at all levels of instruction must include general education, professional preparation, and academic specialization, the report described in some detail what that education might look like in programs for elementary and secondary school teachers of English. Acknowledging that the MA degree would have to be recognized as the terminal degree for an increasing number of college teachers of English, given supply and demand at the time, the report recommended that the PhD in English continue to represent the highest kind of scholarship but that it also provide prospective college teachers with supervised teaching experience in a first-year writing or literature course. The report also outlined a vision of the purposes of inservice programs, a vision that included improving the entire educational program and narrowing the gap in knowledge between generations of teachers.

Converging Alliances

As university and school teachers of English worked together in the CEEB Commission on English, the NDEA summer institutes, and professional associations across the 1950s and early 1960s, their appreciation for one another grew. In his important history, *English in a Decade of Change* (1968), Michael F. Shagrue, then assistant secretary for English in MLA, reports that one strand of salutary work that grew out of these mutual efforts began with the 1962 Allerton Park Conference, sponsored by Project English. Participants from both college and university departments of English initiated steps and studies acknowledging their responsibility to prepare teachers of English for all levels of education. Building on these initiatives, at a meeting in 1963 Erwin R. Steinberg, chair of English at Carnegie Mellon University, called for studies of the curriculum for the PhD in English, the PhD in English education, and the EdD in English education. Steinberg, who succeeded J. N. Hook as the coordinator of Project English, observed that there was no group better equipped to address itself to the teaching of language, literacy, and the traditions of our society than "members of college and university departments of English working with their counterparts in the public schools" (Shagrue 39). A study conducted in 1966–67 by Don Cameron Allen, professor of English at Johns Hopkins University, subsequently advanced the commitment of departments of English to teacher education for all levels of instruction and recommended the development of doctoral programs in English education in which the research emphasis would be on the teaching of English (Shagrue).

In the same year that Erwin Steinberg called for developing the PhD in English education, NCTE sponsored a meeting of English educators at Indiana University to discuss issues of teacher preparation. The success of the meeting and the planners' desire to build on a decade of renewed energy in NCTE's Committee on the Preparation and Certification of Teachers of English led a year later to the establishment within NCTE of the Conference on English Education (CEE). Early editors of *English Education*, the journal that CEE began publishing in 1967, named two of the reasons why the conference and its journal were needed. On college and university campuses, there is often only one faculty member in English education, sometimes located in the department of English, sometimes located in the department, school, or college of education, sometimes jointly appointed in English and education. State and local language arts coordinators typically find themselves in the same situation. CEE and its journal were conceived to serve as a forum for peer review and community use of developing practice and research into issues of concern to professionals preparing and certifying teachers of the English language arts.

Another project that grew out of collaboration between professional associations of English language arts educators during the 1950s and 1960s was the English Teacher Preparation Study (ETPS), undertaken to develop guidelines for preparing teachers of English at all levels of instruction.[4] Initiated in 1965, the ETPS was conducted by the National Association of State Directors of Teacher Education and Certification (NASDTEC), NCTE, and MLA, with support from the U.S. Office of Education. The study's advisory board viewed ETPS work as building upon a foundation constructed by numerous committees, studies, and reports that preceded it, among them:

- The fourth report of NCTE's Commission on the English Curriculum, *The Education of Teachers of English for American Schools and Colleges* (Grommon)

- The work of NCTE's Committee on the Preparation and Certification of Teachers of English
- NCTE bibliographies for *The Preparation and Certification of Teachers of English*, edited since 1957 by Autrey Nell Wiley
- The work of the CEEB Commission on English
- Recommendations for teacher preparation, certification, and working conditions advanced in the CEEB commission's report, *Freedom and Discipline in English* (1965)
- Earlier work to write guidelines for the preparation of secondary school teachers that had been sponsored by the U.S. Office of Education and directed by J. N. Hook in the Illinois Statewide Curriculum Study Center (ISCPET)
- Work to develop guidelines for teacher preparation that NASDTEC had undertaken with other professional associations in other disciplines beginning in 1958

In the fourteen months during which the ETPS was conducted, the advisory board, chaired by NCTE's Executive Secretary James R. Squire, distributed successive drafts of the guidelines to associations of schoolteachers and administrators, college and university faculty in English and education, deans of instruction in colleges and universities, state-level school officials, and in one national and four regional ETPS conferences. Just as efforts to design subject English in the 1892 Vassar Conference had occurred in the context of the Committee of Ten's work to define secondary school studies, so too the work of the ETPS to design guidelines for the preparation of teachers of English occurred in the context of similar work to establish guidelines for the preparation of teachers of other subjects.

Many in the field of English education saw in the ETPS a convergence of efforts, collaborations, and alliances that promised to have a dramatic impact on the preparation of teachers of English and on the quality of English teaching. A product of inevitable compromises between parties with common goals and different needs, the 1967 ETPS "Guidelines for the Preparation of Teachers of English" (Viall) did not result in the dramatic changes that some had anticipated. What the guidelines did was to codify understandings and goals for the teaching of English developed during the 1950s and early 1960s by subject area specialists working within the broader field of education and the larger society. Much the same may be said for guidelines prepared across the next half-century by the NCTE Standing Committee on Teacher Preparation and Certification. These documents, published in 1976, 1986, 1996, and 2006 respectively, reflect the Council's ongoing collaborative work to address the question, How are teachers of English best prepared for their professional work?

Because these various guidelines testify to the field's and society's changing understandings of the nature of subject English and how it might best be taught and learned, I use them as reference points to tell the story of the second half-century of NCTE's work to shape meaningful and purposeful preparation of teachers of the English language arts. From 1967 to 2006, the guidelines document from each decade can be read as evidence of English educators' sense of what was needed at the time to prepare themselves and newcomers to the field for their work. Beginning with the 1976 edition of the guidelines, each successive document reflects a growing tension that the Council and its colleagues have felt as public policy and governmental agencies have exercised increasing control over certifying teachers and accrediting teacher education programs. Across the last half-century, teacher educators, including English educators, have conducted an impressive body of research, much of it labor-intensive qualitative research (e.g., case studies, ethnomethodological studies, phenomenological studies) upon which they have built a persuasive body of theory to guide their practice. As English educators have gained sophisticated understandings of the content knowledge and skills needed to teach subject English, public policy has recommended and, in some cases, required that the practice of English education fly in the face of this scholarship.

Guidelines for the Preparation of Teachers of English: 1967 to 2006

The introduction to the eleven-page 1967 "Guidelines for the Preparation of Teachers of English" developed by the ETPS indicates their intention to do the following: (1) to help state departments of education evaluate preparation programs offered by institutions seeking accreditation and by individuals seeking certification, (2) to help colleges and universities develop and evaluate programs for elementary and secondary school teachers, and (3) to encourage institutions to select and recruit strong candidates for the profession (Viall 885). The introduction to the document notes further that the guidelines are intended to set a context within which teacher preparation programs might be evaluated with discretion and imagination, to encourage programs to experiment with promising curricula, and to encourage departments of English and of education to work together to design courses and programs of study (Viall 885). In keeping with conceptions of the teacher of English in place since the beginning of the century and the conception of subject English firmly established in the commissions and committees of the 1950s and early 1960s, the seven guidelines set forth by the ETPS focus on "the teacher's personality and general education; his skills in listening, speaking, reading, and writing; and his knowledge about and ability to teach language, literature, and composition" (Viall 885).

The 1967 guidelines document goes on to define components of the subject:

> By language is meant the structure and historical development of present-day English. By literature is meant chiefly British and American writing of distinction, but also any other writing of distinction in English or in English translation. By children's literature or literature for adolescents is meant literature which has particular interest and value for children or adolescents. By composition is meant oral and written composition and the relation of these two modes to rhetorical theory. (Viall 886)

While the document avoids prescribing a specific program of study to prepare teachers of English, it does recommend at least fifteen hours (or equivalent) of course work in English above the first-year level for the elementary classroom teacher and at least thirty-six hours of course work (or equivalent) for the secondary school teacher. In addition, not unlike the late nineteenth-century report of the NEA Committee of Fifteen, the document recommends that programs for elementary and secondary teachers provide supervised teaching experience, course work in methods of teaching, and a fifth year of study.

Federal and foundation funding that became available in the 1950s and early 1960s encouraged professional associations of English educators to work together to reform the secondary school English curriculum. To support the postsecondary tripod curriculum in English, these funds enabled summer and yearlong institutes that prepared teachers to work with new curricular materials, plan scholarly projects, and develop the 1967 "Guidelines for the Preparation of Teachers of English," work that English educators hoped would improve the teaching of English. By the late 1960s, however, dramatic social changes shifted the agenda. The Civil Rights Movement, the women's movement, the environmental movement, and the Vietnam War led these associations of English educators to reexamine the aims and directions of their work. This redirection is acknowledged in the opening words of the thirteen-page *A Statement on the Preparation of Teachers of English* (1976), issued by NCTE's Standing Committee on Teacher Preparation and Certification:

> In the middle sixties, when the Guidelines for the Preparation of Teachers of English were being developed, "English" was defined by the College Entrance Examination Board's Commission on English as a discipline comprising language, literature, and composition—the familiar "tripod." Today, that metaphor has all but disappeared as a definition of English; our subject is viewed not only as a body of knowledge and as a set of skills and attitudes but also as a process, an activity—something one does (i.e., one uses and responds to language, in a variety of ways in a variety of contexts). . . .
>
> The idea that "English" includes whatever one does with language (maybe even: whatever one does with symbols) has broadened the activities of the English classroom beyond what most of us would have envisaged ten years ago (NCTE Standing Committee, *A Statement* 1)

Societal change, together with changes in the profession accompanying the rising influence of teachers' unions, provided the context within which subject English was reexamined beginning in the late 1960s. However, many English educators point to the

Anglo-American Seminar on the Teaching and Learning of English held at Dartmouth College in 1966 as the occasion prompting the redefinition of subject English and the work of English educators.

The Anglo-American Seminar on the Teaching and Learning of English was convened in 1966 because representatives of the MLA, NCTE, and the United Kingdom's National Association for the Teaching of English (NATE) believed that English as a school subject was facing similar critical challenges in the United States and the United Kingdom. A meeting in which representatives of these organizations exchanged experiences and ideas would help teachers of English better address those challenges. To that end, the Carnegie Corporation provided financial support for fifty scholars—university professors of language, literature, composition, and language arts teacher education—to come together in a monthlong seminar. Consultants—other teachers of English across the levels of instruction but overwhelmingly from higher education—joined the seminar for various periods of time. Although the seminar was not charged to address specific questions, issues for study were identified in advance of the conference, including the overarching question, What is English? (Dixon viii).

Summarizing his understanding of the answers to this overarching question that were proffered at Dartmouth, British educator John Dixon named three conceptions of subject English and claimed that two, what he called the "skills model" and the "cultural heritage model," were outdated. In effect, Dixon's summary and analysis of the conference, published in his important book *Growth through English* (1967), argued for a "personal growth model" and an overarching conception of subject English that integrated the teaching of speech, drama, imaginative writing, and response to literature, a conception of English in which many members of NCTE saw shades of the 1935 experience curriculum published by NCTE's first curriculum commission. In an essay written some time after this personal growth/integrated language arts model had become widely accepted by English language arts educators, James Britton of the University of London, whose voice was among the most influential at Dartmouth, and Merron Chorny of the University of Calgary, claimed that Dartmouth had replaced a view of English that focused on product with a view that focused on process, a view of language learning as a means to literacy. This view recognized the role of language in all learning and perceived learning as active meaning making (Britton and Chorny 110).

This new view of English that Britton and Chorny describe is everywhere obvious in the statement that NCTE's Standing Committee on Teacher Preparation and Certification issued in 1976. In its description of the knowledge, abilities, and attitudes that teachers of the English language arts must acquire throughout their professional lives, the committee outlined areas of knowledge of language, literature, and composition not named in the 1967 guidelines, among them the processes by which children "acquire" language; the relationship between students' language learning and the "social, cultural, and economic conditions within which they are reared"; the processes by which individuals learn to read; the body of literature in English (including literature for children and adolescents, popular literature, oral literature, non-Western literature, and literature by women and minority groups); and activities that make up the processes of oral and written composing (NCTE Standing Committee, *Guidelines,* 1976, 5–6).

The arguments of British scholars advanced at Dartmouth and afterward challenged the "academic model" of subject English then current in the United States. The new perspective was received enthusiastically not only by NCTE's community of teacher educators but also by its maturing Conference on College Composition and Communication (CCCC). At the time of the Dartmouth Conference, CCCC, established within NCTE in 1949, was in the process of reclaiming the Western world's rich rhetorical tradition, developing qualitative research methodologies, and nurturing the work of researchers who were, in turn, building an impressive body of scholarship in the emerging field of composition studies. Distinguishing their work from rhetorical studies that focused on reception, scholars and researchers in composition studies concerned themselves with the processes of producing oral and written texts. Committed to developing a scholarship of the teaching of writing, researchers in composition studies inquired into their students' writing processes as well as the processes of writers in a variety of workplaces. Student texts and works-in-progress took their place alongside the texts of published writers in composition courses as compositionists replaced reductive pedagogies that focused exclusively on correctness with pedagogies that focused on composing processes and how rhetorical constraints shape effective texts. Especially emphasized were rediscovered and newly developed processes of "invention." Studies designed to advance this teaching agenda began to appear in increasing numbers across the 1960s and 1970s.

Just as textbooks written by NCTE leaders in the early years of the twentieth century informed teachers about what the new subject English was and how it might be taught, research studies and textbooks developed by NCTE leaders working in CCCC charted directions for developing scholarship in the teaching of writing. Among these influential studies and textbooks changing composition instruction in schools, colleges, and universities were Ann E. Berthoff's *Forming/Thinking/Writing: The Composing Imagination* (1982) and *The Making of Meaning: Metaphors, Models, and Maxims for Writing Teachers* (1981); Richard Braddock, Richard Lloyd-Jones, and Lowell Schoer's *Research in Written Composition* (1963); William E. Coles's *The Plural I: The Teaching of Writing* (1978); Edward P. J. Corbett's *Classical Rhetoric for the Modern Student* (1971); Peter Elbow's *Writing without Teachers* (1973); Janet Emig's *The Composing Processes of Twelfth Graders* (1971); Donald H. Graves's *Balance the Basics: Let Them Write* (1978); Ken Macrorie's *Telling Writing* (1970); James Moffett's *Teaching the Universe of Discourse* (1968); and Donald M. Murray's *A Writer Teaches Writing: A Practical Method of Teaching Composition* (1968).

One research study, perhaps more than any other at the time, provided schoolteachers, teacher educators, and teachers of college composition and communication a vision of how they might integrate their developing uses of writing as a means of discovery and learning with a rhetorical approach to the teaching of composition. *The Development of Writing Abilities (11–18)* (1975) was sponsored by the Schools Council Project and conducted by a team of English educators associated with the University of London's Institute of Education: James Britton, Tony Burgess, Nancy Martin, Alex McLeod, and Harold Rosen. Resting their work on theories developed in James Britton's earlier work, *Language and Learning* (1970), those associated with the Schools Council Project used their research to argue—in the name of writing across the curriculum—that students should have opportunities in all subject areas to use language to learn and to write in a variety of genres for a variety of audiences and purposes.

In part because the quality of students' writing had become a national concern following *Newsweek*'s 1975 article "Why Johnny Can't Write" (Shiels), the writing across the curriculum movement quickly took hold in the United States, making it possible for the research, theory, and practice developing in composition studies to persuade teachers of other disciplines, not just teachers of subject English, of the importance of composing in their fields. Foundations supported programs in which college and university teachers of composition offered workshops to prepare their colleagues across the curriculum not just to assign and grade writing but also (1) to use writing as a means of teaching, (2) to teach writing by explicitly introducing their students to the forms of argument and textual conventions of their various disciplines, and (3) to respond to students' work-in-progress. At the same time, the University of California at Berkeley funded the first site of what has become the longest-lasting, most widespread, university–schools professional development program for teachers of writing: the National Writing Project (NWP).

Founded in 1974 by James Gray, a former secondary school teacher who was at the time teaching and supervising student teachers at the University of California at Berkeley, and several colleagues, among them Miles Myers, later to become the seventh executive director of NCTE, the NWP today has more than two hundred sites. Gray developed NWP's summer institute, the project's centerpiece, in response to his earlier work as a consultant and codirector in NDEA summer institutes. Convinced that four- to six-week institutes of competitively selected teachers were excellent venues for professional development, Gray was not persuaded that those institutes were best directed by academics who had never taught the students and subjects they were preparing teachers to teach. Consequently, he revised the model. In NWP institutes, teachers—selected on a competitive basis—engage one another in the study of their own classroom-tested teaching practices. They also write and make that writing public, and they read current research in composition studies. Over time, Gray's major prediction about this kind of professional development work has proved true: it has produced a body of knowledge about the teaching of writing that would otherwise be unavailable for peer review and community use (for additional information, see Gray). The model of teacher learning and teacher research, and the ethic that NWP established in the early 1970s, found enthusiastic support in NCTE, which had been founded on similar principles. Any number of NCTE leaders are active in NWP; eight of the ten most recent NCTE presidents are directors of NWP sites. Furthermore, the model of professional development on which NWP was constructed has influenced more than the teaching of writing in subject English. The impact of the model on the teaching of literature, for example, is richly illustrated in the work of NCTE Past President and NWP site director Sheridan Blau, author of *The Literature Workshop: Teaching Texts and Their Readers* (2003) and co-founder of the National Literature Project, which replicates the NWP model for teachers of literature.

Accountability, Standards, and Testing

In addition to drawing attention to changes in subject English that shaped recommendations in the 1976 *A Statement on the Preparation of Teachers of English*, the NCTE Standing Committee on Teacher Preparation and Certification noted developments in the wider environment that were beginning to effect changes in teacher education. The committee drew specific attention to public demands for "accountability" in education, demands that were producing a move toward performance-based and competency-based certification of teachers, and to governmental units that were increasingly involving themselves in setting standards and procedures for teachers' certification.

A decade later, when the committee issued the 1986 version of *Guidelines for the Preparation of Teachers of English Language Arts*, it did so from the perspective of a profession responding to a flood of reports calling for "radical reforms of public school curricula and the preparation and professional advancement of teachers" (NCTE Standing Committee, *Guidelines*, 1986, 2). Among these reports were Ernest Boyer's *High School: A Report on Secondary Education in America* (1983); John Goodlad's *A Place Called School: Prospects for the Future* (1983); the National Commission on Excellence in Education's *A Nation at Risk: The Imperative for Educational Reform* (1983); and Theodore Sizer's *Horace's Compromise: The Dilemma of the American High School* (1984). The committee also was aware of a decade of profession-altering studies conducted and published in the field of teacher education (see, for example, Grossman, Wilson, and Shulman) and the work of the Holmes Group, which published its influential *Tomorrow's Teachers: A Report of the Holmes Group* (1986), calling for postbaccalaureate, research-based teacher education.

In this context, the committee that prepared the 1986 edition of the guidelines introduced with the following words the knowledge, pedagogical abilities, and attitudes needed by prospective teachers of the English language arts during their preservice education:

> Though we certainly must respect the traditions of our own profession, we must also be aware of its inadequacies. We must promote changes in teacher education that respond to societal demands and keep abreast of new knowledge in our field. Recognizing, then, that the teacher of English language arts must respect and nurture students' intellects and imaginations, as well as help them find significant places in society, the Standing Committee on Teacher Preparation and Certification recommends the following guidelines for the preservice preparation of teachers of English language arts. (NCTE Standing Committee, *Guidelines,* 1986, 6)

The 1986 guidelines reinforce the 1976 guidelines' emphasis on the teaching of English as both a body of knowledge and a process, an activity involving the interrelatedness of speaking, listening, reading, and writing. However, the twenty-one page 1986 guidelines discuss, in more detail than in previous versions, recommendations not only for the kinds of pedagogical preparation preservice teachers of English should have on campus and in schools but also for opportunities to experience effective models of instruction—to observe, analyze, and practice effective teaching. In effect, the 1986 guidelines signal a shift in emphasis taking hold in the larger educational community. Drawing to a close was the time when transcripts documenting successful completion of subject area courses were recognized as qualifying teachers for their work; course offerings alone would no longer serve as evidence of a program's effectiveness in preparing teachers for their work.

Like the 1967 guidelines, the 1986 guidelines name audiences that the NCTE Standing Committee on Teacher Preparation and Certification hoped would be influenced by their work: administrators, curriculum planners, state departments of education, state and federal legislators, and agencies responsible for accreditation of institutions preparing teachers, one of which, the National Council for the Accreditation of Teacher Education (NCATE), was in the process at the time of redesigning its evaluation procedures.[5] Recognized currently by the U.S. Department of Education and the Council for Higher Education Accreditation as a national accrediting body for departments, colleges, and schools of education, NCATE was established in 1954. In the late 1970s, as part of a response to criticism of the nature and quality of its work, NCATE established a Specialty Areas Studies Board (SASB) for specialized professional associations (SPAs) such as NCTE.[6] In 1980, NCTE joined NCATE's SASB. In 1987, when NCATE reframed its standards to account for pedagogical content knowledge in specialty areas, NCTE's Standing Committee on Teacher Preparation and Certification developed a matrix of program standards adapted from the Council's 1986 guidelines to use in evaluating English education programs applying to NCATE for recognition. Later, in 2001, when NCATE again reframed its evaluation criteria for recognizing teacher preparation institutions, shifting from a focus on program offerings to the competence and performance of candidates completing those programs, NCTE's standing committee developed performance standards for the initial preparation of teachers of the English language arts.

While NCTE has developed guidelines and standards for influencing the teaching of English and programs in which English teachers are prepared, the Council's work as an SPA in NCATE reveals the challenge that subject area educators face in an accrediting agency consisting of thirty-three member organizations of teachers, teacher educators, content specialists, and local and state policymakers, each with special interests. Within NCATE, NCTE has worked to ensure that English teacher preparation programs are developed in keeping with the findings of theory and research in its subject field. NCATE itself functions in an environment in which policymakers have increasingly equated assessment with testing (McCracken and McCracken) and in which a Teacher Education Accreditation Council (TEAC), established in 1997, has offered an alternative accreditation process focusing on internal review and continuous growth that is more palatable to many colleges and universities. Amid these challenges, subject area organizations such as NCTE are striving today, as they did in the late 1970s, to ensure that differences among the subject areas they represent and the pedagogical content knowledge needed by teachers of different subjects are recognized by accrediting agencies and addressed in teacher preparation programs.

For these reasons, from time to time NCTE members have questioned the value of the Council's work within NCATE. Supporters of that work argue that, before NCTE's guidelines for the preparation of teachers of the English language arts became standards for NCATE program reviews, they had been used at the discretion of departments, colleges, and schools of education, as well as states. After these guidelines were adopted and became the basis for NCTE–NCATE reviews of English education programs, they led to demonstrable and beneficial adjustments in English teacher preparation programs. Critics argue that NCTE's participation in an accreditation program that directs faculty to engage in labor-intensive administrative and fact-gathering tasks not always considered the best indicators of their programs' quality is misdirected energy. Nevertheless, each time an NCTE committee or task force has assessed the value of the Council's participation in NCATE, the Council has decided that the benefits of participation—the benefits of having NCATE evaluators use

NCTE guidelines and standards for the preparation of teachers of the English language arts to determine the quality of English teacher preparation programs—outweigh the drawbacks.

By the time NCTE's seventy-two page *Guidelines for the Preparation of Teachers of the English Language Arts* appeared in 1996, standards and standards certification projects had taken hold across the profession. The 1987 English Coalition Conference also had taken place. During this three-week conference, representatives from the various organizations that had worked together in the midtwentieth century to define subject English came together again to chart new directions for the field. These English educators concerned themselves with the social constructions of language learning and language use, which educators need to understand, respect, and draw on if they are to teach students to live fulfilling lives in America's multicultural society and in a global economy (Lloyd-Jones and Lunsford).

In light of new understandings in English education, the lengthier set of recommendations and fuller discussions in the 1996 guidelines drew attention to the correlation of the guidelines with other national standards projects being developed at the same time. Among these projects were the Interstate New Teacher Assessment and Support Consortium (INTASC), the National Board for Professional Teaching Standards (NBPTS), the National Association of State Directors of Teacher Education and Certification (NASDTEC), the New Standards Project, the Educational Testing Service, the College Board Pacesetter Project, state-level projects to develop standards for learning and assessment funded by the Clinton administration's 1993 *Goals 2000*, and the joint project of NCTE and IRA to identify what English language arts students should know and be able to do. The IRA–NCTE *Standards for the English Language Arts*, reprinted in Appendix H in this volume, are grounded in principles emerging during the last half of the twentieth century and in discussions during the English Coalition Conference. They signal new skills and knowledge required of English language arts teachers.

In keeping with the IRA–NCTE *Standards*, the 1996 teacher preparation guidelines acknowledge that agreement within the profession had grown increasingly difficult to find but nevertheless describe what beginning teachers should know, believe, and be able to do. Significantly, these guidelines make a distinction not found in earlier guidelines documents between "what a program for English majors should require as outcomes and what, in addition or differently, a program to prepare English language arts teachers should require" (NCTE Standing Committee, *Guidelines,* 1996, 3). The standing committee's declared purpose for making this distinction is to emphasize the 1986 guidelines' assertion that "all language processes are integrated and, hence, that language study should be approached holistically" (NCTE Standing Committee, *Guidelines,* 1986, 3). The distinction also draws attention to the disciplinary nature of collegiate studies. Departments of English are often departments specializing in literary studies. Even when language studies and composition studies are also featured, literature, language, and composition are often taught by faculty who are considered specialists in the different areas, who distinguish their tripod of studies from one another. By contrast, teachers of English language arts in elementary, middle, and secondary schools are expected to teach language, literature, and composition; to teach listening, speaking, reading, and writing all at once and all together; and to do so with reference to the variety of languages, images, and experiences of the students with whom they work.

Remaining consistent with previous documents, the 1996 guidelines document does not call for an English language arts program with a predetermined set of courses or experiences; however, it does offer constructed portraits of exemplary English education programs in different types of teacher preparation institutions. It also identifies outcomes that all programs designed to prepare English language arts teachers should produce. In addition, for the first time, the guidelines present a set of basic principles—diversity, content knowledge, pedagogical knowledge and skills, opportunity, and dynamic literacy—underlying the entire document (NCTE Standing Committee, *Guidelines,* 1996, 5). While content knowledge and pedagogical knowledge and skills had been discussed in earlier versions of the guidelines, discussions of diversity, opportunity, and dynamic literacy had been incorporated into other discussions, not separated out for elaboration. By identifying core principles underlying the guidelines, the NCTE standing committee drew attention to defining characteristics that permeate all of NCTE's activities.

From its earliest days, the Council's commitment to diversity has been one of its constitutive characteristics. At the turn of the nineteenth to the twentieth century, this commitment took shape in its work to define subject English; to ensure, for example, that American literature be taught in the English curriculum, to call—as Fred Newton Scott did in *The Teaching of English in the Elementary and Secondary School* in 1903 (Carpenter, Baker, and Scott)—for instruction in the English language that valued language-in-use rather than abstract prescriptions for language use. Later in the twentieth century, this commitment took shape in the Council's emphasis on students' right to read, students' right to their own language, students' having access to a literature curriculum that included works written by people of color and women (see Stephen Tchudi's; Jacqueline Jones Royster's; and Arthur N. Applebee, Judith A. Langer, and Marc A. Nachowitz's chapters in this volume for fuller discussions of these issues). When the 1996 guidelines drew attention to "opportunity standards," they repeated a call first published in the National Interest reports and echoed a call for the opportunity to learn advanced in the IRA–NCTE *Standards in the English Language Arts* (1996).

When the 1996 Standing Committee on Teacher Preparation and Certification named principles of dynamic literacy as underlying the attitudes, knowledge, and pedagogy needed by teachers of the English language arts, it drew attention to NCTE's constitutive mission to support teachers' lifelong learning. In keeping with developing scholarship, the 1996 NCTE standing committee appended to the guidelines two reports developed by CEE commissions that highlight the field's nascent attempts to shape preservice teacher preparation as the first phase of teachers' lifelong professional development: "Effective Transition to Teaching" (1988) and "Inservice Education: Ten Principles" (1994). In making these reports part of the 1996 guidelines, the committee prefigured two significant changes that would appear in the 2006 guidelines document: first, an extended discussion of how teachers' knowledge and competencies develop across their careers, and second, the grounding of recommendations and discussions in published research and scholarship.

Issued four decades after the 1967 guidelines, the 2006 *Guidelines for the Preparation of Teachers of English Language Arts* is a different kind of document. In the 1967 edition, seven guidelines for the preparation of teachers of English language, literature, and composition, K–12, and the rationale undergirding them were presented in eleven outlined pages. Though built on thinking documented in the reports of conferences, commissions, and committees in which NCTE played an influential role during the 1950s and early 1960s, the bases of the 1967 guidelines were determined across fourteen months of consultation between interested parties and vetted by all concerned professional associations. Shaped by the consensual wisdom of a wide range of educators, rationales for the 1967 guidelines were not cited in the document itself. They were assumed. No one questioned the authority of the ETPS to speak for the field of English education. A half-century later, the 2006 guidelines appear as an eighty-four-page, six-chapter discussion of (1) underlying principles to guide the preparation of teachers of the English language arts; (2) recommendations for the dispositions, content knowledge, and pedagogical knowledge that teachers should acquire during their professional preparation; and (3) guidelines for building effective preparation programs for teachers of the English language arts. All claims, discussions, and recommendations are grounded in published research and scholarship, most of which emerged from the field of English education and the broader field of teacher education.

Explaining that it wanted to compose the guidelines document differently from the way it had been shaped in the past, the NCTE Standing Committee on Teacher Preparation and Certification collapses what had previously been many guidelines into a few overarching statements, supporting those statements and the guidelines with evidence-based discussions. The committee notes that its recommendations emerged from classrooms, case studies, and experimental and correlational work, and from fields and disciplines that included teacher education, linguistics, developmental psychology, reading, and English education (NCTE

Standing Committee, *Guidelines,* 2006, 8). In effect, the committee's emphasis in the 2006 document on the theory and research underlying the guidelines reveals the distance traveled by teacher educators who formed the Conference on English Education in NCTE in 1965 to develop a body of scholarship upon which to build their work. When the standing committee notes that amid this scholarship is classroom-based research, it highlights the extent to which the late-twentieth-century teacher-research movement and the postsecondary scholarship-of-teaching movement—both of which have deep roots in NCTE—have contributed to the influence of context-based research on teacher education in the English language arts.

Inspired by principles and practices developed in action, cooperative action, and participatory research movements during the late twentieth and early twenty-first centuries, teacher-researchers of the English language arts have produced a number of studies demonstrably impacting English teacher preparation. These studies highlight the contrast between situation-specific research conducted by individuals responsible for putting the findings of that research into practice, and research conducted apart from actual classrooms by classroom visitors who are not themselves responsible for translating research into practice. Furthermore, these studies draw attention to a theme introduced in the 1996 guidelines and discussed more fully in the 2006 document: the importance of preparing teachers to be students of their own practice. Persuaded that teaching should be guided by research and that research should address problems of actual practice, teacher research—as realized in the late twentieth century by a number of active NCTE members—took shape in "thick" descriptions of teaching and learning. As teacher-researchers in the English language arts described specific teaching and learning moments in their classrooms, they dramatized the dynamic, organic nature of teaching–learning interactions and drew attention to the interplay of social, cultural, and academic forces at work in these interactions. In so doing, they revealed the ways in which (1) teachers' knowledge of subject matter and students; (2) students' interests, competencies, and resources; and (3) the material conditions of teaching and learning (e.g., classrooms, supplies, student–teacher ratios, high-stakes testing programs, etc.)—all at once, all together—determine the nature and quality of education in specific contexts. In effect, even as the teacher research discussed in the 2006 guidelines offers models of teachers' lifelong commitment to learning for and with their students, it also portrays the kind of teaching that the NCTE standing committee envisioned emerging from English teacher preparation programs.

Reconceived as a research-based position statement, the 2006 guidelines also advance a vision of how English teacher preparation programs might be conceived broadly, mindful of pre- and inservice teachers' developing and changing needs across their careers. The committee calls for the development and field-testing of a set of assessments in English education that might be used to validate the content of the guidelines over time (NCTE Standing Committee, *Guidelines,* 2006, 8). Urging the field to undertake this research, the 2006 standing committee does two things: it addresses current calls from public policy officials for such information and invites English educators—the profession—to develop that information.

Even as the 2006 guidelines document reshapes the genre into an evidence-based position statement, advises English educators how to go about constructing teacher preparation programs, and calls for a program of future research, it also preserves generic traditions. Across the years, the committees that have prepared each decade's edition of the guidelines have made it clear that just as those involved in the ETPS were indebted to mid-twentieth-century conferences, committees, commissions, and collaborations of English educators, they are indebted to the authors of the previous decades' guidelines. Speaking for the standing committee in the introduction to the 2006 guidelines, Chair Lois T. Stover acknowledges that, although the time is different, the profession in 2006 is still grappling with issues identified in the 1986 guidelines:

- Increased use of standardized testing for both students and teachers
- Growing influence of psycholinguistics and sociolinguistics on the teaching of English as a second language
- Pedagogy for exceptional students

- Developments in technology
- Learning theories in composition
- Process-oriented approaches to the teaching of writing
- Influential literary theories developed since the "New Criticism"
- Research investigating connections between language and cognition
- The language-for-learning movement (NCTE Standing Committee, *Guidelines,* 1986, 1)

and with issues identified in the 1996 guidelines:

- Challenges of working in the electronic age
- Rising criticism of schools and teachers
- Declining levels of funding for education at all levels
- Increasing demands for accountability and standardization (NCTE Standing Committee, *Guidelines,* 1996, 2)

To these issues, the 2006 standing committee adds others that surfaced in the last years of the twentieth and the first years of the twenty-first century: challenges facing the profession posed by No Child Left Behind legislation, Reading First, narrow definitions of *scientific research* in education established by the U.S. Office of Education, and under- and unfunded mandates, to name a few.

Reading across the guidelines documents, one can easily see how each decade's edition built on and updated earlier ones. Incremental changes in the guidelines reveal the profession's continuing work during the second half of the twentieth century to revise subject English, to make current its understandings of how English is best taught and learned, and to keep current what teachers of English must know and be able to do. The documents also reflect an emerging professional discourse indebted not only to scholarship in the teaching of the English language arts but also to scholarship in fields as diverse as anthropology, composition studies, cultural studies, education, linguistics, literary studies, psychology, and sociology. And they reveal the profession at work in a broader, continually changing society. In these documents, discussions of the knowledge needed by teachers of the English language arts developed, for example, from understandings of the history of the English language, to its varieties, to how it is acquired and learned by native and second language speakers. Discussions of what teachers of the English language arts must be able to do have developed, for example, from reading widely for different purposes and writing in a variety of genres for different audiences and purposes, to reading and writing in different media and symbol systems, to reading and writing in digital environments. Discussions of the nature of teacher preparation programs have developed, for example, from outlines of general education, professional education, and specialized course work for teachers, to contexts in which teacher preparation might beneficially take place, to preparing teachers to engage in their own professional development across their careers. Discussions of the personal attitudes, beliefs, and dispositions that teachers need to work effectively with students have developed, for example, from catalogs of personal traits to outlines of competencies that may be learned and nurtured.

These developing discussions, reflected in the guidelines documents, echo understandings conceived and nurtured in NCTE sections, conferences, committees, commissions, task forces, affiliates, associations, and assemblies, as well as in similar colloquies in other organizations in which NCTE leaders have served, such as those colloquies convened by groups such as the CEEB, the International Federation of Teachers of English, MLA, NBPTS, and NWP. The story of the development of these discussions across the last century, the story related in this essay, accounts for one strand of the work of NCTE to prepare both teachers of the English language arts and their teachers.

To tell this strand of the story, I have reviewed a trail of reports emerging from committees, commissions, task forces, and influential scholars, beginning with reports of NEA committees in the late 1800s on which NCTE founders served and ending with the most recent *Guidelines for the Preparation of Teachers of English Language Arts*, prepared by the 2006 NCTE Standing Committee on Teacher Preparation and Certification. Immersed in resonances of these reports, I have relived vicariously the experiences of a profession forming and maturing within America's changing society and its developing field of education. I have traveled across the last century with English educators identifying the preparation needed for the work we ourselves have defined and realized as we have worked with particular students, in particular places, at particular moments in time.

The essays that constitute this volume, taken together, tell the fuller, richer story of which this chapter is an embedded part, the story of NCTE's first century of work—work that has enabled teachers of the English language arts to prepare themselves and one another to do good work well throughout their careers.

Acknowledgment

I am deeply indebted to the generosity of colleagues within and beyond NCTE, with whom I consulted in person, by telephone, online, and in letters, whose experience, scholarship, wisdom, and insight have informed and enriched this essay: Arthur Applebee, Sheridan Blau, Leila Christenbury, Charles Duke, Edmund Farrell, Cathy Fleischer, Anne Ruggles Gere, David Imig, Julie Jensen, Steven Koziol, Erika Lindemann, Hugh Thomas McCracken, Nancy Mellin McCracken, Ben Nelms, Jacqueline Jones Royster, Charles Suhor, and Kent Williamson.

Notes

1. Arthur N. Applebee names three of the most influential of these texts: Hinsdale; Chubb; and Carpenter, Baker, and Scott (45).

2. See Lawrence A. Cremin's discussion of the writings of Bernard Iddings Bell; Arthur Bestor; Robert Maynard Hutchins; Albert Lynd; Hyman G. Rickover; Mortimer Smith; Mark Van Doren; and Paul Woodring, for example, in *The Transformation of the School: Progressivism in American Education, 1876–1957* (338–47).

3. In 1961, colleges and universities were graduating only approximately 58 percent of the new teachers needed to staff the nation's public schools. The teacher shortage also affected colleges and universities. Increasing college enrollments meant that for every ten college teachers employed in 1955, sixteen to twenty-five would be needed in 1970 (Grommon, *Education* 7).

4. As early as the mid-1940s, organizations beyond the community of English educators—among them the American Council on Education (ACE), the American Association of Colleges for Teacher Education (AACTE), the National Council for the Accreditation of Teacher Education (NCATE), and the NEA—were also working to address issues of teacher preparation. NCTE became part of this work in 1958 in response to a call issued by the NEA National Commission on Teacher Education for interested parties to come together to study the preparation of teachers. Between 1958 and 1961, representatives of eight educational organizations, including the American Association for the Advancement of Science (AAAS) and the American Council of Learned Societies (ACLS), as well as representatives of forty subject matter organizations, including NCTE, met in four conferences to study a broad range of concerns. In *The Education of Teachers of English for American Schools and Colleges* (1963), Alfred Grommon acknowledges that report's indebtedness to work accomplished in the NEA-initiated conferences on teacher education.

5. Across the twentieth century, a number of organizations combined with one another to become in 1948 the American Association of Colleges for Teacher Education (AACTE). These organizations are the American Association of Normal Schools, the American Association of Teachers Colleges, the Association of Deans of Colleges of Education, the National Association of Colleges and Departments of Education, the National Association of Teacher Institutes in Metropolitan Districts, the National Council of Teachers Colleges, the National Education Division of the Association of American Colleges, the Normal School Section of the NEA, and the North Central Council of Normal School Presidents. Since 1948 other agencies have joined AACTE; they include land-grant institutions, teachers colleges, state colleges and universities, and small liberal arts colleges. From the 1920s until 1954, AACTE served as the accrediting body for teacher education, a service provided earlier by the American Association of Teachers Colleges (AATC), an organization composed for the most part of college and university presidents (Cimburek 11).

Faced with the competing demands placed on it as both an accrediting body and a professional organization, AACTE worked with the NEA, the Council of Chief State School Officers (CCSSO), and the National Association of State Directors of Teacher Education (NASDTE) to establish the National Council for the Accreditation of Teacher Education (NCATE) in 1954. Having ceded its role as an accrediting organization to NCATE, AACTE and its 280 members became NCATE's first accredited institutions (Cimburek 11). Currently, NCATE has accredited 632 institutions and has relationships with fifty states, the District of Columbia, and Puerto Rico. Its program standards—in the case of

English language arts, standards developed within NCTE—are used by twenty-two states in lieu of their own.

6. In 1978 the Association of Colleges and Schools of Education in State Universities and Land Grant Colleges and Affiliated Private Universities called for NCATE to redesign its accreditation processes and procedures, indicating that if NCATE did not, it would develop an alternative accreditation system. Anticipating this call, NCATE in 1977 asked Michigan State University's Institute for Research on Teaching to conduct a study of its work and to make recommendations for its improvement. In 1980 the study by Christopher W. Wheeler, *NCATE: Does It Matter?*, recommended among other things that NCATE's accreditation processes be redesigned in light of the body of emerging research demonstrating the importance of teachers' need for pedagogical content knowledge. Eight years later, NCATE's announced redesign included a Specialty Areas Study Board (SASB) of specialized professional associations, including NCTE.

Works Cited

Allen, Don Cameron. *The Ph.D. in English and American Literature.* New York: Holt, 1968. Print.

Applebee, Arthur N. *Tradition and Reform in the Teaching of English: A History.* Urbana, IL: NCTE, 1974. Print.

Bell, Bernard Iddings. *Crisis in Education.* New York: McGraw, 1949. Print.

Berthoff, Ann E. *Forming/Thinking/Writing: The Composing Imagination.* Montclair, NJ: Boynton/Cook, 1982. Print.

———. *The Making of Meaning: Metaphors, Models, and Maxims for Writing Teachers.* Montclair, NJ: Boynton/Cook, 1981. Print.

Bestor, Arthur. *Educational Wastelands: The Retreat from Learning in Our Public Schools.* Urbana: U of Illinois P, 1953. Print.

Blau, Sheridan D. *The Literature Workshop: Teaching Texts and Their Readers.* Portsmouth, NH: Heinemann, 2003. Print.

Boyer, Ernest L. *High School: A Report on Secondary Education in America.* New York: Harper, 1983. Print.

Braddock, Richard, Richard Lloyd-Jones, and Lowell Schoer. *Research in Written Composition.* Champaign, IL: NCTE, 1963. Print.

Britton, James. *Language and Learning*. Harmondsworth, Eng.: Penguin, 1970. Print.

Britton, James, Tony Burgess, Nancy Martin, Alex McCleod, and Harold Rosen. *The Development of Writing Abilities (11–18)*. London: Macmillan, 1975. Schools Council Research Studies. Print.

Britton, James, and Merron Chorny. "Current Issues and Future Directions." Flood, Jensen, Lapp, and Squire 110–20. Print.

Carpenter, George R., Franklin T. Baker, and Fred N. Scott. *The Teaching of English in the Elementary and Secondary School*. New York: Longmans, 1903. Print.

Chubb, Percival. *The Teaching of English in the Elementary and Secondary School*. New York: Macmillan, 1902. Print.

Cimburek, Susan, ed. *Leading a Profession: Defining Moments in the AACTE Agenda, 1980–2005*. Washington, DC: American Association of Colleges for Teacher Education, 2005. Print.

Coles, William E., Jr. *The Plural I: The Teaching of Writing*. New York: Holt, 1978. Print.

College Entrance Examination Board Commission on English. *Freedom and Discipline in English*. New York: The College Entrance Examination Board, 1965. Print.

Corbett, Edward P. J. *Classical Rhetoric for the Modern Student*. 2nd ed. New York: Oxford UP, 1971. Print.

Cremin, Lawrence A. *The Transformation of the School: Progressivism in American Education, 1876–1957*. New York: Knopf, 1961. Print.

Dixon, John. *Growth through English*. Reading, Eng.: National Association for the Teaching of English, 1967. Print.

Elbow, Peter. *Writing without Teachers*. New York: Oxford UP, 1973. Print.

Emig, Janet. *The Composing Processes of Twelfth Graders*. Urbana, IL: NCTE, 1971. Print. NCTE Research Report No. 13.

"English Teacher Preparation Study: Guidelines for the Preparation of Teachers of English–1968." *English Journal* 57.4 (1968): 527–36. Print.

Flood, James, Julie M. Jensen, Diane Lapp, and James R. Squire, eds. *Handbook of Research on Teaching the English Language Arts*. New York: Macmillan, 1991. Print.

Gerber, John C., John H. Fisher, and Curt A. Zimansky, eds. *The College Teaching of English*. New York: Appleton, 1965. Print. NCTE Curriculum Ser. 4.

Goodlad, John I. *A Place Called School: Prospects for the Future*. New York: McGraw, 1983. Print.

Graves, Donald H. *Balance the Basics: Let Them Write*. New York: Ford Foundation, 1978. Print.

Gray, James. *Teachers at the Center: A Memoir of the Early Years of the National Writing Project*. Berkeley, CA: NWP, 2000. Print.

Grommon, Alfred H., ed. *The Education of Teachers of English for American Schools and Colleges*. New York: Appleton, 1963. Print. NCTE Curriculum Ser. 5.

———. "A History of the Preparation of Teachers of English." *English Journal* 57.4 (1968): 484–524. Print.

———. "Teachers as Language Learners: A History of English Language Arts Teacher Education." Flood, Jensen, Lapp, and Squire 380–93. Print.

Grossman, Pamela L., Suzanne M. Wilson, and Lee S. Shulman. "Teachers of Substance: Subject Matter Knowledge for Teaching." *Knowledge Base for the Beginning Teacher*. Ed. Maynard C. Reynolds. New York: Pergamon, 1989. 23–36. Print.

Harvard University Committee on the Objectives of a General Education in a Free Society. *General Education in a Free Society: Report of the Harvard Committee*. Cambridge, MA: Harvard UP, 1945. Print.

Hinsdale, B. A. *Teaching the Language Arts: Speech, Reading, Composition*. New York: Appleton, 1896. Print.

The Holmes Group. *Tomorrow's Teachers: A Report of the Holmes Group*. East Lansing, MI: 1986. Print.

Hook, J. N. *A Long Way Together: A Personal View of NCTE's First Sixty-Seven Years*. Urbana, IL: NCTE, 1979. Print.

Hosic, James Fleming, comp. *Reorganization of English in Secondary Schools: Report by the National Joint Committee on English Representing the Commission on the Reorganization of Secondary Education of the National Education Association and the National Council of Teachers of English*. Washington, DC: GPO, 1917. Print. Dept. of the Interior, US Bureau of Education, Bulletin 1917, No. 2.

Hutchins, Robert Maynard. *The Conflict in Education in a Democratic Society*. New York: Harper, 1953. Print.

International Reading Association, and National Council of Teachers of English. *Standards for the English Language Arts*. Newark, DE: IRA; Urbana, IL: NCTE, 1996. Print.

Joint Committee of the Faculty of Harvard College and the Graduate School of Education. *The Training of Secondary School Teachers, Especially with Reference to English*. Cambridge, MA: Harvard UP, 1942. Print.

Lloyd-Jones, Richard, and Andrea A. Lunsford, eds. *The English Coalition Conference: Democracy through Language*. Urbana, IL: NCTE; New York: MLA, 1989. Print.

Lucas, Christopher J. *Teacher Education in America: Reform Agendas for the Twenty-First Century*. New York: St. Martin's, 1997. Print.

Lynd, Albert. *Quackery in the Public Schools*. Boston: Little, 1953. Print.

Macrorie, Ken. *Telling Writing*. New York: Hayden, 1970. Print.

McCracken, Nancy M., and H. Thomas McCracken. "A Closer Look at Standards." *Ohio Journal of the English Language Arts*, 20.1 (1993): 7–11. Print.

Miller, Thomas P. *The Formation of College English: Rhetoric and Belles Lettres in the British Cultural Provinces*. Pittsburgh, PA: U of Pittsburgh P, 1997. Print.

Moffett, James. *Teaching the Universe of Discourse*. Boston: Houghton, 1968. Print.

Murray, Donald M. *A Writer Teaches Writing: A Practical Method of Teaching Composition*. Boston: Houghton, 1968. Print.

National Commission on Excellence in Education. *A Nation at Risk: The Imperative for Educational Reform*. Washington, DC: GPO, 1983. Print.

National Council of Teachers of English. *The Basic Issues in the Teaching of English: Being Definitions and Clarifications Presented by Members of the American Studies Association, College English Association, Modern Language Association, and National Council of Teachers of English from a Series of Conferences Held throughout 1958*. Champaign, IL: NCTE, 1959. Print.

National Council of Teachers of English Commission on the English Curriculum. *The English Language Arts.* New York: Appleton, 1952. Print. NCTE Curriculum Ser. 1.

———. *The English Language Arts in the Secondary School.* New York: Appleton, 1956. Print. NCTE Curriculum Ser. 3.

———. *Language Arts for Today's Children.* New York: Appleton, 1954. Print. NCTE Curriculum Ser. 2.

National Council of Teachers of English Committee on National Interest. *The National Interest and the Continuing Education of Teachers of English.* Champaign, IL: NCTE, 1964. Print.

———. *The National Interest and the Teaching of English: A Report on the Status of the Profession.* Champaign, IL: NCTE, 1961. Print.

National Council of Teachers of English Curriculum Commission. *An Experience Curriculum in English: A Report of the Curriculum Commission of the National Council of Teachers of English.* New York: Appleton, 1935. Print.

National Council of Teachers of English Standing Committee on Teacher Preparation and Certification. *Guidelines for the Preparation of Teachers of English Language Arts.* Urbana, IL: NCTE, 1986. Print.

———. *Guidelines for the Preparation of Teachers of English Language Arts.* Urbana, IL: NCTE. 1996. Print.

———. *Guidelines for the Preparation of Teachers of English Language Arts.* Urbana, IL: NCTE. 2006. Print.

———. "A Statement on the Preparation of Teachers of English." *English Education* 7.4 (1976): 195–210. Print.

National Education Association Committee of Fifteen. *Report of the Committee of Fifteen on Elementary Education with the Reports of the Sub-Committees: On the Training of Teachers; On the Correlation of Studies in Elementary Education; On the Organization of City School Systems.* New York: American Book, 1895. Print.

National Education Association Committee of Seventeen on the Professional Training of High-School Teachers. "Report of the Committee of Seventeen on the Professional Preparation of High-School Teachers." *Journal of Proceedings and Addresses of the Forty-Fifth Annual Meeting Held at Los Angeles, California, July 8–12, 1907.* Winona, MN: National Education Association, 1907. 523–668. Print.

National Education Association Committee of Ten. *Report of the Committee of Ten on Secondary School Studies, with the Reports of the Conferences Arranged by the Committee.* New York: American Book, 1894. Print.

National Education Association Committee of Twelve. *Report of the Committee of Twelve on Rural Schools Appointed at the Meeting of the National Education Association, July 9, 1895, with Appendices.* Chicago: U of Chicago P, 1897. Print.

Palmer, David J. *The Rise of English Studies: An Account of the Study of the English Language and Literature from Its Origins to the Making of the Oxford English School.* London: Oxford UP, 1965. Print.

Parker, William Riley. "Where Do English Departments Come From?" *College English* 28.5 (1967): 339–51. Print.

Rickover, Hyman G. *Education and Freedom.* New York: Dutton, 1959. Print.

Shagrue, Michael F. *English in a Decade of Change.* New York: Pegasus, 1968. Print.

Shiels, Merrill. "Why Johnny Can't Write." *Newsweek* 8 Dec. 1975: 58–65. Print.

Sizer, Theodore R. *Horace's Compromise: The Dilemma of the American High School.* Boston: Houghton, 1984. Print.

Smith, Dora V. *Evaluating Instruction in English in the Elementary Schools of New York: A Report of the New York Regents' Inquiry into the Character and Cost of Public Education.* Ed. C. C. Certain. Chicago: Scott 1941. National Conference on Research in English Research Bulletin No. 8. Print.

———. *Evaluating Instruction in Secondary School English: A Report of a Division of the New York Regents' Inquiry into the Character and Cost of Public Education in New York State.* New York: Appleton, 1941. NCTE English Monograph No. 11. Print.

———. *Instruction in English.* Washington, DC: GPO, 1932. National Survey of Secondary Education Monograph No. 20, Bulletin No. 17. Print.

Smith, Mortimer. *And Madly Teach: A Layman Looks at Public School Education.* Chicago: Regnery, 1949. Print.

Squire, James R. "The History of the Profession." Flood, Jensen, Lapp, and Squire. 3–17. Print.

———. "The Impact of New Programs on the Education of Teachers of English." *New Trends in English Education: Selected Addresses Delivered at the Fourth Conference on English Education.* Ed. David Stryker. Champaign, IL: NCTE, 1966. 7–14. Print.

Van Doren, Mark. *Liberal Education.* New York: Holt, 1943. Print.

Viall, William P. "English Teacher Preparation Study: Guidelines for the Preparation of Teachers of English." *English Journal* 56.6 (1967): 884–95. Print.

Wheeler, Christopher W. *NCATE: Does It Matter?* East Lansing, MI: Institute for Research on Teaching, 1980. Research Series No. 92. Print.

Woodring, Paul. *Let's Talk Sense about Our Schools.* New York: McGraw, 1953. Print.

NCTE 100 YEARS READING THE PAST. WRITING THE FUTURE.

A Blast from the Past

Did you know that "National English Council" was suggested as an alternate name for the National Council of Teachers of English? The name change was proposed in a constitutional amendment presented at the 1912 NCTE Annual Convention—but was tabled and never revisited.

NCTE in Action

Chapter Ten

Savory Alliances: Ethos and Action in the Historical Development of NCTE

Jacqueline Jones Royster
The Ohio State University

On 1–2 December 1911, an estimated group of sixty-five educators (classroom teachers, college professors, and school and college administrators) from at least twelve states[1] convened in Chicago, Illinois, at the Great Northern Hotel. The call for organization sent out for this meeting by James Fleming Hosic[2] stated the following:

> The English Round Table of the National Education Association [NEA], at its recent meeting in San Francisco, passed a resolution calling upon the Committee on College-Entrance Requirements which was appointed in Boston the year before, to organize a National Council of Teachers of English. The intention was to create a *representative* body, which could reflect and render effective the will of the various local associations and of individual teachers, and, by securing concert of action greatly improve the conditions surrounding English work. (Hook 16)

At the meeting, thirty-seven attendees signed the roster of charter members, thus initiating the National Council of Teachers of English (NCTE, or the Council). The core mission was simple and straightforward: "to increase the effectiveness of school and college work in English" (Hook 286).[3]

A century later, there is much to celebrate about NCTE's consistency over the decades in fulfilling this mission. However, a theme within the larger story that is worthy of more critical attention is the necessary confluence of protest,[4] alliance, and responsive professional leadership that has characterized the organization from the beginning. NCTE was born, in fact, in an environment of protest and was predicated on a set of savory alliances,[5] not only between individual colleagues across educational levels but also between a variety of other organizations that shared a common purpose. The intention of this chapter, therefore, is to view NCTE's history from the perspective of ethos formation and action by highlighting several instructive moments during which a set of originary values emerged in the making and marking of organizational ways of being and doing that we recognize today as NCTE. These values include

- A commitment to **democratic principles** in accepting the challenge of recognizing, protesting, and responding to inequity and injustice in academic endeavors
- Linking with colleagues inside the organization (individuals, subgroups, and affiliated groups) and beyond the organization (other professional groups, governmental agencies, private agencies, and community organizations) to form **alliances for action** that are capable of impact and consequence
- Serving as a staunch **advocate for the exercising of agency and authority by English professionals and their students** in matters related to teaching and learning—

all of which have been and continue to be grounded in a core mission of marshalling and monitoring **quality and effectiveness in English language arts.**

Over the decades, these values have converged dynamically to establish the operational habits of NCTE, as exemplified by the specific historical moments selected for the following analysis. While these particular moments do not exhaust the many illustrative choices available, each does offer an instructive example of this convergence of values, shedding light on ways in which NCTE has functioned productively and consistently in honor of an abiding desire for excellence and effectiveness in the English language arts.

A Defining Moment

The catalyst for the founding of NCTE and setting in motion this type of ethos formation was a substantial dissatisfaction in American education that surfaced by the turn of the twentieth century, according to J. N. Hook (3–28), in three primary ways:

- Secondary teachers and many colleagues at other educational levels as well believed that educational policy was being set without the input of public school teachers and administrators.
- Teachers and scholars with a specific interest in writing, oral language, and rhetoric believed that the English studies curriculum was too dominated by the teaching of literature and not well balanced over other areas in the field, as evidenced particularly in overly specific college entrance examination requirements in literature that were dictating high school curricula in English.
- With the rise in the late nineteenth century of publicly funded high schools and a concomitant increase in the democratization of secondary education, many educators and others (e.g., the Carnegie Foundation for the Advancement of Teaching) were deeply concerned about the shape, nature, and competing agenda of high school curricula.

Exacerbating these issues was the fact that there was no permanent national organization for English education that could be called upon to negotiate such thorny issues or to provide recommendations and coherent leadership in developing sustainable strategies and solutions. There were, however, many local and state groups. Thus, the environment of protest by English professionals from which NCTE emerged was multidimensional, and so were opportunities for collaboration in addressing the challenges. (For additional information on the history of education in the United States, see Applebee; Boyer; and Mondale and Patton.)

Within an environment of educational need and professional desire, the organizational ethos for NCTE took shape. Its ways of doing and being were set in motion right from the beginning, as exemplified by the way in which the leadership emerged. James F. Hosic, head of the Department of English at Chicago Teachers College, now Chicago State University, was appointed by Edwin L. Miller, assistant principal of Central High School in Detroit, Michigan, and outgoing chair of the NEA English Round Table, to chair a committee to survey English educators across the nation about the highly contentious issue of college entrance requirements. To accomplish this task, Hosic and Miller enlisted help from Fred Newton Scott, professor of rhetoric at the University of Michigan, and John M. Clapp from Lake Forest College in Illinois. Their questionnaire successfully fleshed out in a more grounded way critical issues in testing and English education from the perspective of experts—teachers and school administrators. Simultaneously and unexpectedly, however, the study also revealed professional attitudes toward existing policies that the surveyors had not anticipated, policies that suggested the need for more inclusive and more concerted action in monitoring and increasing effectiveness in English teaching and education.

When the group reported on the pattern of response to the English Round Table, the information inspired a resolution that this group readily adopted. The resolution called for the English Round Table chair (who by that point was Hosic) to take leadership in establishing an independent national society of English teachers. Ultimately, the survey brought to the attention of the group not only the views of English professionals on the thorny challenge of college entrance examinations but also a consistently articulated desire for change from teachers across the nation. The respondents saw a critical need for teachers, particularly those in public schools, to participate actively in setting agenda and educational policy in English studies and, indeed, for them to take the leadership in developing strategies to increase the effectiveness of teaching and learning in the English language arts.

The primary consequence of this initiative and the resulting resolution was that the four key orchestrators of the survey process also became key players in a critical effort to secure concerted organized action for development and change. Hosic, the official leader of the group, had multiple professional connections within the National Education Association (NEA) that permitted him to offer a unique cross-pollinating leadership in this enterprise. He had served as chair of the survey committee, been a founder of the Chicago English Club, and, in 1911, after Miller's service, became chair of the English Round Table. When the first meeting of NCTE convened, all four men became charter members of the new organization; Hosic was confirmed as secretary, and Fred Newton Scott was confirmed as the first president (NCTE, Board of Directors Meeting Minutes, 2 Dec. 1911). In becoming leaders in the new Council, these men brought to bear a core matrix of relationships—their own small alliance as well as a broader set of connections—in forming the cooperative networks for action that ultimately enabled the establishment and growth of NCTE.

The main point to be made here is that the ethical matrix of the Council formed within an alliance, a network of professional and personal relationships. Miller (seventh president of NCTE) appointed Hosic as chair of the survey committee, and also turned over to him leadership of the English Round Table. Miller and Hosic had taught together at Englewood High School in Chicago. Fred Newton Scott, one of Miller's former teachers, joined the survey committee and was elected ultimately as the first and second president of NCTE (NCTE, Board of Directors Meeting Minutes, 2 Dec. 1911; NCTE, Board of Directors Meeting Minutes, 29 Nov. 1912). John M. Clapp was a colleague of Miller's and Hosic's in Chicago and leader of the Illinois Association of Teachers of English. This matrix of professional colleagues and friends was amplified by the professional connections of other charter members, including those of Edwin M. Hopkins, professor of rhetoric and English language at the University of Kansas. Hopkins was chair of the Modern Language Association (MLA) committee to study the teaching load in English, especially in the teaching of composition. In carrying out the MLA study, Hopkins worked closely with the new NCTE leadership, as evidenced by the fact that one of the first resolutions passed by the Council in its first organizational meeting was one that endorsed

> the work of Hopkins and the MLA committee and also directed the Executive Committee to obtain further ammunition for Hopkins by asking "state officers, including high school inspectors," to furnish information on "the comparative cost of equipment and instruction for the various departments of the high schools"—data that would later show English to be the least well supported financially. (Hook 19)

In 1916, Hopkins became the fifth president of NCTE.

The point in chronicling these relationships is to underscore the extent to which a habit of cooperation and collaboration, especially between individual members with multiple alliances, was established as fundamental to NCTE operations right from the start.

From this organizational foundation developed two primary frameworks within which NCTE was able to grow beyond the charter group: the organization's constitution and its organization into sections. The 1911 constitution made a place for three kinds of Council membership: individual teachers and supervisors of teaching; associations of English teachers, who would be entitled to "one delegate for each one hundred members or fraction thereof" (Hook 287); and individuals other than teachers and administrators who wished to identify with the Council's work. This model allowed membership to grow dynamically. Certainly, with the constitution in place, increasing numbers of English educators joined the new organization. Just as lively, however, if not more so, were the connections formed at the local level through affiliate organizations, a set of alliances that have proved over the decades to be a particular strength for the Council in establishing its national scope and reach.

As reported in *English Journal* during NCTE's twenty-fifth anniversary year, encouraging the formation of local affiliate organizations as branches of the national organization was a fortuitous decision. It served to

> . . . extend the influence of the Council into the uttermost parts . . . [to] enable the humblest worker to have a voice in national affairs through his representatives. The delegates of the local associations were to be given a voice in the management of the Council. Thus the national body, which might otherwise fall into the hands of an oligarchy, benevolent or otherwise, would be democratized. And it was so. ("The National Council, 1911–36" 813)

With this vision and framework of democratic access and participation, local organizations joined NCTE as affiliate organizations, starting with the already powerful New England, Illinois, and Indiana associations. Since then the number of local organizations for teachers and administrators, as well as some student affiliates for preservice teachers, has grown nationwide and beyond. Currently, groups are active in forty-eight states, the District of Columbia, and Canada (including Alberta, British Columbia, Manitoba, Quebec, and Saskatchewan). They form "a partnership for the teaching of English language arts at a national and grassroots level" (NCTE, "Join Your Local Affiliate" n. pag.). Their local activities complement activities at the national level with regard to hosting local and regional conferences, offering leadership development opportunities, networking in support of local and state issues, publishing journals and newsletters, etc. At the national level, through their representation on the NCTE Board of Directors and various committees and task forces, these members also have played important roles in addressing issues with a national scope, such as in the leadership that NCTE has provided on censorship issues since the 1950s.

A second framework for growth and development was established at NCTE's second annual meeting. The program included sectional meetings and conference sessions devoted to specific educational levels: Elementary, Secondary, and College. In addition to what are now a core set of NCTE sections were two other sections that sponsored sessions at the second meeting, the Normal School Section and the Public Speaking Section; a few years later, a Library Section was formed.[6] These groups provided focused mechanisms for professional development, for addressing issues specific to the particular group, and also for offering distinctive opportunities for members with a broad range of interests and concerns to participate in national conferences and meetings. The move toward sectionalized involvement overtly recognized that, while all educational levels and interest areas hold similar goals and values, each has different issues and challenges. This early acknowledgment of academic diversity made a deliberate place for differences to coexist in the Council and for alliances to be struck, a practice that would prove quite productive in subsequent decades.

Quite early in its history, then, NCTE developed a habit of making room for internal alliances and transformed this habit into a basic operational practice, as demonstrated again in subsequent decades by the formation of various conferences within NCTE, including the

- Conference on College Composition and Communication (CCCC), formed in 1949, which "supports and promotes the teaching and study of college composition and communication by (1) sponsoring meetings and publishing scholarly materials for the exchange of knowledge about composition, composition pedagogy, and rhetoric; (2) supporting a wide range of research on composition, communication, and rhetoric; (3) working to enhance the conditions for learning and teaching college composition and to promote professional development; and (4) acting as an advocate for language and literacy education nationally and internationally" (CCCC)
- Conference on English Education (CEE), formed in 1963, which "serves those NCTE members who are engaged in the preparation, support, and continuing education of teachers of English language arts/literacy" (CEE)
- Two-Year College English Association (TYCA),[7] formed in 1996, which "unites teachers committed to the teaching and study of English in the two-year college, to advancing the profession, and providing a national voice for the two-year college in postsecondary education" (TYCA)

The latter half of the twentieth century also saw the development of a significant group of caucuses (Black, Latina/o, Asian/Asian American, Jewish, and American Indian), all of which hold distinctive, special interests within the larger array of concerns related to the teaching and learning of English.

As suggested by 1966 NCTE President Muriel Crosby, the NCTE constitution (much like the United States Constitution) provided

> the means for NCTE to meet changing demands and needs while supporting the founding principles. Here, I believe, is NCTE's key to the consistency it has maintained through the years in its provision for dissent, its recognition of the value of different points of view, its belief in the common humanity all men share. (qtd. in Hook 17)

I would argue also that the actions of early NCTE leadership helped to engender (whether consciously or not) an organizational ethos that encouraged the Council to be nimble in its capacity to absorb and adjust to complexity and calls for change, as indicated by the creation of a proactive membership framework that permitted active participation by cohorts of members with different experiences and different points of view. This ethos embraced by principle a tolerance of others, and by practice produced both sure and sometimes uneasy alliances (as suggested in subsequent sections). More important, perhaps, in doing so, it permitted the Council

- to address complex issues in well-grounded ways, taking advantage of various sets of knowledge, experience, and expertise, and
- to respond, sometimes enthusiastically, sometimes not, to changing conditions and needs in the larger society.

A Diversity Within

The preceding account easily documents, on the one hand, that the original, core leadership of NCTE began as an alliance that operated on democratic principles as a fundamental value. On the other hand, it just as easily suggests that the founding group was an "old white boys" network with a power base centered in public institutions in the Midwest. However, the latter is not totally the case. What is quite true is that this early group was significantly midwestern and that there was little participation in the early days from the southern and western states or even the eastern states, other than New York. There was, in fact, also no participation by people of color, a situation that would remain constant for almost twenty years and that would continue to be problematic for several decades thereafter, particularly in terms of visible leadership.

However, among the original thirty-seven charter members, there was indeed considerable diversity with regard to gender. Notably, eleven of the thirty-seven charter members can be identified[8] as women:

Emma J. Breck, head of the English Department, Oakland High School, Oakland, California

Flora Elsie Hill, head of the Department of English, Michigan State Normal School, Marquette, Michigan

Elizabeth Graeme Barbour, head of the English Department, Louisville Girls High School, Louisville, Kentucky

Sally S. Maury, Louisville Girls High School, Louisville, Kentucky

Ida M. Windote, head of English, Oak Park, Illinois

Elvira D. Cable, Department of English, Chicago Teachers College, Chicago, Illinois

Eva Levy, Farrew School, secretary, Chicago English Club

Sara D. Jenkins, Madison High School, English and French, Madison, Wisconsin

Mary Newell Eaton, Central High School, Grand Rapids, Michigan

Martha E. Clay, Central High School, Grand Rapids, Michigan

Grace Darling, Bowers High School, Chicago, Illinois

Notable also is that in the first meeting, Emma J. Breck was elected the first vice president, becoming the leading edge for the many other women who would follow her in this position over the next twenty years: Grace Shepherd, Mary Hargrave, Essie Chamberlain, Alice L. Marsh, and Sophia Camenisch. Joining this group of women leaders were women who served as second vice president, including (again) Emma J. Breck (elected to the second vice presidency in both 1915 and 1922), Cornelia S. Hulst, Mary B. Fontaine, Claudia E. Crumpton, Olive Ely Hart, Mary Percival, Elizabeth N. Baker, and Stella S. Center (Hook 288). A point to keep in mind, however, is that during this era, the vice presidential positions did not automatically lead to presidential leadership, so, despite whatever experience, expertise, or abilities the women leaders may have exhibited, they were in effect relegated to secondary positions and functioned essentially within the sexist context of their times. Typically, with NCTE being no exception, the professional strengths and leadership potential of women was unlooked for, unseen, and unrecognized (as was certainly the case for racial minorities, since they were not included at all). The reality of such gender presuppositions is substantiated by a reflection by W. Wilbur Hatfield, secretary-treasurer of the Council from 1919 to 1953 and editor of *English Journal* from 1922 to 1955. In response to a question regarding the leadership abilities of Rewey Belle Inglis, the first female president of NCTE, Hatfield stated,

> Until five years ago or so I thought it was very little. She was the youngest president we ever had. She was a very pretty woman. You see a pretty young woman getting ahead pretty fast, you sometimes wonder how much is the face and how much is something else. I went back and looked at the minutes as they were reported in the *English Journal* and more happened in the organization of the Council that year—not more outside the Council, but more happened in the organization that year than most other times, so I was evidently mistaken about that. (qtd. in Gerlach 20)

Hatfield's attitude was typical of his time rather than unusual. Even in a professional organization such as NCTE that espoused democratic principles, such viewpoints situated the professional participation and leadership of women within a framework that tended to limit their voices, constrain the scope of their levels of engagement, and render their contributions cloudy, if not altogether invisible. The historical record, however, verifies that women members were committed to active involvement, they were persistent in exercising their interests, and they worked arduously and with considerable integrity to support NCTE's goals. (See Gerlach and Monseau for more detailed information about the work and national leadership of women in NCTE and in English education more generally.) Recognized or not, women's presence and attitudes mattered, and with the advocacy of key members in the core leadership who accomplished the nomination of a female candidate, the Council elected its first female president in 1928, seventeen years after its founding.

Rewey Belle Inglis, the successful candidate, was a classroom teacher at University High School in Minneapolis, Minnesota, and an expert on language development, classroom pedagogies, and teacher training. She published several articles in Council journals and became the senior editor for Harcourt's Adventures in Literature series. As Hatfield suggests, her presidency was successful. (For additional information on Inglis, see Gerlach.) Inglis stimulated membership growth, diversified convention program offerings, and brought greater attention to the relationship between teaching and research. In addition, she championed strengthening the Council's relationships with other professional organizations, such as the National Association of Teachers of Speech and the National Association of Teachers of Journalism. As she asserted, "We cannot escape the responsibilities of speech because another organization bears the main burden. Two horses pulling together move a bigger load than one, but woe to the wagon when one pulls east and the other pulls west" (qtd. in Gerlach 23). This statement suggests that Inglis recognized the advantage of cooperative effort, good communication, collective action, and shared authority and responsibility.

This spirit of humane cooperative leadership continued the next year when Ruth Mary Weeks from Kansas City, Missouri, assumed the presidency. (For additional information on Weeks, see Byers.) Weeks was a social activist, classroom teacher, and advocate for vocational training. As a scholar, she wrote books for teachers, including *Socializing the Three Rs* (1919), *Primary Number Projects* (coauthored in 1923 with Rosamond Losh), and *A Correlated Curriculum* (1936). She also coedited two literature anthologies, *World Literature* (1938) and *English Literature* (1941). As president of NCTE, Weeks had several notable achievements, but two of them have had long-lasting impact over the decades:

> With the support of the Executive Committee, she arranged for the Council to become a not-for-profit corporation so that it could assume responsibility for "its own business transactions." . . . Weeks [also] initiated one of the Council's first transactions in its newly incorporated form, "the approval of a contract between the National Council and the *English Journal* providing for publication of the *Journal* as a Council organ, for the maintenance of a joint office, and for the purchase of the *Journal* by the Council in the case of Mr. Hatfield's[9] death or his desire to sell the *Journal* during his lifetime." (Byers 42–43)

In another pioneering effort between these two early women leaders, the Council was convinced during Inglis's presidential term to hold its Annual Convention for the very first time west of the Mississippi River. Weeks made a persuasive case to a deeply doubtful Council leadership about the strength of her networking abilities and about what she could accomplish as the coordinator of local arrangements—if the meeting were held in her hometown. Together, then, Inglis and Weeks blazed new trails. First, they succeeded in bringing the Annual Convention to Kansas City, Missouri, and with Weeks's leadership, enthusiasm, and networking talents, they increased conference attendance significantly. This meeting would stand for several years as the most well-attended Convention ever. Second, the official registrants in Kansas City included for the first time African American teachers and administrators.

In reflecting on the professional guidance provided by early NCTE leaders, three points can be easily extrapolated:

- The new organization benefited greatly from a small circle of very active professional friends who, through their multiple alliances, facilitated cooperative, concerted action with English colleagues nationwide and with various other organizations to accomplish mutual goals.
- The original leaders were monochromatic with regard to race but included a significant number of women in visible positions. Many of these women were leaders in their local settings and active as teachers, administrators, and scholars. Within the sexist social environment of their era, however, they made a presence for themselves in the new organization, but they did not rise to presidential leadership until 1929.
- Whether consciously or not, the early leadership established an enduring ethos for NCTE, enhanced by a constitutional framework that centralized democratic principles. Membership was broadly defined, with membership development a cooperative spirit that encouraged multidimensional collective action. Thus (much like the framers of the United States Constitution), this leadership created a deliberate space and process for engagement within which differences (the nature of which they could not predict) might coexist.

Advocacy and Professional Leadership

Additional evidence of the formation of an originary ethos within NCTE, anchored in democratic principles, alliance, advocacy, and professional leadership, is embedded in two resolutions that passed during the first organizational meeting (in addition to the one endorsing the work of Hopkins's MLA committee on teaching loads). One of these resolutions authorized the Council to present a request to the National Conference on Uniform Entrance Requirements in English (NCUER) to include "in their several delegations an adequate number of representatives from public high schools" (Hook 19). The request supported the NCTE founders' basic belief in democratic principles, in resonance with the nation's founding commitment to the idea of "no taxation without representation." From the perspective of NCTE leaders, those affected by policies should have an active role in the process of decision making about those policies, an ideological view that would constitute a vibrant ethical thread within NCTE in subsequent decades, as evidenced by a steady stream of subsequent resolutions that have exercised the Council's commitment to advocacy for both teachers and students.

NCUER was first convened in 1894 to address the issue of a uniform basis for testing high school applicants' qualifications for postsecondary education. NCUER's charge followed the earlier efforts of a conference between two groups, New England Colleges and the Association of Colleges and Preparatory Schools of the Middle States and Maryland. As their names suggest, these decision-making bodies had consisted primarily of colleagues from colleges and private schools in the East, with minimal participation by colleagues from public schools or other regions, in keeping with general practices and the typical power structure in educational arenas during the nineteenth century. According to Hook, NCUER developed a list of readings that was widely accepted, particularly by the College Entrance Examination Board after its establishment in 1900 and by the North Central Association accrediting agency. The NCUER list "recommended some literary works for 'deep' study and others for 'wide' study (the works listed did vary over time). The NCUER was influential, especially in the East, until its demise in 1931" (Hook 9).

While standardization of entrance requirements was a complicated issue then as now, by the end of the nineteenth century, a critical factor in developing workable strategies was the sociocultural landscape of the United States. Historically, both secondary schooling and higher education had been essentially elite enterprises. During the nineteenth century, however, times and conditions changed dramatically:

- With the end of the Civil War and chattel slavery, definitions of United States citizenship were officially encoded in the Thirteenth (1865), Fourteenth (1868), and Fifteenth (1870) Amendments to the United States Constitution, issuing into law a recognition of not only millions of African Americans as citizens but also all persons born or naturalized in the United States, and barring, as well, any denial of the rights of citizenship based on race, color, or previous condition of servitude.
- The late nineteenth and early twentieth century was a time of massive immigration, including immigrants from all sectors of Europe as well as significant numbers from across Asia, South and Central America, and Africa.
- Within the United States, even discounting new immigration, there were also significant internal population shifts: from the South to the North, as evidenced by the great migration of African Americans from rural southern plantations to urban factories, and from the East to the West, as immigrants from Europe (especially farmers and craftspeople) moved from the eastern states to the Midwest and the far West.
- In the nineteenth century, there was a considerable effort by power elites to forge a strong national identity for the United States and to move a relatively new nation to a place of prominence on the world stage, not only by energizing the nation's participation in international markets and political arenas but also through cultural movements, such as Ralph Waldo Emerson's call for the recognition and production of an "American" literature in his 1837 address, "The American Scholar," to Phi Beta Kappa at Harvard University.
- With the rise of technological inventions and American industrialization, economic structures and processes in the United States were changing rapidly.

As the United States transitioned from its founding as a nation to its second century, the combination of all the above factors and more signaled dynamic social, political, economic, and cultural change. As might be predicted, such multilayered shifting had a tremendous impact on the education system and on the roles that it should and could play in meeting the relatively new nation's educational challenges and opportunities. Passionate calls for educational opportunities came from a broad spectrum of the population as well as from the power elites seeking mechanisms by which to manage and control the masses. During this era, there was in fact a steady increase in both publicly funded high schools and, as evidenced by the Morrill Acts, publicly funded higher education.

Greater access to education offered evidence of a growing democratization of educational opportunity—by class, gender, and race. The question, therefore, of representation in professional organizations and groups charged with setting recommendations for schooling came to be viewed as particularly problematic because colleges and private schools had habitually dominated these efforts, leaving the public school sector without adequate representation. Although NCTE's request for a more inclusive approach to participation and decision making did not specifically address class, race, and gender diversity in schools, colleges, or universities, the request to NCUER was still a critical one that set in motion a habit of calling for more equitable participation in policymaking processes by English professionals from a broader spectrum of institutional types.

The second NCTE resolution that demonstrated NCTE's early advocacy for quality and effectiveness in the teaching and learning of English called for the abolition of prescribed literary works as the basis for college entrance examination questions. According to Hook, several members of the Council leadership preferred that students who graduated from certified high schools not have to pass an entrance examination at all. The Council body, however, accepted the idea that "if examinations in English for admission to college are to be held at all, the tests suggested in this [New York] circular will obviate many of the present evils" (Hook 20). The New York circular was an open letter to teachers of English distributed by the New York State Association of Teachers of English. This statement recommended "a thorough revision of college entrance examinations in English, advocated elimination of a set list of books, and urged examinations not on 'the acquisition of information but [on] the power to read and express'" (Hook 13). Its acceptance by NCTE marked the beginning of the care, attention, resources, and leadership that the Council would persistently provide as a watchdog for enterprises related to standardized testing, particularly at state and national levels.

A Response to Changing Demands

Through these two resolutions, which serve as illustrative examples of NCTE's originary values, advocacy for the teaching and learning of English was immediately established as a primary function of NCTE. To sustain a high level of commitment to this particular concept, however, the Council needed to be nimble in its capacity to set a vibrant, multidimensional, and democratic vision for academic effectiveness. The Council also needed to be innovative in finding ways for all manner of English professionals across educational levels and institutional types to participate actively in crafting appropriate and effective responses in support of English studies, both as a tool of the social order and as an arena for professional work. The duality of this mission reflected the dynamic changes within American society and underscored a fundamental question that has lingered throughout NCTE's centurylong history: advocacy for whom in particular?

NCTE's efforts to achieve substantial flexibility in accomplishing its goals—including advocacy in support of democratic principles, alliance for concerted action, and, given the public trust that is deeply embedded in NCTE's societal mandates, responsive and socially responsible professional leadership—have become the hallmark of its ethical operations, with these efforts over the decades being tested and retested time and again. One peak moment of challenge came on 4 April 1968 with the assassination of Dr. Martin Luther King, Jr., in Memphis, Tennessee, which occurred while the NCTE Annual Convention was in progress in Milwaukee, Wisconsin. This moment of challenge, however, was not the first. Throughout the history of NCTE, the Council has been encumbered by the racist and sexist elements of the nation in which it exists. The assassination of Dr. King, therefore, constituted a flashpoint, but one that had been flickering, as it were, for several decades.

To retrace a few milestones using the African American professional experience generally as an illustrative example, consider the following:

1911. NCTE was founded without the participation of colleagues of color, a fact that did not change until Rewey Belle Inglis, the first female president of NCTE, in 1929 encouraged participation by educators of color.

1922. Chattanooga, Tennessee, was the site of NCTE's first Annual Convention to be held in the South. The fact that Chattanooga was a racially segregated city did not factor into its selection, if the issue was considered at all. The bottom line was that, despite the numbers of African American colleagues in schools and colleges across the South, these colleagues were not accepted as official conference registrants.

1929. The Kansas City, Missouri, meeting was the site of several firsts. Rewey Belle Inglis was the first female president of NCTE, this meeting was the first to be held west of the Mississippi, and NCTE welcomed its very first official African American registrants. Inviting attendance, however, did not ensure a smooth and substantive inclusion of racial minorities going forward, and this milestone did not erase the complex array of sociopolitical challenges that African Americans and other racial minorities continued to face in their efforts in subsequent decades to participate actively in Council activities.

1932. The Annual Convention was held in Memphis, Tennessee. Stella S. Center was the NCTE president (the third woman to hold this position). She was southern-born but spent her career in the Northeast. In 1932 she was head of the English department of Theodore Roosevelt High School in New York and renowned for her teaching and scholarship in reading. The meeting was held in the prestigious Peabody Hotel. African American members were not permitted to enter the Peabody as either residential guests or patrons for food service. As noted by Sue Ellen Holbrook, the details and challenges of this meeting remain unclear and undocumented, but the result of the racist discourtesies directed toward African American members at this site was that Center invited this group to attend a *separate* meeting in another building on the other side of the street. The African Americans identified speakers they wished to hear, and those speakers were directed to give their presentations a second time at the alternate site. Hook points out two ironies: (1) Center's theme for the conference was that "all education proceeds by the participation of the individual in the social consciousness of the race," and (2) racist images appeared in conference advertisements that would today be incendiary (128).

1941. The Annual Convention was held in Atlanta, Georgia. Robert C. Pooley, professor of English at the University of Wisconsin at Madison, was NCTE president. As in Memphis, African American colleagues could not reside at the conference hotel, nor were they admitted to meals. A small difference between the 1932 and 1941 experiences was that, while these colleagues still could not take full advantage of conference activities, they were permitted to occupy balcony seats to hear the banquet addresses. A more significant change, however, was not in the details of NCTE's holding the meeting in what remained a racially segregated South, but in the Council members' response to the situation. Some members were outraged by the treatment of professional colleagues, and the discord eventually gave rise to a resolution at the 1945 Convention. This resolution constituted

> the Council's first official firm stand on the matter of segregation: a resolution to the effect that no Council convention would thereafter be held in any place in which any Council member would be discriminated against in any way. As a result no NCTE convention was held again in the South until 1962, when I [J. N. Hook] arranged for a Miami Beach convention that was managed by Executive Secretary James R. Squire. (Hook 129)

As this chronology indicates, NCTE's first organizational advocacy for colleagues of color who were seeking to exercise their rights and commitments as Council members and as professionals in English studies took more than thirty years, but in 1945 the Council did indeed take a distinctively supportive action that provided the context for the participation and involvement of colleagues of color over the next twenty years.

With the earlier examples of challenges as backdrop, the historic moment of the King assassination comes into bolder relief as a firestorm that, in effect, had been building for fifty-eight years. When the news of the assassination reached conventiongoers in Minneapolis on 4 April,[10] a memorial service was quickly organized by Elliott Evans and Ernece B. Kelly for the following day. This moment of tragedy and memorialization served as inspiration for African American colleagues to push forward more energetically their preexisting desires for organizational changes.

Some changes were to some extent already coalescing. At the 1967 Convention in Hawaii, William A. Jenkins (then a professor at the University of Wisconsin at Milwaukee and the first African American to edit a Council journal, *Language Arts* [1961–1968]) had won the election for president-elect and was slated to become the first African American president of NCTE in 1969. Other African American colleagues in attendance in Hawaii included Margaret L. Arnold, Charlotte Brooks, Elizabeth Burgess, Marianna White Davis, Marjorie Farmer, Nick Ford, Charles G. Hurst, Thomas D. Jarrett, Ione V. Jones, Lorena E. Kemp, Delores Kendrick, Delores Minor, Alvin Rucker, Darwin T. Turner, and Rosa Lee Winchester. This group, encouraged by Delores Minor, began conversations about the lack of meaningful participation in the Council by African American colleagues. While they recognized the roles of Jenkins and a few other African American leaders, they felt that the participation of African American colleagues was overwhelmingly both small and limited mainly to the role of observers, rather than participants, in the Convention. There was little or no participation on panels and little or no opportunity to learn the ways of the Council and to groom oneself for leadership. This group also was concerned about the representations of African American students at the Convention and of African American literature in textbooks and other publications. Discussions of such issues continued at the 1968 Convention in Milwaukee; at the annual business meeting, the group supported a resolution moved by Elizabeth Burgess and seconded by William Jenkins. It was adopted with the following wording:

- That the National Council of Teachers of English call upon all teachers of English language arts to recognize that they must do far more than they have done to meet the needs of young people in minority groups within this multi-cultural society.
- That the membership support the intention of the Executive Committee to commit a higher proportion of the resources of the Council to find new and imaginative solutions to the language needs of these young people.
- That each member of the committees and commissions of the Council take immediate steps to reconsider the goals and priorities of the committee or commission, so as to devote greater energy toward finding and implementing solutions which will meet the needs of these young people.
- That each member of NCTE be exhorted to reflect on his responsibilities in the present crisis, to act within his competence to resolve that part of the crisis that is within his reach. ("Resolution Passed")

Except for the call for a greater allocation of resources by NCTE, this resolution was primarily and significantly ideological, asking for advocacy and for the Council to stand resolute in its commitment to act innovatively in responding to pressing challenges in the field. This call for advocacy and action supported the foundational values upon which NCTE had formed, but for the first time, the call was for advocacy and action on behalf of students from minority groups.

In effect, this resolution represented the first moment of collective activism by African American members, signaling that collective action by African American colleagues was well on its way. In short order, this group formed its own alliance, the Black Caucus, and drew in not only colleagues who attended the NCTE Annual Convention but also those who attended the CCCC Annual Convention. The purpose of the Black Caucus, like the purpose of NCTE itself, was simple and straightforward:

> The Black Caucus of NCTE/4Cs has as its primary goal the following: to promote and insure the active involvement and participation of Black educators (particularly teachers of composition, literature, languages, and reading) in decision and policy making roles and in the programs and activities of NCTE and 4C's. (Gibbs n. pag.)

The Black Caucus was joined by other caucuses—including the Latina/o, Asian/Asian American, American Indian, and Jewish caucuses—and was also followed by a broad range of other special interest groups, initiated especially by members of CCCC (e.g., the Progressive Caucus), thus embodying in a dynamic way the notion of a space and process within NCTE and its internal organizations for dissent and difference, and also for the opportunity, again, for savory alliances.[11]

One of the specific results from the call for Council action in support of minority issues was the establishing in 1969 of the NCTE Task Force on Racism and Bias in the Teaching of English. Led by Ernece B. Kelly, members included José A. Carrasco, Carlota Cárdenas Dwyer, James Lee Hill, Adolfo McGovert, Philip D. Ortego, and Montana H. Rickards, as well as a group of colleagues who served as advisors: Gabriel Cardova, Marianna W. Davis, Janet Emig, William A. Jenkins, and Roxanne Knudson. One distinctive initiative of the task force was its establishment of a Textbook Review Committee composed of Alexander Boyd, José A. Carrasco, Jeffrey Chan, Frank Chin, Charles J. Evans, Ernece B. Kelly, Sophia P. Nelson, Philip D. Ortego, Montana H. Rickards, and Antonia Valcarcel (Kelly, *Searching for America* viii). The committee's charge was to survey high school and college anthologies as well as readers in American literature to assess how inclusive these volumes were of literature from a broad spectrum of perspectives, including those of underrepresented minority groups. On 26 November 1970, the NCTE Board of Directors adopted the "Criteria for Teaching Materials in Reading and Literature of the NCTE Task Force on Racism and Bias in the Teaching of English." This document called for "the truth and reality of our nation's history and literature [to] be embodied in its texts and other teaching materials, and that includes the fact of the racial and ethnic diversity of its peoples" (Kelly, *Searching for America* xv), and it presented a set of seven criteria related to the creation and selection of textbooks.

Through its advocacy and leadership, this task force provided critical leverage in the Council's efforts to usher in an era of direct and specific activism in support of social justice within the Council. Among many signs of change during these years was the hiring in 1973 of Sandra E. Gibbs as director of the

NCTE Office of Minority Affairs. And in 1977, social change was much in evidence at the Annual Convention in New York City, as Hook reports:

> Charlotte Brooks of Washington, D.C., was president; . . . Marjorie Farmer of Philadelphia, was the incoming president. A black woman novelist, Toni Morrison, was, along with Brooks, the featured speaker at the opening general session; another black woman author, Alice Walker, was the speaker at the College Section meeting, which was chaired by a black man, Hobart Jarrett of Brooklyn College; black actors Ossie Davis and Ruby Dee were the speakers at the annual banquet. And almost exactly half of the names listed in the index of convention participants were identifiable as female. (233)

During this era of alliance, activism, and leadership within NCTE on behalf of diversity, another important initiative that symbolized the Council's commitment to advocacy and action was the passing of the "Resolution on the Students' Right to Their Own Language," adopted at the 1974 Annual Convention in New Orleans and endorsed by several other professional organizations that shared NCTE's mission and purpose. The resolution resulted from initiatives led by CCCC, and especially from the commitment and dedication of members of the Black Caucus, who worked with other CCCC members to take a proactive professional stance on a complicated challenge. The resolution was adopted by CCCC, NCTE, and ultimately other professional organizations as well. It included background information and other explanatory details, and began with the following statement:

> Resolved, that the National Council of Teachers of English affirm the students' right to their own language—to the dialect that expresses their family and community identity, the idiolect that expresses their unique personal identity[.]

The history and impact of this resolution are chronicled comprehensively in *Affirming Students' Right to Their Own Language: Bridging Language Policies and Pedagogical Practices* (2009) edited by Jerrie Cobb Scott, Dolores Y. Straker, and Laurie Katz. This collection of essays discusses the "Students' Right" resolution as a sterling example of how advocacy, alliance, and responsive, socially responsible professional leadership have converged within NCTE and affected not only research in the English language arts and classroom practice but also educational and social policy.

A Second Century

Through their initial actions, the originary leadership of NCTE made bold moves that fostered a sense of organizational ethos whereby the Council functioned as a democratic organization committed to working cooperatively with its members and others in advocating excellence and effectiveness in the teaching and learning of English. Much of the early work was responsive to pressing needs rather than proactive, and in cooperation with more established organizations and agencies. As chronicled by Applebee as well as Hook, these external alliances began with the founding of NCTE. The National Education Association provided noteworthy leadership and support in enabling the establishment of NCTE and in working with this new group to produce in 1917 the report *Reorganization of English in Secondary Schools* (Hosic). This and other alliances involved jointly sponsored committees, conferences, meetings, reports, research projects, special initiatives, policy statements, etc. They included various working relationships with organizations such as the Modern Language Association, the College Language Association, the International Reading Association, the Speech Communication Association, the National Association of Journalism Directors, and more. In addition, NCTE worked collaboratively with colleges and universities, the U.S. Department of Education, academic publishers, and various funding agencies (such as the Carnegie Foundation for the Advancement of Teaching and the Ford Foundation). Three examples of these accomplishments include

- The founding of Teachers of English to Speakers of Other Languages (TESOL), an independent professional organization established in 1966 through the allied efforts of five organizations variously concerned with second language learning: the Center for Applied Linguistics, MLA, the National Association of Foreign Student Affairs, NCTE, and the Speech Association of America

- The first copublishing arrangement—for Studies in Writing and Rhetoric, one of the first scholarly book series to focus on the teaching of writing—in 1980 between CCCC and Southern Illinois University Press

- The collaboration of the International Reading Association and NCTE in 1996 to produce the *Standards for the English Language Arts*

International alliances have been formed as well, beginning in the 1960s with the National Association for the Teaching of English (British) and then with other organizational leaders and teachers in Canada and Great Britain.

A perennial challenge for organizations committed to alliance and responsive and responsible professional leadership is sustaining organizational focus and identity, and such has been the case for NCTE. Periodically, it is necessary to ask hard questions: What is NCTE and what is its relevance to members, their students, the profession, and society at large? What distinguishes NCTE from other professional organizations with similar interests and goals? What is the nature of the leadership that it provides? What constitutes its proactive, rather than its responsive, agenda as it moves into its second century? NCTE has the habit of addressing such questions through the work of committees and task forces, of which we have had a considerable number, and this moment of centennial celebration offers us yet another opportunity to reexamine our steadfast values, priorities, and commitments going forward.

An embedded question in this process is how we shall use this milestone moment. In a nation that hungers for even more than a rhetoric of hope in the face of devastating conditions—an economic recession within the nation and around the world, two wars in the Middle East and unrest globally, and critical challenges in all sectors of our lives, including the sustaining of a high-quality educational experience for all the nation's children—what will we say? What will we do? We are, in fact, hard-pressed to use this moment in good conscience, good faith, and with good vision as we look both back on a laudable past and forward on a complex social, political, and economic landscape.

Basic values have sustained the Council over the decades:

- A commitment to **democratic principles** in accepting the challenge of recognizing, protesting, and responding to inequity and injustice in academic endeavors
- Linking with colleagues inside the organization (individuals, subgroups, and affiliated groups) and beyond the organization (other professional groups, governmental agencies, private agencies, and community organizations) to form **alliances for action** that are capable of impact and consequence
- Serving as a staunch **advocate for the exercising of agency and authority by English professionals and their students** in matters related to teaching and learning
- Grounding all of this in a core mission to marshal and monitor **quality and effectiveness in the English language arts**

These values have engendered, as suggested here, an ethos of which as an organization we can be proud. It has nurtured and sustained the Council through decades of growth, and it is capable of doing so still. Perhaps not so surprising even for the second century, our challenges remain basic: how, when, under what conditions, and by what innovations will we continue to do the work of advocacy, alliance, and responsive and responsible professional leadership in the interest of the highest quality and effectiveness in the teaching and learning of the English language arts? We are called upon to renew and reaffirm our mission and to inspire ourselves and those who will follow in continuing our causes.

As has been said many times before in times of reflection and speculation and at moments of decision, the nature of our journey has been written, not our destination. We know where we've been and we've gained strength from those experiences. But at the end of the day, at the end of a century, where do we go from here?

Notes

1. In *A Long Way Together*, J. N. Hook lists two different numbers for the states represented: twelve (16) and nineteen (19). The discrepancy may be explained by the published proceedings of the first meeting: "[a]bout sixty-five delegates and representative teachers from twelve states responded to the call in person, and letters were received from

many more. In all, some twenty states were interested in the movement" (NCTE, "National Council" 32).

2. James Fleming Hosic was head of the Department of English at Chicago Teachers College (now Chicago State University). As explained later in this essay, in 1911 the English Round Table of the Secondary Division of the National Education Association appointed a committee to survey college entrance requirements. Hosic was named the chair of the committee and also chair of the English Round Table for the remainder of 1911 and 1912. Results of a nationwide questionnaire led to the conclusion that there was a pressing need for a permanent nationwide organization of teachers of English (the English Round Table was not a permanent organization). At the same time, a commission on the reorganization of secondary education was forming, and Hosic was named chair of the commission's subcommittee on English (Hook 13–15).

3. J. N. Hook was a professor of English at the University of Illinois who served as the first executive secretary of the Council.

4. As Hook reports, the call for an organization for teachers of English arose from growing concerns among teachers and educational leaders nationwide about the lack of voice and visibility for teachers in the making and shaping of educational policies in the teaching of English, about the rigidity of the curriculum and overly specific college entrance requirements imposed by colleges and universities on American high schools, and about a lack of uniformity in the preparation of students in English (3–28).

5. I purposely chose *savory* as the descriptor here to indicate that the alliances in which NCTE has engaged over the decades have been based fundamentally on ideological concerns about secondary education in general and the teaching and learning of English across levels and institutions in particular; on ethical concerns about quality and excellence; and on a tacit respect for both the complexity of the challenges and the strengths that might obtain from a cooperative approach. From the beginning, while these relationships have typically been full-bodied and flavorful, they also have been just as likely to be spicy and salty, a feature of the dynamic of alliance-building, a strategy through which excellence in the field of English has endured and thrived.

6. According to Hook, in 1928 the Normal School Section was renamed the Teachers College Section and operated under that rubric until 1941, when colleges gained a broader power base; the vibrancy of the Public Speaking Section faded after the founding of a national speech teacher association; and the Library Section did not build vibrancy within NCTE, given the existence of a very strong American Library Association (ALA)

(25–27). In this last case, instead of NCTE's establishing its own strong library section, it developed a cooperative relationship with the ALA.

7. Note that while TYCA formed officially within NCTE in 1996, there had existed since 1966 a network of regional conferences for two-year college English faculty, established by NCTE and CCCC, in which two-year college colleagues had been particularly active since its formation. With the generous support of both NCTE and CCCC, regional TYCAs gained strength, with members continuing actively to participate nationally in all of the NCTE college groups (CCCC, College Section, and CEE). By the 1990s, TYCA had gained considerable organizational strength, with seven quite viable regional organizations. With this strength, these groups recognized the need for a stronger, more coherent national voice through a national TYCA organization. For additional information, see the series of historical articles written by Andelora ("Forging," "Professionalization," "TYCA: 1991–1993," "TYCA: 1994–1997").

8. The NCTE charter, which provides names, addresses, and positions of the charter members, appears in a handwritten ledger. Several of the signatures are difficult to decipher. I apologize for any misinterpretations of the handwriting or misspellings of names.

9. In 1921, James Hosic, the original owner–editor of *English Journal*, sold it to W. Wilbur Hatfield, who served as owner–editor from 1922 to 1955, when it became, with the foresight of Weeks, an official publication of NCTE.

10. The details that follow about the founding of the NCTE Black Caucus are based on Marianna White Davis's *History of the Black Caucus of the National Council of Teachers of English* (1994); an essay prepared by Ernece B. Kelly (at the time, professor of English at Kingsborough Community College in New York) for the seventh issue of the NCTE–CCCC *Black Caucus Newsletter* ("Twenty Years"); and personal correspondence from Sandra E. Gibbs, longtime director of special programs at NCTE.

11. See Hook (233–34) for his assessment from an organizational perspective of the gains achieved by African Americans within the Council over the five years following the establishment of the Black Caucus. See Davis for an account of actions and achievements from the perspective of a member of the Black Caucus. Note also an initiative in progress, currently entitled *Writing and Working for Change: A Digital Archive of Social Activism by Teachers of NCTE*, a collection being edited by Samantha Blackmon, Cristina Kirklighter, and Steve Parks that seeks to document the collective work of English teachers to support NCTE's commitment to social justice and equality.

Works Cited

Andelora, Jeffrey. "Forging a National Identity: TYCA and the Two-Year College Teacher-Scholar." *Teaching English in the Two-Year College* 35.4 (2008): 350–62. Web. 11 Aug. 2009.

———. "The Professionalization of Two-Year College English Faculty: 1950–1990." *Teaching English in the Two-Year College* 35.1 (2007): 6–19. Web. 11 Aug. 2009.

———. "TYCA and the Struggle for a National Voice: 1991–1993." *Teaching English in the Two-Year College* 35.2 (2007): 133–48. Web. 11 Aug. 2009

———. "TYCA and the Struggle for a National Voice: 1994–1997." *Teaching English in the Two-Year College* 35.3 (2008): 252–65. Web. 11 Aug. 2009

Applebee, Arthur N. *Tradition and Reform in the Teaching of English: A History*. Urbana, IL: NCTE, 1974. Print.

Boyer, Ernest L. *High School: A Report on Secondary Education in America*. New York: Harper, 1983. Print.

Byers, Judy Prozzillo. "Ruth Mary Weeks: Teaching the Art of Living." Gerlach and Monseau 30–48. Print.

Conference on College Composition and Communication (CCCC). "Newcomers—learn more!" *National Council of Teachers of English*. NCTE, n.d. Web. 11 Aug. 2009.

Conference on English Education (CEE). Home page. *National Council of Teachers of English*. NCTE, n.d. Web. 11 Aug. 2009.

Davis, Marianna White. *History of the Black Caucus of the National Council of Teachers of English*. Urbana, IL: NCTE, 1994. Print.

Emerson, Ralph Waldo. *Emerson: Essays and Lectures*. Ed. Joel Porte. New York: Literary Classics, 1983. Print.

Gerlach, Jeanne Marcum. "Rewey Belle Inglis: A Crystal-Ball Gazer." Gerlach and Monseau 3–29. Print.

Gerlach, Jeanne Marcum, and Virginia R. Monseau, eds. *Missing Chapters: Ten Pioneering Women in NCTE and English Education.* Urbana, IL: NCTE, 1991. Print.

Gibbs, Sandra E. Letter with attachment to Jacquelyn Harris. 5 Aug. 1991. TS. Personal collection of Jacqueline Jones Royster.

Holbrook, Sue Ellen. "Stella Stewart Center: Proceeding under Their Own Power." Gerlach and Monseau 49–68. Print.

Hook, J. N. *A Long Way Together: A Personal View of NCTE's First Sixty-Seven Years*. Urbana, IL: NCTE, 1979. Print.

Hosic, James Fleming, comp. *Reorganization of English in Secondary Schools: Report by the National Joint Committee on English Representing the Commission on the Reorganization of Secondary Education of the National Education Association and the National Council of Teachers of English*. Washington, DC: GPO, 1917. Print. Dept. of the Interior, US Bureau of Education, Bulletin 1917, No. 2.

International Reading Association, and National Council of Teachers of English. *Standards for the English Language Arts*. Newark, DE: IRA; Urbana, IL: NCTE, 1996. *National Council of Teachers of English*. Web. 11 Aug. 2009.

Kelly, Ernece B., ed. *Searching for America*. Urbana, IL: CCCC/NCTE, 1972. Print.

———. "Twenty Years Later—Time for Assessments." *The Black Caucus Newsletter* 7 (March 1988): 1–6. Print.

Losh, Rosamond, and Ruth Mary Weeks. *Primary Number Projects*. Boston: Houghton Mifflin, 1923. Print.

Mondale, Sarah, and Sarah B. Patton. *School: The Story of American Public Education*. Boston: Beacon Press, 2001. Print.

"The National Council, 1911–36." *English Journal* 25.10 (1936): 805–36. Print.

National Council of Teachers of English. Board of Directors Meeting Minutes. 2 Dec. 1911. MS. University of Illinois Archives (Record Series 15/70/003, Box 1), Urbana, IL.

———. Board of Directors Meeting Minutes. 29 Nov. 1912. MS. University of Illinois Archives (Record Series 15/70/003, Box 1), Urbana, IL.

———. "Join Your Local Affiliate of NCTE." *National Council of Teachers of English*. NCTE, n.d. Web. 11 Aug. 2009.

———. "Names, Addresses, and Positions of the Charter Members of the National Council of Teachers of English." [1911.] MS. University of Illinois Archives (Record Series 15/70/003, Box 1), Urbana, IL.

———."Resolution on the Students' Right to Their Own Language." *National Council of Teachers of English.* NCTE, 1974. Web. 8 Aug. 2009.

———. "A Resolution Passed by the National Council of Teachers of English at the Fifty-eighth Annual Meeting, 1968." *English Journal* 58.3 (1969): 398. Print.

"National Council of Teachers of English: Proceedings of the First Annual Meeting, Chicago, December 1 and 2, 1911." *English Journal* 1.1 (1912): 30–45. Print.

Scott, Jerrie Cobb, Dolores Y. Straker, and Laurie Katz, eds. *Affirming Students' Right to Their Own Language: Bridging Language Policies and Pedagogical Practices.* New York: Routledge; Urbana, IL: NCTE, 2009. Print.

Studies in Writing and Rhetoric. Home page. *Duke University.* Duke University, n.d. Web. 11 Aug. 2009.

Teachers of English to Speakers of Other Languages. Home page. *Teachers of English to Speakers of Other Languages.* TESOL, n.d. Web. 11 Aug. 2009.

Two-Year College English Association (TYCA). Home page. *National Council of Teachers of English.* NCTE, n.d. Web. 11 Aug. 2009.

The United States Constitution. U.S. House of Representatives, n.d. Web. 11 Aug. 2009.

Weeks, Ruth Mary. *A Correlated Curriculum: A Report of the Committee on Correlation of the National Council of Teachers of English.* New York: D. Appleton-Century, 1936. Print.

———. *Socializing the Three Rs.* New York: Macmillan, 1919. Print.

Weeks, Ruth Mary, Rollo La Verne Lyman, and Howard C. Hill, eds. *English Literature.* New York: Scribner's, 1941. Print.

———. *World Literature.* New York: Scribner's, 1938. Print.

NCTE 100 YEARS READING THE PAST. WRITING THE FUTURE.

A Blast from the Past

Did you know that most NCTE members did not participate in selecting the organization's president until 1974? Prior to a constitutional amendment permitting members at large to elect NCTE officers, they were chosen by the NCTE Board of Directors, who represented associations of English teachers affiliated with NCTE.

How NCTE Serves the Public Interest

NCTE develops and advances sound teacher practices that enrich student learning. We advocate for policies that draw on the collective knowledge and wisdom of accomplished educators in English language arts and English studies.

We do this by:

- Providing professional development tailored to various career stages and to all levels of education from preschool through graduate school
- Developing a national knowledge base on policy in literacy education and its impact on students in English language arts classrooms from early childhood through college
- Broadening assessment practices so that students' ongoing learning inside and outside of classrooms is visible to teachers, schools, and the public
- Preparing teachers and students to think, express themselves, and communicate through a mixture of text, images, video, sound, and digital media
- Conducting and making accessible to educators research on innovative teaching practices that improve student learning and on changes in the demands for reading and writing in today's world
- Advancing the teaching of English language learners by building upon their cultural and linguistic strengths to foster their success in reading and writing
- Leading efforts to improve adolescent literacy at the classroom level and to reform policy at the national level
- Forming alliances and partnerships to strengthen our impact on literacy education policies and practices, preschool through university

(2005)

NCTE'S 2020 VISION

NCTE will have transformed the public understanding of the connection between teacher knowledge and student learning. To accomplish this, NCTE will develop a system that provides rich opportunities for career-long teacher learning and that documents the growth of both literacy teachers and their students. Teachers who choose to participate in this system will be celebrated for their achievements by community leaders and the media. Policymakers also will rely upon these teachers for their expertise in literacy teaching and learning.

(2005)

CHAPTER ELEVEN

Visions of the Future

JOHN S. MAYHER
New York University

"Children are the living messages we send to a time we will not see."

NEIL POSTMAN, *The Disappearance of Childhood*, 1982

English teaching lost a great prognosticator when Neil Postman died too young. As his colleague, I loved to speculate with him about the future, which he viewed with a mixture of hope and alarm. He cared deeply about children and was profoundly worried about the changes he saw in our culture, especially the effects of new and emerging media on their minds and hearts. I first "met" Neil when I read *Teaching as a Subversive Activity* (Postman and Weingartner) shortly before joining him on the New York University faculty in 1969. He was a kindred spirit to those of us who worried that schools had become too bogged down in mindless routines of drill and regurgitation.

Postman's call for change was powerful, but only ten years later, he seemed to have changed his mind when he published *Teaching as a Conserving Activity.* Careful comparison of his educational goals, however, reveals that he really hadn't changed much—what had changed was his sense of the roles schools had to play in an increasingly non-print-literate culture. His sense was that we had to define the kind of schooling our culture needs in terms of a thermostatic look at the culture's commitment to literacy: too concentrated, as in the 1950s and 1960s—get progressive, open up the canon, encourage many media, and develop student-centered curricula. And if that went too far and got too diffuse, as in the 1970s and 1980s—conserve the powers of print literacy and promote reading and writing.

I tell this story to illustrate how complicated it is to predict the educational future in a rapidly changing culture. But as Larry Cuban has shown, schooling itself has remained much more stable than most other aspects of that culture over the past century. Ted Sizer has often pointed out that the structure of American high schools—which enshrined the teaching of English as a central curricular mission—was designed by a Committee of Ten in 1892. And that continues to be a problem because the schools envisioned in 1892 were elite affairs expecting only a small percentage of the population to enter, much less complete, high school, and fewer still to go on to higher education. Schools then and schools now do not serve the children of the poor, the children of immigrants, or the children of color as well as they serve their more economically advantaged peers. Rhetoric about leaving no child behind to the contrary, it still seems clear that choosing your parents wisely is the best predictor of school success.

A similar committee in 1992 probably would still have erected English as one of the curricular pillars, but English might have been somewhat different than it was in 1892 or 1911, even if still recognizable. More important, if subject English is to survive, how should the *English* of the twenty-first century be defined? One of the dilemmas faced by curriculum writers and policymakers is that English remains a label that different people confidently think they can use, only to discover that many of the people they are talking to define it differently. It is clear, for example, that the English taught in college English departments and the demands on secondary English teachers have had little in common since 1892, and as secondary teachers have embraced new media, the disparity has grown. And when early childhood and elementary education are included, as they must be, still other aspects of English language arts teaching and learning come into focus.

Ben Nelms pointed out in his reflections on the history of subject English since 1892 that the original formulation of English as a secondary school subject had brought together disparate strands—labeled in the 1950s as the tripod of language, literature, and composition. He showed that the overall conception had been successful and had lasted for a century, but he simultaneously quoted Arthur N. Applebee, who contends that the continuing tensions have meant that "the English language arts have a long-standing predisposition to come unglued—to separate into the individual studies from which they were assembled" (Applebee 49). Indeed, as the twentieth century rolled on and became the twenty-first, more and more content and processes were added: film and television studies, computer connectivity, and a much broader range of literatures to be considered and included—young adult fiction, world fiction in translation, and literature written by an ever-wider range of contemporary writers threatening to squeeze out many of the "classics" of the past. The chapters in this volume also reflect these many strands but still embody the core attachment to the old tripod as well as the newer concerns of diversity, assessment, political advocacy, and the explosion of the electronic media.

The Council's Progressive Stance

These same tensions have consistently roiled the organization of professional English language arts teachers whose centennial this volume celebrates. As the previous chapters have shown, these controversies and disputes have not been dull, but while unanimity has never been sought or achieved, and even consensus often has been difficult, as I read these chapters and have myself experienced the second half of the National Council of Teachers of English's first one hundred years, I'm impressed by the overwhelmingly progressive pattern that has informed the positions, beliefs, and practices of the Council.

When looking back at NCTE's past as described in earlier chapters, several consistent themes emerge that suggest directions for the Council's future. These include:

- A growing concern for all children, not just the best and the brightest, or the native speakers, or the standard-dialect speakers
- A consistently accepting attitude toward language varieties (despite the common caricature of English teachers as grammar-obsessed Miss Fidditches), exemplified in *Students' Right to Their Own Language*

- A growing flexibility regarding canonical texts (no longer exclusively *Beowulf* to Virginia Woolf but instead including diverse contemporary American and British works as well as world Englishes, literature in translation, and children's and adolescent literature)

- A growing concern for social justice for both students and teachers and a recognition of human dignity and worth (e.g., the IRA–NCTE project on standards lost its federal funding in part because it insisted on including equity and access standards as well as competence and performance standards)

- A consistent support for freedom of expression and access to texts; fighting censorship of the books students read and the texts they write

- A consistent support for the professionalism of teachers: recognizing the complexity of teaching and learning and the importance of professional teacher preparation and continuing education, including advocating for professional standards in teacher education and certification, advocating for accreditation of teacher education programs, and formulating critiques of quick-fix alternative pathways to the classroom

- A consistent recognition of the importance of research as a crucial factor in understanding how English is best taught and learned at all levels and with all students; in addition, and of crucial recent importance, advocating a flexible and inclusive set of definitions for research methodologies accepted as "scientific"

- Consistent willingness to explore and advocate changing definitions of *English* and *literacy education*, including recently developing a new set of definitions of the demands of twenty-first-century literacies

- Consistent support for beleaguered teachers through policies recommending limits on class size, on numbers of students that teachers should meet each week, and on the importance of adequate planning time; consistent support for teachers' ongoing professional development through conferences, journals, and, more recently, online systems designed to nurture beginners and revitalize the experienced

- A growing recognition that the Council's positions need to be actively pursued in the political arena locally and nationally (including the recent opening of a Washington, DC, office, hiring a lobbyist, sponsoring annual trips to DC to lobby, and speaking out strongly against the limits and distortions of the No Child Left Behind Act)

- Ongoing willingness to experiment with how the organization is structured and run: interest groups, assemblies, task forces, conferences, sections, etc.

This fundamentally progressive record does not mean there has been universal assent to all of these ideas within the membership of NCTE. Consider, for example, the Assembly for the Teaching of English Grammar's advocacy of grammar teaching or those who support required phonics for all—or, more crucially, those who doubt that we have had a significant impact on the larger profession or the public. Dennis Baron recently questioned why his teaching of progressive language attitudes—and that of most of the rest of us who have been teaching teachers—has not had much (any?) effect on our students as teachers. In my own work (Mayher, *Uncommon Sense*), I've tried to show that many of these progressive ideas have not been able to affect deeply the commonsense conceptions of English language teaching and learning held by the profession as well as by the public and policymakers.

When I talk to civilians, they still complain about the spelling and grammar of the graduates they hire, still believe that teachers are lax and lazy and have no standards. And they generally have no clue about how complex teaching and learning are: "After all, you're done at three o'clock, aren't you?" Even more deeply held is their conviction that their own school experience makes them experts on education, causing them, among other misguided beliefs, to cast doubt on the necessity for teacher education, to believe that children too are lazy and must be threatened with punishment if they are to work hard and achieve, and to ignore all of the nonclassroom factors that affect teacher and student performance, including money, time, facilities, community support, and student background.

One important aspect of NCTE's deeply progressive stance has been its openness to debates about the what, why, and how of English teaching, as well as who should teach and whom those people should teach. Even when the organization passes resolutions or formulates policies or sets standards, there is little likelihood of unanimous adherence to them by the membership. Some of this can make the organization less effective with congresspeople, governors, and other officials. It is easier to get legislative and administrative backing for consensus stances than for issues in dispute. But pretending unanimity when none exists would, in the long run, violate and weaken the progressive stance that has characterized NCTE for the past century as the organization welcomed debate and supported controversy. The paradoxical consequence is that our expertise as communicators and teachers has not been effectively used to educate the broader public. The consistency with which the same issues resurface suggests a failure to communicate, and if NCTE is going to become a more effective advocate in its second century, new approaches will need to be tried.

Most important is the reality that NCTE has not been sufficiently focused on or effective in working with some of the biggest issues still facing American education: racism and racial profiling, the long-term effects of poverty on learning and learners, and the difficulties facing immigrants and other second language learners. As the earlier chapters have shown, the Council has struggled to overcome its own racial biases and to protest discrimination, but this is an effort that must be consistent and ongoing. One area that needs greater Council resources is recruiting teachers from large urban school districts to make special efforts to develop programs that support their work with children in need of extra help and support. The Conference on College Composition and Communication has had a strong record in this area, but neither the teacher education Conference on English Education nor the NCTE sections have been as focused as they need to be. Demographic predictions of the school-age population project the strong growth of what will no longer appropriately be labeled "minority" populations in more and more school districts, but that future is already here in the major cities of the United States, and the issues raised must get a bigger part of NCTE's focal energy. Many individual members of the Council have the experience and the linguistic, rhetorical, and pedagogical expertise to play significant roles in helping to solve these problems, but the solutions will continue to be piecemeal and sporadic unless a clear and powerful spotlight keeps shining on these problems and leads to Council-sponsored initiatives that work.

The Politics of Education: Standards and Testing

To some degree, the ideological and pedagogical disputes within the profession and the tensions between its various branches pale before the larger challenges of education and, in particular, its political context. One of the great ironies of the past twenty-five years is that the Reagan administration, which came into office determined to eliminate the then relatively recently formed U.S. Department of Education, ended up reinvigorating the federal role in education, which led to the enormous expansion of federal involvement in the recent past. The publication in 1983 of *A Nation at Risk*, written by a committee appointed by Reagan Education Secretary Terrell Bell, announced yet another crisis in education that demanded deep and powerful reforms (National Commission on Excellence in Education). In some respects, the report echoed the response to the "crisis" provoked by the Soviet Union's launch of *Sputnik* in 1957, which led to the passage of the National Defense Education Act.

A Nation at Risk, which compared the threat to America's prosperity and leadership caused by the failures of our schools to an invasion by a foreign power, triggered an avalanche of breast-beating, finger-pointing, and cries of alarm. The biggest concern expressed by the report was for the level of excellence reached by our best students in comparison to those of our major economic rivals, principally Japan. The committee's consensus seemed to be that schools and teachers were lax in their demands and that even the best students were too willing to coast through what was characterized as a watered-down curriculum. This in turn led to a call to raise standards and improve accountability to measure how well students were achieving them. The wildfire of reform spread within and without the profession as governors (led by then-Governor Bill Clinton) and the incoming George H. W. Bush administration vied to be first on their block with ever higher bars for students and teachers. States and the federal government both got involved in sponsoring different standards projects.[1]

Projects setting subject matter standards were funded by the U.S. Department of Education, and NCTE joined with the International Reading Association (IRA) to compete to develop the

English language arts standards. The NCTE–IRA consortium won the three-year grant in October 1992, began its work, and then, after a review by the U.S. Department of Education in 1994, saw the money withdrawn halfway through the project. The full tale of what happened has not, to my knowledge, been written, and in the chronology of the project appended to the published, final version of the standards, no comment is provided as to why the application for continued funding was rejected in March 1994. What seemed to be the issue was NCTE's and IRA's insistence on including equity and access standards along with achievement standards. The two organizations persevered without the federal funds and published their version of the standards after substantial internal disputes in March 1996 (IRA and NCTE).[2] By then it was too late for the "national" standards to have the hoped-for effect, since most of the states had gone ahead and written their own and because the federal government had not yet insisted on common standards (or tests) across the country. The delay also cost both organizations considerable revenues since the sale of books and other supporting materials never reached anticipated numbers.

In this context, the important policy connection is the line that runs from *A Nation at Risk* through setting state (and national) standards, to the development of state accountability tests and, following the respective elections of the governors of Arkansas and Texas to the presidency, to the passage of the No Child Left Behind Act (NCLB). Despite its benign and even progressive title (stolen from the Children's Defense Fund), NCLB has had a mostly pernicious effect on schools that were serving the most challenging and challenged populations: the poor. While the law includes some good features, such as increased funding and, potentially, the disaggregating of student data so that problems cannot be hidden under averages, the law's insistence on annual testing and its methods of determining progress toward its goals have exacerbated the gap between the haves and the have-nots. Pressures for school choice also widen the gap because they have helped to support charter schools, regarded by some as an opening wedge for school vouchers to be used at private schools.

The tests used to demonstrate adequate yearly progress have been developed by each state, based, at least in principle, on state standards. Since the standards vary widely, it is not surprising that the tests do too, and so do the real measures of pupil achievement. National comparisons can be made only with National Assessment of Educational Progress (NAEP) data, which is widely regarded as both more rigorous and more comprehensive than state assessments. NCLB legislation did not interfere with the states' determination of their own tests and passing rates, thereby failing to challenge the educational differences between them. While some states have done better than others to develop a meaningful set of standards and goals in their testing programs, almost all observers agree that the fill-in-the-bubble tests used don't speak to the full range of abilities that the standards movement was attempting to capture. The best literacy tests, such as the New York State Regents Exam in English, do require substantial writing samples, but even so, timed writing on demand does not exhaust the competencies students need to master. Until NCTE wins its battle to broaden literacy assessment to include work done during the school year to meet a variety of assignments in a range of genres, the testing system will remain too limited.

NCTE has taken a strong stance within the coalition of professional organizations urging dramatic changes in NCLB. The statements in the "2008 NCTE Legislative Platform" call for alternatives to many of the most problematic features of the law, starting with:

- Change Adequate Yearly Progress Measurement.

> A shift from single, high stakes measures to multiple measures is needed to produce a more accurate portrait of yearly progress toward academic achievement. More nuanced assessments can provide better information on achievement without increasing the testing burden and wasting valuable instructional time. Therefore, NCTE calls upon Congress to fund pilot studies by local education agencies to explore how combinations of multiple measures provide a better understanding of student achievement. These should include a variety of plans incorporating state level assessments; classroom, school, or district tests; extended writing samples; tasks, projects, performances, exhibitions; and collected samples of student work, portfolios or learning records. Teachers in these districts should gain access to assessment data from these pilots in a timely fashion so they can use it to shape instruction. (n. pag.)

These critiques had a powerful effect on Congress, to the extent that all efforts to renew the law were stymied pending the results of the 2008 presidential election. But, sadly, as I write this chapter, the standards jinni has once more emerged from the bottle in the form of a draft set of Common Core State Standards being written by teams appointed by the National Governors Association and the Council of Chief State School Officers and so far endorsed by forty-six states and, apparently, Secretary of Education Arne Duncan. NCTE President Kylene Beers released an open letter to the NCTE membership in July 2009 discussing how, if at all, NCTE should get involved in the process, since we were not initially invited. First responses from members varied, with some in favor of a seat at the table but most opposed to either the standards or NCTE's involvement—or both. On 17 August 2009, Beers described in a second letter the range of views NCTE members held on the matter:

> We each bring to the table our own beliefs concerning such a document. Some of us acknowledge the importance of commonly held standards that could serve as high goals for all in this nation; others of us resist any standards that are not created by individual classroom teachers for their individual classrooms. And many of us fall somewhere along that continuum. We see value in educational standards that are consistent from state to state and yet understand that each student deserves the right to an education that best suits his or her unique needs. We worry about national standards that could result in a national test and see immediately the problems with a national curriculum. And all of us—no matter our personal positions on common standards—find a place and space at the National Council of Teachers of English. (Beers)

It's too early to know how the Common Core State Standards will work their way into law and practice, but it does seem clear that in this and many other policy areas dangers lurk in all directions, in terms of both the actions to be taken and the arguments to be made. It does seem significant that most of the members of the writing teams for the draft Common Core State Standards were test-makers from college admissions test sponsors. While some of the language of the early draft could ultimately commend and encourage good practice, there is no evidence of thoughtful endorsement of the multiple measures called for in NCTE's 2008 legislative platform, quoted earlier. And, most important from an NCTE perspective, there is no evidence of teacher (or student) involvement in the process of standard setting. As Susan Ohanian, an NCTE member most consistent in her critique of the process and effects of such standard setting, has noted,

> I would point out that a belief in and adherence to the notion of something arbitrarily termed "grade level" is a serious part of the problem in the whole Standards game. It gets people thinking that ALL students should learn commas in apposition in 2nd grade, the semi-colon in 6th, and write fiction in 4th. I don't mention these casually but pull them from my serious study of standards. Anybody who has more than one child knows that they develop at different rates, not to mention different abilities and dispositions.

This most recent standards initiative on the part of the National Governors Association and the Council of Chief State School Officers opens the door to developing a whole new round of tests—to the great profit of the test-makers, the professional tutoring schools, and the sellers of test prep materials. Stephen Krashen has reflected on the huge cost of a new round of test development and argued that we should

> not invest 4.5 billion on new standards and tests. Instead, work on improving the NAEP to get a picture of how our students are performing, and continue to use teacher evaluation to evaluate individual student performance. We should begin by cutting back testing, not adding testing. . . . Teacher evaluation does a better job of evaluating students than standardized testing: The repeated judgments of professionals who are with children every day is more valid than a test created by distant strangers. Moreover, teacher evaluations are "multiple measures," are closely aligned to the curriculum, and cover a variety of subjects.

Krashen's position echoes the "2008 NCTE Legislative Platform," and his stance on testing and the principle of No Unnecessary Testing (NUT) could be a strong, communicable, and effective position for NCTE to adopt. What is problematic about all of the standards efforts has not been the processes or even the formulations of the standards; it has been the constraining effect of testing technologies, along with their high-stakes applications to children, schools, and teachers, that have had the powerful noxious effect challenged by critics of NCLB.

Since literacy and math have been the major foci of testing, these subjects have quite naturally become the major foci of teaching as well. Teachers of social studies, the arts, and even the sciences have quite rightly complained about the diminished time and attention given to their subjects because they aren't "on the test." NCTE needs to continue working with other humanities and social science organizations to help strengthen a broader and more diverse curriculum, kindergarten through grade 12. Further, the implicit definitions of literacy embodied in many of the tests, especially those for the youngest learners, have limited the "skills" being taught to those being tested. And, not surprisingly, when these children are later assessed by more broad-based and meaningful measures, whatever gains were found in the early grades have evaporated. The assumption underlying most direct instruction test preparation programs intended to show success on the fill-in-the-bubble tests is, in effect, "all testing, all the time." Even if scores go up, the knowledge and the attitude that students need to be successful academically and in the world extend far beyond the scope of these tests. Breadth and depth of reading and fluency, as well as power and thoughtfulness in writing, are just a few of the characteristics that few tests measure.

When noneducators dictate educational policy and in some cases get hired to run school districts, as is true in many big cities including New York, the only evidence that seems to count for them is bubbled test results. If, as NCTE and many other educators have long maintained, such test scores only minimally reveal achievement or effective instruction, we are trapped in a vicious cycle of teaching to inadequate tests in self-defense while knowing that even good test scores don't really reveal the kinds of deep learning and thoughtful achievement that NCTE stands for and that students need. Since this kind of short-term test prep "teaching" is insisted on most strongly in schools with poor test scores—and poor children—this population is doubly penalized by being denied access to the kind of instruction and learning that would help to bridge the achievement gaps that limit successful access to higher education and meaningful employment.

R-E-S-P-E-C-T

The only way fully to resist the reductive effect of these tests on English language arts teaching and learning (as well as other subjects) is to return classroom teachers to the central role in assessment they once had. Ever since *A Nation at Risk*, teachers have been scapegoated as the problem. Most of the efforts at "reform" following the report have involved controlling teachers through mandated, often scripted, curricula and methods that reduce teacher autonomy and leave little room for innovation, creativity, and individualization. Teachers got some of the blame after *Sputnik* too, but in those days, most of the federal monies supporting that particular cycle of "reform" went into professional development for teachers, not punishment. NCTE now bills itself as "the professional home of the English language arts community," so it has an enormous stake in teachers' being treated as professionals.

The professional treatment of teachers will be most effectively addressed in collaboration with a broad spectrum of other professional associations, as happened in the recent debate over the reauthorization of NCLB. Teachers of all subjects and grade levels and schools have been systematically disrespected over the years since *Sputnik* and, especially, since the publication of *A Nation at Risk*. This is especially true of teachers in urban schools, which for some mysterious reason have failed to overcome the effects of poverty, inadequate resources, crumbling school buildings in decaying neighborhoods, bureaucratic mismanagement, and a consistent starvation diet of inadequate support. Even many middle-class and suburban schools have been labeled as failures by the punitive demands embodied in the definition and single-test measurement of "adequate yearly progress." These forces have combined to make teaching a less and less attractive profession as a long-term career, and one of the severest problems facing education is the high attrition rate of teachers, including many of the most capable.

Disrespect has manifested itself not only in the use of standardized testing to replace teacher judgment of student progress but also in the regrowth of the kind of scripted "teacher-proof" curricula that first surfaced in response to the *Sputnik* "crisis." NCTE has a been a consistent advocate for teacher autonomy and creativity as the best guarantee of quality education and innovation, which "all testing, all the time" threatens to stifle. Another development that may threaten teacher autonomy and creativity in the future is the use of online instruction. While I can understand the appeal for students of the convenience (and privacy) of online instruction, by reifying the notion that transmission is the basic framework of teaching, such online course work threatens both community-building and human interactivity, essential hallmarks of classroom instruction. And I wonder whether the continued de-skilling of teachers will threaten membership in organizations such as NCTE, since it would seem unnecessary to pay dues, subscribe to journals, or attend conventions unless teachers are free, even encouraged, to apply the ideas acquired through these venues in their own classrooms and to collaborate with professional colleagues in improving instruction.

The lack of respect for teachers and teaching is amplified in the lack of respect for teacher education and teacher educators. The general perception that such programs are at best a waste of time and at worst actually useless has led to a variety of efforts to permit people to teach without going through any kind of education or certification program. Indeed, for many in the public and the press, the unprepared "teachers" of Teach for America are preferred to graduates who chose teacher education. Certification does not guarantee high quality, of course, and completing a teacher education program does not mean that teachers can stop learning more about becoming effective in the classroom, but simply knowing one's subject, or being bright, does not guarantee competence either. Because I've spent forty years as a teacher educator, this is, quite naturally, a personal sore point with me. While no one would argue that all teacher education programs are effective and of high quality, most teachers would endorse their learning experience in teacher education even as they recognize that graduation does not yet earn them the label of "master teacher." Most of the research supports this view of teacher education (see Darling-Hammond and Bransford).

NCTE Policy Advocacy

The relevance of this history to the future of NCTE speaks to the increasing importance of political action by the organization and by its members acting locally and nationally. As education has become more overtly political, what have come to be called "stakeholders" have become and must continue to be more active. While NCTE's ultimate concern is with the children we teach, we also must be supportive of our membership since, without the kind of teaching excellence that NCTE advocates and supports, the students of America will suffer. And supporting excellent teaching means doing so throughout the process of teacher development, from preservice teacher education through improving working conditions and providing professional development for experienced teachers. These urgent issues demand that NCTE continue and even step up its political activity as well as the political education of its members. They may also involve rethinking and recasting the relationship between the national organization and its state and, in some cases, local affiliates. Affiliates have differed in their representativeness, activities, and political effectiveness, but given the important role of the states in setting curriculum and, especially, testing policy, it may be important to find ways to renew and coordinate national and local advocacy activities.

NCTE has made efforts of this sort in the past in, for example, activities that resulted in publication of *The National Interest and the Teaching of English: A Report on the Status of the Profession* (1961; NCTE Committee on National Interest), which got English teaching supported under the National Defense Education Act (NDEA). Originally, NDEA supported teacher preparation in mathematics, the sciences, and foreign languages, but James Squire and others made a convincing case for the importance of reading and writing, and in 1965 English was added to the list of supported subjects, together with reading and various branches of social studies. (I was personally grateful for this support because I spent a wonderful summer at the University of the Pacific at an NDEA workshop, enjoyed a productive year at the University of Illinois as an NDEA Experienced Teacher Fellow, and received additional NDEA fellowship support for my doctorate at Harvard.)

This sense of the privileged status of science and mathematics for the national interest, and especially the national economy, is still with us. As I write this, President Obama and the U.S. Congress seem poised to include support for preparing science and mathematics teachers as part of the economic stimulus bill. No one questions the value of these subjects, but to single them out distorts the nature of education and the importance of the social sciences and the humanities in preparing productive citizens. Once again, as with *The National Interest and the Teaching of English* report, it seems important for NCTE and its sister organizations in the humanities and social sciences to develop the case for broad-scale funding across the curriculum. In view of the widespread economic ignorance and the shoddy ethical dealings of those who led us into the economic crisis of 2008 that is still with us today, helping students and teachers become critical citizens, prudent investors, discriminating consumers, and ethical actors seems as valuable as any other goals of education. And beyond that, it seems clear that many other human needs and abilities required for mental, emotional, spiritual, and moral health have never been adequately addressed by schools and colleges. It might be a good time for NCTE to form another committee to explore drafting a new version of *The National Interest and the Teaching of English* to help make that case, enlisting, while we're at it, colleagues from other disciplines as well as organizations such as the Center for Social Emotional Education, Educators for Social Responsibility, and Facing History and Ourselves.

Reformulating National Goals for Education

Indeed, this might be a good time to rethink the national goals of education. When the standards movement emerged from the perceived crisis described in *A Nation at Risk*, it was not accompanied by a process of national goal setting. As a result, standards were set in terms of the subjects of the curriculum that were traditional at the end of the nineteenth century, a curriculum whose dimensions had been largely set by the Committee of Ten in 1892–93. While NCTE eagerly joined other subject matter organizations in reaching for its slice of the curricular pie, nowhere in the standard-setting process was there a call to question the then-current organization or goals of the curriculum. Should the ends and means of education be the same in the twenty-first century as they were at the end of the nineteenth? This conflict affects education at all levels. In higher education, the traditional disciplines still define both the curriculum and the organization of colleges and universities. Secondary schools are organized and staffed according to these subject areas, and even in primary schools the pressure is on for teachers to have a "content major," defined as one of the disciplines taught in the secondary schools, as well as the breadth of coverage needed to teach all subjects.

Given myriad changes in the culture, it seems likely that few educators or noneducators would argue very long or hard for the status quo if they were appointed to design a twenty-first-century curriculum in 2012. However, as I've argued in *Uncommon Sense* (Mayher), we all have difficulty imagining educational alternatives. Our own 14,000 or more hours of schooling have developed what I've come to call an educational commonsense conception of the norms of education. This educational common sense is particularly powerful because it functions almost completely unconsciously and was acquired experientially. But if education is to play the part we hope it will in the twenty-first century, we must learn to question our educational assumptions and take up the struggle to determine what citizens and workers will need and how education can help them attain the necessary competencies. While this is clearly not going to be done by English language arts teachers alone, our vantage point as language educators gives us a perspective that can provide knowledge and experience for NCTE and its members, individually and collectively, to take leadership roles in a process of reimagining education for our next century.

The states' collective effort to formulate new national "common core" standards could be reframed to begin such a dialogue. The current relatively secretive process could be opened up to begin a national dialogue on the goals and ends of education. Doing so collectively, with people inside and outside of education, might result in dramatically refocusing the content and processes of schooling. New or combined disciplines and a stronger emphasis on social and emotional as well as cognitive development might lead to serious questioning of whether one academic size fits all students. Fairness, equity, and access need not mean identical programs for all students, but rather the opportunity for all students to get an appropriate education. What should be common? What could be individualized? Who has a voice in the decision making? How do we continue to build the community necessary to sustain a free democracy while at the same time maximizing the chance of each child to develop his or her own interests and talents to the fullest?

Such a national revisioning would threaten the educational status quo and would undoubtedly be resisted by many, including, potentially, subject matter teachers and their organizations, even NCTE. The Council has endorsed expanding the curricular mandate of English language arts teachers to include what has been defined as *21st century literacies*, just as it once did with drama, film, and television (NCTE, *21st Century*). But what if a new vision of education suggests we don't need English teachers, or even literacy teachers, old or new? What if the "skills" of the English language arts were seen as distributed across the disciplines without the need for literacy specialists? Or what if the "content"—literature especially, but also language study—of English in schools and colleges were to be amalgamated into a more interdisciplinary grouping, say, a version of humanities that incorporated the arts, the social sciences, and philosophy, as well as more traditional English content? Would we welcome or resist such reconceptualizing? And, most important, how long can we continue to educate children who will live and work in the second half of the twenty-first century with schools that were designed in essence at the end of the nineteenth?

While education has always been political, in the post–*Nation at Risk* era it has become more partisan because, especially at the federal level, monies for and control of education have grown dramatically since 1983 (McDonnell). Additionally, different segments of the political spectrum have adopted distinct curricular stances of their own, including how to teach beginning reading, what texts are appropriate for classrooms and school libraries, what the nature and definition of *scientific* research are, and how (or whether) to educate teachers. While some of these controversies may permeate the ranks of NCTE members, generally NCTE's official positions consistently have advocated openness, pluralism, and freedom of inquiry. As James Moffett attests in *Storm in the Mountains* (1988), his account of the controversy over and eventual removal of his curricular materials in Kanawha County, Charleston, West Virginia, freedom of inquiry itself is controversial, and there are many school stakeholders whose sense of certainty does not welcome multiple voices. The election of Barack Obama as president of the United States seemed to suggest that openness is in the ascendancy, but the threat of closure and rigidity will always be with us, especially when our own self-interests are threatened, as they would be by a genuinely dramatic rethinking of the purposes and processes of schooling. So far, at least, President Obama's education policy has been as regressive and test-driven as his predecessor's, and his endorsement of charter schools poses a threat to the public schools, which historically have been the backbone of American democracy and economic opportunity.

The Future of NCTE as an Organization

The future of NCTE as an organization is connected to the likely evolution of the disciplines it embodies, to changes in the perception and role of teachers at all levels, and to the political and social climate locally, regionally, and nationally. While many of these developments are difficult to predict, it seems safe to say that the explosive growth of information technology will continue to have enormous effects on English language arts teaching and, directly and indirectly, on NCTE's membership, conventions, journals, and all other ways in which members communicate with one another, with their students, and with the public. The last decade has already seen significant changes in NCTE, consistent with new roles for the Internet and other electronic communication media. New websites, blogs, wikis, electronic versions of journals, and a variety of online participatory professional development opportunities already exist and will undoubtedly grow and evolve.

Their impact on the Council's budget is more difficult to predict, but the general sense among Internet users that its content should be available for free is potentially problematic for all content providers. Journals are not likely to go the way of the music business in the short run, but as electronic texts proliferate, it is less and less clear where the money will come from to support their production. Will advertisers pay for electronic-only journals? Will members? Similarly, the high cost of face-to-face meetings and conventions threatens to put pressure on attendance and to suggest the need for alternative "meeting" formats, or the development of face-to-face formats that accomplish learning experiences that can't be replicated electronically. NCTE (and many other professional organizations) has already struggled with alternative formats for convention sessions, but the presentation format continues to dominate such meetings, a format that too often features either reading a written text or presenting PowerPoint slides—either of which easily could be transmitted online. These formats continue to reflect the commonsense conception of knowledge as something produced and published (mostly in universities), such presentations representing important semi-publication credits for tenure-aspiring professors. As one who has tried for many years to help NCTE and the Conference on English Education open up its formats for convention sessions to make them more participatory and less presentational, more interactive and less reactive, I know how hard it is to challenge the established ways of doing "convention." But if conventions are to thrive, more must be done to provide reasons for attending that call on the collective energy of all participants, both as learners and as experts.

New Challenges in the Twenty-First Century

The earlier chapters in this volume spelled out both the conflicts within and outside of NCTE and the overwhelmingly progressive base that encouraged and dealt with them. As we look forward, however, it seems clear that new challenges are emerging, with new threats to the organization and its mission(s). Demographic shifts that are bringing more and more nonnative speakers of English into mainstream schools will continue to challenge an organization overwhelmingly devoted to native speakers.[3] NCTE also must continue its efforts to diversify its membership and, especially, to develop its presence in urban schools, widely regarded as problems in American education. If we, with Neil Postman, are committed to the children who are the future, we must be sure that we are helping all teachers reach and effectively teach all children.

None of these changes will come easily to an organization whose membership has been (1) drawn from former English majors devoted to classic literature and standard language, (2) overwhelmingly white, and (3) either suburban or rural in background. This demographic also has inclined English teachers to be keepers of the flame of "Standard English." Even the young and mostly politically liberal future teachers in my classrooms often have been reluctant to recognize the legitimacy of nonstandard dialects and are convinced that speakers with "foreign" accents or other-than-standard patterns of speech must be "corrected" if they are to achieve academic or economic success. These views continue to be debated within and outside of the Council and are likely to be so for the foreseeable future. But while arguing about them among ourselves is both valuable and enjoyable, we must find better ways to help parents, administrators, test makers, policymakers, and the press understand where we agree—we value all students' language—and what we debate—how best to help all students gain access to what Geneva Smitherman-Donaldson calls the "language of wider communication."

Given the recent attention to the "achievement gap" between black and white students, one wonders how much of it is an artifact of a language/literacy-testing process that demands a single register of the written language. In the second half of the twentieth century, NCTE as an organization has been consistently on the side of tolerance of language variety and respect for diverse languages and dialects. Such stances, however, have had limited effect on either the public perception of what English teachers ought to do in teaching language or, indeed, on the perceptions and practices of many in the profession. Will the next century see a change in expectations for language success? Will schooling be less monolingual as the student body becomes less so? If NCTE is to succeed in becoming a presence in urban schools and others with large populations of non-English speakers, it will need to develop outreach strategies that speak to the complexities and conflicts of urban education.

The story of subject English as embodied by NCTE and explicated in the chapters of this volume has most often been a tale of a college-bound subject, intended in part to provide access for students from nonelite backgrounds to higher education and the upper levels of the workplace. High school education was a level reached by only a small percentage of the population at the beginning of the twentieth century, when NCTE was founded. Attendance grew steadily throughout the century until the expectation now is that every student should earn a high school diploma and most should go on to some kind of higher education. Success in English—in both reading and writing—therefore became one of the key hurdles that students needed to overcome in order to move on in school. As a result, the traditional literature-centered subject was extended and to some extent modified, but rarely radically revised, to reach the greatly expanded secondary school population.

The most dramatic challenge to NCTE, however, comes from the extraordinary and ongoing development of electronic media that have been welcomed by America's schoolchildren in ways that have still not been fully understood or appreciated. Most of the adults who teach in and administer schools have been slow to grasp what these technologies are doing to the minds and learning styles of the kids who have come to master them. Younger and younger children now have cell phones, their own Internet-connected computers, or the kind of hybrid/Internet devices that allow instant emailing from anywhere to anywhere. All of these technologies—especially the Internet—have the potential to be powerful learning tools, but they are also potentially dangerous. Think of cyberbullying or sexting in an environment in which cell phone camera pictures are widely distributed, even posted on the Internet. No one fully understands the long-range consequences of social networking systems such as MySpace or Facebook in terms of their effect on kids' minds or sense of self.

This challenge will grow during NCTE's second century as visual media and other technologies continue to threaten the hegemony of print literacy, with consequences that we can't anticipate for students, teachers, and the larger culture. Neil Postman worried about these consequences of the media environment, and the impact of such changes may be dire, promoting what Susan Jacoby characterizes as "unreason." Others recognize the challenges but see cognitive virtues in video games (Gee), for example, and multimodal discourse (Kress and van Leeuwen, *Multimodal; Reading Images*), which would require some substantial shifts in both the content and the processes of the English curriculum. NCTE has already begun to confront these challenges by defining *21st century literacies* ("NCTE Definition"), but it will be a struggle to modify the English curriculum to help students learn to interpret and use the wide range of media and technologies that will be available to them. And such changes also present challenges to preservice and inservice teacher education. How do we enable teachers to understand and productively use the rapidly changing media environment?

The media world itself is in flux, as newspapers and magazines shrink or disappear and as online blogs and e-zines take their place. Whatever protection the standard editing process provided newspaper readers can be lost or weakened and sometimes overrun by the need for speed. Both news and rumors spread at the speed of light over all of these devices, and are then augmented by verbal rumormongering, the spread of partial or inaccurate information, and superficial explanations. None of us is immune from these influences, but students have fewer alternative fact-checking resources to fall back on and may be most vulnerable to these forces.

Some of these media seem easily interpretable, such as movies and television, but that apparent ease may be deceptive, especially in terms of developing the kind of critical response that guards against more or less subtle manipulation. Helping students learn to take a critical but noncynical stance toward the media that surround them is clearly an important role for schools as a whole, but it is less clear how this guidance fits into the traditional roles of subject-matter-based organizations. Is this part of the English language arts teacher's role? NCTE has institutionally said yes, and is moving to support its members as they learn how to help children learn in these new ways and with new technologies.

Prospects in Retrospect

All of these changes and challenges are putting enormous pressure on schools and teachers to conform to the kind of test-based teaching that reduces teacher autonomy and stifles both student and teacher creativity. Is this a passing trend or the harbinger of an even more confining model of education? NCTE's historic positions have been in favor of enhanced teacher authority, but in recent years the respect for teachers on which such authority depends has been systematically eroded. It is difficult to imagine how it can be restored, but if it can be, it will depend on articulating clearly the need for such respect, defining explicitly why it is deserved, and being plain about the consequences of its being denied. As I look back on the second half of NCTE's first century, I don't see a golden age, but I do see a period in which teachers were able to make their own pedagogical decisions and in which schools and schooling were not the political football they have since become.

By no means have schools ever been perfect; indeed, many of us in NCTE have been strong voices for change and strong challengers of the status quo throughout the century. But the critique of schooling made by teachers and other education insiders differs substantially in quality, tone, and emphasis from criticisms made by those who have spent no time at the chalkface (now the SMART Board). Schools undoubtedly need to change, but productive and constructive change must be based on an accurate analysis of the means of schooling in terms of clearly defined ends of education. Determining ends must be a community-wide project, but the means should be left to the professionals who have experience with children and adolescents. We won't always agree, but our debates will always take the complex realities of children and classrooms into account, and we will never argue that one size fits all. See, for example, the dialogue between Peter Smagorinsky and George Hillocks in the July 2009 issue of *English Journal* on the question of whether there are such things as "best practices."

The combination of changes wrought by the explosion of digital media, by the challenges of bringing high-level schooling to all children, and by the growing determination of nonprofessionals to dictate not only policy but also practice makes this an extraordinary time to be a teacher or administrator, student or parent, member or leader of a professional teachers organization such as NCTE. Teachers need help, and a strong NCTE could be a valuable resource to provide it, but they must have allies as well, which requires finding ways to reach out to parents and even to students so that they can become articulate co-advocates for the kind of education that truly will enable all children to grow and learn for a lifetime.

Acknowledgment

Thanks to Sue Ruskin-Mayher for her help and support with this chapter, her consistent advocacy for the children who most need schools to help them overcome poverty and racism, and her extraordinary modeling of how teacher education should be done.

Notes

1. There is considerable disagreement within the education community as to whether there really was a crisis, whether the committee had identified the right problems, and whether standards were the best solution. For a discussion, see Berliner and Biddle.

2. The chronology also omits any mention of the firestorm of protest that arose when the "consensus draft" was distributed at the NCTE Spring Convention in March 1995. The response led NCTE leadership to bring Michael Kibby of SUNY Buffalo and me together to write a new set of standards in the summer of 1995. This process is not mentioned in the chronology, nor is the identity of the individuals who wrote a competing set of standards that summer, which were those eventually adopted, nor any details as to how theirs got substituted for ours. I describe my experience in "Reflections on Standards and Standard Setting," but I know of no thorough, published history of the project (but see Kelly). The IRA–NCTE *Standards for the English Language Arts* were published by the two organizations in 1996.

3. Both TESOL and, earlier, IRA splintered off from NCTE, and there have been periods when the college composition folks have threatened to do so as well.

Works Cited

Applebee, Arthur N. "Toward Thoughtful Curriculum: Fostering Discipline-Based Conversation." *English Journal* 83.3 (1994): 45–52. Print.

Baron, Dennis. "Language and Education: The More Things Change." 2008. TS.

Beers, Kylene. "An Open Letter to NCTE Members about the Common Core State Standards." *National Council of Teachers of English.* NCTE, 17 Aug. 2009. Web. 20 Aug. 2009.

Berliner, David C., and Bruce J. Biddle. *The Manufactured Crisis: Myths, Fraud, and the Attack on America's Public Schools.* Reading, MA: Addison-Wesley, 1995. Print.

Cuban, Larry. *How Teachers Taught: Constancy and Change in American Classroom, 1890–1990.* 2nd ed. New York: Teachers College, 1993. Print.

Darling-Hammond, Linda, and John Bransford, eds. *Preparing Teachers for a Changing World: What Teachers Should Learn and Be Able to Do.* San Francisco: Jossey-Bass, 2005. Print.

Gee, James Paul. *What Video Games Have to Teach Us about Learning and Literacy.* New York: Palgrave-Macmillan, 2003. Print.

Hillocks, George, Jr. "Some Practices and Approaches Are Clearly Better Than Others and We Had Better Not Ignore the Differences." (A Response to Peter Smagorinsky). *English Journal* 98.6 (2009): 23–29. Print.

International Reading Association, and National Council of Teachers of English. *Standards for the English Language Arts.* Newark, DE: IRA; Urbana, IL: NCTE, 1996. Print.

Jacoby, Susan. *The Age of American Unreason.* New York: Pantheon, 2008. Print.

Kelly, Kathryn H. "National English Language Arts Content Area Standards: Process and Emergent Trends in Revisions." Diss. Florida State U, 1997. Print.

Krashen, Stephen. "NUT: No Unnecessary Testing." 2009. skrashen@yahoo.com.

Kress, Gunther R., and Theo van Leeuwen. *Multimodal Discourse: The Modes and Media of Contemporary Communication.* London: Arnold, 2001. Print.

———. *Reading Images: The Grammar of Visual Design.* 2nd ed. New York: Routledge, 2006. Print.

Mayher, John S. "Reflections on Standards and Standard Setting: An Insider/Outsider Perspective on the NCTE/IRA Standards." *English Education* 31.2 (1999): 106–21. Print.

———. *Uncommon Sense: Theoretical Practice in Language Education.* Portsmouth, NH: Boynton/Cook, 1990. Print.

McDonnell, Lorraine M. *Politics, Persuasion, and Educational Testing.* Cambridge, MA: Harvard UP, 2004. Print.

Moffett, James. *Storm in the Mountains: A Case Study of Censorship, Conflict, and Consciousness.* Carbondale: Southern Illinois UP, 1988. Print.

National Commission on Excellence in Education. *A Nation at Risk: The Imperative for Educational Reform.* Washington, DC: GPO, 1983. Print.

National Council of Teachers of English. "The NCTE Definition of 21st Century Literacies." *National Council of Teachers of English.* NCTE, 15 Feb. 2008. Web. 28 July 2009.

———. *Students' Right to Their Own Language.* Spec. issue of *College Composition and Communication* 25.3 (1974): 1–32. Print.

———. *21st Century Literacies: A Policy Research Brief Produced by the National Council of Teachers of English.* Urbana, IL: NCTE, 2007. Print.

———. "2008 NCTE Legislative Platform." *National Council of Teachers of English.* NCTE, 14 Feb. 2008. Web. 18 Aug. 2009.

National Council of Teachers of English Committee on National Interest. *The National Interest and the Teaching of English: A Report on the Status of the Profession.* Champaign, IL: NCTE, 1961. Print.

Nelms, Ben F. "Reconstructing English: From the 1890s to the 1990s and Beyond." *English Journal* 89.3 (2000): 49–59. Print.

Ohanian, Susan. "Common Core Writing Teams." N.d. *eddrra@yahoo groups.com.* 28 July 2009.

Postman, Neil. *The Disappearance of Childhood.* New York: Delacorte, 1982. Print.

———. *Teaching as a Conserving Activity.* New York: Delacorte, 1979. Print.

Postman, Neil, and Charles Weingartner. *Teaching as a Subversive Activity.* New York: Delacorte, 1969. Print.

Sizer, Theodore. *Horace's Compromise: The Dilemma of the American High School.* Boston: Houghton, 1984. Print.

Smagorinsky, Peter. "Is It Time to Abandon the Idea of 'Best Practices' in the Teaching of English?" *English Journal* 98.6 (2009): 15–22. Print.

Smitherman-Donaldson, Geneva. "Toward a National Public Policy on Language." *College English* 49.1 (1987): 29–36. Print.

NCTE READING THE PAST. WRITING THE FUTURE. 100 YEARS

A Blast from the Past

Have you ever heard of the NCTE Commission on Dreams? It never existed—but it was actually proposed in 1977 by former NCTE Executive Director J. N. Hook, who urged the Council to consider the challenges of the future. Its members, according to Hook, would be recognized for their breadth of vision, imagination, the ability to look forward, and affirmative thinking. "There should probably be a poet in the group," Hook concluded, "and a range in age from college [students] to old but alert."

Afterword

Edmund J. Farrell
The University of Texas at Austin

In light of scientific estimates that the universe has existed for 13½ billion years and planet Earth for 4½ billion years, one century is an infinitesimal period, less than a subatomic particle in the eye of time. But what a century it has been!

Of those who gathered in Chicago one hundred years ago to found the National Council of Teachers of English (NCTE), who among them could have anticipated that the Council only a century later would have more than 52,000 members diverse in gender, ethnicity, race, and sexual orientation; that it would contain various sections, assemblies, committees, and caucuses; that it would sponsor and cosponsor conventions, conferences, and affiliates throughout the nation; that it would not only publish sectional journals and hundreds of books but also provide a variety of websites, all to enable its membership to keep constantly abreast of their field?

Who among the founders might have foreseen the shift from an agrarian society to an urban one; the rise in the nation's population, from roughly 95 million to 308 million; the development of talking motion pictures and of Technicolor; the frequent cinematic use of four-letter words and highly sexual scenes; the widespread ban on smoking in bars and public buildings; the increase in citizens' longevity from forty-seven years to seventy-eight years; the ubiquity of automobile and semitrailer, the decline of railways, and the existence of interstate highways, giving birth to gridlock and suburban sprawl; the creation of automatic washers and dryers, credit cards and ballpoint pens, refrigerators and freezers, synthetic fibers and plastic, jet airplanes, radar, laser, and air-conditioning, this last precipitating wholesale migration into Sun Belt states; the inception of the Internet and World Wide Web, permitting instantaneous global communication as well as use of personal blogs and Nings, YouTube, Facebook, MySpace, Second Life, and Twitter; the growth of nanotechnology, making available ever smaller and ever more sophisticated electronic media—computers and television sets, FM and satellite radios, cell phones, iPods and iPhones, Blackberries and Palm Pilots, CDs and DVDs, and e-books?

Who a century ago might have foreseen the explosive growth of public and higher education, from 6 percent graduating from high school in 1900 to 70 percent today, from 2 percent of eighteen- to twenty-four-year-olds enrolled in higher education at the turn of the last century to approximately 60 percent of that age group now enrolled in two-year or four-year colleges or in universities; of an influx of immigrants from around the globe, making necessary widespread ESL and bilingual educational programs; of the growth of Advanced Placement courses and of special education for children with special needs; of educational vouchers, magnet and charter schools, and online programs of teacher certification; of local programs of educational assessment giving way to statewide and national assessments?

No Council founder would have had the prescience to know that in the century ahead the nation would participate in a number of major wars, some in far-off lands largely unfamiliar to those gathered in Chicago; that it would experience both a Great Depression and a number of serious recessions; that its scientists would develop atomic bombs, annihilators of populations in Hiroshima and Nagasaki, and space ships that would transport astronauts to the moon; that England would decline as a world power and that China would emerge as a major economic and military power; that American English would become the foremost international language; that well-armed and violent drug cartels would manage an intercontinental flow of illegal drugs; that assassins in one decade would cut short the lives of three of this country's foremost leaders—President John F. Kennedy, Robert F. Kennedy, and Rev. Martin Luther King, Jr.; that the nation's courts and its Congress would ensure voting rights for women and African Americans, protect the civil rights of minorities and gays, integrate schools, make available retirement and medical benefits for the elderly, and permit access to abortions and pornography; that American citizens would observe an act of terrorism that would topple two high-rise icons in its most metropolitan city; that a large share of American factories and businesses would migrate to foreign shores, leaving jobless tens of thousands of workers; that shopping malls and huge box stores would eliminate small local businesses; that the nation's strongest telescope would transmit astounding pictures of far-distant galaxies in a complex and ever-expanding universe; that one century after NCTE's founders met in Chicago, three women would have been named to the nation's highest court and an African American president would occupy its White House.

Which of the founders might have had sufficient foreknowledge to expect the medical and scientific accomplishments that lay in the decades ahead? Who could have envisioned, for example, the development of a vaccine that would end fears of getting polio; of antibiotic drugs that would fight infections and of psychotropic drugs that would empty asylums of the mentally ill; of the unraveling of DNA and of the promises of stem-cell research; of the possibility of altering human biological inheritance through genetic engineering or of human behavior through social engineering; of the cloning of animals and plants; of the transplantation of human hearts, livers, and kidneys; of titanium replacements of knee, hip, and shoulder joints; of artificial insemination and the existence of surrogate parents; of the ready availability of pills for women to prevent pregnancy and of ones for men to overcome impotence?

The consequence of rapid social, technological, and scientific changes during the century past is that the pace of life of Victorians appears closer to that of the Greeks and Romans than to the pace of life of time-pressed, multitasking contemporary Americans. As remarkable as the last century has been in its accomplishments, it has left in its wake a number of critical problems, problems that I believe education, including the subject of English, must help to address in the decades ahead. Among them are issues related to population growth, poverty, privacy and human worth, weaponry and terrorism, national infrastructure and debt, and the future of the American family, each of which I can sketch only briefly.

Population growth. Since 1911 the population of the United States has increased by more than 200 million. The world's population a century ago was less than 2 billion; now estimated to be approaching 7 billion, the global total is expected to level off by 2050 at almost 9.5 billion, with most of the growth occurring in less-developed countries. Because population growth is the prime cause of loss of habitat and extinction of species, diminution of natural resources, pollution of the environment, and climatic change, I believe it to be the foremost problem facing the human species.

Poverty. Poverty is both an international and a domestic problem, with income of citizens in developed nations far outstripping that of individuals in underdeveloped and developing countries. Impoverished citizens in the latter nations receive less than adequate subsistence income, the result being rampant disease, inadequate health care, and high mortality rates. In the United States, CEOs of large corporations have been awarded in recent years incomes more than four hundred times larger than salaries earned by average workers; millions of American children and their parents are malnourished; and gated communities or guarded condos increasingly separate the wealthy from the poor. In September 2009, the National Center for Education Statistics reported that students from low-income families are ten times more likely to drop out of school than those from higher-income families.

Privacy and human worth. Because of electronic technology, most Americans now live open lives. Credit card companies and stores document their buying habits; miniature cameras record their presence in, outside of, and within buildings; doctors' offices share their medical records with insurance companies; the government records their incomes, tracks their flights, and at times listens in on their conversations; persons known or unknown to them can photograph their activities and submit these to YouTube for viewers' delectation; their ideas and emotions are shared on cell phones, tweets, Facebook, and MySpace. Citizens can nightly view TV programs on which characters are stabbed, shot, eviscerated, and autopsied; and teenagers can play video and computer games in which mock human beings are pulverized with the push of a button. Under teachers' guidance, students might consider whether privacy is worth preserving, and if so, why, when, and how? If not, why not? They might discuss whether Americans have become so inured to violence that individual lives are no longer sacred, and, if so, whether individual human worth is worth preserving. Again, if so, why and how? If not, why not?

Weaponry and terrorism. Billions of dollars are involved annually in the international arms trade, with tens of thousands of jobs nationally and internationally dependent on the making and selling of fighter planes, armored tanks and trucks, and such assault rifles as AK-47s. Religious sects and anti-Western groups have been using suicide bombers, improvised explosive devices, gas attacks, and conventional weapons as agencies of terrorism. About the globe, thousands of laboratories can legally create new toxic strains of pathogens immune to current antibiotics or vaccines. Huge stores of nuclear warheads currently are held by the United States and Russia, with China, England, France, India, and Pakistan known to be other nuclear powers. Suspected nuclear states are Israel and North Korea, with Iran ambitious to be yet another. How to reduce, if not put an end to, arms races, international terrorism, and the spread of nuclear weaponry will require the deepest and most creative thinking of the nation's future leaders, now our students.

National infrastructure and debt. The nation's debt has been rising, while its infrastructure has been crumbling. In a population of 308 million people, each citizen's share of the national debt, estimated to be $12 trillion in September 2009, was approximately $39,000. To remain solvent in the decades ahead, Medicare and Social Security will require trillions of dollars of additional revenue, while the long-term costs of national health care remain unknown. Furthermore, most of the nation's roads, rails, bridges, levees, dams, and clean water and sewerage systems are old and in need of repair. The American Society of Civil Engineers reported in January 2009 that it would cost $2.2 trillion over the next five years to make America's infrastructure adequate. In short, those now in our classrooms will inherit an immense federal debt for which they will become responsible.

Future of the American family. Whether the traditional American nuclear family can survive is moot. Cohabitation outside of marriage is increasingly common and socially acceptable. According to a report of the National Center for Health Statistics released in May 2009, unmarried mothers accounted in 2007 for 39.7 percent of births in the United States, more than double the percentage in 1980. The instability of marriage, given the high percentage of Americans who divorce, of unmarried couples who cohabit, and of children reared by single parents, gives rise to serious questions about whether this traditional American institution can or should survive and whether future citizens would or would not be adversely affected by its demise.

To ensure that students are informed citizens and voters, I believe that they should all become familiar in secondary school with the problems and issues I have merely sketched here. More able students in the upper years of high school should learn problem-solving techniques that address in multidisciplinary fashion, perhaps in configurations discussed by John Mayher in the preceding chapter, these and other problems that I have overlooked or that have yet to emerge.

In addition to teaching the writing and research skills needed to address critical problems, English teachers could contribute to multidisciplinary courses their knowledge of literature dealing with utopian and dystopian fiction, poverty and wealth, nature, warfare, the family, individual worth, and the making of ethical decisions. Students, in dealing with critical problems and attendant issues, should have at their disposal a full array of technological aids, among them computers, computer and video games, self-paced computer programs, audio/video recorders and players, cameras, interactive whiteboards, and flat-screen TVs. Finally, I believe that NCTE should establish a well-funded Standing Committee on the Future, one charged with monitoring and publicizing legislative, economic, scientific, technological, and demographic events that may affect members' teaching and curricula or the welfare of those in their charge.

As this volume makes evident, the teaching of English and language arts and the preparation and certification of its teachers has continually evolved over the past century. As it continues to do so, I hope that its teachers will help prepare those in their classrooms to deal intelligently with an unstable world, that they will help students shape the kind of nation in which they and their progeny, and their progeny's progeny, would wish to live their lives.

Such matters do not easily lend themselves to standardized tests.

Appendix A

Some Important Dates in the History of American Literacy Education and NCTE

Library of Congress established	1800
Steel pen points manufactured in England	1803
John Quincy Adams, first Boylston Professor of Rhetoric at Harvard University	1805–09
United States war with England	1812–15
William Monroe, early producer of graphite pencils in Boston	1812
Samuel Hall opened first American normal school for teachers in Concord, VT	1823
Noah Webster, *An American Dictionary of the English Language*	1828
Richard Whateley, *Elements of Rhetoric*	1828
Manual pencil sharpener patented	1828
William Lloyd Garrison published the abolitionist newspaper *The Liberator*	1831–65
William McGuffey, *Eclectic Readers*	1836–57
Envelopes for mail first used	1839
U.S. Census included a literacy question	1840
England issued first adhesive postage stamp, developed by Rowland Hill	1840
Samuel F. B. Morse demonstrated the telegraph to Congress	1844
Boston Public Library opened, first library to allow the public to borrow books	1854
Connecticut adopts first literacy test as a qualification for voting	1855
National Teachers Association founded (later NEA)	1857
Pencils with attached eraser manufactured	1858
Charles Darwin, *On the Origin of Species*	1859
American Civil War	1861–65
Morrill Act established agricultural colleges	1862
Twenty colleges founded for African Americans	1865–70
Alexander Bain, *English Composition and Rhetoric*	1866
Metal paper fasteners patented	1866
U.S. Department of Education created	1867
Christopher Latham Sholes, Carlos Glidden, and Samuel Soule patented the typewriter	1868

Transcontinental railroad completed	1869
Tax-supported high schools established	1870s
Essay required for Harvard entrance examination	1874
Alonzo Reed and Brainerd Kellogg, *Graded Lessons in English*	1875
American Library Association (ALA) founded	1876
Alexander Graham Bell patented the telephone	1876
Thomas A. Edison invented the phonograph	1877
Adams Sherman Hill, *The Principles of Rhetoric and Their Application*	1878
Modern Language Association (MLA) founded	1883
Oxford English Dictionary	1884–1928
Harvard established a required first-year composition course	1885
John F. Genung, *The Practical Elements of Rhetoric*	1885
Mimeograph machine introduced	1887
Barrett Wendell, *English Composition*	1891
Fred Newton Scott and Joseph Denney, *Paragraph-Writing*	1891
International Copyright Act passed	1891
Columbian Exposition in Chicago introduced the public to motion pictures	1893
NEA Committee of Ten included English in high school program of study	1893
National Conference on Uniform Entrance Requirements in English organized (dissolved in 1931)	1894
The Parent Teacher Association (PTA) founded in Washington, DC	1897
The Katzenjammer Kids, an early comic strip, appeared in the *New York Journal*	1897
Matthew Schooley patented the bent-wire paper clip	1898
John Dewey, *The School and Society*	1899
Gertrude Buck, *The Metaphor*, an early doctoral dissertation in rhetoric	1899
New England Association of Teachers of English organized	1901
College Board administered first national assessment to 978 students	1901
First Nobel Prize for Literature awarded to Sully Prudhomme	1901
First transatlantic radiotelegraph transmission	1901
Percival Chubb, *The Teaching of English in the Elementary and Secondary School*	1902
Fred N. Scott, "The Philosophy of the Assignment"	1903
Edwin C. Wolley, *Handbook of Composition*	1907
Otto Jespersen, *A Modern English Grammar on Historical Principles*	1909–49
National Council of Teachers of English (NCTE) founded in Chicago, 1–2 December	1911
James F. Hosic elected first NCTE Secretary	1911
English Journal, owned by James F. Hosic, launched	1912

NCTE Board of Directors adopted first constitution	1913
NCTE published first booklist, *Books for Home Reading*	1913
World War I	1914–18
Leaders of NCTE's Public Speaking Section founded the National Association of Academic Teachers of Public Speaking (now the National Communication Association)	1914
Desk-model office stapler manufactured	1914
Quarterly Journal of Public Speaking began publication (renamed *Quarterly Journal of Speech* in 1928)	1915
American Association of University Professors (AAUP) founded	1915
American Educational Research Association (AERA) founded	1916
NCTE and NEA cosponsored *Reorganization of English in Secondary Schools*	1917
NCTE members totaled 1,700	1917
First Pulitzer Prizes awarded	1917
NEA Commission on the Reorganization of Secondary Education, *Cardinal Principles of Secondary Education*	1918
Flu epidemic postponed NCTE Convention to February 1919	1918
NCTE affiliates increased to nineteen	1919
W. Wilbur Hatfield elected NCTE Secretary-Treasurer	1919
NCTE promoted Better Speech Week	1919
American Council of Learned Societies (ACLS) founded	1919
H. L. Mencken, *The American Language*	1919
C. C. Certain, *Standard Library Organization and Equipment for Secondary Schools of Different Sizes*	1920
National Conference on Educational Method founded (became Association for Supervision and Curriculum Development in 1943)	1921
First NCTE Annual Convention in the South (Chattanooga)	1922
ALA awarded first Newbery Medal to Hendrik Willem van Loon's *The Story of Mankind*	1922
Scott, Foresman's Literature and Life Series became model for school literature anthologies	1922
I. A. Richards and C. K. Ogden, *The Meaning of Meaning*	1923
Wilhelm Ritzerfeld invented the Ditto machine, or spirit duplicator	1923
Elementary English Review begun by C. C. Certain	1924
Linguistic Society of America founded	1924
Jean Piaget, *The Language and Thought of the Child*	1926
Scholastic Aptitude Test (SAT) first administered	1926
Workbooks introduced into English courses	1926
Charles Woolbert, *The Fundamentals of Speech*	1927
The Jazz Singer first synchronized dialogue and singing in a feature film	1927
NCTE had 4,877 members and a net worth of $8,280.28	1928
NCTE inaugurated "College Edition" of the *English Journal*	1928

Great Depression in the United States	ca. 1929–39
Rewey Belle Inglis, first woman president of NCTE	1929
First NCTE Annual Convention west of the Mississippi (Kansas City)	1929
First NCTE Curriculum Commission appointed	1930
NCTE incorporated as a nonprofit corporation	1930
Civilian Conservation Corps defined *functional literacy* as completing three or more years of schooling	1930
Cellophane tape patented	1930
NCTE "sections" formally defined	1931
NCTE promoted literary recordings of writers reading their works	1933
NCTE contracted with D. Appleton-Century to publish reports and materials	1933
Leonard Bloomfield, *Language*	1933
CBS and NBC broadcast NCTE convention speakers on radio	1934
NCTE published *An Experience Curriculum in English*	1935
William F. Thrall and Addison Hibbard, *Handbook to Literature*	1936
NCTE's silver anniversary; five thousand members and fifty affiliates	1936
Association of Teachers of English in Negro Colleges founded (later CLA)	1937
NCTE sponsored first spring regional conference in Spokane, WA	1937
College English Association founded	1938
American Library Association awarded first Caldecott Medal to *Animals of the Bible*, illustrated by Dorothy P. Lathrop	1938
Louise Rosenblatt, *Literature as Exploration*	1938
Cleanth Brooks and Robert Penn Warren, *Understanding Poetry*	1938
World War II	1939–45
College English replaced the college edition of *English Journal*	1939
Television broadcasts demonstrated at New York World's Fair	1939
Mortimer Adler, *How to Read a Book*	1940
John C. Hodges, *Harbrace College Handbook*	1941
John Crowe Ransom, *The New Criticism*	1941
Charlemae Rollins, *We Build Together: A Reader's Guide to Negro Life and Literature for Elementary and High School Use*	1941
No NCTE Annual Convention; Board of Directors met in Chicago	1942
No NCTE Annual Convention; business meeting only in New York City	1943
Hungarians Laszlo and Georg Biro patented first ballpoint pen	1943

Chairs of NCTE Elementary, High School, and College Sections joined the NCTE Executive Committee	1944
NCTE offered "junior memberships" to students	1944
G. I. Bill (Servicemen's Readjustment Act, Public Law 78-346) assisted veterans to attend college	1944
NCTE promoted the use of the term *language arts* as a school subject	1945
NCTE adopted a policy to hold conventions in cities providing members "rooms and dining-room services regardless of race or religion"	1945
First NCTE Radio Award given to CBS program "On a Note of Triumph"	1945
NCTE had 8,814 members and a net worth of $24,479.13	1945
Kenneth Burke, *A Grammar of Motives*	1945
ENIAC computer completed	1945
John E. Warriner, *English Grammar and Composition*	1946
NCTE became owner of *Elementary English Review*, renamed *Elementary English* (*Language Arts* in 1975)	1947
Margaret M. Heaton, *Reading Ladders for Human Relations*	1947
U.S. Bureau of the Census defined *functional illiteracy* as completing fewer than five years of schooling	1947
Education Testing Service (ETS) founded	1947
Conference on College Composition and Communication became first NCTE conference	1949
College Composition and Communication began publication	1950
Filmstrips became a popular instructional medium	1950–mid 1970s
Korean War	1950–53
James McKrimmon, *Writing with a Purpose*	1950
U.S. Bureau of the Census defined *functional illiterates* as having fewer than six years of schooling	1952
Fire destroyed NCTE Headquarters at 211 W. 68th St., Chicago	1953
J. N. Hook became NCTE Executive Secretary	1953
McCarthyism flourished; NCTE published *Censorship and Controversy*	1953
Brown v. Board of Education declared segregation in public schools unconstitutional	1954
NCTE Headquarters moved from Chicago to 704 S. Sixth St., Champaign, IL	1954
NCTE bought *English Journal* from editor W. Wilbur Hatfield	1954
National Council for the Accreditation of Teacher Education (NCATE) founded	1954
NCTE's High School Section became the Secondary Section	1955
NCTE published Ideaform theme paper	1955
Sony introduced the transistor radio	1955
College Board launched Advanced Placement (AP) Program	1955
International Reading Association (IRA) founded	1955

Liquid Paper invented	1956
Noam Chomsky, *Syntactic Structures*	1957
NCTE initiated Achievements Awards in Writing	1957
Sputnik launched	1957
National Defense Education Act (Public Law 85-864) passed	1958
NCTE Commission on the Profession appointed	1958
NCTE had 43,831 members and a net worth of $204,922.19	1958
The Basic Issues in the Teaching of English	1958
NCTE distributed *Abstracts of English Studies*	1958
James Bryant Conant, *The American High School Today*	1959
American College Testing (ACT) college entrance assessment first administered	1959
Commercial xerographic copiers available	1959
Woods Hole Conference on science education resulted in Jerome Bruner's *The Process of Education* (1960)	1959
NCTE Advisory Council established to make recommendations to the NCTE Executive Committee	1960
NCTE published *Studies in the Mass Media* (until 1964)	1960
NCTE Headquarters moved to 508 S. Sixth St., Champaign, IL	1960
James R. Squire became NCTE Executive Secretary	1960
Research Foundation established to honor J. N. Hook	1960
U.S. Office of Education defined *functional literacy* as completing eighth grade	1960
Vietnam War (U.S. involvement in)	1961–73
NCTE Commission on the English Language appointed	1961
Wayne Booth, *The Rhetoric of Fiction*	1961
Lawrence A. Cremin, *The Transformation of the School*	1961
NCTE released *The National Interest and the Teaching of English*	1961
Webster's Third New International Dictionary of the English Language, Unabridged	1961
NCTE adopted *The Students' Right to Read*	1962
Lev Vygotsky, *Thought and Language*	1962
College Board sponsored summer institutes for English teachers	1962
J. N. Hook named coordinator of Project English's federally funded curriculum study centers, conferences, and research	1962
Yukio Horie, Tokyo Stationery Company, invented the fiber-tipped marking pen	1962
NCTE and the University of Illinois cosponsored the National Study of High School English Programs	1963–65
Alberta Council of Teachers of English was first Canadian affiliate of NCTE	1963
Walter Loban, *The Language of Elementary School Children*, launched NCTE Research Reports series	1963
Richard Braddock, Richard Lloyd-Jones, and Lowell Schoer, *Research in Written Composition*	1963

President John F. Kennedy assassinated on 22 November	1963
Civil Rights Act (Public Law 88-352) passed	1964
NCTE Board of Directors prohibited racial restrictions on affiliate membership	1964
David H. Russell Research Award established	1964
NCTE Conference on English Education established	1964
Marshall McLuhan, *Understanding Media*	1964
Amendments to the National Defense Education Act (1958) promoted the study of language and composition	1964
NCTE Commission on Literature appointed	1964
NCTE sponsored first International Conference on the Teaching of English	1965
U.S. Congress expanded funding for public education through the Higher Education Act (HEA) (Public Law 89-329) and the Elementary and Secondary Education Act (ESEA) (Public Law 89-10)	1965
National Endowment for the Humanities established	1965
Edward P. J. Corbett, *Classical Rhetoric for the Modern Student*	1965
Regional conferences on English in the two-year college held in Chicago, San Bernardino, San Antonio, Charlotte, Cazenovia, Vancouver, and St. Louis	1966
NCTE held first conference for affiliate leaders, Santa Fe, NM	1966
Harold B. Allen, *TENES: A Survey of the Teaching of English to Non-English Speakers in the United States*	1966
Teachers of English to Speakers of Other Languages (TESOL) founded	1966
Anglo-American Seminar on the Teaching and Learning of English (Dartmouth Conference)	1966
Adult Education Act funded programs for adults lacking secondary school diplomas	1966
NCTE won contract to direct the ERIC Clearinghouse on the Teaching of English	1967
NCTE Commission on Composition appointed	1967
NCTE National Junior College Committee appointed (became the National Two-Year College Council in 1986)	1967
John Dixon, *Growth through English: A Report Based on the Dartmouth Seminar*	1967
Research in the Teaching of English began publication	1967
Jonathan Kozol, *Death at an Early Age*	1967
Robert F. Hogan became NCTE Executive Secretary	1968
Rev. Dr. Martin Luther King, Jr., assassinated on 4 April	1968
NCTE Chicano (later Latino) Caucus organized	1968
Rhetoric Society of America founded	1968
International Baccalaureate (IB) founded	1968
James Moffett, *Teaching the Universe of Discourse*	1968
Donald Murray, *A Writer Teaches Writing*	1968

NCTE had 120,243 members and a net worth of $486,508.84 1969
NCTE Commission on Reading appointed 1969
NCTE Task Force on Racism and Bias appointed 1969
English Education began publication 1969
First national assessment of writing by the National Assessment of Educational Progress (NAEP) 1969
ARPAnet computer network established 1969
United States landed men on the moon 1969
Chaim Perelman and L. Olbrechts-Tyteca, *The New Rhetoric* 1969
William A. Jenkins, first African American president of NCTE 1969
Sunny Decker, *An Empty Spoon* 1969
NCTE Black Caucus founded 1970
NCTE Conference of Secondary School English Department Chairmen (CSSEDC) established (renamed Conference on English Leadership in 1991) 1970
NCTE Executive Committee adopted *Criteria for Teaching Materials in Reading and Literature*, prepared by the NCTE Task Force on Racism and Bias in the Teaching of English 1970
NCTE Promising Researcher Awards established 1970
First national assessment of reading by NAEP 1970
Paulo Freire, *Pedagogy of the Oppressed* 1970
NCTE Headquarters moved to 1111 Kenyon Road, Urbana, IL 1971
Janet Emig, *The Composing Processes of Twelfth Graders* 1971
James Kinneavy, *A Theory of Discourse* 1971
First NCTE Committee on Public Doublespeak appointed 1972
NCTE Executive Committee approved the concept of "assemblies" 1972
Fund for the Improvement of Postsecondary Education (FIPSE) established 1972
William Labov, *Language in the Inner City: Studies in Black English Vernacular* 1972
Freshman English News began publication 1972
Michel Foucault, *The Archaeology of Knowledge* 1972
Eliot Wigginton, *The Foxfire Book* 1972
Constitutional amendments restructured NCTE 1973
Frank O'Hare, *Sentence Combining: Improving Student Writing without Formal Grammar Instruction* 1973
First Wyoming Conference on Freshman and Sophomore English 1973
Peter Elbow, *Writing without Teachers* 1973
NCTE published *Students' Right to Their Own Language* 1974
Members-at-large elected NCTE's president for the first time 1974
Teaching English in the Two-Year College began publication 1974
Writing-across-the-curriculum program established at Carleton College 1974
Bay Area Writing Project established 1974

Arthur N. Applebee, *Tradition and Reform in the Teaching of English: A History* 1974
Personal computers began to be mass-marketed 1974
Support for the Learning and Teaching of English (SLATE) launched 1975
Elementary English Review was renamed *Language Arts* 1975
Newsweek published "Why Johnny Can't Write" 1975
Journal of Basic Writing began publication 1975
National Association for Bilingual Education (NABE) founded 1975
Education for All Handicapped Children Act (Public Law 94-142) enacted 1975
Council of Writing Program Administrators (WPA) founded 1976
Gary Tate, *Teaching Composition: Ten Bibliographical Essays* 1976
NCTE Gay Caucus met at the NCTE Annual Convention 1976
NCTE Commission on the History of the Council appointed 1977
Mina Shaughnessy, *Errors and Expectations: A Guide for the Teacher of Basic Writing* 1977
Geneva Smitherman, *Talkin and Testifyin: The Language of Black America* 1977
E. D. Hirsch Jr., *The Philosophy of Composition* 1977
NCTE and IRA sponsored national and regional conferences on the Impact of Child Language Development Research on Curriculum and Instruction 1979–82
CSSEDC Quarterly began publication (renamed *English Leadership Quarterly* in 1991) 1979
NCTE Commission on Media appointed 1979
NCTE among twenty-four organizations that endorsed *The Essentials of Education* 1979
J. N. Hook, *A Long Way Together: A Personal View of NCTE's First Sixty-Seven Years* 1979
NCTE affiliates fund the filing of a friend-of-the-court brief supporting a student's appeal of a decision in a book-banning case (*Pico v. Island Trees School District*) 1979
U.S. Department of Education became a cabinet-level agency 1980
Journal of Advanced Composition began publication 1980
The Writing Center Journal began publication 1980
Post-It Notes sold nationwide 1980
John C. Maxwell became NCTE Executive Director 1981
The Writing Instructor began publication 1981
National Humanities Alliance (NHA) founded 1981
NCTE Spring Conference replaced separate section and CEE conferences 1982
NCTE published "The Essentials of English" 1982
Rhetoric Review began publication 1982
Classroom Notes Plus began publication 1983
NOTES Plus began publication (ceased in 1999) 1983

NCTE had 67,969 members and a net worth of $774,902	1983
U.S. Department of Education, *A Nation at Risk: The Imperative for Educational Reform*	1983
Donald H. Graves, *Writing: Teachers and Children at Work*	1983
Ernest L. Boyer, *High School: A Report on Secondary Education in America*	1983
Internet created	1983
Written Communication began publication	1984
IDEAS Plus began publication (ceased in 2002)	1984
John I. Goodlad, *A Place Called School: Prospects for the Future*	1984
Theodore R. Sizer, *Horace's Compromise: The Dilemma of the American High School*	1984
National Center for the Study of Writing and Literacy established at Carnegie Mellon University and the University of California at Berkeley (ceased in 1995)	1985
Marjorie N. Farmer, ed., *Consensus and Dissent: Teaching English Past, Present, and Future*	1986
Carnegie Forum on Education and the Economy released *A Nation Prepared: Teachers for the Twenty-First Century*	1986
George Hillocks Jr., *Research on Written Composition: New Directions for Teaching*	1986
NCTE cosponsored the English Coalition Conference	1987
National Board for Professional Teaching Standards formed	1987
Stephen M. North, *The Making of Knowledge in Composition: Portrait of an Emerging Field*	1987
Diane Ravitch and Chester E. Finn, *What Do Our Seventeen-Year-Olds Know?*	1987
Lynne V. Cheney, *American Memory*	1987
Talking Points began publication	1989
Tim Berners-Lee and Robert Cailliau built the World Wide Web	1989
Miles Myers became NCTE Executive Director	1990
NCTE and the NCTE Black Caucus hosted the first African American Read-In	1990
Teach for America began providing teachers for low-income communities	1990
The Council Chronicle began publication	1991
James Flood, Julie M. Jensen, Dianne Lapp, and James R. Squire, eds., *Handbook of Research on Teaching the English Language Arts*	1991
Jeanne Marcum Gerlach and Virginia R. Monseau, eds., *Missing Chapters: Ten Pioneering Women in NCTE and English Education*	1991
National Writing Project authorized as a federal education program	1991
Primary Voices K–6 began publication (ceased in 2002)	1993
Voices from the Middle began publication	1994

School Talk began publication	1995
Asian/Asian American Caucus met at the CCCC Convention	1995
National Two-Year College Council became Two-Year College English Association (TYCA)	1996
NCTE and IRA published *Standards for the English Language Arts*	1996
Oprah Winfrey launched her book club	1996
Faith Z. Schullstrom became NCTE Executive Director	1997
NCTE launched the Reading Initiative	1997
Caucus for American Indian Scholars and Scholarship met at the CCCC Convention	1997
J. K. Rowling, *Harry Potter and the Sorcerer's Stone*	1998
Whole Language Umbrella became an NCTE conference	2000
NCTE Middle Level Section established	2000
The Report of the National Reading Panel: Teaching Children to Read released	2000
Kent Williamson became NCTE Executive Director	2000
Alliance for Excellent Education founded	2001
Apple, Inc., introduced the iPod portable media player	2001
NCTE inaugurated Advocacy Day on Capitol Hill	2002
No Child Left Behind Act (NCLB; Public Law 107-110) reauthorized the Elementary and Secondary Education Act (ESEA)	2002
ReadWriteThink, cosponsored by NCTE, IRA, and MCI Worldcom (later cosponsored by the Verizon Foundation), offered free Internet-based teaching resources	2002
NCTE Jewish Caucus met at the NCTE Annual Convention	2002
Skype, software permitting voice calls over the Internet, developed	2002
Iraq War	2003–
NCTE had 48,125 members and a net worth of $18,576,551	2003
NCTE developed CoLEARN, an online professional development resource	2003
NCTE West office opened at the University of California at Berkeley	2003
NCTE established the Consulting Network	2003
National Endowment for the Arts, *Reading at Risk: A Survey of Literary Reading in America*	2004
NCTE James R. Squire Office of Policy Research in the English Language Arts established	2004
NCTE opened an office at 1410 King St., Alexandria, VA	2005
NCTE released *The Impact of the SAT and ACT Timed Writing Tests*	2005
Leaders wrote NCTE's first legislative platform	2006
Twitter, a micro-blogging service, launched	2006
NCTE began developing Pathways, an online professional development program	2007

Apple, Inc. introduced the iPhone	2007
Amazon launched Kindle, a device for reading electronic books	2007
Executive Committee adopted the *NCTE Definition of 21st Century Literacies* and *NCTE Framework for 21st Century Curriculum and Assessment*	2008
NCTE sponsored the Institute for 21st Century Literacies	2008
The Ohio State University launched the Digital Archives of Literacy Narratives (DALN)	2008
Laurie Katz, Delores Straker, and Jerrie Cobb Scott, eds., *Affirming Students' Right to Their Own Language: Bridging Language Policies and Pedagogical Practices*	2008
NCTE sponsored the National Day on Writing, 20 October	2009

Appendix B

NCTE Presidents

Year	President	Affiliation While Holding Office
1912	Fred Newton Scott	University of Michigan
1913	Fred Newton Scott	University of Michigan
1914	Franklin T. Baker	Teachers College, Columbia University
1915	E. H. Kemper McComb	Manual Training High School, Indianapolis, IN
1916	Edwin M. Hopkins	University of Kansas
1917	Allan Abbott	Teachers College, Columbia University
1918	Edwin L. Miller	Northwestern High School, Detroit, MI
1919	Joseph M. Thomas	University of Minnesota
1920	James Fleming Hosic	Chicago Normal College
1921	H. G. Paul	University of Illinois at Urbana–Champaign
1922	Charles Robert Gaston	Richmond Hill High School, New York, NY
1923	J. W. Searson	University of Nebraska
1924	Thomas C. Blaisdell	Slippery Rock State Normal College
1925	T. W. Gosling	Madison Public Schools, Madison, WI
1926	Sterling Andrus Leonard	University of Wisconsin
1927	Dudley Miles	Evander Childs High School, New York, NY
1928	Charles Carpenter Fries	University of Michigan
1929	Rewey Belle Inglis	University of Minnesota

1930	Ruth Mary Weeks	Paseo High School, Kansas City, MO
1931	Rollo L. Lyman	University of Chicago
1932	Stella S. Center	John Adams High School, New York, NY
1933	Walter Barnes	New York University
1934	Oscar J. Campbell	University of Michigan
1935	Charles Swain Thomas	Harvard University
1936	Dora V. Smith	University of Minnesota
1937	Holland D. Roberts	Stanford University
1938	Marquis E. Shattuck	Detroit Public Schools, Detroit, MI
1939	Essie Chamberlain	Oak Park High School, Oak Park, IL
1940	E. A. Cross	Colorado State College of Education
1941	Robert C. Pooley	University of Wisconsin
1942	John J. DeBoer	Chicago Teachers College
1943	Max J. Herzberg	Weequahic High School, Newark, NJ
1944	Angela M. Broening	Baltimore Public Schools, Baltimore, MD
1945	Harold A. Anderson	University of Chicago
1946	Helene W. Hartley	Syracuse University
1947	Porter G. Perrin	University of Washington
1948	Thomas Clark Pollock	New York University
1949	Marion C. Sheridan	New Haven High School, New Haven, CT
1950	Mark Neville	John Burroughs School, St. Louis, MO
1951	Paul Farmer	Henry W. Grady High School, Atlanta, GA
1952	Lennox Grey	Teachers College, Columbia University
1953	Harlen M. Adams	Chico State College
1954	Lou L. LaBrant	Atlanta University
1955	John C. Gerber	State University of Iowa
1956	Luella B. Cook	Minneapolis Public Schools, Minneapolis, MN
1957	Helen K. Mackintosh	U.S. Office of Education

1958	Brice Harris	The Pennsylvania State University
1959	Joseph Mersand	Jamaica High School, Jamaica, NY
1960	Ruth G. Strickland	Indiana University
1961	Harold B. Allen	University of Minnesota
1962	George Robert Carlsen	State University of Iowa
1963	David H. Russell	University of California
1964	Albert R. Kitzhaber	University of Oregon
1965	Richard Corbin	Hunter College High School, New York, NY
1966	Muriel Crosby	Wilmington Public Schools, Wilmington, DE
1967	Albert H. Marckwardt	Princeton University
1968	Alfred H. Grommon	Stanford University
1969	William A. Jenkins	University of Wisconsin at Milwaukee
1970	James E. Miller Jr.	University of Chicago
1971	Robert A. Bennett	San Diego University School District, San Diego, CA
1972	Virginia M. Reid	Oakland Public Schools, Oakland, CA
1973	Walker Gibson	University of Massachusetts
1974	Margaret Early	Syracuse University
1975	Stephen Dunning	University of Michigan
1976	Charlotte Huck	The Ohio State University
1977	Charlotte Brooks	Washington, DC, Public Schools
1978	Marjorie Farmer	Temple University
1979	Yetta Goodman	University of Arizona at Tucson
1980	Alan Purves	University of Illinois at Urbana–Champaign
1981	Robert Squires	Oneonta High School, Oneonta, NY
1982	John Stewig	Carthage College
1983	William Irmscher	University of Washington
1984	Stephen Tchudi	Michigan State University
1985	Sheila Fitzgerald	Michigan State University
1986	Richard Lloyd-Jones	University of Iowa

1987	Nancy S. McHugh	Grant High School, Van Nuys, CA
1988	Julie M. Jensen	The University of Texas at Austin
1989	Janet Emig	Rutgers University, emerita
1990	Ruth K. J. Cline	University of Colorado
1991	Shirley Haley-James	Georgia State University
1992	James E. Davis	Ohio University
1993	Jesse Perry	San Diego City Schools, emeritus
1994	Janie Hydrick	McArthur Elementary School, Mesa, AZ
1995	Miriam Chaplin	Rutgers University at Camden
1996	Beverly Ann Chin	University of Montana at Missoula
1997	Carol Avery	Millersville, PA
1998	Sheridan Blau	University of California at Santa Barbara
1999	Joan Naomi Steiner	University of Wisconsin at Oshkosh
2000	Jerome C. Harste	Indiana University
2001	Anne Ruggles Gere	University of Michigan
2002	Leila Christenbury	Virginia Commonwealth University
2003	David Bloome	Vanderbilt University The Ohio State University
2004	Patricia L. Stock	Michigan State University
2005	Randy Bomer	The University of Texas at Austin
2006	Kyoko Sato	California State University, Northridge
2007	Joanne Yatvin	Portland State University, emerita
2008	Kathleen Blake Yancey	Florida State University
2009	Kylene Beers	Teachers College, Columbia University
2010	Carol Jago	University of California, Los Angeles
2011	Yvonne Siu-Runyan	University of Northern Colorado, emerita
2012	Keith Gilyard	The Pennsylvania State University

Appendix C

NCTE Executive Directors

Year	NCTE Secretary-Treasurer
1911–19	James Fleming Hosic
1920–53	W. Wilbur Hatfield
	NCTE Executive Secretary
1954–60	J. N. Hook
1960–67	James R. Squire
1968–81	Robert F. Hogan
	NCTE Executive Director
1981–89	John C. Maxwell
1990–97	Miles Myers
1997–2000	Faith Z. Schullstrom
2000–	Kent Williamson

Appendix D

NCTE Section Chairs

Year	Elementary Section	Junior High School/ Middle Level Section	High School/ Secondary Section	College Section	Normal School/ Teachers College Section
1912	Franklin T. Baker TC, Columbia U		Louise B. Stickney Yeatman HS St. Louis, MO	Arthur C. L. Brown North-western U	Alma Blount State NS Ypsilanti, MI
1913	[Met with Normal School Section]		[Met with College Section]	Charles W. Kent U Virginia	Samuel A. Lynch Iowa State TC
1914	J. W. Searson Agricultural College of Kansas		E. H. Kemper McComb Manual Training HS Indiana-polis, IN	Edwin Mims Vanderbilt U	Sarah J. McNary State NS Trenton, NJ
1915	Mary B. Fontaine Supervisor of English Charleston, WV		Cornelia Steketee Hulst Central HS Grand Rapids, MI	Karl Young U Wisconsin	Florence U. Skeffington Eastern Illinois NS
1916	George A. Myrick Cambridge, MA		Oscar C. Gallagher West Roxbury HS Boston, MA	F. N. Scott U Michigan	Willis H. Wilcox Maryland State NS

1917	[Met with Normal School Section]		Claudia E. Crumpton Alabama Girls' Institute Monte-vallo, AL	J. M. Thomas U Minnesota	D. O. Coate State NS La Crosse, WI
1918	Convention postponed	Convention postponed	Convention postponed	Convention postponed	Convention postponed
1919	Burr F. Jones Massachu-setts Board of Education		A. B. Sias West HS Rochester, NY	Ashley H. Thorndike Columbia U	
1920			Margaret Sleezer Senn HS Chicago, IL	Allan Abbott TC, Columbia U	
1921			William N. Otto Shortridge HS Indiana-polis, IN	Hardin Craig U Iowa	
1922	T. W. Gosling Superinten-dent of Schools Madison, WI	[First mention; met with Elementary School Section]	Grace Rotzel Fairhope, AL	Hardin Craig U Iowa	
1923	Clara Beverley Detroit, MI		C. C. Certain Detroit, MI	Hardin Craig U Iowa	[Met with Elementary School Section]
1924	H. H. Ryan Ben Blewett JHS St. Louis, MO	[Met with Elementary School Section]	Ida T. Jacobs Des Moines, IA, and Ward H. Green Tulsa, OK	C. C. Fries U Michigan	Constance Mitchell Arkansas State TC
1925		Claudia E. Crumpton Hutchinson Intermediate School Detroit, MI	L. A. Hutchens New Trier Township HS Kenilworth, IL, and E. R. Clark East HS Rochester, NY	C. C. Fries U Michigan	S. A. Lynch State TC Cedar Falls, IA

1926	C. C. Certain U of North Carolina	Dora V. Smith U Minnesota	Max J. Herzberg Central HS Newark, NJ, and Olive Ely Hart South Philadelphia HS for Girls Philadelphia, PA	C. C. Fries U Michigan	Thomas C. Blaisdell State NS Slippery Rock, PA
1927	C. C. Certain Detroit TC	Claudia E. Crumpton Hutchinson Intermediate School Detroit, MI	James M. Spinning West HS Rochester, NY, and Susan E. Wilcox Springfield HS Springfield, IL	C. C. Fries U Michigan	Conrad T. Logan State TC Harrisonburg, VA
1928	C. C. Certain Detroit TC	James M. Grainger State TC Farmville, VA	Sarah E. Simons Supervisor of English Washington, DC	Thomas A. Knott Springfield, MA	[Met with Element-ary School Section]
1929	C. C. Certain Detroit TC	Charles S. Pendleton Peabody College for Teachers Nashville, TN	Ward H. Green Tulsa Public Schools	Thomas A. Knott Springfield, MA	
1930	Frances Dearborn Johns Hopkins U	Florette McNeese Classen HS Oklahoma City, OK	M. Aline Bright Mobile HS Mobile, AL	John S. Kenyon Hiram College	
1931	C. C. Certain Detroit TC	Florette McNeese Oklahoma City HS	Harry E. Coblentz South Division HS Milwaukee, WI	Oscar J. Campbell U Michigan	

1932	Florence E. Bamberger Johns Hopkins U	Angela Broening Dept. of Research Detroit, MI	Marquis E. Shattuck Director, Language Education Detroit, MI	Oscar J. Campbell U Michigan	
1933	[Met with Teachers College Section]	Roland A. Welch Durfee Intermediate School Detroit, MI	Imelda Stanton Central HS Memphis, TN	Oscar J. Campbell U Michigan	Rebecca Pollock West Virginia U
1934	Maude McBroom State U of Iowa	Menetta E. Koenig Garrison Junior HS Baltimore, MD	Imelda Stanton Central HS Memphis, TN	Roscoe E. Parker U Tennessee	
1935	Eloise Ramsey Wayne U	Eliza F. Hoskins West Side HS Little Rock, AR	Harold A. Anderson University HS Chicago, IL	Atwood H. Townsend New York U	
1936	Ruth Bristol Milwaukee State TC	Gladys Persons Theodore Roosevelt HS New York, NY	Winifred H. Nash Roxbury Memorial HS Roxbury, MA	Robert M. Gay Simmons College	
1937	Mary D. Reed Indiana State TC Terre Haute, IN	Myrtle Gustafson Claremont Junior HS Oakland, CA	Orren H. Smith Roxbury Memorial HS for Girls Roxbury, MA	Oscar J. Campbell Columbia U	
1938	Mary D. Reed Indiana State TC Terre Haute, IN	Roland A. Welch Durfee Intermediate School Detroit, MI	Harold A. Anderson University of Chicago HS Chicago, IL	Oscar J. Campbell Columbia U	

1939	Mary D. Reed Indiana State TC Terre Haute, IN	Jane Souba Isaac Young HS New Rochelle, NY	Luella B. Cook Central HS Minneapolis MN	Oscar J. Campbell Columbia U	
1940	Mary D. Reed Indiana State TC Terre Haute, IN	George W. Norvell Supervisor of English Albany, NY	Eugene Seubert Maplewood-Richmond Heights HS Maplewood, MO	Warner G. Rice U Michigan	
1941	Mary D. Reed Indiana State TC Terre Haute, IN	Mildred M. Finch Alexander Hamilton Junior HS Cleveland, OH	Angela M. Broening Baltimore Public Schools	Warner G. Rice U Michigan	
1942	No Convention	No Convention	No Convention	No Convention	No Convention
1943	No Convention	No Convention	No Convention	No Convention	No Convention
1944	Dora V. Smith U Minnesota		Ward H. Green Supervisor of English Tulsa, OK	George B. Parks Queens College	
1945	Dora V. Smith U Minnesota		Ward H. Green Supervisor of English Tulsa, OK	Porter G. Perrin Colgate College U Washington	
1946	Dora V. Smith U Minnesota		Irvin C. Poley Germantown Friends School Philadelphia, PA	Roy B. Basler Peabody College for Teachers U Arkansas	
1947	Bernice E. Leary Board of Education Madison, WI		Irvin C. Poley Germantown Friends School Philadelphia, PA	Tremaine McDowell U Minnesota	

1948	Ruth Strickland U of Indiana		Helen F. Olson Queen Anne HS Seattle, WA	Tremaine McDowell U Minnesota	
1949	Ruth Strickland U of Indiana		Helen F. Olson Queen Anne HS Seattle, WA	Margaret M. Bryant Brooklyn College	
1950	Hannah M. Lindahl Mishawaka Public Schools Mishawaka, IN		Hardy R. Finch Greenwich HS Greenwich, CT	Margaret M. Bryant Brooklyn College	
1951	Hannah M. Lindahl Mishawaka Public Schools Mishawaka, IN		Hardy R. Finch Greenwich HS Greenwich, CT	Theodore Hornberger U Minnesota	
1952	Mildred A. Dawson Appalachian State TC Boone, NC		Leon C. Hood Clifford J. Scott HS East Orange, NJ	James F. Fullington The Ohio State U	
1953	Mildred A. Dawson Appalachian State TC Boone, NC		Leon C. Hood Clifford J. Scott HS East Orange, NJ	Barriss Mills Purdue U	
1954	Edna L. Sterling Seattle Public Schools		Luella B. Cook Minneapolis Public Schools	Brice Harris The Pennsylvania State U	
1955	Edna L. Sterling Seattle Public Schools		Virginia Belle Lowers Los Angeles City Schools	Brice Harris The Pennsylvania State U	

1956	Alvina T. Burrows New York U		Virginia Belle Lowers Los Angeles City Schools	T. A. Barnhart St. Cloud State College	
1957	Alvina T. Burrows New York U		Hardy R. Finch Greenwich HS Greenwich, CT	T. A. Barnhart St. Cloud State College	
1958	Elizabeth Guilfoile Cincinnati Public Schools		Hardy R. Finch Greenwich HS Greenwich, CT	George Arms U New Mexico	
1959	Elizabeth Guilfoile Cincinnati Public Schools		Richard Corbin Peekskill HS Peekskill, NY	George Arms U New Mexico	
1960	Muriel Crosby Wilmington Public Schools Wilmington, DE		Richard Corbin Hunter College HS New York, NY	William S. Ward U Kentucky	
1961	Muriel Crosby Wilmington Public Schools Wilmington, DE		Robert A. Bennett Minneapolis Public Schools	William S. Ward U Kentucky	
1962	Miriam E. Wilt Temple U		Robert A. Bennett Minneapolis Public Schools	Autrey Nell Wiley Texas Woman's U	
1963	Miriam E. Wilt Temple U		Jarvis E. Bush Wisconsin State College at Oshkosh	Autrey Nell Wiley Texas Woman's U	

1964	Virginia M. Reid Oakland Public Schools Oakland, CA		Jarvis E. Bush Wisconsin State College at Oshkosh	Glenn Leggett U Washington	
1965	Virginia M. Reid Oakland Public Schools Oakland, CA		Frank E. Ross Oakland County Schools Pontiac, MI	Glenn Leggett U Washington	
1966	Walter J. Moore U Illinois at Urbana–Champaign		Frank E. Ross Eastern Michigan U	Robert M. Gorrell U Nevada	
1967	Walter J. Moore U Illinois at Urbana–Champaign		John C. Maxwell Upper Midwest Regional Educational Laboratory Minneapolis, MN	Robert M. Gorrell U Nevada	
1968	Charlotte S. Huck The Ohio State U		John C. Maxwell Upper Midwest Regional Educational Laboratory Minneapolis, MN	Henry W. Sams The Pennsylvania State U	
1969	Charlotte S. Huck The Ohio State U		Mildred E. Webster St. Joseph Senior HS St. Joseph, MI	Henry W. Sams The Pennsylvania State U	
1970	Robert Dykstra U Minnesota		Mildred E. Webster St. Joseph Senior HS St. Joseph, MI	Walker Gibson U Massachusetts at Amherst	

1971	Robert Dykstra U Minnesota		Robert E. Palazzi Burlingame HS Burlingame, CA	Walker Gibson U Massachusetts at Amherst	
1972	Bette J. Peltola U Wisconsin at Milwaukee		Robert E. Palazzi Burlingame HS Burlingame, CA	Blyden Jackson U North Carolina at Chapel Hill	
1973	Bette J. Peltola U Wisconsin at Milwaukee		Evelyn M. Copeland Fairfield Public Schools Fairfield, CT	Blyden Jackson U North Carolina at Chapel Hill	
1974	Jerome Green The Ochs School New York, NY		Evelyn M. Copeland Fairfield Public Schools Fairfield, CT	Kenneth S. Rothwell U Vermont	
1975	Jerome Green The Ochs School New York, NY		Robert Squires Oneonta HS Oneonta, NY	Kenneth S. Rothwell U Vermont	
1976	Eileen Tway Miami U of Ohio		Robert Squires Oneonta HS Oneonta, NY	Hobart Jarrett Brooklyn College–CUNY	
1977	Eileen Tway Miami U of Ohio		James Sabol Bellevue Washington Public Schools Bellevue, WA	Hobart Jarrett Brooklyn College–CUNY	
1978	Sr. Ann Redmond College of St. Catherine		James Sabol Bellevue Washington Public Schools Bellevue, WA	Hobart Jarrett Brooklyn College–CUNY	

1979	Sr. Ann Redmond College of St. Catherine		Frances M. Russell Winchester HS Winchester, MA	Hobart Jarrett Brooklyn College–CUNY	
1980	Dianne Monson U Wisconsin at Madison		Frances M. Russell Winchester HS Winchester, MA	Harry Brent Rutgers U at Camden	
1981	Dianne Monson U Wisconsin at Madison		Jonathan Swift Stevenson HS Livonia, MI	Harry Brent Rutgers U at Camden	
1982	Angela Jaggar New York U		Jonathan Swift Stevenson HS Livonia, MI	Harry Brent Rutgers U at Camden	
1983	Angela Jaggar New York U		Skip Nicholson Burbank HS Burbank, CA	Harry Brent Rutgers U at Camden	
1984	Rudine Sims The Ohio State U		Skip Nicholson Burbank HS Burbank, CA	Edward P. J. Corbett The Ohio State U	
1985	Rudine Sims The Ohio State U		Theodore Hipple U Tennessee	Edward P. J. Corbett The Ohio State U	
1986	Sr. Rosemary Winkeljohann Millersville U		Theodore Hipple U Tennessee	Lynn Quitman Troyka Queens-borough CC–CUNY Bayside, NY	

1987	Sr. Rosemary Winkeljohann Millersville U		George B. Shea Jr. Belleville West HS Belleville, IL	Lynn Quitman Troyka Queens-borough CC–CUNY Bayside, NY	
1988	Janie Hydrick McArthur Elementary School Mesa, AZ		George B. Shea Jr. Belleville West HS Belleville, IL	Janice M. Lauer Purdue U	
1989	Janie Hydrick McArthur Elementary School Mesa, AZ		Faith Z. Schullstrom Guilderland Central School District Guilderland, NY	Janice M. Lauer Purdue U	
1990	Barbara Kiefer The Ohio State U		Faith Z. Schullstrom Guilderland Central School District Guilderland, NY	Tilly Warnock U Wyoming	
1991	Barbara Kiefer The Ohio State U		Jackie Swensson Meritt Hutton Junior HS Thornton, CO	Tilly Warnock U Wyoming	
1992	Barbara Flores California State U		Jackie Swensson Metropolitan State College Denver, CO	Cynthia Selfe Michigan Technological U	
1993	Barbara Flores California State U		Mildred Miller Perris Union HS District Perris, CA	Cynthia Selfe Michigan Technological U	

1994	Barbara Flores California State U		Mildred Miller Perris Union HS District Perris, CA	James L. Hill Albany State College	
1995	Kathy G. Short U Arizona		Joan Naomi Steiner Menasha HS Menasha, WI	James L. Hill Albany State College	
1996	Kathy G. Short U Arizona		Joan Naomi Steiner Menasha HS Menasha, WI	Frank Madden Westchester CC Valhalla, NY	
1997	Patricia Cordeiro Rhode Island College		Carolyn Lott U Montana at Missoula	Frank Madden Westchester CC Valhalla, NY	
1998	Patricia Cordeiro Rhode Island College		Carolyn Lott U Montana at Missoula	Frank Madden Westchester CC Valhalla, NY	
1999	Yvonne Siu- Runyan U Northern Colorado		Charleen Silva Delfino East Side HS District San Jose, CA	Kathleen Blake Yancey U North Carolina at Charlotte	
2000	Yvonne Siu- Runyan U Northern Colorado		Charleen Silva Delfino East Side HS District San Jose, CA	Kathleen Blake Yancey Clemson U	
2001	Vivian Vasquez American U	Kathryn D. Ramsey River Oaks Baptist School Houston, TX	Dave Wendelin Jefferson County Public Schools Golden, CO	Kathleen Blake Yancey Clemson U	

2002	Vivian Vasquez American U	Kathryn D. Ramsey River Oaks Baptist School Houston, TX	Dave Wendelin Jefferson County Public Schools Golden, CO	Patricia Harkin U Illinois at Chicago	
2003	Kathryn Mitchell Pierce Glenridge School Clayton, MO	Kathryn D. Ramsey River Oaks Baptist School Houston, TX	Rebecca Bowers Sipe Eastern Michigan U	Patricia Harkin U Illinois at Chicago	
2004	Kathryn Mitchell Pierce Glenridge School Clayton, MO	Howard Miller Lincoln U	Rebecca Bowers Sipe Eastern Michigan U	Dickie Selfe Michigan Technological U	
2005	Curt Dudley-Marling Boston College	Howard Miller Lincoln U	Niki Locklear Kenton County Schools Kenton, KY	Dickie Selfe Michigan Technological U	
2006	Curt Dudley-Marling Boston College	Sandy Hayes Becker Middle School Becker, MN	Niki Locklear Kenton County Schools Kenton, KY	Brian Huot Kent State U	
2007	Franki Sibberson Albert Chapman Elementary School Powell, OH	Sandy Hayes Becker Middle School Becker, MN	Diane Waff WestEd Oakland, CA	Brian Huot Kent State U	
2008	Franki Sibberson Albert Chapman Elementary School Powell, OH	Sandy Hayes Becker Middle School Becker, MN	Diane Waff U Pennsylvania	Jude Okpala Howard CC Columbia, MD	

2009	Debra Goodman Hofstra U	Nancy Patterson Grand Valley State U	Wanda Porter Kailua, HI	Jude Okpala Howard CC Columbia, MD	
2010	Debra Goodman Hofstra U	Nancy Patterson Grand Valley State U	Wanda Porter Kailua, HI	Mike Palmquist Colorado State U	

CC = Community College
HS = High School
JHS = Junior High School
NS = Normal School
TC = Teachers College
U = University

Appendix E

NCTE Journal Editors

Abstracts of English Studies

1958–62	H. Lewis Sawin	University of Colorado at Boulder
1962–74	John B. Shipley	Ohio University University of Illinois at Chicago
1974–77	J. Wallace Donald	University of Colorado at Boulder

College Composition and Communication

1950–52	Charles W. Roberts	University of Illinois at Urbana–Champaign
1953–55	George S. Wykoff	Purdue University
1956–58	Francis E. Bowman	Duke University
1959–61	Cecil B. Williams	Oklahoma State University Texas Christian University
1962–64	Ken Macrorie	Western Michigan University
1965–73	William F. Irmscher	University of Washington
1974–79	Edward P. J. Corbett	The Ohio State University
1980–86	Richard Larson	Herbert H. Lehman College–CUNY
1987–93	Richard C. Gebhardt	Findlay College Bowling Green State University
1994–99	Joseph Harris	University of Pittsburgh
2000–04	Marilyn M. Cooper	Michigan Technological University
2005–09	Deborah H. Holdstein	Governors State University Northern Illinois University Columbia College, Chicago
2010–	Kathleen Blake Yancey	Florida State University

College English

1939–55	W. Wilbur Hatfield	Chicago Teachers College
1956–59	Frederick L. Gwynn	University of Virginia Trinity College, CT
1960–65	James E. Miller Jr.	University of Nebraska University of Chicago
1966–77	Richard Ohmann	Wesleyan University
1978–85	Donald Gray	Indiana University
1986–92	James C. Raymond	University of Alabama
1993–98	Louise Z. Smith	University of Massachusetts at Boston
1999–2005	Jeanne Gunner	Santa Clara University Chapman University
2006–	John Schilb	Indiana University

English Education

1969–73	Oscar M. Haugh	University of Kansas
1973–79	Ben R. Nelms	University of Missouri
1979–86	Allen Berger	University of Pittsburgh
1986–93	Gordon Pradl Mary K. Healy	New York University University of California at Berkeley
1994–96	Patricia Lambert Stock	Michigan State University
1996–2000	David Schaafsma Ruth L. Vinz	Teachers College, Columbia University University of Illinois at Chicago Teachers College, Columbia University
2001–05	Dana L. Fox Cathy Fleischer	Georgia State University Eastern Michigan University
2005–10	Michael Moore	Georgia Southern University

English Journal

1912–21	James Fleming Hosic	Chicago Teachers College
1922–55	W. Wilbur Hatfield	Chicago Teachers College
1955–64	Dwight E. Burton	Florida State University
1964–73	Richard S. Alm	University of Hawaii at Manoa

1973–80	Stephen N. Tchudi	Michigan State University
1980–87	Ken Donelson Alleen Pace Nilsen	Arizona State University Arizona State University
1987–94	Ben F. Nelms	University of Missouri University of Florida
1994–98	Leila Christenbury	Virginia Commonwealth University
1998–2003	Virginia R. Monseau	Youngstown State University
2003–08	Louann Reid	Colorado State University
2008–	Ken Lindblom	Stony Brook University

English Leadership Quarterly*

1971–72	Thomas D. Ragan	Rio Mesa High School, Oxnard, CA
1973	Melvin Merzon	Oak Park High School, Oak Park, MI
1973–75	Edward Longanecker	Junior High School, Mount Pleasant, IA
1976–79	Louis M. Papes	Chagrin Falls High School, Chagrin Falls, OH
1980–82	Roberta McFarland	Jeb Stuart High School, Falls Church, VA
1983	Leslie A. Kent	Robert Frost Middle School, Fairfax, VA
1984–89	Driek Zirinsky	Eastern Washington University Boise State University
1990–94	James Strickland	Slippery Rock University
1994–2001	Henry Kiernan	Bellmore-Merrick Central High School District North Merrick, NY
2001–07	Bonita L. Wilcox	Cambridge Springs, PA
2007–	Lisa Scherff Susan L. Groenke	University of Alabama University of Tennessee at Knoxville

*Begun in 1979 as the *CSSEDC Quarterly* and published by the NCTE Conference for Secondary School English Chairpersons, the journal was retitled *English Leadership Quarterly* in 1991, when the conference became the Conference on English Leadership.

*Language Arts**

1925–41	C. C. Certain	Detroit Teachers College Northwestern High School, Detroit, MI
1941–42	Julia L. Certain	Detroit, MI
1942–61	John J. DeBoer	Chicago Teachers College University of Illinois at Urbana–Champaign
1961–68	William A. Jenkins	University of Wisconsin at Milwaukee
1968–72	Rodney Smith	State of Florida Department of Education, Tallahassee, FL
1972–76	Iris Tiedt	University of Santa Clara
1976–83	Julie M. Jensen	The University of Texas at Austin
1983–90	David Dillon	University of Alberta McGill University
1990–97	William H. Teale	The University of Texas at San Antonio University of Illinois at Chicago
1997–2001	Curt Dudley-Marling	York University, North York, ON, Canada Boston College
	Sharon Murphy	York University, North York, ON, Canada
2001–06	Kathy G. Short	University of Arizona at Tucson
	Jean Schroeder	Tucson Unified School District
	Gloria Kauffman	Tucson Unified School District
	Sandy Kaser	Tucson Unified School District
2006–	Laurie Katz	The Ohio State University
	Barbara Kiefer	The Ohio State University
	Patricia Enciso	The Ohio State University
	Detra Price-Dennis	The Ohio State University
	Melissa Wilson	Beck Urban Academy, Columbus, OH

*Established as *Elementary English Review* in 1925, the journal became *Elementary English* in 1947 and *Language Arts* in 1975.

Primary Voices K–6

1993–94	Kathy Meyer Reimer Diane Stephens Karen Smith	Goshen College University of Hawaii at Honolulu NCTE Staff, Urbana, IL
1994–99	Diane Stephens Kathy Meyer Reimer Jennifer Story	University of Hawaii at Honolulu Goshen College Dole Intermediate School, Honolulu, HI
1999–2002	Lester L. Laminack Katie Wood Ray	Western Carolina University Western Carolina University

Research in the Teaching of English

1967–72	Richard Braddock	University of Iowa
1973–78	Alan Purves	University of Illinois at Urbana–Champaign
1978–83	Roy C. O'Donnell	University of Georgia
1984–91	Judith A. Langer Arthur N. Applebee	University of California at Berkeley Stanford University State University of New York at Albany
1992–97	Sandra Stotsky	Harvard University
1997–2003	Peter Smagorinsky Michael W. Smith	University of Oklahoma University of Georgia Rutgers University
2003–08	Anne DiPardo Melanie Sperling	University of Iowa University of California at Riverside
2008–	Mark Dressman Sarah McCarthey Paul Prior	University of Illinois at Urbana–Champaign University of Illinois at Urbana–Champaign University of Illinois at Urbana–Champaign

School Talk

1995–96	Andrea Butler Regie Routman	Chicago, IL Shaker Heights, OH, City School District

1996–97	Regie Routman	Shaker Heights, OH, City School District
	Donna Maxim	The Center for Teaching and Learning, Edgecomb, ME
1997–98	Kathryn Egawa	Madrona Elementary School, Seattle, WA
	Donna Maxim	The Center for Teaching and Learning, Edgecomb, ME
	Cora Lee Five	Edgewood School, Scarsdale, NY
1998–99	Cora Lee Five	Edgewood School, Scarsdale, NY
	Marie Dionisio	Louis M. Klein Middle School, Harrison, NY
1999–2001	Kathy Egawa	NCTE Staff, Urbana, IL
	Joanne Hindley Salch	Manhattan New School, New York, NY
	Marianne Marino	Central Elementary School, Glen Rock, NJ
2001–02	Jane Hansen	University of New Hampshire
	Marianne Marino	Central Elementary School, Glen Rock, NJ
2002–03	Kathryn Egawa	NCTE Staff, Urbana, IL
	Jane Hansen	University of New Hampshire
	Vivian Vasquez	American University
	Marianne Marino	Central Elementary School, Glen Rock, NJ
2003–04	Curt Dudley-Marling	Boston College
	Vivian Vasquez	American University
	JoAnne Wong-Kam	Punahou School, Honolulu, HI
2004–05	Shari Frost	Norwood Park School, Chicago, IL
	Franki Sibberson	Eli Phiney Elementary, Dublin, OH
2005–06	Franki Sibberson	Eli Phiney Elementary, Dublin, OH
	Susi Long	University of South Carolina at Columbia
2006–07	Susi Long	University of South Carolina at Columbia
	Linda K. Crafton	Benedictine University
2007–08	Linda K. Crafton	Benedictine University
	Nancy Johnson	Western Washington University

2008–09	Nancy Johnson	Western Washington University
	Frank Chiki	Double Eagle Elementary School, Albuquerque, NM
2009–10	Frank Chiki	Double Eagle Elementary School, Albuquerque, NM
	Andrea García	Hofstra University

Studies in the Mass Media

1960–64	Joseph Mersand	Jamaica High School, Jamaica, NY

Talking Points

1989–94	Debra Goodman	Detroit Public Schools, Detroit, MI
1994–98	Jane Bartow	Breck School, Minneapolis, MN
	Jerry Bartow	Minnetonka Middle School East, Minnetonka, MN
1998–2000	Shirley R. Crenshaw	Westminster College
	Dorothy F. King	Westminster College
2001–04	Peggy Albers	Georgia State University
	Allen Koshewa	Lewis and Clark College
2004–07	Bess Altwerger	Towson University
	Prisca Martens	Towson University
2007–08	James Wygant	San Roque School, Santa Barbara, CA
	Edie Lanphar	San Roque School, Santa Barbara, CA
2008–09	James Wygant	San Roque School, Santa Barbara, CA
	Edie Lanphar	San Roque School, Santa Barbara, CA
	Kelly Welch	San Roque School, Santa Barbara, CA
2009–10	Phil Fitzsimmons	University of Wollongong, Australia
	Edie Lanphar	San Roque School, Santa Barbara, CA
2010–	Carol Gilles	University of Missouri, Columbia
	Jennifer Wilson	University of South Carolina at Columbia

Teaching English in the Two-Year College

1974–76	Ruth Fleming Shaw W. Keats Sparrow	East Carolina University East Carolina University
1976–77	W. Keats Sparrow	East Carolina University
1977–79	Bertie E. Fearing W. Keats Sparrow Frieda W. Purvis Holmes	East Carolina University East Carolina University Pitt Technical Institute, Greenville, NC
1979	Bertie E. Fearing W. Keats Sparrow	East Carolina University East Carolina University
1980	Bertie E. Fearing	East Carolina University
1980–87	Bertie E. Fearing John C. Hutchens	East Carolina University Pitt Community College, Greenville, NC
1987	John C. Hutchens	Pitt Community College, Greenville, NC
1988–94	Nell Ann Pickett	Hinds Community College, Raymond, MS
1994–2001	Mark Reynolds	Jefferson Davis Community College, Brewton, AL
2002–05	Howard Tinberg	Bristol Community College, Fall River, MA
2006–	Jeff Sommers	West Chester University, West Chester, PA

Voices from the Middle

1994–99	Maureen Barbieri Linda Rief	Spartanburg Day School, Greenville, SC Marymount School, New York, NY Oyster River Middle School, Durham, NH
1999–2006	Kylene Beers	University of Houston Yale University
2006–	Janis Harmon Roxanne Henkin Elizabeth Pate	The University of Texas at San Antonio The University of Texas at San Antonio The University of Texas at San Antonio

Appendix F

NCTE Assemblies and Commissions

NCTE Assemblies

Assembly on Literature for Adolescents of NCTE (ALAN)—established in 1973

Children's Literature Assembly (CLA)—established in 1975 as Assembly on Children's Literature

Junior High/Middle School Assembly—established in 1975 and dissolved in 2000 to become the Middle Level Section of NCTE

Assembly on International Exchange—established in 1976

International Assembly—established in 1977 and dissolved in 1995 to merge with the International Consortium and then, in 2000, to become the NCTE Standing Committee on International Concerns

International Writing Centers Association: An NCTE Assembly—established in 1982 as National Writing Centers Association, an NCTE Assembly

Assembly for Research—established 1983

Emeritus Assembly—established in 1983

Assembly on Computers in English (ACE)—established in 1985

English as a Second Language Assembly (ESLA)—established in 1985

Doctoral Student Assembly—established in 1986 and dissolved in 2001

Assembly on Media Arts (AMA)—established in 1988

Whole Language Assembly—established in 1989 and dissolved in 1997 to become the Whole Language Umbrella

Assembly of State Coordinators of English/Language Arts (ASCE-LA)—established 1990

Assembly on American Literature (AAL)—established in 1990

Assembly for Civic Education—established in 1990 and dissolved in 1993

Assembly for Science and Humanities—established in 1990 and dissolved in 1996

Assembly for Advisers of Student Publications/Journalism Education Association (AASP/JEA)—established in 1991, formed from the Journalism Education Association, an NCTE-affiliated association

Assembly of Rural Teachers of English—established in 1991 and dissolved in 2001

Assembly on Literature and Culture of Appalachia (ALCA)—established in 1991

Women in Literacy and Life Assembly (WILLA)—established in 1991

Assembly for Expanded Perspectives on Learning (AEPL)—established in 1993

Assembly for the Teaching of English Grammar (ATEG)—established in 1993

Assembly on Alternatives for English Language Arts Instruction for Students with Diverse Academic Needs—established in 1993 and dissolved in 1998

Gay Straight Educators' Alliance (GSEA)—established in 1994 as the Assembly for Gay Lesbian Academic Issues Awareness (AGLAIA)

Assembly for National Board Certified Teachers (ANBCT)—established in 2006

Early Childhood Education Assembly (ECEA)—established in 2009

NCTE Commissions

NCTE Curriculum Commission appointed	1930
NCTE Commission on the English Curriculum appointed	1945
NCTE Commission on the Profession appointed	1958
NCTE Commission on the English Language appointed	1961
NCTE Commission on Literature appointed	1964
NCTE Commission on Composition appointed	1967
NCTE Commission on Reading appointed	1969
NCTE Commission on the History of the Council appointed	1977
NCTE Commission on Media appointed	1979
NCTE Commission on Assessment appointed	2009

Appendix G

NCTE Annual Convention Sites and Themes

Year	City	Headquarters Hotel	Convention Theme
1911	Chicago	Great Northern Hotel	
1912	Chicago	Auditorium Hotel	
1913	Chicago	Auditorium Hotel	
1914	Chicago	Auditorium Hotel	
1915	Chicago	Auditorium Hotel	
1916	New York	Hotel Astor	
1917	Chicago	Congress Hotel	
1919	Chicago	Hotel LaSalle	Postponed from Nov. 1918 to 26–27 Feb. 1919
1919	Boston	Brunswick Hotel	
1920	Chicago	Auditorium Hotel	
1921	Chicago	Auditorium Hotel	
1922	Chattanooga	Hotel Patten	
1923	Detroit	Hotel Statler	
1924	St. Louis	Hotel Statler	
1925	Chicago	Auditorium Hotel	
1926	Philadelphia	Benjamin Franklin Hotel	
1927	Chicago	Palmer House	
1928	Baltimore	Southern Hotel	
1929	Kansas City	Hotel Baltimore	
1930	Cleveland	Hotel Statler	
1931	Milwaukee	Hotel Schroeder	

1932	Memphis	Hotel Peabody	I believe that all education proceeds by the participation of the individual in the social consciousness of the race. John Dewey
1933	Detroit	Hotel Statler	Recent Experiences and Experiments in Teaching English
1934	Washington, DC	Mayflower Hotel	
1935	Indianapolis	Claypool Hotel	The Teaching of English in a Changing Curriculum
1936	Boston	Hotel Statler	American Youth and English
1937	Buffalo	Hotel Statler	Re-Creating Life through Literature and Language
1938	St. Louis	Jefferson Hotel	Evaluating the Program in English
1939	New York	Hotel Pennsylvania	Unifying the English Program for the Individual
1940	Chicago	Stevens Hotel	
1941	Atlanta	Biltmore Hotel	Our Defense of American Traditions
1942	Chicago	Palmer House	Board of Directors meeting only
1943	New York	Hotel Pennsylvania	Business meeting only
1944	Columbus	Deshler-Wallick Hotel	English Today and Tomorrow
1945	Minneapolis	Hotel Radisson	The Emerging English Curriculum
1946	Atlantic City	Hotel Claridge	English for These Times
1947	San Francisco	St. Francis Hotel	Realism in English Teaching
1948	Chicago	Stevens Hotel	English for Maturity
1949	Buffalo	Hotel Statler	English for Every Student
1950	Milwaukee	Hotel Schroeder	The Work Is Play for Mortal Stakes
1951	Cincinnati	Sheraton-Gibson Hotel	English and Human Personality

1952	Boston	Hotel Statler	Great Traditions, Widening Horizons
1953	Los Angeles	Hotel Statler	Turn East, Turn West
1954	Detroit	Hotel Statler	I taught them the grouping of letters, to be a memorial and record of the past, the mistress of the arts and mother of the Muses. Aeschylus, *Prometheus Bound*
1955	New York	Commodore Hotel	Now understand me well—it is provided in the essence of things that from any fruition of success, no matter what, shall come forth something to make a greater struggle necessary. Walt Whitman, *Song of the Open Road*
1956	St. Louis	Hotel Sheraton-Jefferson	Ah, but a man's reach should exceed his grasp, Or what's a heaven for? Robert Browning, "Andrea del Sarto"
1957	Minneapolis	Hotel Leamington	How Wide Is Your World?
1958	Pittsburgh	Penn-Sheraton Hotel	Honour and shame from no condition rise; Act well your part, there all the honour lies. Alexander Pope, *Essay on Man*
1959	Denver	Cosmopolitan Hotel	English Meets the Challenge
1960	Chicago	Morrison Hotel	
1961	Philadelphia	Bellevue-Stratford Hotel	I fling my soul on high with new endeavor And ride the world below with a joyful mind. William Rose Benet, "The Falconer of God"

1962	Miami Beach	Americana Hotel	The way of the spirit and the way of the mind Edith Hamilton, *The Greek Way*
1963	San Francisco	Mark Hopkins Hotel	
1964	Cleveland	Sheraton-Cleveland Hotel	
1965	Boston	Sheraton-Boston Hotel	
1966	Houston	Rice Hotel	
1967	Honolulu	Ilikai Hotel	
1968	Milwaukee	Sheraton-Schroeder Hotel	
1969	Washington, DC	Sheraton-Park Hotel	Dreams and Realities
1970	Atlanta	Regency Hyatt House	Imagination is not a talent of some men but is the health of every man Ralph Waldo Emerson, *Letters and Social Aims*
1971	Las Vegas	Stardust Hotel	The young men of this land are not, as they are often called, a "lost" race—they are a race that never yet has been discovered. And the whole secret, power, and knowledge of their discovery is locked within them—they know it, feel it, have the whole thing in them—and cannot utter it. Thomas Wolfe, *The Web and the Rock*
1972	Minneapolis	Radisson Hotel	That each child may learn who he is, what he is, and what he may become—what it is, in fact, to be a full human being. Margaret Mead

1973	Philadelphia	Sheraton Hotel	Seeing Ourselves
1974	New Orleans	Marriott Hotel	. . . The prey of fear, he, always curtailed, extinguished, thwarted by the dusk, work partly done, says to the alternating blaze, "Again the sun! anew each day; and new and new and new, that comes into and steadies my soul." Marianne Moore, "The Pangolin"
1975	San Diego	El Cortez Hotel	The orientation of English, her magnetic North, should be to the profound needs of all people. Stephen Dunning, "Making Connections"
1976	Chicago	Palmer House	Beginnings
1977	New York	Americana Hotel	Working Together
1978	Kansas City	Radisson Muehlebach Hotel	Widening the Circle of Communication
1979	San Francisco	Hilton Hotel	Respect for the Language Learner
1980	Cincinnati	Stouffer Hotel	Unity in Diversity
1981	Boston	Sheraton-Boston Hotel	Sustaining the Essentials
1982	Washington, DC	Washington Hilton Hotel	Let the Best of the Past Inform the Future
1983	Denver	Hilton Hotel	Quality for All
1984	Detroit	Westin Hotel	Renaissance Art and Science
1985	Philadelphia	Wyndham Franklin Plaza Hotel	Listening to the Past, Speaking to the Present
1986	San Antonio	Hyatt Regency Hotel	What We Will Be
1987	Los Angeles	Hilton Hotel	Making Connections
1988	St. Louis	Adam's Mark Hotel	Taking Language to Heart

1989	Baltimore	Stouffer Harbor-place Hotel	Celebrating Diversity
1990	Atlanta	Atlanta Hilton Hotel	Educating the Imagination
1991	Seattle	Seattle Sheraton Hotel	Free to Teach, Free to Learn
1992	Louisville	Galt House	How Infinite in Faculties: Celebrating Ourselves as Teachers
1993	Pittsburgh	Hilton Hotel	Democracy through Language
1994	Orlando	Clarion Hotel	Defining Ourselves and Our Work in a Changing World
1995	San Diego	Town and Country	Teaching for Lifelong Learning
1996	Chicago	Hilton Hotel	Honoring All Our Stories
1997	Detroit	Westin Hotel	Language as Moral Action
1998	Nashville	Gaylord Opryland Hotel	Learning with Our Students: Growing as Teachers
1999	Denver	Adam's Mark Hotel	Reimagining the Possibilities
2000	Milwaukee	Hilton Hotel	Teaching Matters
2001	Baltimore	Wyndham Baltimore Inner Harbor	Recreating the Classroom
2002	Atlanta	Atlanta Hilton and Marriott Marquis	Celebrating the Languages and Literacies of Our Lives
2003	San Francisco	Marriott Hotel	Partners in Learning
2004	Indianapolis	Marriott Hotel	Significance
2005	Pittsburgh	Hilton Hotel	On Common Ground
2006	Nashville	Gaylord Opryland Hotel	The Compleat Teacher: Bringing Together Knowledge, Experience, and Research
2007	New York	Marriott Marquis	Mapping Diverse Literacies for the Twenty-First Century: Opportunities, Challenges, Promising New Directions

2008	San Antonio	Marriott Rivercenter and Riverwalk	Because Shift Happens: Teaching in the Twenty-First Century
2009	Philadelphia	Philadelphia Marriott	Once and Future Classics: Reading Between the Lines
2010	Orlando	Disney Coronado Springs Resort	Teachers and Students Together: Living Literate Lives
2011	Chicago	Palmer House and Chicago Hilton	

Appendix H

IRA–NCTE Standards for the English Language Arts

1. Students read a wide range of print and nonprint texts to build an understanding of texts, of themselves, and of the cultures of the United States and the world; to acquire new information; to respond to the needs and demands of society and the workplace; and for personal fulfillment. Among these texts are fiction and nonfiction, classic and contemporary works.

2. Students read a wide range of literature from many periods in many genres to build an understanding of the many dimensions (e.g., philosophical, ethical, aesthetic) of human experience.

3. Students apply a wide range of strategies to comprehend, interpret, evaluate, and appreciate texts. They draw on their prior experience, their interactions with other readers and writers, their knowledge of word meaning and of other texts, their word identification strategies, and their understanding of textual features (e.g., sound-letter correspondence, sentence structure, context, graphics).

4. Students adjust their use of spoken, written, and visual language (e.g., conventions, style, vocabulary) to communicate effectively with a variety of audiences and for different purposes.

5. Students employ a wide range of strategies as they write and use different writing process elements appropriately to communicate with different audiences for a variety of purposes.

6. Students apply knowledge of language structure, language conventions (e.g., spelling and punctuation), media techniques, figurative language, and genre to create, critique, and discuss print and nonprint texts.

7. Students conduct research on issues and interests by generating ideas and questions, and by posing problems. They gather, evaluate, and synthesize data from a variety of sources (e.g., print and nonprint texts, artifacts, people) to communicate their discoveries in ways that suit their purpose and audience.

8. Students use a variety of technological and information resources (e.g., libraries, databases, computer networks, video) to gather and synthesize information and to create and communicate knowledge.

9. Students develop an understanding of and respect for diversity in language use, patterns, and dialects across cultures, ethnic groups, geographic regions, and social roles.

10. Students whose first language is not English make use of their first language to develop competency in the English language arts and to develop understanding of content across the curriculum.

11. Students participate as knowledgeable, reflective, creative, and critical members of a variety of literacy communities.

12. Students use spoken, written, and visual language to accomplish their own purposes (e.g., for learning, enjoyment, persuasion, and the exchange of information).

Source: International Reading Association, and National Council of Teachers of English. *Standards for the English Language Arts*. Newark, DE: IRA; Urbana, IL: NCTE, 1996. Print.

Index

Editor

Erika Lindemann is associate dean for undergraduate curricula at the University of North Carolina at Chapel Hill, where she directed the writing program for many years and taught writing courses and courses for writing teachers. Among other works, she is the author of *A Rhetoric for Writing Teachers* and *True and Candid Compositions*, the latter an extensive website featuring the writings of antebellum college students. She inaugurated the *Longman Bibliography of Composition and Rhetoric* and then the *CCCC Bibliography of Composition and Rhetoric* and is the recipient of the 2005 CCCC Exemplar Award. She has served as NCTE's parliamentarian since 1990.

Contributors

Donna E. Alvermann is the University of Georgia's appointed distinguished research professor of language and literacy education. She studies young people's literacies and popular culture in a digital environment. Her publications include *Reconceptualizing the Literacies in Adolescents' Lives* (2nd ed.) and *Adolescents and Literacies in a Digital World*. Alvermann co-directed the National Reading Research Center, edited *Reading Research Quarterly*, and served as president of the National Reading Conference (NRC). Elected to the Reading Hall of Fame, she is the recipient of NRC's Oscar Causey Award for Outstanding Contributions to Reading Research and the International Reading Association's William S. Gray Citation of Merit.

Arthur N. Applebee is distinguished professor and chair of the Department of Educational Theory and Practice at the University at Albany–SUNY, where he also directs the National Research Center on English Learning and Achievement. He has published widely on the teaching and learning of language and literacy across grade levels and has been a longtime consultant to the National Assessment of Educational Progress. A past president of the National Conference on Language and Literacy, he is a member of the Reading Hall of Fame. His book *Curriculum as Conversation* earned the NCTE David H. Russell Research Award.

Deborah Brandt is professor of English at the University of Wisconsin at Madison, where she teaches undergraduate writing and graduate courses in literacy and writing studies. She has been a recipient of the NCTE Promising Researcher Award (1983), the David H. Russell Research Award (1993), and the CCCC Outstanding Book Award (2003). In 2003 she also received the Grawemeyer Award in Education. Her latest book is *Literacy and Learning: Reflections on Writing, Reading, and Society* (2009).

Mary T. Christel teaches Advanced Placement literature and composition as well as media and film studies at Adlai E. Stevenson High School in Lincolnshire, Illinois, where she has been a member of the communication arts department since 1979. In 2001 she published her first book on media literacy with Ellen Krueger, *Seeing and Believing: How to Teach Media Literacy in the English Classroom*, and she coedited with Scott Sullivan *Lesson Plans for Creating Media-Rich Classrooms* in 2007. In 1996, Christel was recognized by the Midwest Chapter of the National Academy of Television Arts and Sciences with a special award for her efforts in promoting media literacy education.

Leila Christenbury is professor of English education at Virginia Commonwealth University in Richmond, where she teaches English methods, young adult literature, applied English linguistics, and a seminar for student teaching interns. She is past president of NCTE and former editor of *English Journal*. The author or coauthor of ten books, she recently received the NCTE Distinguished Service Award, the David H. Russell Research Award, and the James N. Britton Award for Educational Research. As chair of the NCTE Task Force on Council History and 2011, she has been active in all aspects of the NCTE centennial and in efforts to preserve the NCTE archives.

Edmund J. Farrell is a former teacher of English and department chair at James Lick High School in San Jose, California; supervisor of secondary English at the University of California at Berkeley; associate executive director of NCTE; and professor of English education at The University of Texas at Austin. A past president of the California Association of Teachers of English and the Texas Council of Teachers of English and Language Arts, he has been the recipient of both the NCTE Distinguished Service Award and the NCTE James R. Squire Award for Extraordinary Contributions to Teaching and Learning in the English Language Arts.

Anne Ruggles Gere joined NCTE when she was a high school English teacher in 1967; her department chair said it would be a good idea. Stephen Dunning, director of the University of Michigan's Joint PhD Program in English and Education (JPEE), which she entered in 1970, said the same. Since then, she has served as CEE representative to the Secondary Section, member of the Standing Committee on Research, chair of the Research Foundation, chair of CCCC, president of NCTE, and director of the James R. Squire Office of Policy Research in the English Language Arts. The author of ten books and more than seventy articles, Gere is Gertrude Buck Collegiate Professor at the University of Michigan at Ann Arbor, where she directs JPEE and the Sweetland Writing Center.

With her passion for young adult literature and her delight in working with kids on technology projects, **Sandy Hayes** has never really left eighth grade; she teaches at Becker Middle School in Becker, Minnesota. She has edited the student writing issue of the Minnesota

NCTE affiliate, *MCTE Journal*, and has served as the Technology Toolkit editor for *Voices from the Middle.* She was elected to the NCTE Executive Committee as the Middle Level representative-at-large (2003–05) and as chair of the Middle Level Section (2005–07). From 2005 to 2009, she served on the Middle Level Section Steering Committee.

Judith A. Langer is distinguished professor at the University at Albany–SUNY, where she is founder and director of the Albany Institute for Research in Education and director of the Center on English Learning and Achievement. Her research, focusing on the development of the literate mind, has had a strong national and international impact on policy and practice. She has published extensively, including ten books. A second edition of *Envisioning Literature* will soon be released, along with her latest book, *Envisioning Knowledge: Gaining Literacy in Disciplinary Coursework.* She holds an honorary doctorate from the University of Uppsala and a Creative Scientists of the World award from Lund University.

Carol D. Lee is professor of education and social policy in the Learning Sciences Program at Northwestern University. She is president of the American Educational Research Association (2009–10), a member of the National Academy of Education, past president and fellow of the National Conference of Research on Language and Literacy, former vice president of Division G of the American Educational Research Association, a former fellow at the Center for Advanced Study in the Behavioral Sciences, former chair of the NCTE Standing Committee on Research, and recipient of the NCTE Distinguished Service Award. She is a founder of four schools in Chicago.

John S. Mayher is professor emeritus of English education at New York University, where he directed the doctoral and teacher education programs for many years and was awarded the university's Distinguished Teaching Medal in 1998. His *Uncommon Sense: Theoretical Practice in Language Education* won the NCTE David H. Russell Research Award in 1992. Long active in NCTE, he was chair of the Conference on English Education from 1990 to 1992 and received the NCTE Distinguished Service Award in 1998. He also convened the Fifth Conference of the International Federation for the Teaching of English at New York University in 1995.

Marc A. Nachowitz is a PhD candidate in the University at Albany–SUNY's Department of Educational Theory and Practice. He received his BS and MA in English education from the University of Connecticut. After teaching high school English for thirteen years and providing professional development workshops on teaching the explicit processes of effective readers, he retired from the classroom to pursue research interests in adolescent literacy. He is particularly interested in studying the cognitive processes of adolescent readers and in understanding how the habits of effective readers might be explicitly taught and modeled in the classroom.

Jacqueline Jones Royster, professor of English at The Ohio State University, has been an active member of NCTE and CCCC, serving as CCCC chair in 1995. The author of scholarship on rhetorical, literacy, cultural, and women's studies, she is the recipient of numerous prestigious awards, including the Braddock Award (2000) for the best article in *CCC*, the Mina P. Shaughnessy Prize (2001) for *Traces of a Stream*, the CCCC Exemplar Award (2004), the Nancy Dasher Award (2006) from the CEA of Ohio for *Calling Cards*, and the ADE Frances Andrew March Award (2006) for distinguished service to the profession. She currently serves as coeditor of the *Norton Anthology of Rhetoric and Writing* and as coauthor of *Tectonic Shifts in Feminist Rhetorical Practices.*

Anika Spratley is assistant professor in the Department of Teacher Preparation at Johns Hopkins University. Before teaching at the university level, she was a high school English teacher and administrator in urban schools. She has worked in Prince Georges County, Maryland, and in Chicago. Her work focuses primarily on issues of literacy and struggling adolescent readers. She is also interested in teacher knowledge and specifically in how teachers' content knowledge and beliefs about students impact learning situations.

Patricia Lambert Stock is currently visiting professor at the University of Maryland at College Park, director of the University of Maryland Writing Project, and professor emerita at Michigan State University, where she served as founding director of Michigan State's Writing Center and co-founder of the Red Cedar Writing Project. An NCTE past president and former editor of *English Education*, she has written books and articles about literacy teaching and learning, teacher research, the scholarship of teaching, writing centers, and contingent faculty in higher education. Her work has been recognized with the James Britton, Richard A. Meade, Janet Emig, and the CCCC Outstanding Book Awards.

Stephen Tchudi joined NCTE in 1963 while in graduate school at Northwestern University. He subsequently taught English at Northwestern, Michigan State, and the University of Nevada at Reno. He edited *English Journal* from 1973 to 1980 and was NCTE president in 1984. His books include two NCTE publications: *The Astonishing Curriculum: Integrating Science and Humanities through Language* and *Alternatives to Grading Student Writing*. After retiring in 2004, he moved to Yankee Hill, California, where his family is creating a sustainable organic farm. He is a writer and editor for the Chico Peace and Justice Center and co-hosts a weekly radio program, *Ecotopia*, with Susan Tchudi.

Kathleen Blake Yancey, Kellogg W. Hunt professor of English at Florida State University, directs the graduate program in rhetoric and composition studies. Former chair of the NCTE College Section and former chair of CCCC, she is the immediate past president of NCTE. The author, coauthor, or editor of eleven scholarly books and more than sixty book chapters and refereed articles, Yancey recently edited *Delivering College Composition: The Fifth Canon* (2006), which received the Best Book Award from the Council of Writing Program Administrators. She will serve as the editor of *College Composition and Communication* from 2010 to 2014.

This book was typeset in Sabon by Barbara Frazier.
Typefaces used on the cover include Garamond Book Condensed
and Univers 67 Condensed Bold.
The book was printed on 50-lb. Williamsburg Offset paper
by Versa Press, Inc.